LONGSTREET HIGHROAD GUIDE
— TO THE —

TENNESSEE MOUNTAINS

BY VERNON AND CATHY SUMMERLIN

LONGSTREET

ATLANTA, GEORGIA

Published by

LONGSTREET PRESS, INC.

a subsidiary of Cox Newspapers,
a subsidiary of Cox Enterprises, Inc.
2140 Newmarket Parkway
Suite 122
Marietta, Georgia 30067

Great efforts have been made to make the information in this book as accurate as possible. However, over time trails are rerouted and signs and landmarks can change. If you find a change has occurred to a trail in the book, please let us know so we can correct future editions.
A word of caution: Outdoor recreation by its nature is potentially hazardous. All participants in such activities must resume all responsibility for their own actions and safety. The scope of this book does not cover all potential hazards and risks involved in outdoor recreation activities.

Printed by RR Donnelley & Sons, Harrisonburg, VA

1ˢᵗ printing 1999

Library of Congress Catalog Number 98-87787

ISBN: 1-56352-475-9

Book editing, design, and cartography
by Lenz Design & Communications, Inc., Decatur, Georgia

Cover illustration by Granville Perkins, *Picturesque America*, 1872

Cover design by Richard J. Lenz, Decatur, Georgia

Illustrations by Danny Woodard, Loganville, Georgia

Talk of mysteries! Think of our life in nature—daily to be shown matter, to come in contact with it—rocks, trees, wind on our cheeks! the *solid* earth! the *actual* world! the *common sense! Contact! Contact! Who* are we? *where* are we?

—Henry David Thoreau, *The Maine Woods, Ktaadn [1848]*

Contents

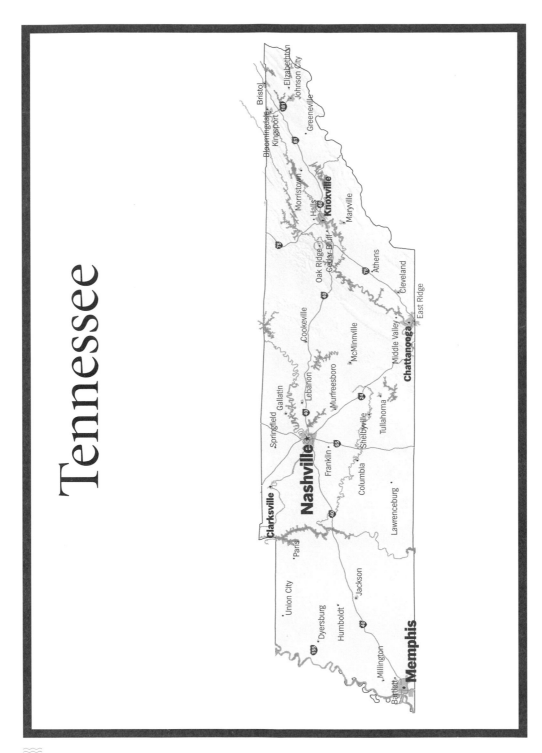

Tennessee

How Your Highroad Guide Is Organized

Upper Unakas
Pages 149–200

Great Smoky Mountains
National Park Pages 245–298

Lower Unakas Pages 201–244

Valley and Ridge
Pages 123–148

Upper Cumberland Plateau Pages 19–80

Lower Cumberland Plateau Pages 81–122

How to Use Your Longstreet Highroad Guide

The *Longstreet Highroad Guide to Tennessee* includes a wealth of detailed information about the best of what the Tennessee mountains have to offer, including hiking, camping, fishing, canoeing, cross-country skiing, mountain biking, and horseback riding. The *Longstreet Highroad Guide* also presents information on the natural history of the mountains, plus interesting facts about Tennessee's flora and fauna, giving the reader a starting point to learn more about what makes the mountains so special.

This book is divided into six major sections using Tennessee's main physiographic regions, plus three additional sections. One is an introduction to the natural history of the mountains, one details the Appalachian Trail in Tennessee, and the other introduces visitors to the lakes of the Tennessee Valley Authority.

The maps in the book are keyed by figure numbers and referenced in the text. These maps are intended to help orient both the casual and expert mountains enthusiast. Below is a legend to explain symbols used on the maps. Remember, hiking trails frequently change as they fall into disuse or new trails are created. Serious hikers may want to purchase additional maps from the US Geological Service before they set out on a long hike. Sources are listed on the maps, in the text, and in the appendix.

A word of caution: the mountains can be dangerous. Weather can change suddenly, rocks can be slippery, and wild animals can act in unexpected ways. Use common sense when in the mountains so all your memories will be happy ones.

Legend

Amphitheater	Wheelchair Accessible	Misc. Special Areas	
Parking	First Aid Station	Town or City	
Telephone	Picnic Shelter		
Information	Horse Trail	Physiographic Region/ Misc. Boundary	
Picnicking	Horse Stable	Appalachian Trail	
Dumping Station	Shower	Regular Trail	
Swimming	Biking	State Boundary	
Fishing	Comfort/Rest Station	70 Interstate	
Interpretive Trail	Cross-Country Ski Trail	522 U.S. Route	
Camping	Snowmobile Trail	643 State Highway	
Bathroom	Park Boundary	SR2010 State Route	
		T470 Township Road	

Preface

This book gives an overview of Tennessee's three easternmost physiographic provinces. Although these were often the first areas visited by white settlers, they remain the most remote. Protected by their geologic ramparts, these lands offer a wealth of opportunities to immerse yourself in the sights and sounds of vast public acreage. This book guides you from the rugged Cumberland Plateau, across the undulating Valley and Ridge province, to the Unaka Mountains.

From the gorge of the Big South Fork River to the dramatic, misty peaks of the Great Smoky Mountains, we describe the geology and natural history of each area while directing you to hiking trails, campgrounds, fishing holes, bicycle and horse-back-riding trails, whitewater, and scenic highlights.

As we travel through each region, we uncover historic sites and recreation areas as varied as the remains of historic Utopian societies on the Cumberland Plateau and the site of the 1996 Olympic whitewater event on the Ocoee River.

We share with you the knowledge of countless park rangers, geologists, and naturalists, as well as tidbits from our combined 45 years of personal experiences in Tennessee's mountains. We hope that you'll be inspired to learn and experience this beautiful portion of the Southeast yourself. Our appendixes furnish you with good sources for more information.

Carpe diem!

—Vernon and Cathy Summerlin

Acknowledgments

We wish to acknowledge Doug Markham with the Tennessee Wildlife Resources Agency; Michael Hoyal and Albert Horton with the Tennessee Department of Environment and Conservation Division of Geology; Andrea Shea with Tennessee's Division of Natural Heritage; Donnie Cable, Pete Irvine, Verne Maddux, Cheryl Sommers, and Delce Dyer in the Cherokee National Forest; Nancy Gray and Bob Miller at Great Smoky Mountains National Park; Judith Bartlow with TVA; Randy Hedgepath with South Cumberland State Recreation Area; and Brian King with the Appalachian Trail Conference.

A special thanks to Russ Manning, Sondra Jamieson, Robert Brandt, Kelly Roark, Evan Means, and William Skelton, and the many hikers who blazed the trails before us. Thanks to Ron Wilson and Howard Duncan at Big South Fork National River and Recreation Area, and to Barbara Stagg at Historic Rugby who helped us step into Rugby's past.

We extend great appreciation to two of the finest editors we have ever worked with, Pam Holliday and Richard Lenz, for their untiring patience and direction. They shared their knowledge of the mountains with us and we are grateful. Thanks also to our publisher, Longstreet Press, and especially to Marge McDonald, director of the Highroad Guide series, for her confidence in us throughout this arduous project, and Steve Gracie, General Manager, for his patience and understanding.

—Vernon and Cathy Summerlin

Tennessee Physiographic Regions

Tennessee has 14 distinct physiographic regions.

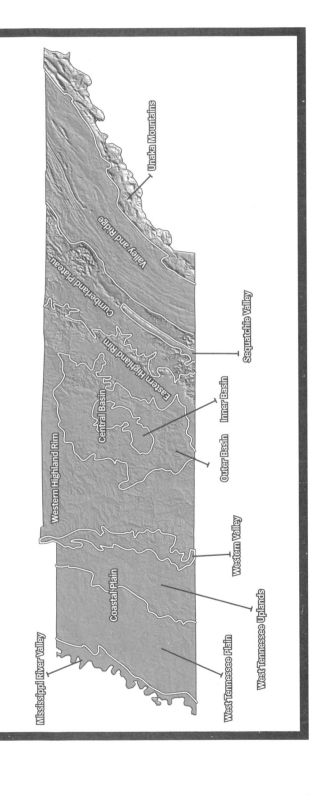

The Natural History of East Tennessee

From a perch on Tennessee's rooftop, Clingmans Dome, the Appalachians stretch into the distance as what seems to be one vast, green, and uniform landscape. But there is more to these mountains than first meets the eye. The Appalachians, extending from Alabama to Newfoundland, contain a complex mixture of specialized habitats. There are rich mountain coves, boulderfields, balds, and boreal forests, all with their own unique assemblage of flora and fauna. This diverse landscape has been created over millions of years by complex geologic events and now harbors a diversity of plants and animals that is legendary—a diversity perhaps unequalled outside the tropical rain forests.

Even by a geologist's standards, the Appalachians are old mountains: The bedrock was formed 1 billion years ago and the mountains are 500 million years old, 10 times older than the Rockies, Sierras, and Andes. They have been created, worn down, and

[*Above:* Whitewater rushes over boulders on a winter morning]

Geologic Time Scale

Era	System & Period	Series & Epoch	Some Distinctive Features	Years Before Present
CENOZOIC	**Quaternary**	Recent	Modern man.	11,000
		Pleistocene	Early man; northern glaciation.	1/2 to 2 million
	Tertiary	Pliocene	Large carnivores.	13 ± 1 million
		Miocene	First abundant grazing mammals.	25 ± 1 million
		Oligocene	Large running mammals.	36 ± 2 million
		Eocene	Many modern types of mammals.	58 ± 2 million
		Paleocene	First placental mammals.	63 ± 2 million
MESOZOIC	**Cretaceous**		First flowering plants; climax of dinosaurs and ammonites, followed by Cretaceous-Tertiary extinction.	135 ± 5 million
	Jurassic		First birds, first mammals; dinosaurs and ammonites abundant.	181 ± 5 million
	Triassic		First dinosaurs. Abundant cycads and conifers.	230 ± 10 million
PALEOZOIC	**Permian**		Extinction of most kinds of marine animals, including trilobites. Southern glaciation.	280 ± 10 million
	Carboniferous	Pennsylvanian	Great coal forests, conifers. First reptiles.	310 ± 10 million
		Mississippian	Sharks and amphibians abundant. Large and numerous scale trees and seed ferns.	345 ± 10 million
	Devonian		First amphibians; ammonites; Fishes abundant.	405 ± 10 million
	Silurian		First terrestrial plants and animals.	425 ± 10 million
	Ordovician		First fishes; invertebrates dominant.	500 ± 10 million
	Cambrian		First abundant record of marine life; trilobites dominant.	600 ± 50 million
	Precambrian		Fossils extremely rare, consisting of primitive aquatic plants. Evidence of glaciation. Oldest date algae, over 2,600 million years; oldest dated meteorites 4,500 million years.	

created again as a result of tectonic and weathering forces. Continental drift, a phenomenon that continues on earth's surface today, has played a major role. Continental drift is explained by the plate tectonics theory, which holds that earth's continents are not part of one contiguous piece of crust, but rather are individual pieces, or tectonic plates. These plates float across earth's semifluid mantle, and when they collide, the result is an orogeny or mountain-building event.

Geologists believe three orogenies are responsible for forming the Appalachians. The first, the Taconic orogeny, occurred 440 million years ago, and the second, the Acadian orogeny, occurred during the Age of Fishes, 380 million years ago when amphibians were first exploring dry land. These first two orogenies raised the northern Appalachians, while the third, the Alleghenian orogeny, shaped the southern Appalachians, including eastern Tennessee. This tectonic event began 290 million years ago and lasted for 50 million years.

During the Alleghenian orogeny, the continents were not aligned as they are today. North America was part of Laurentia, a landmass that also included Europe. Laurentia collided with the supercontinent of Gondwana, comprised of Africa, South America, Antarctica, Australia, and parts of Asia. When Africa slammed into the eastern side of North America, rocks on the ocean floor were driven under continental crust rocks in a process called subduction. The force of the collision slid, or thrust, rocks over other rocks and raised the southern Appalachians. When the continental movement stopped, the last of the Paleozoic oceans had disappeared and one landmass, Pangea, floated on earth's surface. Pangea did not begin to break apart until early in the Age of Dinosaurs, 225 million years ago.

Geologists attempting to piece together this complex history of the Appalachians have a difficult task. As continental drift built mountains, it destroyed or distorted the original bedding planes of ancient sediments, making it tough to distinguish exactly what happened over the past 500 million years.

In the 100-million-year period between the Acadian and Alleghenian orogenies and during much of the Mesozoic Era, Laurentia existed in the tropical latitudes and was covered by lush vegetation. The land became home to primitive seed-ferns, giant horsetails, and tree clubmosses. Animal life included insects and other arthropods as well as numerous amphibians, and for a time Laurentia was covered by a shallow inland sea alive with marine creatures. By the beginning of the Age of Mammals, North America drifted north into the Temperate Zone but not before accumulating a wealth of decomposing microorganisms that created a rich layer of organic material.

Heat and pressure transformed this organic material into rich natural resources—fossil fuels—that would bring humans to the Appalachians looking for wealth. Carbon was converted to coal, and marine organisms became natural gas.

Tennessee's Mountain Region

The legacy of these tectonic events in Tennessee is three mountainous physiographic provinces. From west to east they are the Cumberland Plateau, the Valley and Ridge, and the Unakas.

The Cumberland Plateau is the southern portion of the Appalachian Plateau that extends into Tennessee and south into Alabama. The eastern side is marked with a distinct escarpment 900 feet high while the western edge has been made more irregular by erosion. The plateau is essentially a wide and flat tableland trending northeast to southwest. The region is composed of hard sandstones that did not experience uplifting and fracturing and have resisted erosion, and the plateau is underlain by moderately abundant coal deposits. Where resistant sandstone strata overlie softer shales and coals, there are numerous waterfalls, including Fall Creek Falls in Van Buren County, the highest east of the Rockies.

The Valley and Ridge takes its name from its long ridges and valleys oriented in a northeast-southwest direction. This topography was shaped by folding and faulting that occurred during the Paleozoic Era. Great force from the east, possibly from northern Africa ramming into eastern North America, rippled the landscape like a rug pushed against a wall from one side. Then erosion set in, shaping more resistant rock into ridges and cutting valleys into weaker ones. The area is dominated by dolomite and highly erodible limestone, making caves numerous. The region has great habitat diversity and supports an especially diverse fish fauna, including the Upper Clinch River (*see* page 127), which holds one of the most diverse fish faunas in North America.

The portion of the Appalachians known elsewhere as the Blue Ridge is called the Unakas in Tennessee. The Unakas characteristically display waterfalls, steep stream gradients, and forested slopes within rugged terrain. Valleys range from 1,500 feet elevation in the north to 1,000 feet in the south, and peaks rise to over 6,000 feet. This region includes such mountains as the Chilhowee, English, Bean, Holston, Roan, and Smokies. The Great Smoky Mountains are part of the Unakas restricted to the area of the Great Smoky Mountains National Park.

Biological Diversity in the Southern Appalachians

The southern Appalachian region is the most diverse in the Appalachian chain. In terms of flora, the southern Appalachians are home to at least 400 species of moss, 130 species of trees, and over 2,500 species of flowering plants, hundreds of which are found nowhere else in the world. When it comes to fauna, the southern Appalachians are equally rich. Field scientists have counted 175 species of terrestrial birds,

65 species of mammals, and 25,000 species of invertebrates. Here there are 39 species of Plethodontid salamanders, more than are found anywhere else in the world. These mountains are home to 167 snails—many of them endemics (found nowhere else). In the snail family Zontidae, there are 38 species native only to the southern Appalachians, and in the family Polygyridae, there are 30 endemic species in these mountains. The southern Appalachians are also the global center for millipedes: 234 species have been described, with an estimated 250 undescribed.

One major factor contributing to this diversity is water. The southern Appalachians are second in the U.S. only to the Pacific Northwest in the amount of rainfall they receive. Five to eight feet of water pours onto these mountains from the skies each year. This rainfall, combined with a mild climate, grows lush mountain forests, which manage the water and send what isn't soaked into the ground off as rivers and streams.

Mountains also need water—the force that eventually erodes them away—for the formation of life-giving soil. The topography and the types of soils derived from rock types determine the plant and animal communities that thrive in the southern Appalachians. Soil is a combination of weathered rocks and minerals, as well as living creatures and organic detritus. The type of rock that it is eroded determines the pH or acid/base value of the soil that is formed and in turn, the plants the soil will support. As plants decompose they add their organic matter to eroded rock and concentrate nutrients in the top layer of soil, or topsoil. Topsoil helps soil retain water and nutrients instead of allowing them to wash away with rain water, and plants keep topsoil in place. An abundance of rich soil means greater plant life, so throughout the mountains, areas with rich, black topsoil, like coves, support a more diverse vegetative community than exposed ridgetops, which are covered in a thin soil layer and home to only the hardiest of plants.

Water in the form of glaciers has also affected the southern Appalachians. Over the past 2 million years, glaciers have not extended farther south than Pennsylvania, but Tennessee and the rest of the southern Appalachians have felt their effects. During the numerous cold glacial and warm interglacial times, boreal and temperate species have advanced and retreated up and down the mountain chain. Not all of the plants and animals who migrated south returned north when the glaciers receded. These northern species found niches for survival and contribute to the southern Appalachians' biological diversity. Species that remain as remnants of the ice ages are called relicts and can be found especially in north-facing coves where it is moist and cool. Examples of marooned species include yellow birch, sugar maple, and the New England cottontail.

Another remnant of the ice ages is a unique habitat called boulderfields—collections of jumbled, now moss-covered boulders usually on north-facing coves above 3,200 feet. During glacial periods, the Appalachian bedrock was subjected to freezing and thawing, and these are places were the rock eventually fractured. Today boulderfields are home to prolific displays of spring wildflowers and trees such as yellow birch and basswood.

The southern Appalachians are also diverse because not all of the mountains' plants and animals originated here. When North America was part of larger landmasses like Laurentia and Pangea, it shared species with other continents. When landmasses broke apart, species found ways to survive in new habitats on new continents. Today, red foxes and weasels are shared with Europe, while black bear, deer, and copperheads are shared with Asia. Animals that came from tropical areas include the short-tailed shrew, raccoon, and gray fox. Some of the plants found in these mountains that have their closest relatives in eastern Asia include hemlock (*Tsuga*), tulip poplar (*Liriodendron*), sweetshrub (*Calycanthus*), and foamflower (*Tiarella*).

Topography, elevation, and sunlight—along with water, soil, and history—determine what species live where. Visitors don't have to travel north to visit a variety of habitats; they can simply travel up a mountain in the Appalachians. A trip up a 6,000-foot mountain is the equivalent to driving 1,000 miles north and will lead through a variety of life zones or biomes that support unique plant and animal communities. A life zone is shaped by a variety of factors including elevation, the direction it faces and how much sunlight it receives, and rainfall. A high, north-facing valley and stream might be home to wood frogs, spring salamanders, hemlocks, and rosebay rhododendrons, while a cliff face is a more likely place for peregrine falcons, ravens, green salamanders, Carolina hemlock, and table mountain pine.

Mountains also have a way of carving up the landscape and separating species from one another, similar to the effect islands have in an ocean. On these "islands in the sky," species are genetically isolated. Mountains and valleys prevent them from mixing with other species groups, until eventually the isolated species becomes a new species. In this way, mountains contribute to their own biodiversity.

Tennessee's Mountain Flora

The unique conditions found in the southern Appalachians create a wide range of natural communities. Each natural community contributes to biodiversity by acting as home to a unique assortment of flora and fauna. There are dozens of distinctive habitats in the southern Appalachians, including heath balds, grassy balds, bogs, and rocky summits, but mostly there are forests. Eastern deciduous forest covers 70 percent of these southern mountains, and within the deciduous forest are several major forest types. The major forest types in Tennessee are discussed below and include the cove hardwood, oak-hickory, chestnut oak, red oak, white oak, hemlock, pine, and spruce-fir forests.

Depending on elevation and other growing conditions, every forest develops layers of plants, from the tallest trees to the fungi. Dominant trees are the tallest, with medium and smaller trees under them. Shrub layers develop under the small trees and then there are the vascular (herbaceous) and nonvascular plants growing on the forest floor.

Cove Hardwood Forest

Growing in the coves below 4,500 feet, the cove hardwood forest is the most diverse forest type in North America. These communities can support as many as 30 species of canopy trees and a great variety of shrubs and wildflowers in the understory. The reasons for this diversity are water and soil.

Coves are formed as rainfall and melted snow pour down mountain slopes carrying soil and gravel. When this water reaches a valley, it deposits its load in a fan delta. Vegetation takes root, stabilizing the soil and eventually decomposing to add its own nutrients to the collection. Coves are also usually protected from nature's elements from the rear and on each side by ridges, and they make good homes for plants and animals, as well as humans. The fertile black soil makes coves precious to mountain farmers, and in the 1800s and early 1900s, many Appalachian coves were harvested for their rich timber. However, in some remote and inaccessible areas, coves flourished untouched and now contain awesome old-growth timber.

In the Appalachians, coves are most often found on western slopes, which face into the prevailing wind and consequently receive heavier precipitation and erosion. Nowhere is cove development more legendary than in the Great Smokies, especially on the Tennessee slopes. One of the most famous coves of its kind is Cades Cove near Gatlinburg.

Eastern hemlock (*Tsuga canadensis*), silver bell (*Halesia carolina*), buckeye (*Aesculus octandra*), basswood (*Tilia americana*), sugar maple (*Acer saccharum*), yellow poplar (*Liriodendron tulipfera*), beech (*Fragus grandifolia*), and yellow birch (*Betula alleghaniensis*) are the dominant trees in cove hardwood forests. The old-growth trees may reach 75 feet to 100 feet high with crowns sometimes reaching 200 feet. White ash (*Fraxinus americana*), green ash (*Fraxinus pennsylvanica*), northern red oak, cucumbertree (*Magnolia acuminata*), bitternut hickory (*Carya cordiformis*), red maple, and wild black cherry (*Prunus serotina*) are other trees that may grow among the dominant trees.

The shadowed understory consists of small and medium trees including umbrella magnolia (*Magnolia tripetala*), blue beech (*Carpinus caroliniana*), Fraser magnolia (*Magnolia fraseri*), yellowwood

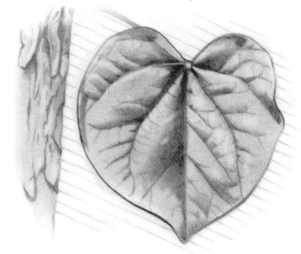

EASTERN REDBUD
(Cercis canadensis)
This tree can be identified by its thick, leathery, heart-shaped leaves and clusters of pink flowers.

(*Calrastris lutea*), holly (*Ilex opace*), and hop hornbeam (*Ostrya virginiana*). The shrub layer is usually missing or sparsely developed. Strawberry bush (*Euonymus americanus*) and spicebush (*Lindera benzoin*) may grow in the cove hardwood forest at lower elevations. At higher elevations the shrubs may be alternate leaf dogwood (*Cornus alternifolia*), hobblebush (*Viburnum alnifolium*), and doghobble (*Leucothoe fontanesiana*). Wild hydrangea (*Hydrangea arborecsens*) grows at all elevations and may be a member of the shrub layer.

Throughout the southern Appalachians, but especially in cove hardwood forests, there is a large variety of wildflowers. In spring, blue cohosh (*Caulophyllum thalictroides*), squirrelcorn (*Dicentra canadensis*), Dutchman's breeches (*Dicentra cucullaria*), bleeding heart (*Dicentra eximia*), umbrella leaf (*Diphylleia cymosa*), trout lily (*Erythronium americanium*), wild geranium (*Geranium maculatum*), sharp-lobed hepatica (*Hepatica acutiloba*), dwarf crested iris (*Iris cristata*), bishop's cap (*Mitella diphylla*), showy orchis (*orchis spectabilis*), mayapple (*Podophyllum peltatum*), solomon's seal (*Polygonatum biflorum*), bloodroot (*Sanguinaria canadensis*), black snakeroot (*Cimicifuga racemosa*), false solomon's seal (*Maiantheumum racemosum*), giant chickweed (*Stellaria pubera*), foamflower (*Tiarella cordifolia*), trillium (*Trillium* sp.), and many violet species (*Viola* sp.) can be seen. In summer, white snakeroot (*Ageratina altissima* var. *roanenis*), black cohosh (*Cimicifuga racemosa*), blue cohosh, jewelweed (*Impatiens pallida*), wood fern (*Dryopteris cristata*), giant chickweed , foamflower, bedstraw (*Galium aparine*), and strawberry bush are usually found.

Oak-hickory Forests

Oak-hickory forests thrive between 2,500 feet and 3,000 feet elevation and occupy slightly drier areas than the cove hardwoods. Northern red oak (*Quercus rubra*), pignut hickory (*Carya glabra*), white oak (*Quercus alba*), and mockernut hickory (*Carya tomentosa*) are the dominant species with black oak (*Quercus velutina*), sweet pignut hickory (*carya ovalis)*, chestnut oak (*Quercus prinus*), black gum (*Nyssa sylvatica*), and tulip poplar joining in.

Understory trees are commonly red maple (*Acer rubrum*), flowering dogwood (*Cornus florida*), and sourwood (*Oxydendrum arboreum*). The shrub layer contains mostly huckleberry (*Galussacia ursina*) and mountain laurel (*Kalmia latifolia*), but rosebay rhododendron (*Rhododendron maximum*) and flame azalea (*Rhododendron calendulaceum*) may live among the dominant trees.

Few herbaceous plants survive on the oak-hickory forest floor. Of those that may occur are the Christmas fern (*Polypodium virginianum*), goldenrod (*Solidago* sp.), false foxglove (*Aureolaria laevigata*), galax (*Galax aphylla*), pipsissewa (*Chimaphila umbellata*), downy rattlesnake plantain (*Goodyera pubescens*), false solomon seal, and bellwort (*Uvularia grandifloria*).

Chestnut Oak Forests

Chestnut oak forests, once known as chestnut oak-chestnut forests, live well at 4,500 feet elevation or less. In the early 1900s, the chestnut blight removed the chestnut tree, which historically made up half of the tree count in this forest classification. Chestnut oak, northern red oak, and red maple filled about half the niche left vacant by the demise of the large chestnut trees. White oak, black oak, black gum, red maple, tulip poplar, and a small percentage of hickories enter the mix.

Above 2,500 feet in chestnut oak forests, mountain laurel, flame azalea, rosebay rhododendron, and huckleberry are the main shrubs. Also above 2,500 feet, sweetshrub (*Calycanthus floridus*) and highbush blueberry (*Vaccinium simulatum*) may be members of the shrub layer.

False foxglove, gall-of-the-earth (*Prenanthus trifoliata*), wood betony (*Pedicularis canadensis*), downy rattlesnake plantain, hellebore (*Veratrum viride*), and galax make up the herb layer, but at higher elevations this layer's coverage drops from 30 percent down to about 1 percent.

Red Oak and White Oak Forests

Red oak forests and white oak forests are not appreciably different below 4,500 feet. At higher elevations the red oak forest will have American beech and silver bell (*Halesia monticola*) growing in it. Red maple, basswood, black cherry, yellow birch (*Betula lutea*), buckeye, and white ash are found in the red oak forests and white oak forests below 4,500 feet. In white oak forests above 4,500 feet, white oak usually dominates some exposed southwestern ridges, and pignut hickory and chestnut oak will generally be present.

The shrub layers for these two forests are also similar, consisting most commonly of highbush blueberry, flame azalea, and mountain laurel.

Herbs under the red oak forests are similar to those in chestnut oak forests below 4,500 feet, whereas the white oak forests have a sparse smattering of herbs, usually ferns and grasses. In the red oaks forests and white oaks forests above 4,500 feet, the herb layers are similar, sparse with mostly sedges.

Hemlock Forests

More often than not, the hemlock forests occur in dense stands between 2,500 feet and 4,500 feet elevation. They grow from mountain peaks to along streams, and they are found on north-facing slopes. The hemlock normally reaches more than 3 feet in diameter with its crown rising over 100 feet. The higher the elevation the more likely these trees will be nearly homogenous, dominating all other tree species.

If hemlock forests have a shrub layer, it will consist mostly of rhododendrons at higher elevations. Other understory shrubs include rosebay rhododendron, mountain rosebay, doghobble, wild hydrangea, and mountain laurel. The denseness of the hemlock forest and its thick understory species usually prevent a herbaceous layer. Where there are openings among the heaths, wood fern, partridgeberry (*Mitchella repens*), rattlesnake plantain, and foamflower may grow.

Pine Forests

Virginia pine (*Pinus virginiana*) forests dominate at low elevations, 3,000 feet or less, in stands on south-facing slopes and in old fields. Mountain laurel and lowbush blueberries (*Vaccinium vacillans*) are usually the dominant shrubs. Herbs include little bluestem (*Andropogon scoparius*), broomstraw (*Andropogon geradii*), bracken fern (*Pteridium aquilinum*), goat's rue (*Tephrosia virginiana*), wild indigo (*Baptisia tinctoria*), tickseed sunflower (*Coreopsis tinctoria*), asters (*Aster* sp.), and goldenrod.

Pitch pine (*Pinus rigida*) forests dominate at elevations between 2,200 feet and 3,200 feet. Scarlet oak may sometimes share dominance. Mountain laurel and low-bush blueberry are the main shrubs under these pines, and the sparse herbs consist of little bluestem, bracken fern, trailing arbutus (*Epigaea repens*), and wintergreen (*Gaultheria procumbens*).

SUGAR MAPLE
(Acer saccharum)
Sugar maple's sap is the source of maple syrup and sugar.

Spruce-fir Forests

Spruce-fir forests are usually found from 4,500 feet to over 6,000 feet elevation. Red spruce (*Pices rubens*) and Fraser fir (*Abies fraseri*)—boreal species typical of more northern latitudes—dominate here. Some red spruce are known to live more than 300 years. Yellow birch, mountain maple, striped maple, serviceberry, and mountain ash (*Sorbus americana*) may also be found in this high forest. The shrub layer of bearberry (*Arctostaphylos uva-ursi*) and hobblebush hovers over herbs, including woodfern, bluebeard lily (*Clintonia borealis*), aster, wake-robin (*Trillium erectum*), twisted stalk (*Streptopus roseus*), Rugel's ragwort (*Rugelia nudicaulis*), and mosses.

The American Chestnut

The grand and generous American chestnut, *Castanea dentata*, once made up 40 to 50 percent of forests in the southern Appalachians, but today, for all practical purposes, it is gone. Tiny saplings still spring from old root systems, but the trees succumb to the chestnut blight before they grow large enough to reproduce. The story of this tree's disappearance is one of the most dramatic in the history of these mountains and speaks to the power of even the smallest forest invader.

These were giant canopy trees that rose to heights of more than 100 feet and had trunks 10 feet across. The chestnut's nearly rot-resistant wood was light and easily worked, and settlers used it to build everything from cabinets to barns to homes. Maybe most importantly, American chestnuts were prolific nut-producers that provided a bountiful mast crop each fall. People as well as wildlife depended on the sweet nut for food.

The American chestnut blight first appeared in the Bronx Zoo in 1904, and it is believed to have been brought to the United States around 1890 via some Oriental chestnuts. Within 10 years the blight had spread to the Shenandoah National Park. Within another 15 years it was in the Smokies, and by 1938, 85 percent of the chestnuts there were dead. Most were dead by the 1940s. It has been estimated that $400 billion worth of trees were lost in 9 billion acres of forests.

The chestnut fungus (*Cryphonectria parasitica*) invades the tree through any tiny opening in its bark such as a cut or bruise. The fungus spreads filaments into the cambium layer and destroys it, thereby cutting off water and nutrients to the tree. In about four years the fungus circles the tree, essentially girdling it. The roots are not infected because the fungus can't live below the soil. The wind, birds, and insects easily spread the fungus spores.

Mostly white oak and red oak have filled the niche left vacant by the dying mast-producing trees, but work continues to revive the American chestnut. The United States Department of Agriculture and other researchers have tried to hybridize the chestnut with blight-resistant Oriental species, but there is not any success to report. Work with a virus to render the fungus less virulent has been successful in Europe, and it is hoped that this hypovirulent strain can be introduced in the United States with similar results. The flaws with this less lethal strain are that is does not spread as readily as the deadly strain, and it can revert back to the potent strain.

Genetic work may yet save the majestic tree. The American Chestnut Foundation is optimistic that backcrossing techniques may make blight-resistant trees and nuts available within a few years. Mapping of the chestnut's genes has aided in telling which plants have resistance to the blight.

Balds

Balds are one of the greatest mysteries in the southern Appalachians. More than 80 of these high-altitude, treeless, open areas exist from Virginia south to Georgia, some as large as 20 acres, and no one is certain why. They defy the natural laws of succession, a process vegetative communities go through as they develop into ultimate climax communities. In the southern Appalachians, that climax community is usually one of the forest types previously discussed. However, balds have not been invaded by surrounding forests and instead have remained open grassy or heathlike areas for thousands of years. Altitude does not cause these openings because in no place do they approach treeline.

The explanations and speculations for why balds exist range from natural conditions such as fungi, parasitic insects, drought, fire, ice, and/or winds to man clearing the areas for grazing animals. It is known that some of them existed when the first white settlers arrived and that settlers used the open areas for grazing their livestock. Indians may have been the first to burn such areas to attract grazing game animals or to create places of worship.

Grassy balds are distinguished by an abrupt transition from forest to bald. Good examples of grassy balds can be seen in Tennessee in the Highlands of Roan Mountain and at Andrews Bald. Mountain oak grass is usually dominant on these balds with some introduced grasses, sedges, and various herbs. The most abundant herbs are five fingers (*Potentilla canaddensis*), hedge nettle (*Stachys* sp.), goldenrod, rattlesnake root, catbriar (*Smilax rotundifolia*), bluets (*Houstonia caerulea*), coneflower, gentian (*Gentiana quinquefolia*), and giant chickweed.

EASTERN RED CEDAR
(Juniperus virginiana)
Cedar chests are made from the fragrant wood of this tree.

Rhododendrons (*Rhododendron maximum* or *R. carolinianum*) commonly dominate heath balds at lower elevations, with purple laurel (*R. catawbiense*) and mountain laurel (*Kalmia latifolia*) at higher elevations. Heath balds are also covered by blueberry and other heath shrubs, the particular species depending on the elevation. Sometimes the shrubs grow so densely (up to 10 feet high) that they become known as "hells," such as the fabled Jeffery Hell in the Tellico Ranger District of the Cherokee National Forest. Beauty Spot is an excellent example of a health bald on Unaka Mountain in the Unaka Ranger District of the Cherokee National Forest (*see* page 175).

Herbs rarely become significant under these dense heath balds, but wintergreen, galax, cow wheat (*Melampyrum lineare*), Indian cucumber root (*Medeola virginiana*), and painted trillium (*Trillium undulatum*) may get a toehold.

The continuance of prehistoric balds is not understood, but it has been suggested that thick grasses and the thick root systems of the heath prevent tree seedlings from surviving and that historic grazing on the balds has limited plant succession. Now that many balds in national forests and national parks are protected from grazing and maintenance activities like fire are prohibited, some scientists are concerned trees and shrubs will invade and balds will disappear.

Bogs

Bogs occur more often at lower elevations and are rare in Tennessee's Appalachian Mountains. Bogs are waterlogged areas that usually have certain plants associated with them, most frequently sphagnum moss (*Sphagnum* spp).

Poor drainage causes bogs to form and the stagnant environment becomes so acidic that only very specialized plants and animals can survive. Vegetative matter collects and decays, creating acidic leftovers. Swamp pink (*Helonias bullata*), bog laurel (*Kalmia carolina*), Carolina saxifrage (*Saxifraga caroliniana*), cinnamon fern (*Osmunda cinnamonea*), and an interesting group of carnivorous plants survive here.

Carnivorous plants such as sundew (*Droscera rotundifolia*) and pitcher plants (*Sarracenia* spp.) have adapted to living in nutrient-poor soil by developing ways to capture and eat animals. Their large tubular leaves attract and collect insects. Some plants have hoods with translucent spots that insects try to escape through but cannot, and they die of exhaustion. Other pitcher plants have recurved hairs in the tubular leaves to keep insects from crawling out. Insects drown in the water collected in the plant's base. The organisms decay or are digested by secreted enzymes that some of these carnivorous plants produce. The insect provides nitrogenous compounds that the plants need.

Bogs are disappearing due to eutrophication, water deprivation, and other conditions. Many of the bog plants and animals are on the endangered or threatened species list. Four such animals are the bog lemming (*Synaptomys cooperi*), water shrew (*Sorex palustris*), smokey shrew (*Sorex fumes*), and bog turtle (*Clemmys muhlenbergii*).

Tennessee's Mountain Fauna

Along with luxuriant plant growth comes interesting and unique animals. Faunal communities, like flora, vary up and down the Appalachians according to elevation and climatic conditions. Typically, some animals are more visible than others, but with a little patience, there is lots of wildlife to see here.

Wildlife often hides in their habitats from intruders, such as hikers. Some wild animals may show themselves if visitors sit still, concealed, and remain quiet for awhile. Usually it takes about 30 minutes for an animal to feel comfortable about going about its business after being disturbed.

The wild turkey (*Meleagris gallopavo*) and the wild boar (*Sus scrufa*) are two critters that will be difficult to see. The reclusive turkey has powerful eyesight and picks out the slightest movement in the woods. It sees in color, so wear camouflage if you want to hunt or photograph the bird, and be very still, using a wide tree as your background.

The wild boar is nocturnal but evidence of its activity is easy to find along some trails through the mountains. It is better to avoid this rough character. It is a charging animal, and its sharp tusks can inflict severe wounds.

Black bears (*Ursus americanus*) are a signature species of the mountains, especially of the Smokies, and it has become more common to see these animals as they've learned to wander into campgrounds and picnic areas in search of human food. Campers should take precautions to avoid a bear encounter by hanging their food so the animals can't reach it. Hikers should make enough noise when walking that a bear has the opportunity to avoid them.

Hikers and those touring the mountains in automobiles may see the white-tailed deer (*Odocoileus virginianus*), especially at dawn and dusk. Cades Cove in the Smokies is a popular spot for viewing this animal.

Some of the animals that are more difficult to see are the elusive red fox (*Vulpes fulva*), gray fox (*Urocyon cinereoargenteus*), southern flying squirrel (*Glaucomys volans*), and northern flying squirrel (*Glaucomys sabrinis*). The flying squirrels are nocturnal, and the foxes, like the turkey, avoid humans.

The nocturnal bobcat (*Lynx rufus*), another rarely seen animal, usually makes a meal of rabbits and rodents but it also eats birds, mice, eggs, reptiles, and squirrels. Although bobcats are able to kill deer, they rarely feed on deer.

The gray squirrel (*Sciurus carolinensis*), fox squirrel (*Sciurus niger*), and red squirrel (*Tamiasciurus hudsonicus*) are usually easy to find among nut-bearing trees. Other mammals in the mountains include mink (*Mustela vision*), raccoons (*Procyon lotor*), opossums (*Didelphis marsupialis*), groundhogs (*Marmota monax*), beaver (*Castor canadensis*), skunks (*Mephitis mephitis*), cottontail rabbits (*Sylvilagus floridanus*), long-tailed weasels (*Mustela freneta*), and river otters (*Lutra canadensis*). Some of the smaller mammals are the pine vole (*Microtus pinetorum*), southern bog lemming (*Synaptomys cooperi*), woodland jumping mouse (*Napaeozapus insignis*), silver-haired bat (*Lasionycteris noctivagans*), Keen's myotis (*Myotis keenii*), and Eastern pipistrelle (*Pipistrellus subflavus*).

There are more than 120 species of birds that are found in the mountains. Some of the birds that are interesting to photograph are bald eagles (*Haliaeetus leucocdphalus*) and peregrine falcons (*Falco peregrinis*). Hooded warblers (*Wilsonia citrina*), dark-eyed juncos (*Junco hyemalis*), crows (*Corvus brachyrhynchos*), ravens (*Corvus corax*), yellow-throated vireos (*Vireo flavifrons*), black-capped chickadees (*Parus atricapillus*), barred owls (*Strix varia*), Eastern phoebes (*Sayornis phoebe*), and summer tanagers (*Piranga rubra*) are likely to be heard or seen. But, alas, the red-cockaded woodpecker (*Picoides borealis*) is not a bird you are likely to see. These birds require large pine trees with a sparse understory. Fire suppression practices prevented natural forest fires from clearing the understory and took away this bird's habitat.

Many birds are well adapted to second-growth forests of Tennessee, and a few that prefer them are the yellow-throated warbler (*Geothlypis trichas*), wood thrush (*Catharus fuscescen*), Louisiana water thrush (*Seiurus motacilla*), rufous-sided towhee (*Pipilo erythrophthalmus*), and indigo bunting (*Passerina cyanea*). Typical of the birds that inhabit hardwood forests are the whip-poor-will (*Caprimulgus vociferus*), screech owl (*Otus asio*), red-tailed hawk (*Buteo jamaicensis*), black vulture (*Coragyps atratus*), and red-bellied woodpecker (*Centurus carolinus*). Many of the birds that inhabit the hardwood forests will also be found in the hemlock and pine forests.

In the pines are bird species that depend on the food chain that thrives in this habitat, such as the pine warbler, red-breasted nuthatch (*Sitta canadensis*), evening grosbeak (*Hesperiphona vespertina*), and bobwhite quail (*Colinus virginianus*). Hairy woodpeckers (*Picoides villosus*), common flickers (*Colaptes auratus*), and pileated woodpeckers (*Dryocopus pileatus*) prefer the mixed pine-oak habitats.

The mixed hardwood forests are home to many amphibians, including the mountain chorus frog (*Pseudacris brachyphona*), Eastern spadefoot toad (*Scaphiopus holbrooki*), spotted salamander (*Ambystoma maculatum*), Eastern newt (*Notophthalmus viridescens*), and dusky salamander (*Demognathus fuscus*).

Numerous reptiles occupy niches in these mountains. The common snapping turtle (*Chelydra serpentina*), stinkpot (*Sternotherus odoratus*), green anole (*Anolis carolinensis*), coal skink (*Eumeces anthracinus*), northern water snake, Eastern ribbon snake (*Thamnophis sauritus*), brown snake (*Storeria dekayi*), and pine snake (*Pituophis melanoleucus*) are examples.

According to *The Fishes of Tennessee*, Tennessee has the richest freshwater fauna of any state in the U.S. It reports there are between 302 and 319 species of native and introduced fishes alone. This diversity can most likely be explained by the several distinct drainages within Tennessee as well as the numerous physiographic provinces. As the topography changed, certain animal populations were cut off from other members of the same species. If a mountain rises and isolates a lake or stream, fish and other aquatic and semiaquatic species are not able to leave the water and cross the mountain to breed. When these species remain separated from others of their kind long enough, they evolve into new species.

Adding to this aquatic diversity is a host of introduced species. Tennessee's numerous waterways and man-made reservoirs have attracted resource managers and others to introduce exotic fish into them, purposefully and by accident. Game fishermen benefit from some of these introductions, but other exotic fishes are nuisances and are detrimental to native fauna. Carp, rainbow and brown trout, striped bass, and yellow birch are some of the introduced species.

Salamanders

Just as fish isolated by mountains have evolved into new species, so have salamanders. Because 39 salamander species exist in the southern Appalachians, many scientists now believe these mountains are the center for salamander evolution. These lungless creatures spend their lives living beneath logs and loose stones among damp leaf decay. They absorb oxygen directly through their sensitive skin, which must stay moist and cool.

As temperatures rose at the end of the last ice age, salamanders probably migrated up mountainsides in search of cooler habitat. They became isolated on individual summits and evolved into the variety of species that exists today. Now some populations are in danger because of their tiny home ranges. As mountainsides are further subdivided by trails, timbering operations, and roads, individual populations become smaller and smaller and threaten to disappear completely.

People and the Tennessee Mountains

The mountains have always been a desirable place to live and visit because of their natural wealth and beauty. People have shaped the landscape of the southern Appalachians for thousands of years through hunting, farming, grazing, mining, and logging.

A series of prehistoric peoples—of the Paleo-Indians, the Archaic and Woodland cultures, and the Mississippian tradition—lived by hunting on the grasslands and fishing the streams of Tennessee. Native Americans, primarily the Cherokees, valued these lands as hunting grounds, but species including mountain bison (*Bison bison*), gray wolves (*Canis lupus*), and elk (*Cervus elaphus*) were quickly eliminated when white settlers arrived.

The Europeans that arrived included plantation workers, immigrants of Scotch-Irish and German descent, and veterans of the French and Indian Wars and the Revolutionary War who received land grants as payment for service. All came in search of a better life. Eventually they began farming small plots and raising livestock to supplement their diet of wild game.

They learned to use the land to their advantage. Settlers soon discovered that fertile and productive soils made coves some of the best places to raise crops, but as coves became more populous with farms, graziers were left looking for grasslands to feed cattle, sheep, and horses. They turned to the grassy balds. The people of Cades Cove built a long and steep trail up to Gregory Bald, almost 3,000 feet above. Balds like these were subjected to dense clouds and fog, frequent showers, and heavy dews, making them even more succulent grasslands. Coves and balds complemented each other and settlers found ways to make the best use of the land.

Timber had also been flourishing in the southern Appalachians for thousands of years and stood as a valuable resource to be taken by white settlers. The people who lived in Tennessee from the 1830s to the 1880s had very timber-intensive life-styles, using wood for everything from building their homes to building fires. They didn't always cut entire tracts, either. They usually went into the forests and cut the best trees they could find.

Beginning in 1890 and continuing well into the twentieth century, commercial lumbering rocked the South. New forms of transportation (steam power and an expanded railroad), new methods of felling, new mill technology, new materials (steel), and large-scale land ownership led to a new wave of exploitation of forest resources. Commercial loggers also did not usually harvest all of the trees. They took the best trees,

Hikers will find solitude, as well as beautiful scenery, in the Tennessee mountains.

starting at lower elevations and following major streams back and up into the forest. Usually the lands they didn't cut were the highest and roughest tracts. Such practices didn't just remove valuable timber but also left hillsides bare, without vegetation to hold valuable soil in place. Silt and sediments washed into rivers and streams, changing their character and chemistry and killing aquatic species.

Finally, mountain lovers became concerned about conserving natural resources. National forests began to be established to ensure a continuous timber supply for the country but also to preserve some areas from the logger's axe. In Tennessee, the Cherokee National Forest was created in the Unaka Mountains. The National Park Service guards the Great Smoky Mountains National Park, the largest undeveloped region in the southern Appalachians and an International Biosphere Reserve. Along with state parks and numerous other management areas in Tennessee, there are unique approaches to conservation like the Big South Fork National River and Recreation Area. This combination of national river and national recreation area preserves the river gorge as a wilderness area and offers outstanding recreational opportunities.

Eastern Tennessee offers some of the best opportunities to appreciate the lush green landscape of the southern Appalachians. While millions of people live in these hills and millions more flock here to visit, there are still plenty of places where nature's wealth and beauty can be observed. Climb to the top of a heath bald and survey the rhododendron display. Turn over a rock in a cove forest and discover a dusky or spotted salamander. Stand on the banks of the Clinch and reel in the catch of the day. The wild lands of Tennessee are waiting to be discovered.

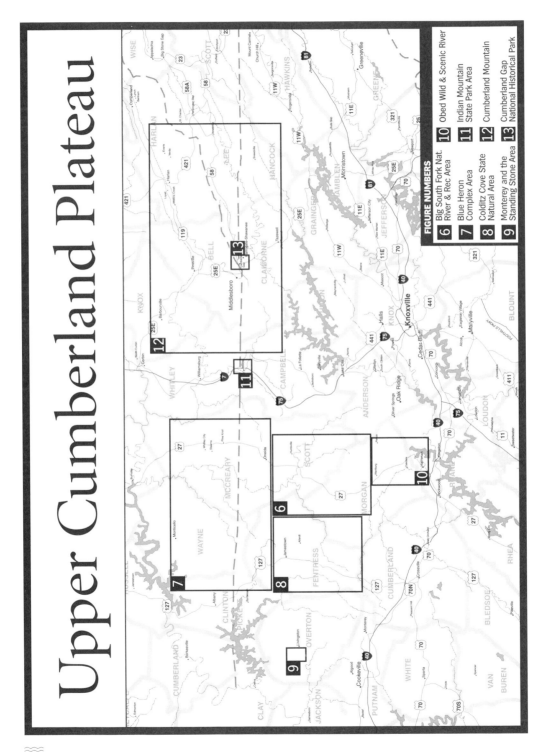

Upper Cumberland Plateau

T he Cumberland Plateau is the name given to the southern part of the Appalachian Plateau that extends from the western border of New York through Tennessee into central Alabama. The Cumberland Plateau contains about 4,300 acres in the swath that is about 55 miles wide on the northern border of Tennessee near the Virginia/Kentucky line and less than 40 miles wide at the state's southern border near Chattanooga.

It is a 2,000-foot high, sandstone-capped tableland bordered on the east by the Valley of East Tennessee, and on the west by the Eastern Highland Rim. Much of the plateau is flat, although there are some rolling hills, a few higher mountains, and numerous deep gorges. Prominent escarpments with an average height of 900 feet mark both sides. The general plateau elevation is approximately 1,700 to 1,900 feet, but a few of the mountains have elevations over 3,000 feet.

[*Above:* White-tailed deer are frequently seen throughout the Upper Cumberland Plateau]

There is considerable difference between the escarpments on each side. The eastern escarpment is abrupt, smooth to slightly curving, and only occasionally notched by drainage that empties into the Tennessee River. It is a line of bluffs that served for many years as a barrier to westward migration.

When James Robertson led the first settlers into the Great Valley in 1776, they were halted by this gigantic wall, which had no apparent gaps or openings. Robertson used what can only be described as extreme measures. To circumvent it, he sent part of his expedition, under the command of Col. John Donelson, by flatboat down the Holston and Tennessee rivers and on to the Ohio River, up the Ohio to the Cumberland River, and up the Cumberland to Nashville. Even after the Cumberland Gap was discovered, and Robertson and Daniel Boone began moving parties through it to Kentucky and Tennessee, there were still people who preferred to go the long way around rather than across the plateau.

Had the topography of the plateau been reversed, access to it would have been a less challenging task because the western edge is ragged and deeply incised by several river systems. The gaps created by these drainages would have provided relatively easy passage.

The differences in the topography between the eastern and western edges of the plateau have to do with how and where the early mountain-building pressures were applied. Approximately 250 million years ago, the forces that formed the plateau came from a southeasterly direction. This resulted in tight folding along the eastern edge of the plateau, but elsewhere the rock was compressed to the point of breaking. Large-scale breaks, properly called faults, allowed large masses of rock to move along the break lines. The entire group of faults is called the Cumberland Overthrust Fault, although it is not a single fault but an interwoven and complex system along which some parts of the plateau moved only slightly while others moved as much as 10 miles. The most prominent movement was the 125-mile-long offset on the northern escarpment that was pushed to the northwest at what is now Lake City. This massive, displaced portion of the plateau that extends into Kentucky and Virginia is known as the Cumberland Block.

The western edge of the Cumberland Plateau is irregular and undefined because the Cumberland, Elk, and Duck rivers and their tributaries have reshaped it. Also, the effects of the thrusting and faulting 250 million years ago diminished over distance. The western edge of the plateau did not suffer the shifting of its hard sandstone cap to an inclined position as occurred on the eastern escarpment.

The rocks on the plateau are primarily sandstone, siltstone, coal, and shale formed during the Pennsylvanian Period. The force from the collision with Africa 250 million years ago did not produce enough pressure and heat on the Cumberland Plateau to metamorphose these rocks.

The extensive folding and faulting of the hard sandstone caprock on the eastern half of the plateau exposed to erosion underlying layers of softer sedimentary deposits laid down during the Paleozoic Era. In one of these layers, which represents the Pennsylvanian Period, deposits of vegetation became carbonized after being subjected to enormous pressure over millions of years. Coal was formed, and its discovery led to widespread exploitation of the plateau, primarily by strip-mining. Although this practice is more tightly regulated today, it is still conducted at some locations.

While coal is found at various places on the plateau, the largest amount of strip-mining has traditionally occurred in Morgan, Scott, Campbell, and Anderson counties in a broad, downwarped area surrounded by resistant caprock. Inside the basins are high mountains carved from folded layers of sedimentary rocks that have long since disappeared from other parts of the plateau.

Initially, the plateau served primarily as a seasonal hunting ground for the Cherokee and Shawnee Indians, who never established permanent village sites. Instead, they used caves and rock houses cut by the streams and rivers along the walls of the steep canyons as their temporary quarters. Some of these homes are important archeological sites. Later, the longhunters of the Daniel Boone era (so named because of the long duration of their hunting forays, or because of the long rifles and long knives they carried) used some of the rock houses for shelter before they built cabins as hunting bases.

Few immigrants settled on the plateau because of its rugged nature, and most knew of the rich farmlands in Middle Tennessee. From the outset until the present day, the plateau has remained Tennessee's last frontier, still sparsely populated in comparison with other parts of the state.

Yet the highland area wasn't totally overlooked. Early on, its natural resources attracted mining and lumber companies, and the plateau was literally stripped of coal and timber. The economic booms these ventures created began in the closing years of the nineteenth century. Early logging involved selective, labor-intensive removal of certain species of trees like oak and poplar located near waterways. Oxen were used to haul wood out of steeper areas to the river where rafts of logs were floated down river during the rainy season to markets in Celina, Carthage, and Nashville.

Later years brought railroads, improved roads, portable sawmills, and widespread commercial logging. Along with commercial logging came the introduction of the practice of clear-cutting, or the removal of essentially all the trees in a particular area, leaving the soil vulnerable to erosion. Due to the rugged terrain, some of the steepest areas remained inaccessible to clear-cutting methods of timber harvesting.

Although residents mined coal on a small scale prior to 1880, interest in commercial coal mining by the timber companies as well as other operators began to grow rapidly in the early 1900s. Early mining activity utilized tunnels cut into hillsides to reach coal seams. Later strip-mining became the primary method of coal extraction. Sediment and refuse from mining activities degraded once crystalline streams.

During the Great Depression, the timber market deteriorated, and by the end of World War II, the coal reserves were becoming depleted. The boom gradually departed the Cumberland Plateau, taking with it many of the families who had settled in the area and leaving the damage created by man's activities to slowly heal.

Second-growth forests have been successful in growing where humans let them, occupying about 75 percent of the area. Unlike the Unaka Mountains with many forest types, the Cumberland Plateau has the upland forests on the tableland and mountain areas with the ravine forests occupying the lower elevations, including gorges.

In the Cumberland Plateau, mixed oak forests dominate the tableland and mountains. Shortleaf pine, white oak, and chestnut oak grow on the ridgetops, with a sprinkling of sugar maple, basswood, buckeye, tulip poplar, and beech. Tulip poplar, red maple, black gum, and sourwood can be found among oaks along wetter areas.

Mixed-oak woods attract the turkey, gray squirrel, and opossum with mast and thick undergrowth. Birds, including the red-eyed vireo (*Vireo olivaceus*), scarlet tanager (*Piranga olivacea*), and tufted titmouse (*Parus bicolor*) prefer the canopy whereas the wood thrush, hooded warbler, and downy woodpecker (*Picoides pubescens*) favor the understory.

The ravine forests, growing in the gorges of the Upper Cumberland Plateau, consist of beech, sugar maple, red oak, tulip poplar, white oak, chestnut oak, basswood, sweet buckeye, white pine (*Pinus strobus*), hemlock, yellow birch, black cherry, white ash, red maple, and umbrella and cucumber magnolias. Sour gum, black walnut, and hickory are occasionally found among these species. The ravine forests' understory includes rhododendron, mountain laurel, dogwood, hop hornbeam, sourwood, redbud, ironwood, serviceberry, and sassafras. Herbaceous flowers include trillium, mayapple violets, delphinium, phacelia, phlox, bloodroot, spring beauty, fire pink, wild iris, anemone, and many others. Not all these herbaceous plants thrive in any one area. Elevation, light, soil, nutrients, and moisture produce different habitats that sustain different plants.

On the edge of the river gorges, pine, chestnut oak, sourwood, and various shrubs hold in the soil. On the floor of the gorges grows sycamore and river birch with wild oats and cane living beneath them. Sugar maple, beech, poplar, basswood, ash, and buckeye grow on the low moist slopes. The understory and groundcover are sparse among hemlock and rhododendron stands. The gorge walls are also sparsely covered with plants because of the lack of soil. Alum root, ferns, and small pines marshal a living among the crevices. Certain animals depend on these walls for their habitat, including vultures, Eastern phoebes (*Sayornis phoebe*), cliff swallows (*Petrochelidon pyrrhonota*), bats, timber rattlesnakes, and copperheads.

The gray fox, skunk, raccoon, barred owl (*Strix varia*), red-shouldered hawk (*Buteo lineatus*), shrews (*Sorex* sp.), Eastern mole (*Scalopus aquaticus*), Eastern woodrat (*Neotoma floridana*), white-footed mouse (*Peromyscus leucopus*), and Eastern chipmunk make their living on the lower slopes of the ravine forest.

The forests at the bottom of the gorges provide food and habitat to beaver, muskrat (*Ondatra zibethicus*), mink, otter, Louisiana water thrush, spotted sandpiper (*Actitis macularia*), and American woodcock (*Philohela minor*). Along the stream banks and in the very narrow floodplains of sand, gravel, and boulders are bullfrogs (*Rana catesbeiana*), southern leopard frogs (*Rana sphenocephala*), pickerel frogs (*Rana palustris*), water snakes (*Nerodia* sp.), and midland painted turtles (*Chrysemys picta*). The belted kingfisher (*Megaceryle alcyon*) and green heron (*Butorides striatus*) are two common water birds living along the streams.

The topography of the plateau causes the rivers to flow in different directions. The Big South Fork, Caney Fork, Calfkiller, and Collins rivers flow north and west into the Cumberland River, while the Obed, Emory, and Sequatchie rivers flow south and east into the Tennessee River.

The rivers of the plateau and their tributaries carved gorges, and the walls are of the gorges exposed sandstone layers. Waterfalls, rock houses, and natural stone arches are results of the erosion of the softer rock under the sandstone layers.

The Upper Cumberland Plateau is bracketed on the west by the western escarpment of the plateau; on the east by the eastern escarpment consisting of Walden Ridge and Cumberland Mountain; on the south by Interstate 40; and on the north by the Tennessee/Kentucky/Virginia state lines. There are two exceptions: all of the Big South Fork National River and Recreation Area that lies in both Tennessee and Kentucky is covered in this chapter, and so is the Cumberland Gap Historic Park that lies in Tennessee, Kentucky, and Virginia.

The Upper Cumberland Plateau contains all or parts of Claiborne, Campbell, Scott, Pickett, Fentress, Overton, Morgan, Putnam, Anderson, Cumberland, and Roane counties.

Sgt. Alvin C. York Historic Site

[Fig. 7(17)] There have been many American military heroes throughout the nation's history, but few, if any, have remained as permanently fixed in people's minds as World War I soldier Sgt. Alvin C. York. Denied conscientious objector status, York went to war reluctantly. Under heavy enemy fire while on patrol in the Argonne Forest of France, York killed more than 20 German soldiers armed with only a Colt .45, a rifle, and his Tennessee backwoods skills. The enemy surrendered 132 men and 35 machine guns to York and the remaining six survivors in his patrol on October 18, 1918. America's most decorated World War I veteran, York was awarded more than a dozen medals, including the Congressional Medal of Honor, the nation's highest award and the Croix de Guerre, the highest award of France.

He returned to his home in the beautiful Wolf River valley at Pall Mall where he married his longtime sweetheart and lived on a 385-acre farm purchased for him with funds raised by grateful Tennesseans.

Later, a movie dramatizing his exploits starring Gary Cooper further enhanced his reputation, but he refused to take advantage of the fame he had earned and used his share of the proceeds to found an interdenominational Bible school. He remained in Pall Mall until his death in 1964. The state historic site includes the York farm and gristmill with picnic sites overlooking the Wolf River. Andrew Jackson York, one of his sons, is the park ranger at the historic site.

Directions: The farm and grist mill are located at Pall Mall, 8 miles north of Jamestown on TN 127.

Activities: Tour York's home and gristmill, picnicking, swimming.

Facilities: Swimming pool, playground.

Dates: Open daily.

Fees: None.

Closest town: Crossville, 45 miles.

For more information: Alvin York State Historic Area, General Delivery, Pall Mall, TN 38577. Phone (931) 879-6456.

Pickett CCC Memorial State Park

[Fig. 7(14)] Nestled against the western side of the Big South Fork National River Recreation Area at the Kentucky state line. Pickett is one of the most botanically diverse parks in the Tennessee State Park system. In the spring there are many wildflowers, including bluets (*Houstonia serpyllifolia*), bloodroot (*Sanguinaria canadensis*), mayapple (*Podophyllum peltatum*), mountain laurel (*Kalmia laifolia*), Catawba rhododendron (*Rhododendron catawbiense*), pinxter flower (*Rhododendron nudiflorum*), trailing arbutus (*Epigaea repens*), and several kinds of violets. In addition, the park has exceptional scenic and geologic attractions.

The 11,752 acres of land turned over to Tennessee by the Kentucky-based Stearns Coal and Lumber Company in 1933 became a state forest. In 1934, the Civilian Conservation Corps (CCC) and National Park Service aided the state in developing the facilities to make it Tennessee's first state park.

Of particular interest are unusual rock formations, natural bridges and tunnels, caves and rock shelters, waterfalls, lush forests, and the 15-acre, man-made Arch Lake, lined with cliffs and named for the natural bridge located on one of the embayments. Pickett is also the southern terminus of the Sheltowee Trace National Recreation Trail (*see* page 44).

Since Pickett is open to all types of hunting in season, safety zones have been established to define the areas closed to hunting.

Directions: From I-40 take the Crossville/Jamestown Exit, travel TN 127 north approximately 30 miles to Jamestown, turn on TN 154 north for 15 miles to the park.

Activities: Hiking, hunting (in Pickett Forest), fishing, boating, swimming, tennis, horseshoes, volleyball, playgrounds, scenic drives, and summer naturalist programs.

Facilities: Cabins, campground (electric and water hookups), grills, group camp, hiking trails, boat rental, lighted tennis courts, picnic tables and shelters, bathhouse.

Dates: Open year-round.

Fees: There is a charge for cabins and camping.

Closest town: Jamestown, 15 miles.

For more information: Pickett CCC Memorial State Park, 4605 Pickett Park Highway, Jamestown, TN 38556. Phone (931) 879-5821.

HIKING TRAILS

There are 14 trails from which to choose, all of them interconnecting. Most are less than 2 miles in length and are easy to moderately difficult. All are accessible from near the park office. Two of the longer trails, Hidden Passage Trail and Rock Creek Trail, are especially popular.

HIDDEN PASSAGE TRAIL

[Fig. 7(15)] This is a trail that is popular year-round, since it offers a wide variety of scenic views and seasonal botanical delights. The profusion of spring wildflowers is particularly impressive. The trail is named for a sandstone tunnel through a bluff.

Features along the trail are evergreen and deciduous forests, wildflowers, waterfalls, large rock shelters, Thompson Creek, Rock Creek, wildlife, and scenic views. A side trail leads to an abandoned railroad tunnel, but park rangers say it is not safe to enter.

Directions: The trailhead is north of the park office on TN 154 on the right (east) side of the road. The trail is marked.

Trail: 10-mile loop.

Elevation: Change, 100 feet.

Difficulty: Moderate.

Surface and blaze: Forest floor and rock. Green blaze.

ROCK CREEK TRAIL

[Fig. 7(9)] Interesting features along this route include streams, waterfalls, deciduous and evergreen forests, and rock bluffs. Much of Rock Creek Trail follows an old railroad bed and there are a couple of good camping spots before it reaches a parking area and more primitive camping spots near TN 154.

Directions: Drive north 1.8 miles from the park entrance on TN 154, turn right before the bridge over Rock Creek, and turn left in 0.1 mile. Get on the Rock Creek Trail where it fords the creek.

Trail: 5 miles, one-way.

Elevation: Change, 250 feet.

Difficulty: Moderate.

Surface and blaze: Forest floor and rock. Brown blaze.

Big South Fork Nat. River & Rec. Area

The Big South Fork National River and Recreation Area is approximately 115,000 acres.

Ref: Delorme Tennessee Atlas & Gazetteer

3 MILES

1	To Alum Ford
2	To Yahoo Falls Trail
3	Angel Falls Overlook Trail, Grand Gap Loop Trail
4	West Entrance Trailhead to Bandy Creek Campground
5	Leatherwood Ford, Leatherwood Ford Bridge to Station Camp or Blue Heron Mine and O&W Bridge Trail
6	Leatherwood Ford Loop and Angel Falls Trail
7	John Litton/General Slavens Farm Loop Trail
8	Big South Fork National River & Recreation Area
9	Bandy Creek Visitor Center in TN, Bandy Creek Campground Loop Trail, North White Oak Loop Trail, Charit Creek Lodge Trail, Duncan Hollow Road to Station Camp Creek, Jack's Ridge Loop, Duncan Hollow Trail, Collier Ridge Loop
10	East Rim Overlook Trail and Oscar Blevins Farm Loop Trail
11	Sunset Overlook Trail
12	Zenith Mine to Leatherwood Ford Bridge
13	New River Bridge to Leatherwood Ford
14	Brewster Bridge to Burnt Mill Bridge
15	Meeting of the Waters Loop
16	White Oak Creek Bridge to Burnt Mill Bridge
17	Burnt Mill Bridge
18	Honey Creek Loop Trail

Big South Fork National River and Recreation Area

[Fig. 6] The Big South Fork National River and Recreation Area (BSFNRRA) is located in some of the most remote and rugged territory on the Cumberland Plateau. Its present size is approximately 115,000 acres, and it encompasses almost all of the drainage area of the Big South Fork of the Cumberland River. The Big South Fork originates in Tennessee at the confluence of the Clear Fork and New River, then flows down through a spectacular 600-foot-deep gorge before emptying into the Cumberland River in Kentucky below Cumberland Falls. Nearly two-thirds of the area lies in Tennessee, the remainder in Kentucky.

The sediments that form the layers of limestone, shale, coal, and sandstone found along the Big South Fork were deposited when the area was covered with a shallow sea more than 360 million years ago. Approximately 285 million years ago, the area began a gradual rise to its present altitude of nearly 2,000 feet above sea level, in some areas.

The dramatic rock formations found at the BSFNRRA are the result of the erosion of underlying softer rock, while harder sandstone cap rock remains behind as arches, rock houses, and spires. The Big South Fork River continues to cut ever deeper into the ancient geologic past of the Cumberland Plateau, now cutting into sandstone deposits more than 320 million years old.

Along the lands bordering the rims of deep gorges, stands of red maple (*Acer rubrum*) blanket the plateau with splashes of brilliant red flowers each spring and yellow to red leaves each fall. Since most of the accessible timber was harvested prior to 1930 second-growth forests of oak, hickory, and Virginia pine (*Pinus virginiana*) compete for the broad flats.

The vegetation in the Big South Fork Gorge varies from rim to gorge with Virginia pine thriving in relatively dry soil, hemlocks (*Tsuga canadensis*) finding a niche beneath the rock bluffs on moist, northern slopes, and sycamore (*Platanus occidentalis*) lining the river's edges.

In the early spring, wildflowers found in the BSFNRRA include trout lily (*Erythronium americanum*), twinleaf (*Jeffersonia diphylla*), rue anemone (*Thalictrum thalictroides*), common cinquefoil (*Potentilla simplex*), trillium, and Dutchman's breeches (*Dicentra cucullaris*). In late spring (May), even more wildflowers add their grace to the rugged landscape. Jack-in-the-pulpit (*Arisaema triphyllum*), showy orchis (*Orchis spectabilis*), coreopsis (*Coreopsis tinctoria*), and Virginia bluebells (*Mertensia virginica*) are some of the best known. In June and July you can expect to see the brilliant orange hues of butterfly weed (*Asclepias tuberosa*) and flame azalea (*Rhododendron calendulaceum*). Black-eyed susan (*Rudbeckia hirta*) persists in August in some areas. Partridgeberry (*Mitchella repens*) and white snakeroot (*Eupa-*

torium rugosum) are also among the more than 40 species blooming.

In late summer and fall, the scarlets and soft lavenders of bergamot or bee balm (*Monarda fistulosa*) fill the spaces along sunlit paths. Goldenrod (*Solidago* sp.) and blazing star (*Liatris scariosa*) are among the fall bloomers. A checklist of wildflowers is available.

A large part of what makes the outdoors experience so rewarding is encountering wildlife in a natural habitat, on their own turf, so to speak. Visitors could see a bobcat, Tennessee's only surviving native cat, setting out in search of an evening meal on a warm summer evening. White-tailed deer (*Odocoileus virginianus)* tracks are ubiquitous along moist edges of clearings and game trails after recent rains. Spotting deer grazing around an old homestead creates a lasting vision of the uplands of Big South Fork country for most visitors. Black bears are also sighted within the BSFNRRA.

It's an unexpected delight to come across the sleek river otter (*Lutra canadensis*) at river's edge. Opossum (*Didelphis virginiana*), wild boar (*Sus scrofa*), fox squirrel (*Sciurus niger*), mink (*Mustela vison*), and coyote (*Canis latrans*) are among the more than 50 animal species inhabiting the Big South Fork area. Wildlife in the BSFNRRA is of special interest to anglers and hunters. Hunting has taken place here for centuries, and in this setting a balance is maintained between hunters, wildlife populations, and habitat. The area offers legal hunting in accordance with state regulations.

This region will please any bird watcher. Permanent residents like the great blue heron (*Ardea herodias*) and belted kingfisher (*Megaceryle alcyon*) are spotted fishing along creeks and rivers, while sharp-shinned (*Accipiter striatus*) and red-tailed hawks (*Buteo jamaicensis*) keep a sharp eye out from above. Neotropical migrants like the yellow billed cuckoo (*Coccyzus americanus*), whip-poor-will (*Caprimulgus vociferus*), wood thrush (*Hylocichla mustelina*), and acadian flycatcher (*Empidonax virescens*) stop here before migrating to the tropics for the winter. A checklist of birds, their habitats, and seasons of occurrence is available at the Bandy Creek Visitor Center.

The BSFNRRA is believed to contain thousands of archaeological sites, some pointing to the presence of humans in the large rock houses and caves around 12,000 years ago during the Paleo-Indian period.

The first white men to penetrate the region were the longhunters in the late 1700s. Among such longhunters was a man born in Virginia in 1779 named Jonathan Blevins. Blevins settled first in Kentucky before establishing his home on Station Camp Creek. Jonathan Blevins' grave is located on Station Camp Creek about 2 miles from Charit Creek Lodge (*see* page 34).

The upland farm of his descendant, Oscar Blevins, may be visited on the Oscar Blevins Farm Loop Trail in the Bandy Creek area (*see* page 31). In addition to subsistence ridgetop farms, early settlement in the Big South Fork area tended to be concentrated in river and stream basins in communities like No Business and Station Camp. Later, emphasis shifted to lumber and mining communities with additional settlement along roadways.

In time, a few settlers developed farming operations, but the area remained sparsely settled due to its rugged terrain. The arrival of the railroad in 1880 brought rapid,

Black Bear Project

Since 1987, managers of the National Park Service, the U.S. Forest Service, the Tennessee Wildlife Resources Agency, and the Kentucky Department of Fish and Wildlife Resources have considered the possibility of re-establishing a population of black bears on the upper Cumberland Plateau in the Big South Fork Area (BSFA) of Tennessee and Kentucky. This area consists of the Big South Fork National River and Recreation Area and the Daniel Boone National Forest. The BSFA is part of the black bears' historic range.

In 1990, a habitat suitability study indicated that the landscape could support black bears, but there was also concern about how the bears would react to human activity and how humans would react to bears. To answer these questions, a study began in 1995 to experimentally release a limited number of bears into the BSFA, with further releases to be followed at intervals. The animals were translocated from the Great Smoky Mountains National Park.

The experiment is continuing, with no conclusions expected for several years, but biologists are optimistic about the project. The possibility of eventually having a huntable population is uncertain.

widespread changes. Dozens of mining and lumber operations sprang up in the water-shed, creating an economic boom that was no longer based on subsistence farming and barter. The first commercial oil well in the United States was said to be accidentally drilled here in 1818 during a search for salt water. Limited oil and gas production continue in the BSFNRRA, now primarily in the area adjacent to the southern rim.

After the timber was exhausted, many families left their homesteads and found work as wage earners in company towns like Stearns, Kentucky. One of the mines owned by the Stearns Company, the Blue Heron Mine, opened in 1937 and operated until 1962. Today, the Blue Heron mining camp has been re-created and the Blue Heron Outdoor Historical Museum features exhibits that tell the story of coal mining and logging in the Big South Fork River area (*see* page 33).

Coal mining peaked in the area in the 1930s. The next decade brought declines in production and employment that forced many families to leave the Big South Fork area in order to find employment.

In the 1930s, a narrow rapids in the Kentucky part of the Big South Fork known as Devil's Jump was considered by the Tennessee Valley Authority (TVA) as the site for construction of the tallest dam east of the Rockies. The dam would have created a 37,000-acre reservoir for recreation and flood control with a 480,000-kilowatt generation capacity, significantly more than any other facility in the Southeast.

Although funding for the project was repeatedly approved in Public Works Bills in the United States Senate, the bills failed to gain approval each time in the House of Representatives. Local conservationists remained firmly opposed to the project and

CORN SNAKE

(Elaphe guttata)
This harmless snake is an excellent climber because of the special shape of its belly scales.

looked for alternatives to protect the Big South Fork while providing a much-needed economic stimulus for the area.

The conservationists in the Tennessee Citizens for Wilderness Planning (TCWP) first tried to stop the proposed dam at Devil's Jump by having the Big South Fork included in the Tennessee Scenic Rivers Bill, but when the legislation passed in 1968 the river had been deleted from the list.

TCWP also managed to have the Big South Fork included in the list for the national Scenic Rivers Bill, but again the river was taken off the list before the bill passed.

Eventually, the efforts of the TCWP, a coalition of additional conservation groups known as the Big South Fork Coalition (BSFC), Tennessee Senator Albert Gore Sr., the United States Army Corps of Engineers, the Department of the Interior, and U.S. Senator Howard Baker found a creative alternative that established a national river and recreation area, protecting the wilderness in the Big South Fork Gorge while providing increased access for recreation in adjacent areas.

The Big South Fork National River and Recreation Area was authorized by the Water Resources Development Act of 1974 as amended by Section 184 of the Water Resources Development Act of 1976 "for the purposes of conserving and interpreting an area containing unique cultural, historic, geologic, fish and wildlife, archeologic, scenic and recreational values." In a very unusual arrangement, the BSFNRRA was developed and constructed by the U.S. Army Corps of Engineers and subsequently turned over to the U.S. Department of the Interior for operation and management.

Because management guidelines in a national recreation area are less restrictive than in a national park, visitors to BSFNRRA may enjoy traditional park activities such as hiking, horseback riding, and primitive camping as well as nontraditional activities including four-wheel driving, hunting, and trapping. Among other activities that can be enjoyed are back-packing, bicycling, canoeing, fishing, kayaking, participating in nature programs, nature walking, picnicking, rapelling, recreational vehicle camping, rock climbing, sight seeing, scuba diving, snorkeling, swimming, and whitewater rafting. Information about these activities is available at the Bandy Creek Visitor Center (*see* page 31).

For more information: Big South Fork National River and Recreation Area, Bandy Creek Visitor Center, 4564 Leatherwood Road, Oneida, TN 37841. Phone (931) 879-3625.

⬛ BANDY CREEK VISITOR CENTER IN TENNESSEE

[Fig. 6(9)] First-time visitors will find information on all aspects of the BSFNRRA at the Bandy Creek Visitor Center. In addition to printed guidelines on BSFNRRA activities and the wealth of information offered by friendly park rangers, the book shop has maps, trail guides, and books about the area. This is also the location of public restrooms and the adjacent Bandy Creek Campground, which offers more than 180 campsites. Facilities include developed campsites with hookups for RVs, tent sites, bathhouses, a swimming pool, and services that include stables for boarding horses. The visitor center is on eastern standard time. Although portions of the BSFNRRA are within the central daylight time zone, the entire park functions on eastern standard time for simplification. Interstates 40 and 75 provide access to the area.

Directions: Travelers on I-40 eastbound from the Nashville area should take the Monterey-Livingston Exit (Exit 300-A) or the Jamestown-Monterey Exit (Exit 301) onto TN 62. Take TN 62 east for 16 miles to US 127 at Clarkrange, then turn left and follow US 127 north 18 miles to Jamestown. Travelers may take US 127 through Jamestown or use the US 127 bypass. Approximately 2 miles north of Jamestown take TN 154 north to the intersection of TN 297. Follow TN 297 east approximately 12 miles to the Bandy Creek Visitor Center.

Travelers on I-75 northbound should take the Oneida-Huntsville Exit (Exit 141) onto TN 63. Follow TN 63 west for 21 miles through Huntsville to US 27. Turn right on US 27 and drive north 7 miles to Oneida. At the first traffic light, turn left on TN 297 west and follow the signs on TN 297 for approximately 15 miles to reach the Bandy Creek Visitor Center. To reach the Kentucky Visitor Center at Stearns, continue north on US 27 through Oneida.

Travelers headed south on I-75 have several options for reaching the area. KY 461 at Mt. Vernon (Exit 62) is signed as a route to the BSFNRRA. Travelers choosing this route should take KY 461 south for 19 miles to KY 80 and follow KY 80 west into Somerset, KY to US 27. Follow US 27 south 47 miles into Oneida, TN. At Oneida take TN 297 west and follow the signs for approximately 15 miles to the Bandy Creek Visitor Center.

Southbound I-75 travelers may also take US 25W (Exit 25) at Corbin, KY. Follow US 25W 8 miles to KY 90. Take KY 90 west for 20 miles through Cumberland Falls State Park to Parker Lake to US 27 and follow it as described above.

KY 92 at Williamsburg, KY (Exit 11 off I-75) is another route that can be used. It is a winding but scenic 21-mile drive west from I-75 to US 27 at Pine Knot, KY. From there, follow US 27 south as described above.

Activities: Camping, hiking, horseback riding, swimming, biking, and volleyball.

Facilities: Visitor center, museum, parking area, camping, RV sites, group camp-sites, comfort stations, swimming pools, playgrounds, riding stables, water system, sewer system, RV dump station, amphitheater, hiking and biking trails.

Dates: Open year-round.

Fees: There is charge for camping.

Closest town: Oneida, TN, 10 miles.

For more information: Big South Fork National River and Recreation Area,

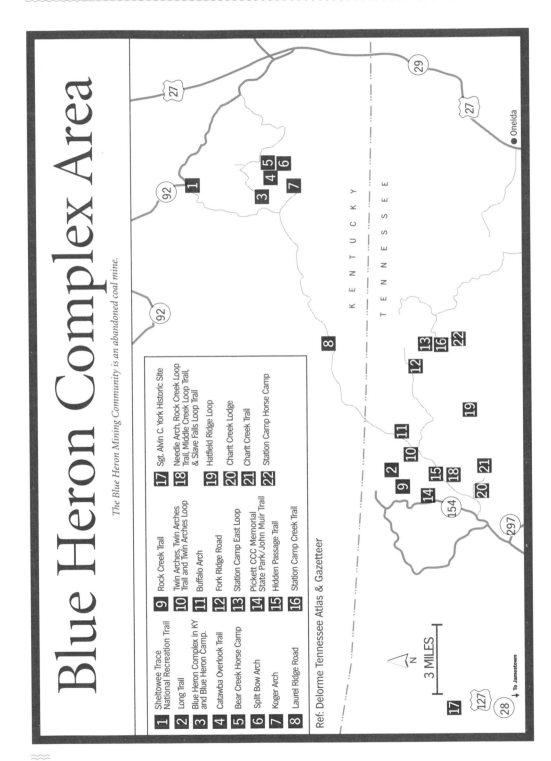

Blue Heron Complex Area

The Blue Heron Mining Community is an abandoned coal mine.

1 Sheltowee Trace National Recreation Trail
2 Long Trail
3 Blue Heron Complex in KY and Blue Heron Camp.
4 Catawba Overlook Trail
5 Bear Creek Horse Camp
6 Split Bow Arch
7 Koger Arch
8 Laurel Ridge Road
9 Rock Creek Trail
10 Twin Arches, Twin Arches Trail and Twin Arches Loop
11 Buffalo Arch
12 Fork Ridge Road
13 Station Camp East Loop
14 Pickett CCC Memorial State Park/John Muir Trail
15 Koger Arch
16 Station Camp Creek Trail
17 Sgt. Alvin C. York Historic Site
18 Needle Arch, Rock Creek Loop Trail, Middle Creek Loop Trail, & Slave Falls Loop Trail
19 Hatfield Ridge Loop
20 Chart Creek Lodge
21 Chart Creek Trail
22 Station Camp Horse Camp

Ref: Delorme Tennessee Atlas & Gazetteer

N

3 MILES

To Jamestown

KENTUCKY
TENNESSEE

Onelda

Bandy Creek Visitor Center, 4564 Leatherwood Road, Oneida, TN 37841. Phone (931) 879-3625.

BLUE HERON COMPLEX IN KENTUCKY

[Fig. 7(3)] The Blue Heron Mining Community is an abandoned coal mine operated by the Stearns Company from 1937 until it was closed in 1962. When production ceased, the buildings were either removed by the company or left to decay. By the time the BSFNRRA was formed, there were no original structures remaining other than the coal tipple, a structure designed to receive coal from mines on both sides of the river and sort it by size into various grades before shipping it out on railroad cars. The U.S. Army Corps of Engineers re-created the location as an interpretive center in the 1980s.

Visitors taking the tour of the complex see a representation of the mining village including the homes, school, and church of Blue Heron as well as one of the entrances to Blue Heron, or Mine 18.

Today there is a paved road to the site as well as a train depot that serves as a landing platform for visitors arriving on the Big South Fork Scenic Railway from Stearns, Kentucky.

The Big South Fork Scenic Railway is an open-air excursion train that travels to Blue Heron from Stearns on the original K&T Railroad line Wednesday through Sunday from May through October, with additional trains running in late April and during the October fall foliage season.

Passengers are loaded first-come, first-serve for the 3-hour, 13-mile round trip. Call (800) GO-ALONG for more information. The Whistle Stop Cafe beside the depot serves breakfast, lunch, and dinner on the days the train is running.

Directions: From Stearns, take KY 1651 to Revelo. Turn right on KY 742 and turn onto Mine 18 Road on the right. Continue straight to Blue Heron. Along Mine 18 Road there are signs directing visitors to two great overlooks, Devils Jump Overlook and Blue Heron Overlook.

Facilities: Parking area with 245-vehicle parking capacity, gift shop, and snack shop.

Dates: Open daily from mid-Apr. through end of Oct.

Closest town: Revelo, KY, 9.5 miles.

For more information: Big South Fork National River and Recreation Area, Bandy Creek Visitor Center, 4564 Leatherwood Road, Oneida, TN 37841. Phone (931) 879-3625. Or the Kentucky Visitor Center, phone (606) 376-5073.

BLUE HERON CAMPGROUND

[Fig. 7(3)] **Directions:** From Stearns, take KY 1651 to Revelo. Turn right on KY 742 and turn onto Mine 18 Road on the right. Turn left at the sign to Blue Heron Campground.

Facilities: 48 improved tent sites and a bathhouse, dump station, electric and water hookups, and play area.

Dates: Open mid-May through mid-Nov.

Fee: There is a charge for tent and trailer sites.

For more information: Big South Fork National River and Recreation Area, Bandy Creek Visitor Center, 4564 Leatherwood Road, Oneida, TN 37841. Phone (931) 879-3625.

CHARIT CREEK LODGE

[Fig. 7(20)] Visitors wishing to enjoy the beauty of the BSFNRRA and primitive accommodations seek reservations at Charit Creek Lodge. It is nestled in a remote wilderness location where Charit Creek joins Station Camp Creek in a small valley framed by high bluffs accessible only on foot or by horseback.

The structure has evolved through the years of habitation, and on the western end there is a log cabin that may have been built in the early 1800s by longhunter Jonathan Blevins. The house became a hunting lodge known locally as "the hog farm" due to the Russian boar imported by owner Joe Simpson in the early 1960s. It was also operated as a youth hostel from 1987 to 1989. Today it's operated by the same folks who operate another well-known Tennessee wilderness retreat, Le Conte Lodge in the Great Smoky Mountains National Park (*see* page 245).

There is running water at the lodge, but no electricity. Each room is equipped with a kerosene lamp and a wood stove. The shower water is heated by solar energy and screened windows and doors provide air conditioning in the summer. There's also a horse stable and you're likely to see groups of riders while you're here. Dinner and breakfast, complete with steaming mugs of coffee, are served. Reservations are needed and you'll receive details on trail choices and directions with your reservation.

Directions: From Bandy Creek Road turn west on TN 297. Continue to TN 154. Turn north on TN 154 for approximately 2 miles. Turn right on Divide Road and continue on Divide Road about 1 mile until it forks. Take the right-hand fork which is Fork Ridge Road and travel 5 miles to the parking area and trailhead. Hike 0.8 mile to the lodge on a steep trail. For a more popular and scenic route, don't take the right-hand fork. Stay on Divide Road approximately 4 miles, until you reach a sign for the Twin Arches Trailhead. Turn and follow that road for 2 miles to a parking area. The trail that starts there is a little longer but isn't as steep, and it leads past the Twin Arches (*see* page 42).

Activities: Hiking, horseback riding, volleyball, and horseshoes.

Facilities: Lodge, cabins, stables, and hiking and horse trails.

Dates: Open year-round.

Fees: There is a charge for the lodge and cabins.

Closest town: Jamestown, 12 miles.

For more information: Charit Creek Lodge, 250 Apple Valley Road, Sevierville, TN 37862. Phone (423) 429-5704.

CHARIT CREEK TRAIL

[Fig. 7(21)] Several switchbacks, a long set of steps, and some stairs aid you on the short, steep, downhill trek to Charit Creek Lodge. In season, you'll see clusters of the delicate rue anemone (*Anemonella thalictroides*), along with chickweed (*Stellaria media*) and trillium (*Trillium* spp.) as the path winds along moist slopes to the stream crossing at Station Camp Creek in front of the lodge.

Charit Creek may have been named for a young girl named Charity who drowned in the creek.

Trail: 0.8 mile, one-way.

Elevation: Change of 500 feet.

Degree of Difficulty: Moderate to strenuous.

Surface and blaze: Rock and forest floor. Red arrowhead blaze.

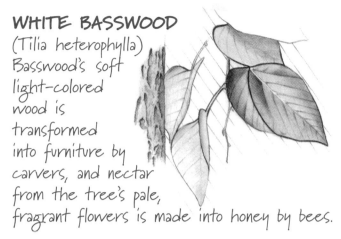

WHITE BASSWOOD
(*Tilia heterophylla*)
Basswood's soft light-colored wood is transformed into furniture by carvers, and nectar from the tree's pale, fragrant flowers is made into honey by bees.

🔲 LEATHERWOOD FORD

[Fig. 6(5)] The Leatherwood Ford is a popular spot on the Big South Fork offering swimming, picnicking, fishing, and interpretive nature trails. There's an easy put-in for canoes with a low-water bridge providing good access to both sides of the river for bank fishermen and hikers. Those who enjoy playing in the water find this a good spot much of the time since the river is often wide, shallow, and gently rippling at this point. Handicapped-accessible boardwalks with benches and footbridges follow the river's edge.

Directions: Take TN 297 to Leatherwood Bridge. Cross the bridge, turn left into the Leatherwood Ford trailhead parking area.

Activities: Hiking, scenic viewing, fishing, picnicking, and boating.

Facilities: Comfort station, viewing platforms, gazebo, pedestrian bridge, hiking trailhead, river access, picnic tables, and a telephone.

Dates: Open year-round.

Closest town: Oneida, 9 miles.

For more information: Big South Fork National River and Recreation Area, Bandy Creek Visitor Center, 4564 Leatherwood Road, Oneida, TN 37841. Phone (931) 879-3625.

LEATHERWOOD FORD LOOP

[Fig. 6(6)] There are several scenic overlooks and rock bluffs along this trail, as well as access to the fantastic Leatherwood Ford Overlook. The trail leads from the rim to the river and back via switchbacks and steps. You may begin your loop at the parking area for the Leatherwood Ford Overlook and Sunset Overlook and descend to the river or begin at the river at the Leatherwood Ford Trailhead below the TN 297 bridge that spans the Big South Fork and climb to the East Rim. The Leatherwood Ford Trail briefly joins the John Muir Trail (*see* page 45) along the river before it

STRIPED SKUNK
(Mephitis mephitis)
Look for the striped skunk's white facial stripe, neck patch, and V on its back.

begins its steady ascent. The moist slopes lining the river are good spots for spring wildflowers in April and May.

Directions: Follow TN 297 approximately 1.5 miles east from the Bandy Creek Road junction to Leatherwood Ford. Turn left on the eastern side of the bridge to the Leatherwood Ford Loop. Or go west from Oneida on TN 297 approximately 14 miles and turn right on the eastern side of Leatherwood Ford Bridge.

Trail: 3.6 miles.
Elevation: Change, 550 feet.
Difficulty: Moderate to strenuous.

ALUM FORD
[Fig. 6(1)] The Alum Ford area is popular for its boat-launching ramp, which gives anglers with power boats access to the river that now flows into Lake Cumberland. People interested in an alternative to RV camping will enjoy primitive camping here at sites with picnic tables. The Yahoo Falls Trails are nearby as well as access to the Sheltowee Trace National Recreation Trail (*see* page 44).

Directions: From Oneida go north on US 27. Take US 70 to KY 700 at Marshes Siding. Turn west on KY 700 and drive approximately 4.5 miles to Alum Ford.

Activities: Hiking, boating, scenic viewing, and fishing.

Facilities: Picnic sites, 8 primitive campsites, pit toilets, boat ramp, car parking area, and hiking trail.

Dates: Open year-round.

Fees: None.

Closest town: Whitley City, KY, 4 miles.

For more information: Kentucky Visitor Center at Stearns, phone (606) 376-5073.

YAHOO FALLS TRAILS—THE TOPSIDE LOOP
[Fig. 6(2)] Yahoo Falls, the tallest waterfall in the BSFNRRA, drops 113 feet as Yahoo Creek tumbles over a gigantic rock shelter. The well-maintained Topside Loop Trail leads from the parking lot at the Yahoo Falls Scenic Area past several overlooks on the way to the top of the falls. Two trails, Cascade (a 1.1-mile loop with blue blazes) and Cliffside (a 1.2-mile loop with green blazes), spur off the Topside Loop (a 1.1-mile loop with yellow blazes). The Cascade Loop follows a portion of the Sheltowee Trace National Recreation Trail (*see* page 44) and Cliffside leads to the base of the falls.

Directions: From Oneida go north on US 27. Take US 70 to KY 700 at Marshes

Siding. Turn west on KY 700, and drive toward Alum Ford River Access but turn right at 4 miles to the Yahoo Falls parking lot and trailhead.

Trail: 0.8 mile, loop.

Elevation: Change, 100 feet.

Degree of Difficulty: Moderate.

Surface and blaze: Yellow blaze.

OTHER HIKING TRAILS

The extensive trail system within the BSFNRRA provides hikers with access to virtually all of the scenic and historic locations and accommodates all ages and levels of experience. Some trails can be walked in less than one hour, while others require a full day or longer, and the degree of difficulty ranges from easy to strenuous, with many of the trails falling in the moderate to strenuous category as a result of length or topography. Due to the presence of high cliffs and the generally rugged nature of the trails, it is recommended that hikers plan to reach their destination well in advance of nightfall. Rain, snow, and ice also increase the difficulty of the trails, making some of them extremely hazardous.

These trails are listed from south to north through the BSFNRRA.

BURNT MILL BRIDGE LOOP

[Fig. 6(17)] Bluffs, rapids, and large boulders are seen along this loop which joins the John Muir Trail as it follows the Clear Fork River, a favored destination for rafters and canoeists. A profusion of wildflowers line the trail in the spring and there are a couple of favorable camping spots along the way.

Directions: From Oneida go south on US 27 and drive 11 miles to Mountain View Road, 0.5 mile on the right south of the New River Bridge. Turn right on Mountain View Road and continue 2 miles to Shoemaker's Store on the right. Turn right at the store, then left at Mountain View Missionary Baptist Church. Drive 2.1 miles to Crossroads Community and turn right at Crossroads Baptist Church at the four-way intersection. Continue 0.3 mile downhill to fork in the road and bear left. Continue an additional 0.5 mile to Burnt Mill Bridge. Trailhead parking is on the left.

Trail: 3.6 miles, loop.

Elevation: Change, 200 feet.

Difficulty: Moderate.

Surface and blaze: Forest floor and rock. Red arrowhead blaze.

HONEY CREEK LOOP TRAIL

[Fig. 6(18)] This is a rugged and strenuous walk involving climbing ladders enclosed in wire, crossing multiple streams, and scrambling over boulders. The trail is very popular with hikers. Along its length the traveler will be pleasantly surprised to see Honey Creek Falls, Moonshine Falls, Hideout Falls, and Boulder House Falls, rock formations, Indian rock shelters, massive boulders, and a series of Class III and IV rapids. Much of the trail passes through what was the Honey Creek Natural Area, a 109-acre pocket wilderness established by Bowater, Inc. prior to the area's incorporation into the BSFNRRA.

Directions: Continue from Burnt Mill Bridge Loop as described in directions above, cross the bridge at the ford, and continue for 3.5 miles to the fork in the road. Take the right fork into the Honey Creek Pocket Wilderness. The Honey Creek Loops Trail begins 0.8 mile down the gravel road. At the end of the road is an outstanding overlook, one of the best in the BSFNRRA.

Trail: 5.5 miles, loop.

Elevation: Change, 460 feet.

Difficulty: Strenuous. (Note: Allow a minimum of 5 hours to complete this trail. Sturdy boots are required. This trail is not recommended after heavy rainfall.)

Surface and blaze: Forest floor and rock. Red arrowhead blaze.

EAST RIM OVERLOOK TRAIL

[Fig. 6(10)] The East Rim Overlook is wheelchair accessible via a paved walkway and provides a scenic overlook 400 feet above the river. A camera with a 200mm lens or larger will provide better details of bluffs and the river below. Retrace your way on the paved portion of the trail or take the short graveled section back to the parking lot.

Directions: The entrance road to the East Rim Overlook is across from the ranger office on TN 297. Continue 0.7 mile to the parking lot for the overlook.

Trail: 0.1 mile, one-way.

Degree of Difficulty: Easy.

Surface and blaze: Paved. Red arrowhead blaze.

SUNSET OVERLOOK TRAIL

[Fig. 6(11)] This trail passes small ponds, leads past a shooting range, and follows a small stream along the ridge on the way to an overlook that provides a nice view of the Big South Fork River gorge from a bare rock bluff.

Directions: Across from ranger office on TN 297 at the Leatherwood Ford Overlook and Sunset Overlook parking area, hike south across the road to the Sunset Overlook Trail.

Trail: 1.3 miles, one-way.

Elevation: No change.

Difficulty: Easy.

Surface and blaze: Forest floor and rock. Red arrowhead blaze.

O&W BRIDGE TRAIL

[Fig. 6(5)] The O&W Bridge Trail follows the river, crosses streams, offers nice views of river bluffs, showcases seasonal wildflower displays, and includes the opportunity to walk across the historic O&W Railroad Bridge. The O&W linked the area with the rest of the world via the O&W Railroad, which carried logs, coal, passengers, and mail between depots in Jamestown and Oneida. Operation of the line ceased in 1954.

Directions: The trailhead is at Leatherwood Bridge on TN 297 east of the Bandy Creek Recreation Area. Cross the bridge, turn left (north) into the Leatherwood Ford trailhead parking area. Park in the parking area and hike south along the east side of the river.

Trail: 2.3 miles, one-way.

Elevation: Change, 100 feet.

Difficulty: Moderate.

Surface and blaze: Forest floor, rock, and railroad bridge. Blue silhouette blaze.

ANGEL FALLS TRAIL

[Fig. 6(6)] This pleasant, level walk features a continuous view of the Big South Fork River, impressive rock bluffs, and Angel Falls. Once an 8-foot cascade that was dynamited in an effort to improve navigation along this section of the river, Angel Falls is now a dangerous Class III or IV rapid. A brochure avail-

FOX SQUIRREL
(Sciurus niger)
During the morning and late afternoon, the fox squirrel buries nuts which it will locate, even under snow, with its keen sense of smell.

able at the Bandy Creek Visitor Center or the gazebo at Leatherwood Ford identifies 30 numbered trees along the trail. The trees range from red mulberry (*Morus rubra*) and umbrella magnolia (*Magnolia tripetala*) to sassafras (*Sassafras albidum*) and shagbark hickory (*Carya ovata*). This is also a good wildflower trail with opportunities for spotting the lovely pink lady's slippers (*Cypripedium acaule*) blooming, usually around Mother's Day.

Directions: The trailhead is at Leatherwood Bridge on TN 297 east of the Bandy Creek Recreation Area. Cross the bridge and turn left (north) into the Leatherwood Ford trailhead parking area. Hike north on the east side of the river.

Trail: 2 miles, one-way.

Elevation: Change, 100 feet.

Difficulty: Easy

Surface and blaze: Rock and forest floor. Red arrowhead blaze.

ANGEL FALLS OVERLOOK TRAIL

[Fig. 6(3)] This trail leads along the west bank of the Big South Fork River and crosses Fall Branch before climbing to the top of a ridge for one of the best scenic views of the Big South Fork River gorge. Hikers should be prepared for steps, a ladder, sheer ledges, and switchbacks. This trail is a portion of the John Muir Trail.

Directions: The trailhead is at Leatherwood Bridge on TN 297 east of the Bandy Creek Recreation Area. Cross the bridge, turn left (north) into the Leatherwood Ford trailhead parking area. Hike north on the west side of river.

Trail: 3 miles, one-way.

Elevation: Change, 450 feet.

Difficulty: Moderate to difficult.

Surface and blaze: Forest floor and rock. Blue silhouette blaze.

GRAND GAP LOOP TRAIL

[Fig. 6(3)] The Grand Gap Loop Trail picks up at the end of the Angel Falls Overlook Trail (*see* above). The loop is 6.8 miles, but reaching it adds 3 or more additional miles since the loop can only be reached via connecting trails. Access from Leatherwood Ford via the Angel Falls Overlook Trail involves a 12.8-mile round trip. Hardwood forests, high cliffs, and overlooks of the Big South Fork and Angel Falls highlight the Grand Gap Loop.

Directions: Trailhead at end of Angel Falls Overlook Trail.

Trail: 6.8 miles, loop.

Elevation: Change, 500 feet.

Difficulty: Moderate.

Surface and blaze: Rock and forest floor. Blue silhouette blaze.

JOHN LITTON/GENERAL SLAVENS FARM LOOP TRAIL

[Fig. 6(7)] Highlights of this trail include rock houses, Fall Branch Falls, and a log house and barn built along a creek in a small cove by John Litton around 1900. The household of General (his name, not his rank) Slavens was the only other family to live on this farm before it was purchased for the BSFNRRA in 1979.

Directions: The trailhead is located at Bandy Creek Campground (*see* page 31) near the swimming pool.

Trail: 6.3 miles, loop.

Elevation: Change, 300 feet.

Difficulty: Easy to moderate

Surface and blaze: Forest floor and rock. Red arrowhead blaze.

BANDY CREEK CAMPGROUND LOOP TRAIL

[Fig. 6(9)] This is a good trail for hikers not up to strenuous climbs up rock ledges or ladders, but wanting a chance to become familiar with the campground and its facilities. This brisk walk in the woods offers the chance to spot birds and occasional deer.

Directions: Bandy Creek Campground trailhead at Bandy Creek Recreation Area's visitor center (*see* page 31).

Trail: 2.3 miles, loop.

Elevation: Change, 80 feet.

Difficulty: Easy.

Surface and blaze: Gravel path. Red arrowhead blaze.

OSCAR BLEVINS FARM LOOP TRAIL

[Fig. 6(10)] A brochure available at the Bandy Creek Visitor Center or from a box near the trailhead discusses plant succession taking place in fields along the trail. The trail passes through fields reclaimed by native grasses, woody plants, and Virginia pine before passing through a forest of poplar, oak, and maple. The honeycombing found on sandstone is explained as the result of differential erosion, a process that leaves behind less erosive materials like mineral deposits and erodes the surrounding sandstone. Evidence shows rock shelters along the path were used by prehistoric visitors 8,000 to 10,000 years ago and more recently as animal pens. The Oscar Blevins homestead consists of a log house built in the 1890s and a frame house built in the 1950s. The Blevins family descended from Longhunter Jonathan Blevins (*see* page 34).

Directions: From the Bandy Creek Visitor Center (*see* page 31) turn left (west) on Bandy Creek Road and go 0.1 mile. The trailhead and parking area are on the left.

Trail: 3.6 miles, loop.

Elevation: Change, 180 feet.

Difficulty: Easy.

Surface and blaze: Rock and forest floor. Red arrowhead blaze.

WEST ENTRANCE TRAILHEAD TO BANDY CREEK CAMPGROUND

[Fig. 6(4)] This trail follows an old logging road along much of its length and intersects the Oscar Blevins Farm Loop Trail after several stream crossings. During May and June hikers may find mountain laurel and rosebay rhododendron in bloom.

Directions: From the Bandy Creek Visitor Center (*see* page 31) go to TN 297, and turn right (west) on TN 297. Go 3.9 miles to the trailhead on the north side of the road.

Trail: 3.2 miles, one-way.

Elevation: Change, 200 feet.

Difficulty: Easy.

Surface and blaze: Rock and forest floor. Red arrow blaze.

MIDDLE CREEK LOOP TRAIL

[Fig. 7(18)] This trail travels through an upland hardwood forest and across rock bluffs before reaching the first large rock shelter. The sandy soil and huge boulders inside rock shelters are the result of water and weathering. Important to prehistoric peoples as well as Indians and early settlers, the rock shelters are also home to a rare plant listed as threatened in Tennessee and Kentucky. Lucy Braun's snakeroot (*Eupaterium Luciae Brauniae*) grows to a maximum height of 3 feet with triangular serrated leaves and tiny tubular white flowers on a stalk at the top of the plant.

Directions: Go north on TN 154 for 2 miles beyond the TN 297 junction. Turn right onto Divide Road. Continue for 0.7 mile to Middle Creek trailhead on the right.

Trail: 3.5 miles, loop.

Elevation: Change, 100 feet.

Difficulty: Moderate.

Surface and blaze: Rock and forest floor. Red arrowhead blaze.

SLAVE FALLS LOOP TRAIL

[Fig. 7(18)] At 1.1 miles, this trail intersects with the Mill Creek Trail. Take this spur trail to see Slave Falls, named for the runaway slaves local legends say once took refuge in the area, and Needle Arch, a sandstone formation molded by runoff and seepage. Back on the Slave Falls Loop Trail, hikers will see Indian Rock House, which at 75 feet deep and nearly 100 feet wide is one of the largest rock shelters in the park.

Directions: Go north on TN 154 for 2 miles beyond the TN 297 junction. Turn right onto Divide Road and in 1 mile take the right-hand fork to Fork Ridge Road. Continue for 1.2 miles to the Sawmill Trailhead on the left.

Trail: 3.4 miles, loop.

Elevation: Change, 300 feet.

Difficulty: Easy.

Surface and blaze: Rock and forest floor. Red arrowhead blaze.

ROCK CREEK LOOP TRAIL

[Fig. 7(18)] Hikers travel along an old railroad bed about 1 mile past the Hattie Blevins Cemetery before joining a 5-mile segment of the John Muir Trail (*see* page 45). The John Muir Trail (JMT) joins the Sheltowee Trace National Recreation Trail and heads up Rock Creek, descending to the creek at a couple of areas deep enough to make nice swimming holes. After the JMT and Sheltowee Trace National Recreation Trail turn to the right, the Rock Creek Loop Trail continues left up a steep path.

Directions: Go north on TN 154 for 2 miles beyond the TN 297 junction. Turn right on Divide Road and go 1 mile to a fork. Follow Divide Road toward Twin Arches. At the junction of Divide Road and Twin Arches Road continue straight ahead on Divide Road for approximately 0.4 mile to Hattie Blevins Cemetery Road. Turn left and continue 2.9 miles to the cemetery and the Rock Creek Loop trailhead.

Trail: 7 miles, loop.

Elevation: Change, 500 feet.

Difficulty: Strenuous.

Surface and blaze: Rock and forest floor. Red arrowhead, blue silhouette JMT, and turtle Sheltowee blazes.

TWIN ARCHES TRAIL

[Fig. 7(10)] The Twin Arches Trail leads to the Twin Arches, massive side-by-side natural bridges that are among the most impressive geological features in Tennessee. The North Arch spans 93 feet and rises 62 feet. The South Arch spans 135 feet and rises 103 feet. Taken together, they are among the largest natural bridges in the world. A steep stairway between the two arches leads to the top.

WHITE ASH

(*Fraxinus americana*) White ash is the most abundant ash in North America. Its bark has a diamond shape.

Directions: Go north

on TN 154 for 2 miles beyond the TN 297 junction. Turn right on Divide Road and go 1.3 miles to a fork. Take left fork of Divide Road and go 2.7 miles to another fork. Take the right fork and follow Twin Arches Road 2.4 miles to Twin Arches trailhead.

Trail: 1.4 miles, one-way.

Elevation: Change, 150 feet.

Degree of Difficulty: Easy–moderate.

Surface and blaze: Forest floor and rock on a well-worn path.

TWIN ARCHES LOOP TRAIL

[Fig. 7(10)] Despite being a strenuous walk, the Twin Arches Loop Trail is one of the most popular in the BSFNRRA because it provides access to the magnificent sandstone formations known as Twin Arches (*see* page 46) and Charit Creek Lodge, a historic site and wilderness accommodation for backpackers and horse trail riders (*see* page 34). Along the way, the trail also passes rock shelters and the sandstone chimney marking the homesite known as Jake's Place, which was named for Jake Blevins, descendant of Longhunter Jonathan Blevins. The Twin Arches Loop Trail is reached by several trails, including the Twin Arches Trail.

Directions: Go north on TN 154 for 2 miles beyond the TN 297 junction. Turn right on Divide Road and go 1.3 miles to a fork. Take left fork of Divide Road and go 2.7 miles to another fork. Take right fork and follow Twin Arches Road 2.4 miles to Twin Arches trailhead.

Trail: 5.9 miles, loop.

Elevation: Change, 150 feet.

Difficulty: Strenuous.

Surface and blaze: Rock and forest floor.

MEETING OF THE WATERS LOOP

[Fig. 6(15)] There are many interesting features on this trail, including historic Laurel Dale Cemetery across from the trailhead. The cemetery contains graves of early members of the Victorian colony at Rugby, including Margaret Hughes, the mother of the founder. The turn-off to the Gentlemen's Swimming Hole is 0.4 mile from the trailhead. This popular swimming hole is where only the men from Rugby (*see* page 56) frolicked in the Clear Fork River, but today everyone enjoys a dip followed by a picnic on a hot summer day. Along the way, a rock shelter known locally as Witch's Cave and spring wildflowers including trailing arbutus (*Epigaea repens*), wild geranium (*Geranium maculatum*), crested dwarf iris (*Iris cristana*), and little brown jugs (*Hexastylis arifolia*) may be seen. The trail continues to the Meeting of the Waters, the confluence of the Clear Fork River and White Oak Creek. A brochure prepared by Historic Rugby and the National Park Service available from the visitor centers at Bandy Creek in the BSFNRRA or the Rugby Schoolhouse warns hikers to beware of timber rattlers, copperheads, ticks, and poison ivy.

Directions: From Oneida take US 27 south to TN 52 at Elgin. Follow TN 52 west 7 miles to Rugby. In Rugby, turn right at sign for Laurel Dale Cemetery. Trailhead is at the cemetery.

Trail: 3 miles, loop.
Elevation: Change, 240 feet.
Difficulty: Moderate.
Surface and blaze: Rock and forest floor. Red arrowhead blaze.

BLUE HERON LOOP TRAIL

[Fig. 7(3)] This trail features scenic overlooks, including one known as Devil's Jump. A portion of the trail that is paved but steep in spots begins about 0.5 mile along the Blue Heron Loop Trail. This portion may be accessed at a parking lot past the one containing the trailhead. The portion accessed from the trailhead in the first parking lot is also paved and is a bit more gentle for those searching for handicapped-accessible trails. The trail passes wildflowers, a rock house, and other geologic formations like Cracks-in-the-Rock, giant rock slabs along the rock bluff joined by narrow stairs. The trail also passes through the historic mining community at Blue Heron.

Directions: In Oneida go north on US 27 and continue to KY 1651 at Pine Knot, KY. Turn left on KY 1651 and drive to Revelo. Turn right on KY 742 at Revelo and turn right (west) in 3.2 miles on Mine 18 Road. Pass the campground on the right and turn left on the Overlooks Road that leads to Blue Heron. The trailhead is at the end of the first parking area but a second paved portion of the trail may also be accessed from the next parking lot on the road leading to the overlooks.

Trail: 6.5 miles, loop.
Elevation: Change, 450 feet.
Difficulty: Moderate.
Surface and blaze: Rock, forest floor, paved portions, and old roadway. Red arrowhead blaze.

CATAWBA OVERLOOK TRAIL

[Fig. 7(4)] The Catawba Overlook provides a scenic view of the Big South Fork River gorge, but the trail to the overlook can be marshy in spots after a rain and requires several creek crossings. In addition to the Catawba rhododendron found at the overlook, wildflowers may be seen along the way.

Directions: At Blue Heron Mining Community (*see* directions page 33) cross tipple bridge to west side of Big South Fork River, turn south and follow signs to overlook.

Trail: 1.6 miles, one-way.
Elevation: Change, 400 feet.
Difficulty: Moderate–difficult.
Surface and blaze: Rock and forest floor.

SHELTOWEE TRACE NATIONAL RECREATION TRAIL

[Fig. 7(1)] The name, *Sheltowee*, means big turtle in Shawnee, and it is a name frontiersman Daniel Boone was given after being captured by the Indians while on a supply mission from Boonesborough to where his men were making salt at Blue Licks. The turtle is the identifying blaze on much of the trail.

Accessed at Pickett CCC Memorial State Park via the Hidden Passage trailhead (*see* page 25), the trail leads past waterfalls, rock shelters, creeks, abandoned mines, railroad trestles, and backcountry camping spots. At the Kentucky state line the trail enters the Daniel Boone National Forest, then swings east and runs along the BSFN-RRA boundary, following the Laurel Ridge Road. The trail continues past natural stone arches, campgrounds, picnic areas, waterfalls, river access points, and rock shelters. It departs the BSFNRRA, heading northward through the Daniel Boone Forest, then enters the BSFNRRA again near the Yamacraw Bridge. This bridge crosses the Big South Fork River near a day-use area off KY 92. Local outfitters describe the river run from Yamacraw Bridge to Alum Ford as easy, or Class I. The trail exits the BSFNRRA for the last time at the headwaters of Lake Cumberland after passing through the Yahoo Falls Scenic Area (*see* page 36).

Portions of the Sheltowee Trace National Recreation Trail north of Cumberland Falls, Kentucky, lie on roads, some of which are open to both off-road vehicles and horses. There are many places where the trail can be accessed, so hikes of whatever length desired can be planned. However, hikers contemplating long trips are urged to obtain up-to-date information from the Stearns Ranger District, POB 429, Whitley City, Kentucky 42653, phone (606) 376-5073.

Trail: Entire length—254 miles. This segment—66.4 miles.

Elevation: Change, 450 feet.

Degree of Difficulty: Strenuous.

Surface and blaze: Rock, gravel road, and forest floor with white turtle blaze and white diamond blaze.

JOHN MUIR TRAIL

[Fig. 7(14)] Named for naturalist and conservationist John Muir (1838–1914), this is one of Tennessee's State Scenic Trails, which, when completed, will extend from Pickett State Park on the Cumberland Plateau to the Appalachian Trail in the southern part of the Cherokee National Forest. At the present time, right-of-way problems stand in the way of connecting the widely separated segments. The trail commemorates the 1867 hike through the plateau by Muir, a conservationist and founder and president of the Sierra Club until his death in 1914.

The western portion of the John Muir Trail (JMT) begins at the Hidden Passage trailhead in Pickett CCC Memorial State Park (*see* page 24) and follows Thompson Creek to a junction with the Sheltowee Trace National Recreation Trail near the Kentucky state line. JMT turns south, then west, back to the southeast, and eventually reaches the Big South Fork River. It follows the river to the Leatherwood Ford Bridge where a short section of the JMT is handicapped accessible. The JMT continues to the old O&W Bridge where it stops until construction is completed. An additional segment to Honey Creek has been partially staked but is not completed at this writing. An 18-mile southern portion of the trail is in the Cherokee National Forest near the Hiwassee State Scenic River (*see* page 218).

Directions: The eastern trailhead is at Leatherwood Ford bridge on TN 297, or the western trailhead is in Pickett CCC Memorial State Park at the Hidden Passage Trail trailhead located 0.3 mile north of the park on TN 154 on the eastern side of the road.

Trail: 42 miles, one-way.

Elevation: Change, 500 feet.

Degree of Difficulty: Moderate.

Surface and blaze: Rock and forest floor. JMT blue blaze.

ARCHES

Arches, or natural bridges, are most often created in the exposed cliffs and ridges of the plateau when the softer rock under the highly resistant sandstone cap erodes. In and around the BSFNRRA there are well over two dozen of these features.

TWIN ARCHES

[Fig. 7(10)] The best known arches in the BSFNRRA are the Twin Arches, which are accessible on the Twin Arches Trail (*see* page 42). The Twin Arches are two of the largest arches in the eastern United States. Steps lead up and across the span.

Directions: Go north on TN 154 for 1.8 miles beyond the TN 297 junction. Turn right on Divide Road and go 1.3 miles to a fork. Take left fork of Divide Road and go 2.7 miles to another fork. Take the right fork and follow Twin Arches Road 2.4 miles to Twin Arches trailhead.

NEEDLE ARCH

[Fig. 7(18)] Needle Arch is a thin, delicate arch that was left standing alone when the back of the rock shelter of which it was once a part eroded. It can be reached from the Slave Falls Loop Trail (*see* page 41). At 1.1 miles along the trail, the Slave Falls Loop Trail turns right to Slave Falls, but go straight on the Mill Creek Trail that leads to Needle Arch.

Directions: Go north on TN 154 for 1.8 miles beyond the TN 297 junction. Turn right onto Divide Road and in 1 mile take the right-hand fork to Fork Ridge Road. Continue for 2.2 miles to the trailhead on the left.

SPLIT BOW ARCH

[Fig. 7(6)] Split Bow Arch is a narrow rock bridge that remained when large chunks of rock eroded and fell from a section of the rock bluff. The arch can be seen from an overlook or a 0.7-mile loop trail leads to and through the arch. The honeycomb rock seen here is formed when groundwater seeps through sandstone, dissolving the iron deposits out of the formation and leaving behind the sandstone.

Directions: To reach the arch from Oneida go north on US 27 and continue to KY 1651 at Pine Knot, KY. Follow KY 1651 to Revelo. Turn on KY 742 at Revelo and turn in 3.2 miles on Mine 18 Road toward Bear Creek Scenic Area. As you continue along the road to Bear Creek, you'll pass a parking area for the Split Bow Arch Overlook before reaching the beginning of the 0.6-mile Split Bow Arch Loop.

YAHOO ARCH

[Fig. 6(2)] Yahoo Arch is another arch formed by erosion at the back of a rock shelter. The 15-foot-high arch with a 60-foot span can be reached from the Yahoo

Falls Scenic Area just off KY 700.

Directions: Take US 70 to KY 700 at Marshes Siding. Turn west on KY 700, and drive toward Alum Ford River Access, but turn right at 4 miles to the Yahoo Falls parking lot and trailhead. Follow the Topside Loop Trail (*see* page 36) for 0.4 mile and turn right on the Yahoo Arch trail.

SPRING SALAMANDER
(Gyrinophilus porphyriticus) This salamander can be found in springs, cool mountain streams, and caves. It is carnivorous and sometimes cannibalistic.

KOGER ARCH

[Fig. 7(7)] Koger Arch is a broad arch resulting from rock shelter erosion. With a clearance of 18 feet, it spans 91 feet. It is accessible from the Sheltowee Trace National Recreation Trail (*see* page 44) and also from a short trail leading up from Devils Creek Road near the Yamacraw area.

Directions: From Stearns go west on KY 92 to Yamacraw Bridge. Turn left (south) on the west side of Yamacraw Bridge on KY 1363 along Rock Creek, and bear to the left (south) at 2.3 miles onto Devil's Creek Road (also called Laurel Creek Road and Beech Grove Road on some maps). The trailhead is on the left 3.1 miles down.

BUFFALO ARCH

[Fig. 7(11)] Buffalo Arch is also accessible from the Sheltowee Trace National Recreation Trail (*see* page 44) near the BSFNRRA/Daniel Boone National Forest boundary on Rock Creek. Buffalo Arch comes out of the hillside, spanning 82 feet and clearing 19 feet.

Directions: Go north from Pickett CCC Memorial State Park (*see* page 24) on TN 154 for 5.4 miles and turn right on FR 562. Continue for 0.8 mile and turn right on FR 6305 (unmarked). Four-wheel-drive vehicles are recommended to go beyond this point. The trail to the arch is 0.3 mile farther down on the left.

EQUESTRIAN CAMPS

Although camping is allowed throughout much of the backcountry accessible by horse trails, BSFNRRA requests that horses be tied on picket lines away from water, trees, and buildings, and all camps should be away from marked safety zones or trails. In addition to the stables at Bandy Creek and facilities for horses at Charit Creek Lodge, there are developed horse camps in both the Kentucky and Tennessee portions of BSFN-RRA. Horses must have current proof of a negative Coggins Test for swamp fever.

BEAR CREEK HORSE CAMP

[Fig. 7(5)] The Bear Creek Horse Camp, operated by a National Park Service concessionaire, services the northern BSFNRRA from its base outside Stearns, Kentucky, but make reservations and inquiries through Oneida in the southern portion of the area.

Directions: From Oneida, go north on US 27 to KY 1651 at Pine Knot, KY. Turn left on KY 1651 to Revelo. At Revelo, take KY 742 approximately 3.2 miles to Mine 18 Road. Continue 2 miles before bearing right at the sign to Bear Creek Horse Camp.

Activities: Horseback riding and camping.

Facilities: 23 developed campsites with water and electricity, tables, grills, tie-outs for 4 horses per site, hot water showers, and modern restrooms.

Fees: There is a charge for camping. Reservations highly recommended.

For more information: Bear Creek Horse Camp, POB 4411, Oneida, TN 37841. Phone (423) 569-3321.

STATION CAMP HORSE CAMP

[Fig. 7(22)] The Station Camp Horse Camp, also operated by a National Park Service concessionaire, services the northern BSFNRRA. It's a good idea to call for reservations at this popular camp west of Oneida.

Directions: From Bandy Creek Visitor Center turn east on TN 297. Drive approximately 10 miles to Station Camp Road. Turn left and follow road to the Station Camp Horse Camp sign on the right.

Activities: Camping and horseback riding.

Facilities: 24 developed sites with water and electricity, tables, grills, tie-outs for 4 horses per site, hot water showers, and modern restrooms.

Fees: There is a charge for camping.

For more information: Station Camp Horse Camp, POB 4411, Oneida, TN 37841. Phone (423) 569-3321.

▓ HORSE TRAILS

The more than 180 miles of horse trails throughout BSFNRRA are marked with a white blaze and a yellow horse head. Some portions of trails are shared by hikers, horses, mountain bikers, all-terrain vehicles (ATVs), and four-by-four vehicles. Although mountain bikes are permitted on horse trails, cyclists are urged to yield to horses and encouraged to remain stationary as horses pass. Horseback riding is forbidden on paved roads and hiking trails not specifically designated for equestrian traffic. Horses, like hikers, are encouraged to stay on the trail because taking short cuts on switchbacks creates paths devoid of vegetation and subject to erosion. To prevent damage to trees, horses should never be directly tied to trees, even for short breaks.

LAUREL RIDGE ROAD

[Fig. 7(8)] This route features upland forests and level to gentle hills with a steep descent to the Big South Fork River at Blue Heron.

Directions: Go north on TN 154 for 1.8 miles beyond the TN 297 junction. Turn right on Divide Road and continue for 3 miles past the Kentucky state line to Peter's Mountain trailhead and parking area on the right.

Trail: 6 miles.

LONG TRAIL

[Fig. 7(2)] This trail features upland forests, Peter's Mountain, and the Blue Heron Mining Community. The trail crosses streams with a ford at the Big South Fork River at Blue Heron.

Directions: Go north on TN 154 for 2 miles beyond the TN 297 junction. Turn right onto Fork Ridge Road. Continue for 1.5 miles to trailhead on the left in parking area.

Trail: Up to 40 miles.

NORTH WHITE OAK LOOP

[Fig. 6(9)] Overlooks, upland forests, old farmlands, and level to gentle hills provide a pleasant ride on this loop trail.

Directions: Bandy Creek Stables/Bandy Creek Equestrian Trailhead near the Bandy Creek Visitor Center off TN 297 (*see* page 31).

Trail: 20.2 miles.

CHARIT CREEK LODGE TRAIL

[Fig. 6(9), Fig. 7(20)] The trail crosses Laurel Fork Creek, passes Charit Creek Lodge, and makes steep descents into Laurel Fork and Station Camp creeks.

Directions: Bandy Creek Stables/Bandy Creek Equestrian Trailhead near the Bandy Creek Visitor Center off TN 297 (*see* page 31).

Trail: 7.1 miles.

JACK'S RIDGE LOOP

[Fig. 6(9)] The trail passes through upland forests on a route that encounters only gentle hills.

Directions: Bandy Creek Stables/Bandy Creek Equestrian Trailhead near the Bandy Creek Visitor Center off TN 297 (*see* page 31).

Trail: 6 miles.

DUNCAN HOLLOW ROAD TO STATION CAMP CREEK

[Fig. 6(9)] This ride features abandoned farmlands, upland forests, and a steep descent to Laurel Fork Creek before reaching Station Camp Creek.

Directions: Bandy Creek Stables/Bandy Creek Equestrian Trailhead near the Bandy Creek Visitor Center off TN 297 (*see* page 31).

Trail: 6 miles.

FORK RIDGE ROAD

[Fig. 7(12)] This trail features a wooded ridgetop, a 1930s railroad grade, a steep descent to the Laurel Fork Creek, and the Big South Fork River.

Directions: Go north on TN 154 for 2 miles beyond the TN 297 junction. Turn right onto Fork Ridge Road and go 4.5 miles. The trailhead is on the left.

Trail: 4.5 miles.

STATION CAMP EAST LOOP

[Fig. 7(13)] The route provides views of old homesites, rock shelters, the Big South Fork River, and wildflowers. There are some steep climbs out of the river gorges. Caution and sound judgment should be used before attempting to ford river at Station Camp East or Big Island at No Business Creek. If in doubt, don't.

Directions: Go east from the Big South Fork River (Leatherwood Ford Bridge) on TN 297 about 6 miles to Station Camp Road. Turn left (north) on Station Camp Road and go 4.3 miles to Station Camp East trailhead.

Trail: 12.8 miles.

STATION CAMP CREEK TRAIL

[Fig. 7(16)] This is a beautiful trip along Station Camp Creek, past old abandoned homesites, and along the Big South Fork River. There are some creek crossings.

Directions: Go east from the Big South River (Leatherwood Ford Bridge) on TN 297 about 6 miles to Station Camp Road. Turn left (north) on Station Camp Road and go 4.3 miles to Station Camp East trailhead.

Trail: 4 miles.

HATFIELD RIDGE LOOP

[Fig. 7(19)] This trail has magnificent overlooks of Charit Creek Lodge, Station Camp Gorge, and the Big South Fork River. The trail has a steep descent into the river gorge.

Directions: Go north on TN 154 for 1.8 miles beyond the TN 297 junction. Turn right on Divide Road. Take Divide Road 4.8 miles to Three Forks. At Three Forks bear right on Terry Cemetery Road, continue to Hatfield Ridge Road, and bear right at the fork. The trailhead is 0.6 mile on the left.

Trail: 9.9 miles.

BACKCOUNTRY CAMPING

Hunters, hikers, mountain bikers, horseback riders, backpackers, and paddlers enjoy roughing it in the backcountry of the BSFNRRA. Although backcountry permits are not required, it is a very good idea for campers to register with the ranger station. Doing so helps the recreation area evaluate backcountry use and locate individuals or parties in case of an emergency. Permits and full information regarding backcountry camping can be obtained from the Bandy Creek Visitor Center.

There are no designated backcountry sites, but existing sites have evolved through repeated use. Camping is allowed in much of the backcountry. Exceptions include areas within 25 feet of a cave, rock house, cemetery, historic site, or the rim of the gorge, or in the path of any trail, roadway, or parking area.

Dead and down trees may be collected for campfires unless temporary restrictions are in effect. Campfires are not allowed in rock shelters, under arches, or near historic structures at any time.

For more information: Big South Fork National River and Recreation Area, Bandy Creek Visitor Center, 4564 Leatherwood Road, Oneida, TN 37841. Phone (931) 879-3625.

FLOATING THE BIG SOUTH FORK

The Big South Fork of the Cumberland River and its major tributaries, Clear Fork, North White Oak, and New River, offer a variety of experiences for canoeing, kayaking, and rafting. Some of the stretches are placid enough for new paddlers, while others require skilled whitewater paddling, so make sure you're competent to handle yourself and your craft from put-in to take-out. The limited access warrants underestimating rather than overestimating your skills and thoroughly researching the area you plan to float.

When water levels are high and the flow rate is increased, the river can be dangerous regardless of the paddlers' experience. Floatation devices should be worn by everyone who floats the river. Helmets should be worn by all kayakers and by open canoeists on Class III and above rapids. The park suggests packing a spare paddle, a throw rope, a bailer, and a first aid kit. All supplies should be secured.

WOOD THRUSH
(Hylocichla mustelina)
The song of the wood thrush is a complex and beautiful series of brief phrases interspersed with a high trill.

For more information such as current river conditions, flow rates, and available commercial operators may be obtained by calling the Bandy Creek Visitor Center, phone (931) 879-3625.

NEW RIVER BRIDGE TO LEATHERWOOD FORD BRIDGE

[Fig. 6(13)] The first 6 miles of the New River are fairly easy paddling, but the next 2 miles have some Class II–III ledges, proving why this is not a beginner's float. The final 7.5 miles are run on the Big South Fork River, which contains several Class III–IV drops. The trip requires enough stamina for a long day of paddling with challenges increasing as the float progresses.

Directions: From Oneida take US 27 south 10 miles to the New River Bridge. River access is immediately south of the bridge.

River distance: 15.5 miles.

Difficulty: I–IV.

ZENITH MINE TO LEATHERWOOD FORD BRIDGE

[Fig. 6(12)] North White Oak Creek is an 8-mile run through short rapids requiring good maneuvering skills. The gorge is lined thickly with second growth including laurel, rhododendron, and hemlock at the base of 400-foot bluffs. Boulders of assorted sizes and shapes must be navigated. This stretch is characterized by low water and is only floatable after rain.

Directions: From Allardt, TN take TN 52 east for 5.5 miles to Mt. Helen Road. Turn left on Mt. Helen Road and drive 4.9 miles to fork in the road at Garrett's Grocery. Take the paved road to the left and drive 0.2 mile to Zenith Road on the left.

Rapid Classification System

The following rapid classification system is designed by the American Whitewater Affiliation. If the ambient temperature is below 50 degrees Fahrenheit or if the trip is an extended one into the wilderness, the river should be considered one class more difficult than normal to allow for the fatigue factor.

Class I: Moving water with a few riffles and small waves. Few or no obstructions. Suitable for beginners.

Class II: Easy rapids with waves up to 3 feet and wide, clear channels that are obvious without scouting. Some maneuvering is required. Suitable for novice boaters.

Class III: Rapids with high, irregular waves often capable of swamping an open canoe. Narrow passages that often require complex maneuvering. May require scouting from shore. Suitable for intermediate boaters.

Class IV: Long, difficult rapids with constricted passages that often require precise maneuvering in very turbulent waters. Scouting from shore is necessary, and conditions make rescue difficult. Generally not possible for open canoes. Boaters in covered canoes and kayaks should have the ability to Eskimo roll. Suitable only for boaters with advanced skills.

Class V: Extremely difficult, long, and very violent rapids with highly congested routes, which should be scouted from shore. Rescue conditions are difficult, and there is a significant hazard to life in the event of a mishap. Ability to Eskimo roll is essential for boaters in kayaks and decked canoes. Suitable only for boaters with advanced skills.

Class VI: The difficulties of Class V carried to the extreme. Nearly impossible and very dangerous. For teams of experts only after close study has been made and all precautions taken.

Follow the road 2 miles to the creek and the access point.

River distance: 7.8 miles.

Difficulty: II.

PETERS BRIDGE TO BREWSTER BRIDGE

[Fig. 8(3)] This is a nice trip for paddlers who know basic canoe strokes and come when there's enough water to run it. Laurel thickets cloak the steep valley walls as the Clear Fork River starts to cut into the Cumberland Plateau. The river is characterized by long, slow segments and short, easy drops.

Directions: The Peters Ford Bridge Road leaves TN 52 at Pleasant View Church of the Nazarene 3 miles east of Allardt and 8 miles east of Jamestown. Turn south on Peters Ford Bridge Road and drive about 5 miles to the access point at Peters Ford Bridge.

River distance: 6 miles.

Difficulty: I–II

BREWSTER BRIDGE TO BURNT MILL BRIDGE

[Fig. 6(14)] This is a very beautiful section featuring rapids with high, irregular waves capable of swamping an open canoe. Some may require scouting from shore and the ability to read water. Paddlers should be capable of whitewater maneuvers.

The only named rapid in this section is Decapitation Fork, formed where the stream passes beneath an undercut rock. Though not particularly dangerous, it requires some maneuvering to navigate.

Those who are tempted to go beyond Burnt Mill Bridge should know the river quickly becomes challenging for expert and advanced canoeists. It features Double Falls with two tumultuous 4-foot drops, Washing Machine which drops into a swirling, boulder-lined pool, and The Ell with its complicated drop. All three rapids are found in a single 200-yard section and more wait downstream.

Directions: Go east from Allardt on TN 52 to Brewster Bridge, crossing the Clear Fork River. River access is at the bridge.

River distance: 10.5 miles

Difficulty: II–III

WHITE OAK CREEK BRIDGE TO BURNT MILL BRIDGE

[Fig. 6(16)] White Oak Creek passes rock houses and scenic bluffs as it heads for the Clear Fork River. The last 0.5 mile of the creek has some Class II rapids, but the float down the Clear Fork River to Burnt Mill Bridge has no major rapids to distract from the surrounding beauty.

Directions: From Oneida take US 27 south to Elgin. Turn right onto TN 52 and drive approximately 5 miles to White Oak Creek Bridge. From Allardt go east on TN 52 to the White Oak Creek Bridge near the Morgan/Scott county line. Access is at the bridge.

River distance: 11 miles.

Difficulty: II.

BURNT MILL BRIDGE TO LEATHERWOOD FORD

[Fig. 6(17)] This is the primary whitewater stretch in the BSFNRRA and is one of the best whitewater runs in the Southeast. It should only be run in the spring when water flow is adequate, and it should only be attempted by those with the proper equipment and experience.

Directions: To reach the Burnt Mill Bridge, follow US 27 south from Oneida. After crossing the New River Bridge, continue approximately 2 miles and turn right at a sign pointing to the Burnt Mill Bridge. Turn left at Mountain View, pass through Black Creek, and continue to the crossroads where there will be a church on the right. Turn right at the crossroads and bear left at the fork. Follow this road to Burnt Mill Bridge.

River distance: Approximately 13 miles.

Difficulty: IV and V rapids.

LEATHERWOOD FORD BRIDGE TO STATION CAMP, OR BLUE HERON MINE

[Fig. 6(5)] This two-day run combines fairly frequent rapids with easy-to-read water and spectacular fall color during October. There are two drops that should be portaged. The first is Angel Falls, 2 miles below Leatherwood, and it should be portaged on the right. Devils Jump, another boulder jam, is located just above the take-out point and should be portaged on the left.

Directions: Take TN 297 approximately 10 miles west from Oneida to Leatherford Bridge. Access is at the bridge.

River distance: 8 miles to Station Camp or 27 miles to Blue Heron Mine.

Difficulty: Angel Falls: III; Devils Jump: III. Depending on flow, these drops may be Class IV.

MOUNTAIN BIKE RIDING

Bikes are not allowed on hiking trails that are blazed with red arrowheads, but bikes share equestrian trails that have a yellow horsehead blaze, although horses have priority. Bikers should stop to let horses pass by to minimize confusion.

It's a good idea to leave your travel plans with someone and you should always wear a helmet. Park rangers recommend carrying your bike over boggy, muddy areas to minimize trail damage.

There are two designated mountain bike trails accessible from the Bandy Creek Visitor Center (*see* page 31), the Duncan Hollow Bike Trail and the Collier Ridge Bike Loop. A map of the trails and other information is available at the visitor center.

DUNCAN HOLLOW TRAIL

[Fig. 6(9)] An old farm site, wooded areas, and a creek crossing are along the route to Station Camp Creek. Portions of the trail are shared with horses.

Directions: Duncan Hollow Road begins near the swimming pool parking lot in the Bandy Creek Campground.

Trail: 5.3 miles, one-way.

Elevation: Change, 720 feet.

Difficulty: Moderate.

Markers: Posts with orange letters and orange arrows.

COLLIER RIDGE LOOP

[Fig. 6(9)] This trail goes by the Katie Blevins Cemetery which is the final resting place of Jacob Blevins, son of early settler Jonathan Blevins and husband of Katie. It crosses the Oscar Blevins Trail, North Bandy Creek, King Branch, and South Bandy Creek, winds through the woods, follows TN 297 for 1.4 miles, and returns to the Bandy Creek trailhead after crossing North Bandy Creek again. It crosses horse trails, and short portions are shared with hikers.

Directions: Trailhead at parking lot 0.2 mile beyond Bandy Creek Campground's visitor center.

Trail: 7.3 miles, loop.

Difficulty: Moderate.

Markers: White arrow on brown metal signs, or orange arrow on four-by-four vertical posts.

OFF-ROAD/HIGHWAY VEHICLES

ATVs, off-road motorcycles, dune buggies, and other off-road vehicles are allowed in the BSFNRRA under certain conditions. In general, the river gorge area is off limits to motorized intrusion and the ridgetop roads are open to multiple use. Multiple use theoretically includes off-road vehicles, but accessible areas are changing as road use is redefined so it's always best to check with the visitor center. A copy of current regulations for Tennessee and Kentucky can be obtained from the Bandy Creek Visitor Center.

For more information: Big South Fork National River and Recreation Area, Bandy Creek Visitor Center, 4564 Leatherwood Road, Oneida, TN 37841. Phone (931) 879-3625.

FISHING

The Big South Fork and its tributaries provide an immense amount of fishing potential for both warm-water and cold-water species. Some parts of the rivers and streams can be reached by automobile or four-wheel-drive vehicle. However, the major part of the system is accessible only on foot or by floating in rafts or canoes. In total there are well over 200 miles of productive water available.

Some species are prevalent from the headwaters to where the Big South Fork leaves the area, while others, notably rainbow trout (*Salmo gairdneri*) and brown trout (*Salmo trutta*), are found only in the higher elevation streams. Neither species is native. They are present in Williams Creek, Laurel Fork, and Station Camp Creek on the upper reaches of the river.

Smallmouth bass (*Micropterus dolomieui*), walleye (*Stizostedion vitreum vitreum*), muskies (*Esox masquinongy*), catfish (*Ictalurus punctatus*), and bluegill (*Lepomis macrochirus*) are found the entire length of the river, and on the extreme lower reaches, sauger (*Stizostedion canadense*), largemouth bass (*Micropterus salmoides*), and white bass (*Roccus chrysops*) occur. These is also a late winter spawning run of walleye from Lake Cumberland that produces some specimens larger than those found year-round in the river.

Fishing licenses from either Tennessee or Kentucky are recognized from Leatherwood Ford Bridge down to the Yamacraw Bridge on the Big South Fork of the Cumberland River. Anglers must follow the regulations of the state in the which the license was issued. However, this reciprocal agreement does not extend to tributary streams. For copies of fishing regulations, contact the Tennessee Wildlife Resource Agency (615-781-6500) or Kentucky Fish and Wildlife Resources (502-564-4336).

HUNTING

The legislation that created the BSFNRRA authorized hunting, which is conducted in accordance with state and federal regulations. Once a favored hunting ground for the Indians who made frequent forays into the territory seeking buffalo (*Bison bison*), elk (*Cervus elaphus*), white-tailed deer, black bear (*Ursus americanus*), and other furbearers for meat and hides, the Cumberland Plateau provided these early hunters temporary camps in caves and rock shelters.

After longhunters Daniel Boone and James Robertson followed game trails through the sheer eastern wall of the plateau, they discovered the rich game bounty of the plateau region and began setting up camps for their sometimes yearlong hunting expeditions. Some of the camps used by Indians, longhunters, and early settlers are now historic sites and popular destinations for hikers.

While many of the big game species that were originally present have long since disappeared, there are now huntable populations of both deer and wild turkeys (*Meleagris gallopavo*) due to restoration programs by the National Park Service and wildlife agencies of Tennessee and Kentucky. Small game hunters seek gray squirrels (*Sciurus carolinensis*), fox squirrels, cottontail rabbits (*Silvilagus floridanus*), bobwhite quail (*Colinus virginianus*), ruffed grouse (*Bonasa umbellus*), opossums, and raccoons (*Procyon lotor*). Trapping is also permitted. Sportsmen and women must comply with the license requirements and regulations of the state in which they are hunting or trapping.

The BSFNRRA also has regulations enforced by National Park rangers. These include a provision that forbids carrying a loaded firearm (including rifles, shotguns, and handguns) in a car, on a horse, or while operating a motorcycle or ATV. Even muzzleloaders must be without gun powder in the pan and cross bows may not be drawn. A weapon may only be fired in pursuit of game during a hunting season, which means target practice is forbidden as is sighting a rifle.

In the interest of public safety, there are a number of safety zones where hunting is not allowed. These are located at the Bandy Creek Campground, East Rim facility complex, Charit Creek Lodge, Blue Heron Recreation Area, Alum Ford, Yahoo Falls, Yamacraw, Worley, Station Camp, Leatherwood Ford, Burnt Mill Bridge, Zenith, Brewster Bridge, and Peters Bridge. Other areas may be added in the future, so current information should be obtained from one of the visitor centers or from a park ranger. All such areas have yellow bands painted on trees to establish a boundary line.

For more information: Big South Fork National River and Recreation Area, Bandy Creek Visitor Center, 4564 Leatherwood Road, Oneida, TN 37841. Phone (931) 879-3625.

Historic Rugby

The picturesque community of Rugby is situated in the forest at the edge of the southern part of the BSFNRRA. Several of the historic buildings are open to the public for tours, including the home of the founder of the last English colony in the United States.

Rugby was founded in 1880 on 75,000 acres of land on the rugged Cumberland Plateau by Thomas Hughes with the financial support of several investors.

Born in 1822 in Uffington, England, Hughes attended England's Rugby School and later wrote the best-selling novel, *Tom Brown's School Days* about his experiences at Rugby. Hughes was inspired by headmaster Thomas Arnold, an education reformer. An elected member of Parliament, Hughes founded trade unions in England, but eventually turned his attention toward the "second sons" of British aristocrats who, by tradition, did not share in their families' accumulated wealth.

Many found themselves poorly prepared to earn a living and forbidden by social convention from seeking their fortune in any occupation that their family considered an embarrassment.

Hughes envisioned a place where these younger sons could use their natural talents in business, trade, or manual arts without social restrictions while preserving many cultural aspects of the society into which they'd been born. By 1879, Hughes was offering younger sons and others wishing to start over in America room and board, the opportunity to be taught to farm by a competent teacher, and loans to purchase land in Rugby.

It was a long and arduous journey to remote Rugby on the Cumberland Plateau, but colonists began to arrive by train at a station about 7 miles from Rugby in 1880. In October 1880, the town officially opened and Hughes's speech talked of "this lovely corner of God's earth" and treating it "lovingly and reverently."

The British Board of Aid to Landownership, the governing board of the colony, set aside park lands, developed bridle trails, and generally encouraged the colonists to explore and enjoy the beauty of the setting and the vast surrounding forest.

Among the first organizations formed was the Library and Reading Room Society. Thousands of books were donated to the colony in honor of Hughes by various publishing houses and private individuals. Of these, 7,000 volumes published between 1687 and 1899 remain in the beautiful Hughes library, one of the finest collections of Victorian literature in America.

Although Thomas Hughes never lived in Rugby, he made several long visits. He stayed with his mother, Margaret Hughes, the unofficial first lady of Rugby, until he built his own home, Kingstone Lisle, in 1884. Kingstone Lisle is open to the public for tours. Margaret Hughes lived in Rugby until her death in 1887. Her grave is located near the trailhead to the Gentlemen's Swimming Hole in Laurel Dale Cemetery.

At its peak, Rugby had more than 70 buildings and a lively social scene, but many of the colonists were unsuited for the hard work needed to tame the Cumberland Plateau wilderness. The board improved the treacherous road from the railroad station to Rugby and built a fine hotel, the Tabard Inn, but misfortune dogged the colony. The severe first winter was soon followed by a typhoid epidemic, a summer drought, and a devastating fire that destroyed the Tabard Inn.

Although its fortunes waned, Rugby was never deserted. Children of the original colonists, Will and Sarah Walton, cared for the remaining buildings until their deaths in the 1950s.

In 1964, a young schoolboy named Brian Stagg visited Rugby and dreamed of preserving and restoring the village. In 1966, the 18-year-old became the director of the nonprofit Rugby Restoration Association and served the community until his death 10 years later. His dreams for Rugby, like those of Hughes before him, live on. Today, Brian's sister, Barbara Stagg continues her brother's work.

Perhaps poet Lois Walker Johnson, in speaking of Rugby, said it best: "...No dream is dead that leaves an afterglow."

Today more than 20 historic structures remain in Rugby. Several are open for tours daily, except Christmas Day and New Years Day. All tours begin at the Schoolhouse Visitor

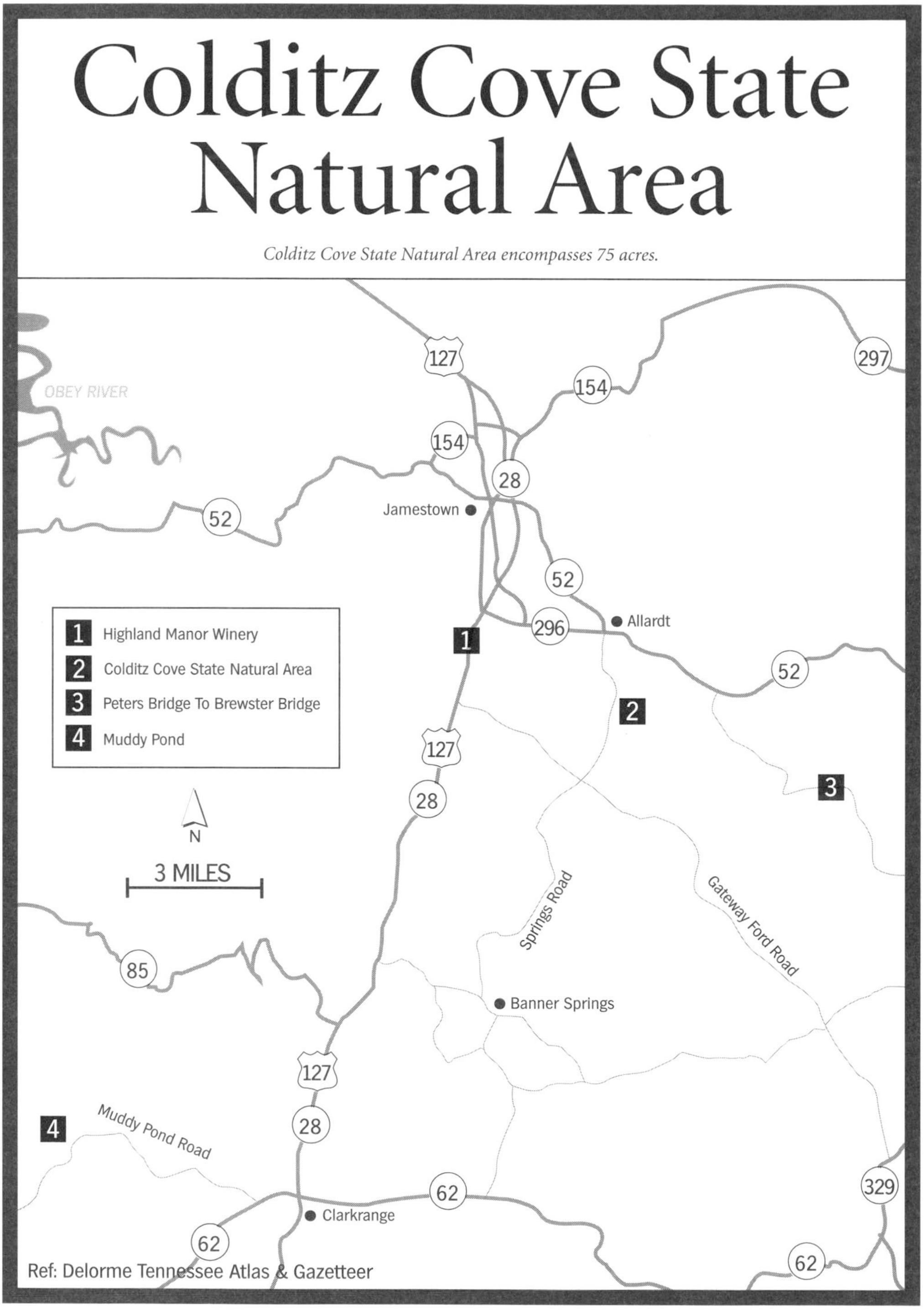

Colditz Cove State Natural Area

Colditz Cove State Natural Area encompasses 75 acres.

OBEY RIVER

297

127

154

154

28

52

Jamestown

52

296 ● Allardt

1 Highland Manor Winery
2 Colditz Cove State Natural Area
3 Peters Bridge To Brewster Bridge
4 Muddy Pond

1

52

2

127

28

3

N

3 MILES

Springs Road

Gateway Ford Road

85

● Banner Springs

127

4 Muddy Pond Road

28

329

62

● Clarkrange

62

62

Ref: Delorme Tennessee Atlas & Gazetteer

Center. The Harrow Road Cafe is open daily and serves specialties like Bubble and Squeak (sauteed mashed potatoes with cabbage) with or without bangers (grilled sausages). Overnight accommodations are available at the historic Newbury House Bed and Breakfast.

There are three major annual events: the Rugby Spring Music and Crafts Festival, the Annual Rugby Pilgrimage, and Christmas at Rugby.

Directions: Rugby is on TN 52 between Elgin and Jamestown. To reach it from the west, take TN 52 off US 127 at Jamestown and travel east for 18 miles. From the east, take TN 52 off US 27 at Elgin and follow it west for 7 miles.

For more information: Historic Rugby, Inc., PO Box 8, Rugby, TN 37733. Phone (423) 628-2441.

Colditz Cove State Natural Area

[Fig. 8] Colditz Cove encompasses 75 lush acres, with its principal attraction being Northrup Falls where Big Branch drops 60 feet in the cove. Northrup Falls takes its name from the family who lived and worked at the falls. The Northrups operated a water-powered mill above the horseshoe-shaped cove.

The land was eventually owned by brothers, Arnold and Rudy Colditz. They allowed anyone to walk their land to see Northrup Falls. The Cumberland Mountain Chapter of the Tennessee Trails Association (TTA) asked permission to build trails on their property so people could easily visit the falls. The brothers thought it seemed like a good idea, so in 1984 the TTA built a loop trail around Northrup Falls.

After the TTA invested a good deal of time and money making the area more easily accessible, the Colditz brothers offered to give the land to the state. Initially, the state rejected the extraordinarily lovely area.

The Nature Conservancy accepted the land to hold in trust until something could be worked out so the state would accept it. The state of Tennessee eventually took possession, but TTA's efforts are visible in the small patches of yellow paint with green arrows painted on them pointing the way along the trails.

From the parking area, visitors hike about 0.5 mile down the old roadway before entering the forest. A tall tree canopy allows only dappled sunlight to fall on the trail. Partridge berries, mosses, mushrooms, lady's slippers, and other shade-loving wildflowers grow among the brown evergreen needles on the forest's floor. Mountain laurel and rhododendrons occupy most of the niches available to shrubs. Majestic hemlocks and pine trees provide most of the shade in this pristine forest.

The green arrows lead you around a waterfall loop that is about 1 mile long. The trail splits at the waterfall and hikers can make the circuit in either direction. To the right the trail crosses the small creek by a wooden bridge and follows the sandstone cliffs. There are good views down into the gorge. There are no guard rails at these sites and the rocks are slippery after a heavy dew, rain, or snow, so be careful.

The trail doubles back as it descends into the cove and leads to the waterfall. There are several areas of deeply undercut banks that Indians inhabited. Indians moved into the plateau region about 12,000 years ago and made use of stone shelters among the cliffs close to streams. As they gave up hunting for agriculture, about 3,000 years ago, they moved into the large river valleys.

During the rainy seasons, hikers will have to watch their step crossing shallow patches of running water, and many springs issue from the cliffs. As hikers walk under the cliffs, water will sprinkle on their heads, especially when they reach the area behind the waterfall. The view is beautiful from behind the falls: hikers look across the pool where the water collects from the falls, through the rocks, and into the huge trees and thick lush underbrush.

There are many large, rough boulders that have fallen from the cliff walls to the east of the falls. The trail is sandy as it leaves the falls area to pass down the cove and turn back up to climb to the top of the gorge. Hikers will want to pause, whether they are huffing and puffing from the climb or not, to enjoy the view. It's a short round trip so take your time. Savor the beauty and the serenity of the quiet woods and the vista from Northrup Falls. Colditz Cove is open year-round. There are no facilities and no ranger station.

Directions: From Jamestown, turn east off US 127 onto TN 52. Drive 5 miles to Allardt. From Allardt, continue east on TN 52 and turn right at sign for Northrup Falls Road. Colditz Cove parking area is about 1 mile farther on the right. From Rugby, the Northrup Falls Road is 11 miles west on TN 52.

Activities: Hiking and viewing waterfalls.

Facilities: None.

Dates: Open year-round.

Fees: None.

For more information: Fentress County Chamber of Commerce, PO Box 1294, Jamestown, TN 38556. Phone (931) 879-9948.

Allardt

[Fig. 8] In the late 1800s, Bruno Gernt and M. H. Allardt founded a community of immigrant Germans at about the same time the British were settling Rugby. German land agent Bruno Gernt envisioned a self-sufficient city on the Cumberland Plateau. Gernt sold 9,000 acres owned by the Clarke family of Nebraska in parcels of 25, 50, and 200 acres at $4 per acre to farmers, miners, and lumbermen.

The town was laid out geometrically and named for Gernt's partner, M. H. Allardt, who died before settlement began. Gernt recruited skilled craftsmen, professionals, and experienced farmers from Germany, and soon Allardt led the region in production of hay, fruits, and vegetables. For more than 50 years, Gernt never ceased his efforts to have Allardt be all he dreamed it could be, and the community prospered for a time. Today, more than a dozen buildings make up the Allardt Historic District.

The Gernt House, home of Bruno Gernt, is listed on the National Register of Historic Places, and the 1891 restored farmhouse can be rented for overnight lodging by calling (931) 879-1176.

October brings the Annual World Pumpkin Federation Weigh-Off and Great Pumpkin Festival, a weekend of pumpkin carvings, paintings, and weighings, as well as bake sales, auctions, craft vendors, music, games, and street dancing.

Directions: Allardt is on TN 52 approximately 5 miles east of Jamestown.

For more information: Upper Cumberland Tourism Association, PO Box 2411, Cookeville, TN 38502. Phone (931) 520-1088. Fentress County Chamber of Commerce, POB 1294, Jamestown, TN 38556. Phone (931) 879-9948.

Jamestown

[Fig. 8] Jamestown, the county seat of Fentress County, was built upon the site of Indian Trails, known to settlers as Sand Springs. Jamestown was home for several years to John Marshall Clemons, father of Samuel Langhorne Clemons, also known as Mark Twain. The elder Clemons was a circuit court clerk of the county and drew the plans for the first courthouse and jail, which were completed in 1828. While living here, John Clemons served as a county commissioner and attorney general. He also acquired thousands of acres of land that he thought would be the making of his family's fortune.

From the sequence of events, it appears undeniable that Samuel, although born in Missouri five months after the family left Tennessee, was conceived in Fentress County. The Mark Twain Spring Park down the street from the Fentress County Courthouse is named to honor this fact. The park, across from the site of the former Clemons home, contains the spring where the Clemons family got its water. The homesite is the present site of the Jamestown Post Office.

Jamestown appears in Mark Twain's writings as Obedstown in *The Gilded Age*. Little did John Clemons realize it would be his son's words rather than his acreage that would make the family fortune.

Directions: Take I-40 to the US 27 Exit. Go north and travel approximately 30 miles.

For more information: Jamestown/Fentress County Chamber of Commerce, POB 1294, Jamestown, TN 38556. Phone (931) 879-9948.

Highland Manor Winery

[Fig. 8(1)] In his autobiography, Mark Twain wrote about "a wild grape of promising sort" that grew on the vast estate his father had purchased on the

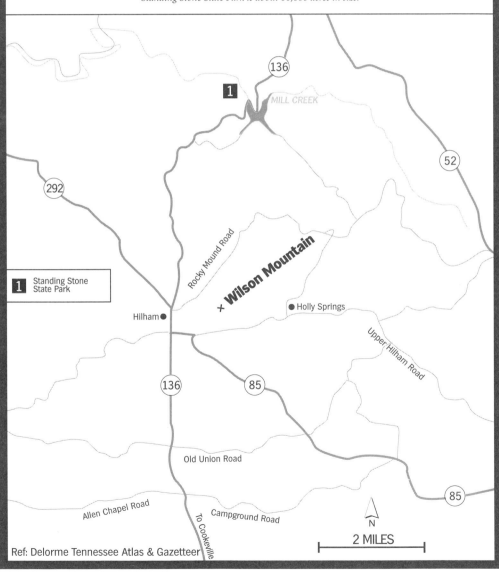

Monterey and the Standing Stone Area

Standing Stone State Park is about 11,000 acres in size.

136

1 MILL CREEK

52

292

Rocky Mound Road

✕ Wilson Mountain

1 Standing Stone
   State Park

● Holly Springs

Hilham ●

Upper Hilham Road

136   85

Old Union Road

85

Allen Chapel Road

To Cookeville

Campground Road

N

2 MILES

Ref: Delorme Tennessee Atlas & Gazetteer

Cumberland Plateau. The grape was muscadine (*Vitis rotundifolia*), and in 1980 a native of the region, Fay Wheeler, and his wife, Kathy, established Tennessee's first licensed winery in this area this century. Today the winery produces limited quantities of muscadine wine, muscadine champagne, and several other varieties of wine. Because of the scarcity of wild muscadine grapes, the winery is sometimes sold out, so it's wise to call ahead if you have your heart set on sampling this particular fruit of the vine.

Highland Manor continues its production of award-winning wines. Visitors are invited to tour the winery, view the wine-making process, and sample the finished products. Picnic areas on the grounds offer the opportunity for an al fresco lunch, complete with the wine of your choice.

Directions: 4 miles south of Jamestown on US 127.

Dates: Open daily for tours and tastings. Closed Sundays during the winter.

For more information: Highland Manor Winery, Highway 127 South, Box 33B, Jamestown, TN 38556. Phone (931) 879-9519.

Monterey and the Standing Stone

Around the beginning of the twentieth century, Monterey was a resort town that boasted seven hotels and drew summer people who came to enjoy the cool temperatures and mountain scenery. The modern Inn at Bee Rock continues this tradition.

The Standing Stone was a 13-foot-tall rock that once stood upright on a sandstone ledge in the area. It was the legendary boundary between Cherokee and Shawnee territory and marked the Cherokee Tallonteeskee Trail. The 8-foot remnant of this stone is preserved in Monterey, where a Standing Stone Celebration of Native American Heritage is held each October.

Standing Stone State Park [Fig. 9(1)], near the historic community of Livingston, contains nearly 11,000 acres and offers cabins, camping, and fishing on the 69-acre Standing Stone Lake. The annual Rolley Hole National Marble Championship takes place in September and earns Standing Stone the title "Marble Capital of the United States." Although Rolley Hole is a team sport played in this area for generations, contenders who take their marble shooting seriously come from far afield. Rolley Hole involves rolling marbles into, you guessed it, holes strategically placed along a 40-foot playing field.

Directions: Standing Stone State Park is 15 miles north of Cookeville via TN 136.

For more information: Upper Cumberland Tourism Association, POB 2411, Cookeville, TN 38502. Phone (931) 520-1088. Cookeville/Putnam County Chamber of Commerce, 302 South Jefferson Avenue, Cookeville, TN 38501. Phone (931) 526-2211.

Catoosa Wildlife Management Area

[Fig. 10(7)] The 82,000-acre Catoosa Wildlife Management Area (WMA) is another of the large tracts on the plateau that has made a comeback from the devastation created by earlier coal and lumber operations. Today it is one of the state's premier nature and wildlife areas.

Catoosa's history is similar to that of many parts of the plateau where such activities were rampant. Initially the area was one of the prized hunting grounds visited seasonally by the Cherokees, Choctaws, Chickasaws, and Shawnees, who often engaged in bitter battles over their individual hunting rights. Later, the longhunters of the Daniel Boone era also came to seek game, and eventually small settlements sprang up.

In the 1870s the first lumber operation got underway, and by 1911, two coal and lumber companies had formed a syndicate that continued to exploit the region until a massive flood in 1929 wiped out the main bridges on their rail lines. In the meantime, the companies were leasing lands where all of the timber had been removed for crops and livestock grazing. The result was an increase in the number of small farms in the area.

The flood and the ensuing Great Depression virtually eliminated the coal and lumber operations, and in 1940 the Crossville Exchange Club appointed a committee to encourage the state to purchase a large tract of the abandoned land for a wildlife management area. In 1942 the Conservation Commission made the initial purchase of 63,000 acres from the Tennessee Mineral and Lumber Company with Pittman-Robertson federal aid funds, which come from federal taxes on guns and ammunition.

In 1949 the Tennessee Game and Fish Commission, now the Tennessee Wildlife Resources Agency (TWRA), established a tentative purchase boundary which encompassed approximately 90,000 acres. A land acquisition program designed to eliminate interior holdings was begun at that time and continues today.

The Catoosa WMA lies within the Emory River drainage, which is divided by a number of major stream drainages, including the Obed River, Daddy's Creek, Clear Creek, and Otter Creek. The terrain is moderately rolling, ranging in elevation from 1,100 feet to 2,300 feet, with deep canyons cut by the streams.

More than 98 percent of the Catoosa WMA is now forested, which is in sharp contrast to what some early travelers observed. In 1797, Francis Bailey wrote, "...about five o'clock we arrived at Crab Orchard. Here we found a large plain or natural meadow, containing many hundred acres covered throughout its whole extent with a tall, rich grass." Two years later, in 1799, Martin Steiner wrote, "...then we crossed barren hills where only bushes grew. Now and then one saw a little tree." There were many other such accounts indicating the open nature of the terrain and the presence of great herds of elk, deer, and bison.

Ecologists believe extensive grazing and periodic burning by the Indians were the reasons for the prairielike conditions. The plant succession that followed when the game and Indians were gone reforested the area, and then, around 100 years later, the lumbering operations again laid the land virtually barren of timber. Now, almost 70 years since that activity halted, the plateau's woodlands are again flourishing.

As a part of the management program, the wildlife populations have been restored, and the Catoosa WMA is one of the most popular places in the region for hunters seeking big or small game. The deer herd is in excellent condition and regularly produces trophy bucks, and wild turkey numbers continue to climb. Also present are the exotic European wild boar, which can be hunted during all of the deer seasons. Small game includes fox squirrels, gray squirrels, ruffed grouse, raccoons, quail, rabbits, and mourning doves (*Zenaidura macroura*).

The streams in the Emory River drainage offer anglers the opportunity to seek a number of game fish. Smallmouth bass, rock bass, bluegill, and muskellunge are the most prevalent species. Many of these waters are in remote and rugged country, and access to them is limited. Parts of some of the streams are floatable, and many of these stretches are included in the Obed Wild and Scenic River System.

Due to the increasing pressure being applied by outdoor users of all kinds, the Tennessee Wildlife Resources Agency (TWRA) has closed Catoosa and several other WMAs to entry between sunset and sunrise. This is intended to reduce the effect of the activities that are considered incompatible to established wildlife management practices.

Since WMAs were purchased by funds generated by hunters, the TWRA regards hunting as the first and foremost priority on these areas. Currently, off-road vehicles and horses are permitted, but only on certain roads and trails. Overnight camping is allowed on designated areas by permission of the area manager. Such camping is subject to the limitation on the permit.

Directions: North of I-40 between Crossville and Harriman and in Cumberland and Morgan counties. TN 298, also called Genesis Road, runs north from Crossville and then goes easterly through the WMA.

For more information: Tennessee Wildlife Resources Agency, 218 Genesis Road, Crossville, TN 38555. Phone (931) 484-9571.

Obed Wild and Scenic River System

[Fig. 10] The Obed Wild and Scenic River system is a unit in the National Wild and Scenic Rivers System, one of only seven such units within the southeastern United States and the only one within Tennessee.

Located in Morgan and Cumberland counties, the Obed winds through a deep sandstone gorge with walls that sometimes tower up to 400 feet above the riverbed. It is a unique scenic resource, with unusual geologic features and an abundance of plant and animal life. The total acreage proposed within the unit is approximately 5,057 acres, which includes portions of the waters, stream bed, and lands adjoining 45.2 miles of the Obed River, two of its tributaries, Clear Creek and Daddys Creek, and the Emory River. To date, over 3,000 acres have been acquired, and it is possible that the total acreage could be expanded in the future to protect the water quality in some of the Obed's major tributary streams.

Obed Wild & Scenic River

The Obed Wild and Scenic River is the only Wild and Scenic River within Tennessee.

1 Panther Branch Trail

2 Frozen Head State Park & Natural Area

3 Chimney Top Trail

4 Obed Wild & Scenic River System

5 Obed/Emory Wild & Scenic River Float Trip

6 North Old Mac Mountain Trail

7 Catoosa Wildlife Management Area

Trail

3 MILES

Pilot Mountain

Wartburg

Obed River

Emory River

Flat Fork Road

Catoosa Road

Noah Hamby Road

Ref: Delorme Atlas & Gazetteer

N

The area has historically rebuffed settlers, mainly because of the rugged terrain and poor soil. However, it was a rich seasonal hunting ground for the Indians and longhunters, and that portion of the river that passes through the Catoosa Wildlife Management Area still abounds with game and fish. This part of the unit is closed during the months of February and March and is closed to all except hunters during the big game hunts in the fall and spring (*see* Catoosa WMA, page 64).

Directions: From Nashville and west, take I-40 to US 127 north. From Knoxville and east, take I-40 to US 27 north. Both US 127 and US 27 connect with TN 62 that skirts the northern edge of the Obed Wild and Scenic River area.

For more information: Obed Wild and Scenic River, 208 North Madien Street, Wartburg, TN 37887. Phone (423) 346-6294.

OBED/EMORY WILD AND SCENIC RIVER FLOAT TRIP

[Fig. 10(5)] The Obed/Emory River system is a free-flowing river system of clean, clear water cut deeply into the Cumberland Plateau and is a major drainage system of the northern half of the plateau. It took millions of years for the streams to cut into the hard sandstone caprock. The rivers are celebrated for their steep gorges with undercut gorge walls, semi-truck–sized boulders, narrow and blind passages, and whitewater drops.

The Obed/Emory requires skillful maneuvering. Many a craft has been bent and broken when water crushed it against the rocks. Much of the river is inaccessible and there is only one way out—walking. Careful planning, studying the route, and meticulous preparations will save you much discomfort, and even your life. But running the river system is the one way to see the natural beauty sculptured and forested over the last 200 million years. Huge hemlocks, white pines, rhododendrons, and mountain laurels make up this canyon forest. Deer, turkey, hawks, bobcats, rattlesnakes, and copperheads make their living here too.

This Obed/Emory River flows without the assistance of dams to provide current. The dry season is the time to plan, not navigate. A good rain will raise the water level within hours, providing exciting whitewater access to the scenic gorges that run through a true wilderness.

It's 35 miles from the put-in at the US 127 bridge on the Obed River to the take-out at Nemo's Bridge on the Emory River. Only the most skilled try the first 10 miles of the run from US 127 to Adams Bridge on Genesis Road north of Crossville. Select the section of river that suits your paddling expertise.

Although there are other rivers in the Obed/Emory River watershed to run, none takes on the mystique or offers better bragging rights than a trip down the Obed/Emory River, which contains the only Class V rapids. Daddys Creek, Lower Islands Creek, Crooked Creek, Crab Orchard Creek, Clear Creek, and White Creek offer exciting runs ranging from Class II to Class IV rides.

US 127 BRIDGE (BISHOP BRIDGE) TO ADAMS BRIDGE

This is the uppermost run on the Obed River, but, of all the runs, this is the one to avoid because of the level of difficulty. Also, this wild and scenic section in Cumberland County is not part of the official National Wild and Scenic River. This 10-mile stretch is known as Goulds Bend Run.

It begins with an easy float until the bottom drops out to a descent of 80 feet per mile. Goulds Bend Run contains the most complex and difficult rapids to negotiate. Knucklebuster and Hellhole rapids rate a Class IV. The rapids named the Esses, or SSS's (two sharp 90-degree turns) should be portaged on the right. Monte Smith, in his book *A Paddler's Guide to the Obed/Emory Watershed,* calls the Esses a Class V. Bob Sehlinger and Bob Lantz in their *A Canoeing and Kayaking Guide to the Streams of Tennessee,* Volume II, rank it a Class IV. To err on the side of safety, consider it a Class V.

River distance: 9.6 miles.

Difficulty: II–V.

ADAMS BRIDGE TO POTTERS FORD

Expect many Class II rapids in this run as well as a couple Class III rapids. The first 1.5 miles could be considered boring, flat with little current, but the middle 1.5 miles are too difficult for novice paddlers. At the end of the middle section is Billy Goat Bluff rapids, a difficult Class III. It should be scouted before attempting to run it. The last section of this run to Potters Ford is fairly placid.

River distance: 4 miles.

Difficulty: III–IV.

POTTERS FORD TO OBED JUNCTION

The run from Potters Ford to the Obed Junction where Daddys Creek flows into the Obed River is a long run with many Class II rides and one Class III. Two dangerous places to be aware of are two undercut rocks. A skillful paddler should be able to avoid these at times of moderate water flow. Smith recommends this section to those running the river for the first time, but he states it is a moderate to difficult run requiring whitewater experience.

River distance: 12 miles.

Difficulty: II–III.

OBED JUNCTION TO NEMO BRIDGE

This is the outstanding run. Below the confluence of Daddys Creek the water volume doubles in the Obed River, the gorge steepens and deepens, the scenery is gorgeous, and there are the 90 Right-90 Left, the Ohmigod!, and the Rockgarden rapids prefaced by many difficult Class II rides. This run is for experienced paddlers only.

The Omigod! is a notorious craft-killer. It should be scouted on the left. Most paddlers forego the thrill of running the Rockgarden, a Class IV ride, and portage around it—it's a man-killer.

Next is the confluence with Clear Creek that forms a long run of rapids, but the life-threatening thrills are over. Many difficult Class II rapids and two Class IIIs are coming, the Keep Right and the Widowmaker. Class IIs complete the last section of the Obed River before it gives way to the Emory River.

The Emory River, much smaller than the Obed River, enters quietly and bends sharply to the right. The remaining river mile to the Nemo Bridge has two Class II rides. About 200 yards below the bridge is a Class III ride called Nemo Rapid.

Before running any of the Obed/Emory River sections consult with an experienced outfitter or the Obed Wild and Scenic River headquarters in Wartburg. Be aware that the class of the rapids will increase with increased river flow.

River distance: 10 miles.

Difficulty: II–IV.

Wartburg

Wartburg rests at an elevation of 1,373 feet at the foot of Ward and Byrd mountains on the Cumberland Plateau. According to the *WPA Guide To Tennessee*, it was named for Wartburg, Germany. Carolyn Sakowski in *Touring East Tennessee Backroads* says it was named for the castle in Thuringia, Germany, where Martin Luther translated the Bible into German.

The colony was founded by George F. Gerding on more than 170,000 acres purchased with the intent of promoting German and Swiss colonization. Prospective colonists were met by agents of the East Tennessee Colonization Company in U.S. port cities or recruited in Germany and Switzerland.

In 1845, the first 50 settlers arrived from Germany. Many stayed at one of the first buildings in town, known as the Immigration House, until land could be cleared and dwellings built.

Between 1846 and 1855, more immigrants followed, most of German or Swiss nationality, and at one time the colony had hundreds of residents. There were several experienced artists and craftsmen in the community, including Frederic Beneike who established a piano factory and artist George Dury, a painter who arrived from Munich in 1849. He painted portraits of Robert E. Lee and Abraham Lincoln and his portrait of Mrs. James K. Polk hangs in the East Room of the White House. Yet despite some successes in wine-making, the poor soil and the isolation of Wartburg from main routes of travel led colonists to eventually begin seeking better lives in the larger cities of middle and eastern Tennessee.

By 1870, Wartburg had been established as the county seat of Morgan County. Today it is the gateway to Frozen Head State Park and Natural Area.

Directions: Wartburg is on US 27, 26 miles north of I-40 between Crab Orchard and Kingston.

For more information: Middle East Tennessee Tourism Council, POB 19806, Knoxville, TN 37939. Phone (423) 584-8553.

Frozen Head State Park and Natural Area

[Fig. 10(2)] The top of Frozen Head Mountain, at 3,324 feet, is often covered in ice and snow in winter, which gives this landmark its name. Of more than a dozen peaks varying from 1,340 feet to more than 3,000 feet, the higher peaks are the result of multiple layers of erosion-resistant rock that remained in place as adjacent parts of the plateau were worn down. The connecting ridges and interlaced valleys are further evidence of this geologic action. The park contains 14 peaks over 3,000 feet elevation, including Frozen Head, the second highest peak on the Cumberland Plateau.

Frozen Head, formerly Morgan State Forest, has a fine trail system with more than 50 miles of trails ranging from easy to strenuous crisscrossing the 11,876-acre Frozen Head State Park and Natural Area. Although heavily logged between 1911 and 1915 and completely burned over by forest fires in 1952, it's now heavily reforested and offers scenic views and an outstanding variety of spring wildflowers. One of the most popular interpretive programs held during the year at Frozen Head is the April wildflower tour.

Trail maps and information about backcountry camping permits are available at the visitor center. There's also a primitive campground with bathhouses and restrooms but no water or electrical hookups.

Directions: Travel east of Wartburg approximately 4 miles on TN 62 to Flatfork Road. Turn left on Flatfork Road and travel 4 miles to the park.

Activities: Hiking, seasonal nature programs, and tours.

Facilities: Campsites (water, grill, fire ring, bathhouse with hot showers), primitive backcountry campsites, restrooms, picnic shelters, playground, trails, and amphitheater.

Dates: Open year-round.

Fees: There is a charge for camping.

Closest town: Wartburg, 8 miles.

For more information: Frozen Head State Park and Natural Area, Rt. 2 Box 1302, Wartburg, TN 37887. Phone (423) 346-3318

HIKING TRAILS

More than 50 miles of trails can be hiked in the 12,000-acre Frozen Head area. Those in the northern end of the park are maintained and most can be reached from the main trailhead near the visitor center and ranger station. Trails in the southern section haven't been maintained in recent years, so only those with map-reading skills should attempt to travel on them. A permit is required for cross-country hiking or overnight camping. Maps of the trails are available at park headquarters.

NORTH OLD MAC MOUNTAIN TRAIL

[Fig. 10(6)] This is one of the trails that leads to the lookout tower atop Frozen Head Mountain, which on a clear day provides a view of the Great Smoky Mountains to the east, Cumberland Mountain to the north, and the Cumberland Plateau to the west. Also within view is Cross Mountain, which at 3,534 feet is the tallest peak in the

Tennessee portion of the plateau. During World War II a radar station was placed atop Cross Mountain to protect the highly secret operations at Oak Ridge from enemy aircraft. The station was abandoned in 1957.

Spring wildflowers, overlooks, yellow poplar (*Liriodendron tulipifera*) stands, fossils, and the lookout tower are the interesting features along the trail.

Directions: The trailhead is at the main parking lot.

Trail: 3.6 miles, one-way.

Elevation: Change, 1,800 feet.

Difficulty: Moderate.

Surface and blaze: Forest floor. Red blaze.

PANTHER BRANCH TRAIL

[Fig. 10(1)] This is the trail that offers the greatest variety of spring wildflowers, and it is interesting at any time of the year because of the other attractions. Features are the DeBord Falls, Flat Fork Creek, and an old railroad bed. Where Panther Branch Trail turns right after leaving the front gate, if you go straight 0.5 mile you reach Emory Gap Falls.

Directions: The trail starts at the front gate of the park.

Trail: 2.1 miles, one-way.

Elevation: Change, 1,000 feet.

Difficulty: Moderate.

Surface and blaze: Forest floor. Blue blaze.

CHIMNEY TOP TRAIL

[Fig. 10(3)] Sandstone cliffs, cap rock formations, and scenic views make this hike worthwhile.

Directions: Main trailhead at the park visitor center.

Trail: 6.9 miles, one-way.

Elevation: Change, 1,700 feet.

Difficulty: Strenuous.

Surface and blaze: Forest floor.

EASTERN WHITE PINE
(Pinus strobus)

Elk Valley

[Fig. 23(1)] One of the prominent physiographic features on the northeastern rim of the plateau is Elk Valley, a straight, narrow valley that was created by the same system that created the much larger Sequatchie Valley on the southern part of the plateau. The valley lies between Walden Ridge and Pine Mountain on the eastern edge of the Cumberland Block and extends from the community of Elk Gap on into Kentucky, for a distance of about 100 miles.

In earlier years the area around Jellico, a town at the northern end of the Tennessee portion of the valley, produced large amounts of high-grade bituminous coal. The coal was strip-mined until the resource was exhausted in the 1950s, leaving more than 200 acres of scarred land.

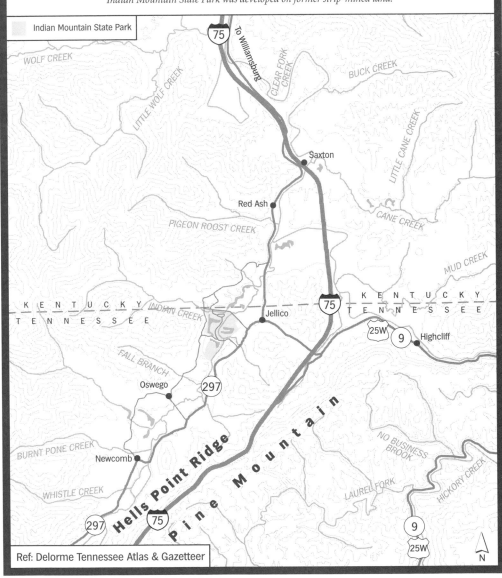

Indian Mountain State Park Area

Indian Mountain State Park was developed on former strip-mined land.

Indian Mountain State Park

Ref: Delorme Tennessee Atlas & Gazetteer

The Elk Valley was also another breach in the formidable eastern escarpment of the plateau, but it, like the one farther south near Rockwood, wasn't discovered until after Cumberland Gap became the mainstream route for settlers moving west into Kentucky and Tennessee.

Directions: TN 297 runs through part of the valley south from Jellico.

Indian Mountain State Park

[Fig. 11] This 200-acre parcel of land containing abandoned strip mine pits was originally acquired in the late 1960s by the city of Jellico using federal funds. Additional grants permitted a reclamation project to occur, and the area was converted into a recreation park containing two small lakes. The entire park is within the city limits of Jellico.

Directions: Take Exit 160 off I-75 North and follow signs to the park.

Activities: Camping, fishing, paddle boating, walking trails, and swimming.

Facilities: Campsites, boat-launching ramp, seasonal boat rentals, walking trails.

Dates: Open year-round.

Fees: There is a charge for camping, paddle boat rental, and swimming.

Closest town: Jellico.

For more information: Indian Mountain State Park, Indian Mountain Road, Jellico, TN 37762. Phone (423) 784-7958.

Lincoln Memorial University

[Fig. 12(2)] Located in the town of Harrogate only a couple miles south of the gap, Lincoln Memorial University is the site of the Abraham Lincoln Museum, one of the largest Lincoln and Civil War collections in the country. The university was founded shortly after the Civil War by Union General Oliver Otis Howard to fulfill Lincoln's wish to help the people of eastern Tennessee who supported him during the war. The museum also serves as a teaching facility for the university.

Directions: On US 25E in the town of Harrogate.

Activities: Viewing collections of Abraham Lincoln's personal items and memorabilia.

Facilities: Museum.

Dates: Open year-round.

Fees: There is a charge for admission.

Closest town: Harrogate.

For more information: Lincoln Memorial University, Harrogate, TN 37752. Phone (423) 869-6237.

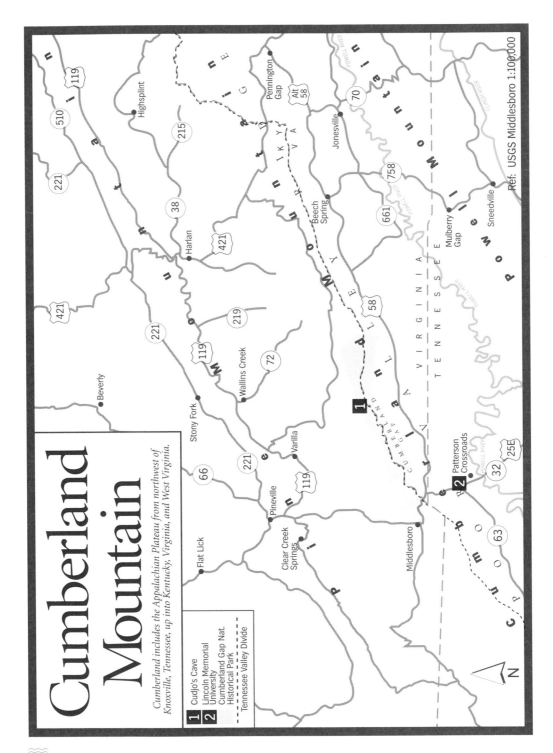

Cumberland Mountain

Cumberland includes the Appalachian Plateau from northwest of Knoxville, Tennessee, up into Kentucky, Virginia, and West Virginia.

1 Cudjo's Cave
2 Lincoln Memorial University
  Cumberland Gap Nat. Historical Park
  - - - Tennessee Valley Divide

Ref: USGS Middlesboro 1:100,000

Cumberland Gap

[Fig. 12] The wall of mountains stretching diagonally from Maine to Georgia known as the Allegheny, or Appalachian, Mountains impeded western expansion during early American colonization. Buffalo and deer established a trail through an unusual gap to the fertile valleys to the west. To understand the unique significance of the gap in American history, it's important to understand the geographic features that combined here to make it the main avenue of migration beyond the Allegheny Mountains.

AMERICAN TOAD
(Bufo americanus)
Despite popular myth, toads do not cause warts.

At one time Yellow Creek flowed south into the Powell River, cutting a gap in Cumberland Mountain as it did so. Cumberland Mountain rose faster than the creek could wear it down and eventually the creek was diverted northward into the Cumberland River. As Yellow Creek flowed out of a large, flat area known as the Middlesboro Basin, it created a valley that led to a second gap at Pine Mountain and beyond to the rolling hills of the bluegrass region of Kentucky.

Indians followed the game to major hunting grounds in what is now Kentucky. This trail became part of a travel route known as the Warrior's Path that led from the Potomac River to the Ohio River.

The gap was first seen by a white man, Dr. Thomas Walker, on Good Friday in 1750, but it remained part of Cherokee lands until the Treaty of Sycamore Shoals was signed 25 years later.

Frontiersman Daniel Boone heard about Cumberland Gap and set out to explore the area in 1769. Suitably impressed with the natural resources, four years later Boone returned with a party of settlers, but his oldest son was killed in a fierce Indian attack before they reached the gap and the party turned back.

Boone's next trip to the gap was in 1775, when he was hired by the Transylvania Land Company to blaze a trail through Cumberland Gap to 20 million acres it had recently acquired from the Cherokee for settlement. He and his crew of 30 back-woodsmen marked and roughly hacked a 208-mile trail from Long Island at Kingsport to Cumberland Gap in less than three weeks during the spring of 1775.

In 1796, the road was widened to support wagons. The migration through the gap was responsible for pushing the westward boundary of the United States to the Mississippi River. Generally, settlers traveled the trail in winter when the water at Cumberland Ford was lower so they could plant spring crops and bring in a harvest the first year. The rugged trail evolved into the Wilderness Road, the safest passage for settlement of the Territory South of the Ohio River.

As westward expansion continued on railroads and steamboats in the 1820s and 1830s, Cumberland Gap lost its importance. That was to change when it was viewed as the Gibraltar of America by General U.S. Grant during the Civil War.

It was a logical point for the Union effort to want to control in predominantly pro-Union east Tennessee, and both the Union and the Confederacy felt it held strategic importance. Though no major battles were fought here, the gap changed hands four times.

Confederate General Felix K. Zollicoffer was dispatched to fortify the gap in May 1861. Two months later, Union General George Morgan was sent to capture the gap. Morgan drew a portion of the Confederate forces defending the gap toward Chattanooga with one brigade while sending the remaining brigade to outflank the remaining defenders at Cumberland Gap. The Confederates evacuated Cumberland Gap on June 17, 1861 and Morgan occupied the important gateway the next morning.

Morgan proceeded to fortify the gap and store supplies in area caves, including Cudjo's Cave, which has been acquired by the National Park Service (*see* below). In September, Confederate General Stephenson engaged Morgan's troops in Tennessee and drove them back to the gap. When the Union general realized the Confederates were maneuvering to turn his flank, he ordered the soldiers to gather what supplies they could take with them and pile everything else in the narrow gap. They set fire to the pile, including exploding munitions, which stopped the Confederate advance and covered their retreat, but once again the gap was in Confederate hands.

In 1863, the tables were turned when Stephenson was met by Union General Burnside in Tennessee and forced to retreat to the gap. The Union forces surrounded the Confederates and forced a surrender. Cumberland Gap remained under Union control for the rest of the war.

The small town of Cumberland Gap is tucked in a hollow on the Tennessee side of the southwestern edge of Cumberland Mountain. Built to house laborers working on a railroad tunnel through the mountains funded by British entrepreneur Col. A. A. Arthur's American Association, Ltd., it has a population of about 220. In the fall of 1996, a new four-lane tunnel rerouted US 25E away from the town of Cumberland Gap, bypassing the town in order to allow the Wilderness Road to be restored to its appearance in Boone's day. It's well worth the short detour into the historic Tennessee town on your way to the 20,271-acre Cumberland Gap National Historical Park (CGNHP) just across the Kentucky line in Middlesboro (*see* page 78). The Wilderness Road hiking trail begins at the remains of the iron furnace off Pennlyn Avenue in Cumberland Gap and climbs gradually through a hardwood forest to the historic gap.

Directions: On US 25E near the junction of Tennessee, Virginia, and Kentucky.

For more information: The Cumberland Gap Towne Hall, North Cumberland Drive at Colwyn Avenue, Cumberland Gap, TN 37724. Phone (423) 869-3860 or (800) 332-8164.

CUDJO'S CAVE

[Fig. 12(1)] Also called Cudjo's Cavern, this cave is noted by Thomas Walker, the first white man to see Cumberland Gap, in his diary. The cave was so well known that the gap we know as Cumberland Gap was known earlier as Cave Gap. Not commonly used as a camping spot by early travelers for fear of being detected by Indians, Gap Cave was often a landmark to be passed by as quickly as possible. The entrance to the cave lay just above a large spring.

The name Cumberland became established after Walker noted a river that was as "crooked as the Duke of Cumberland" flowing through the region. The use of the name Cumberland to describe the region soon followed, and Gap Cave became Cumberland Gap Cave. It was renamed in the 1930s after a novel by J. T. Trowbridge romanticized it as the hiding place for an escaped slave named Cudjo.

Once a popular tourist destination, the cave was closed to tourism until old US 25E was torn up, recycled, and restored to the appearance of the Wilderness Road in the 1700s. The cave has been reopened as Gap Cave as of spring 1999. A hiking trail accesses the cave and the Cumberland Gap National Historic Park has plans to conduct wild cave expeditions to view geologic formations. There are several miles of charted trails to explore.

For more information: Superintendent, Cumberland Gap National Historical Park, PO Box 1848, Middlesboro, KY 40965. Phone (606) 248-2817.

CUMBERLAND TRAIL

[Fig. 13(2)] The Cumberland Trail is a state scenic trail that remains unfinished due to lack of funding and landowner opposition. Most of the trail is privately owned. The project was initiated by the Tennessee Trails Association and was designed to follow a route from Cumberland Gap to a terminus on the Tennessee River south of Chattanooga for a distance of more than 200 miles. From Cumberland Gap the trail ascends Tri-State Mountain, generally follows the plateau's eastern escarpment to Prentice Cooper State Forest, then travels along the rim of the Grand Canyon of the Tennessee River to a point near the Alabama line. Parts of the trail have white blazes.

In the beginning, money for construction of the northern part of the trail was provided by the state and administered by the Department of Environment and Conservation. Since budget cutbacks in 1990 resulted in the funding being withdrawn, this part of the trail has not been maintained. Continuing work on the southern half is being done by members of the Cumberland Trail Conference, Tennessee Trails Association, and several sections are open to hikers.

Trail: 235 miles.

Elevation: Change, 1,800 feet.

Degree of Difficulty: Strenuous.

Surface and blaze: Rock and forest floor with white blaze on a brown background.

For more information: Tennessee Department of Environment and Conservation, 7th Floor, 410 Church Street, L&C Tower, Nashville, TN 37243. Phone (615) 532-0109

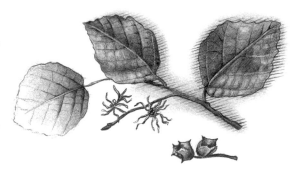

WITCH HAZEL
(Hamamelis virginiana)
This plant blooms after its leaves fall.

Cumberland Gap National Historical Park

Cumberland Gap National Historical Park is a memorial to the Wilderness Road, the Civil War, and the Hensley Settlement.

CUMBERLAND GAP NATIONAL HISTORICAL PARK

[Fig. 12, Fig. 13] Cumberland Gap National Historical Park contains over 20,000 acres in Kentucky, Virginia, and Tennessee, with the majority on the ridgeway north of Cumberland Gap that forms the boundary between Kentucky and Virginia. The park is a memorial to the Wilderness Road, the Civil War, and the Hensley Settlement, a farming community that existed on an isolated plateau from 1904 until 1951. Sherman Hensley arrived in 1904 and, with his family, constructed a home and outbuildings of hewn chestnut logs. At its peak, the settlement included about 100 inhabitants. The National Park Service has restored three of the original 12 farmsteads, and two farmer-demonstrators maintain the properties.

The Pinnacle Overlook [Fig. 13(4)], which affords a splendid view of the town of Cumberland Gap and far beyond, is one of the most popular features in the park. A paved road leads to within about 200 yards of the overlook. There is no road access to many of the other features, such as Sand Cave and White Rocks, but there are about 50 miles of hiking trails. One of these, the Ridge Trail, extends almost the entire length of the park and has four primitive campgrounds that require a permit. Biking and horses are permitted on designated routes.

Directions: Take US 25E from Kentucky or Tennessee, or US 58 from Virginia.

Activities: Hiking, biking, horseback riding, picnicking, and seasonal interpretive programs.

Facilities: Campground, restrooms, amphitheater, and hiking/biking/horse trails.

Dates: Open year-round, except Christmas and Jan. 1.

Fees: There is a charge for camping.

Closest town: Middlesboro, KY, 3 miles.

For more information: Superintendent, Cumberland Gap National Historical Park, PO Box 1848, Middlesboro, KY 40965. Phone (606) 248-2817.

LEWIS HOLLOW TRAIL

[Fig. 13(1)] The trail begins at the Wilderness Road campground and passes Skylight Cave on its way to the top of the Cumberland Mountain. Some hikers prefer to walk only the first half to the cave, since from that point the trail becomes very steep.

Trail: 1.1 miles to picnic area at Skylight Cave. The entire trail is 1.7 miles long.

Elevation: Change, 1,200 feet.

Degree of Difficulty: Moderate to strenuous.

Surface and blaze: Forest floor, no blaze.

TRI-STATE TRAIL

[Fig. 13(3)] The Tri-State Trail intersects the Wilderness Road at Cumberland Gap, and then it passes some Civil War features before ascending the mountain to the point where Tennessee, Kentucky, and Virginia meet. Two side trips may be taken from the Trail: Fort Foote, a Civil War artillery emplacement, is 0.1 mile off the trail about halfway up, and Fort Farragut, also a Civil War fort, is 0.5 mile beyond the Tri-State marker.

Trail: 0.9 mile.

Elevation: Change, 480 feet.

Degree of Difficulty: Moderate.

Surface and blaze: Forest floor, no blaze.

Lower Cumberland Plateau

FIGURE NUMBERS

15 Sequatchie Valley Area
16 Fall Creek Falls State Resort Park
17 South Cumberland St. Recreation Area
18 Grundy Lakes State Park
19 Hawkins Cove State Natural Area
20 Cumberland Caverns
21 Chickamauga & Chattanooga Area

Lower Cumberland Plateau

The lower Cumberland Plateau section is bracketed on the north by I-40, on the west by the plateau's irregular western escarpment, on the east by I-75, and on the south by the Alabama and Georgia state lines. The one exception is the part of Lookout Mountain that extends into Georgia. The Lower Cumberland Plateau includes all or parts of Putnam, White, Cumberland, Van Buren, Bledsoe, Grundy, Franklin, Marion, Sequatchie, Hamilton, Rhea, Meigs, Roane, McMinn, Loudon, and Bradley counties.

The Savage Gulf in the southwestern part of the Cumberland Plateau has the only large virgin tract of typical mixed mesophytic forest in Tennessee. It more closely resembles forests of the northern Cumberland Mountains. This virgin tract of between 1,500 and 2,000 acres was not harvested because of some right-of-way disputes. This is one of the largest virgin tracts in the southeastern United States. In

[*Above:* The South Cumberland State Recreation Area includes many spectacular natural features]

Sequatchie Valley Area

There are 60 floatable miles of water, designated as Class I, on the Sequatchie River.

Ref: Delorme Tennessee Atlas & Gazetteer

1 US 127 Bridge

2 Cumberland County Playhouse

3 The Homesteads

4 Pioneer Loop Trail

5 Cumberland Mountain State Park

6 Ozone Falls

7 Grassy Cove

8 Twin Rocks Nature Trail

9 Stinging Fork Pocket Wilderness & Trail

10 Piney River Trail

11 Laurel-Snow Pocket Wilderness Area

12 Laurel-Snow Trail

13 Crab Orchard

N

5 MILES

Crossville

Crab Orchard

Spring City

WATTS BAR LAKE

Summer City

Summer City Road

SEQUATCHIE RIVER

TENNESSEE RIVER

Dayton

this area are the endangered white fringed orchid (*Platanthera integrilabia*) and Wood's false-hellbore (*Veratrum woodii*).

The most significant feature in the lower portion of the plateau is the Sequatchie Valley, the ruler-straight cleft that bisects the region in Tennessee and extends on into Alabama. The valley is special from a geologic standpoint because it may be the longest and straightest in the world, but it is also important because it subdivides the southern part of the plateau. All of the area west of the valley is referred to as the Cumberland Plateau, but the area to the east is known as Walden Ridge, named after Elijah Walden, one of the longhunters of the Boone era.

The Sequatchie Valley was created during the mountain-building period about 270 million years ago by an overthrust system that pushed rock from the southeast over rock to the northwest. The overriding rock was folded into a gigantic anticline, or arch, the northern part of which is still intact and visible as the Crab Orchard Mountains. The rest of the rocks located southwest of the arch, however, were so fractured that they were easy prey to erosion. The Sequatchie River was able to scoop out the 5-mile-wide Sequatchie Valley.

Unlike most of the land on the plateau, the Sequatchie Valley contains very rich soil, yet the economic boom that began in 1870 and ended with the economic depression of 1893 resulted mainly from the exploitation of the coal, lumber, and iron in the area rather than agricultural products. Several towns sprung up in response to this activity: Pikeville, Dunlap, Whitwell, Kimbal, Victoria, and South Pittsburg. The latter town became the site of a cement factory and a foundry, which helped the area experience some economic recovery during the early part of the century.

Sequatchie Valley

▩ SEQUATCHIE RIVER

[Fig. 15] The Sequatchie River extends for almost the entire length of the Sequatchie Valley, beginning at Devil Step Hollow Cave in Cumberland County and ending at its confluence with the Tennessee River below Nickajack Dam. There are 60 floatable miles of water, designated as Class I, which meander through farmlands and woodlands between College Station and US 64 bridge. There is also good fishing potential with smallmouth bass, rock bass (*Ambloplites rupestris*), and rainbow trout (*Salmo gairdneri*) as the principal species.

The highways generally follow the river all the way through the valley. US 127 parallels it from Pikeville to Dunlap, and TN 28 from Dunlap to Jasper.

For more information: Sequatchie Valley Tourism Area, PO Box 205, Pikeville, TN 37367. Phone (423) 447-2791.

▨ DUNLAP

[Fig. 17] From 1902 to 1927, Dunlap was the site of 268 coke ovens that turned coal into coke, fuel for the smelting of pig iron. The coke was sent to Chattanooga's foundries that transformed pig iron into steel. The beehive-shaped brick ovens, 12 feet in diameter and 6 feet high, were built by the Chattanooga Iron and Coal Company and employed 350 men. Today the ruins of the ovens, which are on the National Register of Historic Places, stand in a 62-acre forest in Coke Ovens Park in Dunlap. Dunlap is at the junction of US 127 and TN 28 in the Sequatchie Valley.

For more information: Sequatchie County Chamber of Commerce, PO Box 595, Dunlap, TN 37327. Phone (423) 949-3479. Dunlap Coke Ovens Historic Site, Mountain View Circle, Dunlap, TN 37327. Phone (423) 949-3483.

Crossville and Greater Cumberland County

[Fig. 15] Crossville got its name around 1856 because of its strategic location on the Cumberland Plateau midway between Nashville, Knoxville, and Chattanooga. The town grew at the crossroads of the old Nashville-Knoxville Road and the Kentucky-Chattanooga Stock Road. The Stock Road brought up to 1,000 horses and mules and the occasional flock of sheep or gaggle of geese through Crossville. Cattle drives from middle Tennessee, Alabama, and Kentucky along this road brought livestock to eastern markets in Virginia.

As you drive south of Interstate 40 and enter Crossville, you'll see many buildings constructed of a locally quarried, durable, mottled sandstone with unusually high silica content known as Crab Orchard Stone.

Long used by residents for chimneys, hearthstones, and walkways, Crab Orchard Stone was once considered scrap because of its hardness and the difficulty in quarrying it. Today, visitors will see Crab Orchard Stone quarries using modern techniques to excavate layers of stone along US 70E between Crossville and Crab Orchard.

Crab Orchard Stone gained public attention when it was used for the Gothic-Revival chapel at Scarritt College off 21st Avenue South in Nashville in 1925 and later at Rockefeller Center in New York. Even Elvis Presley's pool at Graceland is ringed with Crab Orchard Stone.

The coloring of the stone depends on the amounts of iron, titanium, and magnesium, but shades range from tan and buff to gray, blue-gray, and rose. Many houses and public structures in Crossville and the vicinity were built using Crab Orchard Stone including the historic Homestead Tower and the beautiful arched dam built by the Civilian Conservation Corps (CCC) at Cumberland Mountain State Park.

Crossville is also home to Tennessee's largest premium winery in terms of retail sales, the Stonehaus Winery. Founded in 1990, it specializes in regional sweet and semisweet wines produced with grapes from the eastern United States. The winery's best-selling wine is Stonehaus Muscadine wine, which has gained a following throughout the Southeast. The winery is located off I-40 at exit 320.

Directions: Crossville lies just south of I-40 between Nashville and Knoxville, with three exits leading to the city.

For more information: Greater Cumberland County Chamber of Commerce, PO Box 453, Crossville, TN 38557. Phone (931) 484-8444.

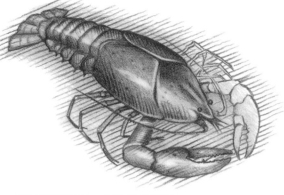

**EASTERN CRAYFISH
(Cambarus bartonii)**

CUMBERLAND COUNTY PLAYHOUSE

[Fig. 15(2)] In 1963, the people of Crossville helped develop an award-winning playhouse after the arrival of veteran television writer, actor, and director Paul Crabtree, his wife, Mary, and their family. Although Tennessee had no professional theaters at the time, the community launched a fund-raising effort that opened the doors of the nonprofit Cumberland County Playhouse in 1965. The high-quality productions quickly began attracting audiences from Chattanooga, Knoxville, and Nashville. Now operated by the Crabtrees' son, Jim, the playhouse has presented a series of plays based on important historic events in Tennessee.

Eighty percent of all revenues are generated by ticket sales to more than 300 performances and concerts on two indoor stages and a seasonal outdoor stage. The presentations are suitable for family audiences. The Cumberland County Playhouse has been designated a major cultural resource by the Tennessee Arts Commission.

Directions: Cumberland County Playhouse is located on US 70 west about 3 miles west of Crossville.

Activities: Plays.

Facilities: Two indoor theaters and one outdoor theater.

Dates: The productions are staged from mid-March into Dec. Contact the theater for play dates.

Fees: There is a charge for plays.

Closest town: Crossville, 3 miles.

For more information: Cumberland County Playhouse, 221 Tennessee Avenue, Crossville, TN 38557. Phone (931) 484-5000.

THE HOMESTEADS

[Fig. 15(3)] South of Crossville at the intersection of TN 68 and US 127/TN 28 is the landmark Homestead Tower. Here, in the museum, is the story of a Depression-era program designed to help more than 200 economically stranded families of miners,

SQUIRRELCORN
(Dicentra canadensis)
Unlike another member of its family, Dutchman's breeches, this plant is not named for its flowers. It is named for the kernel-size yellow corms, swellings in the stem, that develop beneath the soil.

timber workers, and farmers. When the production levels demanded by World War I dropped, men were left unemployed and their families were destitute.

Franklin Roosevelt's administration developed the Division of Subsistence Homesteads program, which purchased 29,000 acres with the intention of putting these folks back on their feet, in decent housing, and on their way to new occupations. Beginning in 1934, the hard-working homesteaders cleared 35-acre tracts and logged the timber to use for building material. They quarried the Crab Orchard Stone and used it to build small stone houses to live in. The houses were owned by the nonprofit Cumberland Homesteaders' Cooperative Association. According to plan, cooperative enterprises including a sorghum mill, a coal mine, and a canning factory created much-needed jobs. The canning factory employed 300 workers in the production of 80,000 quarts of fruits and vegetables annually.

First Lady Eleanor Roosevelt visited the Homestead project. The homesteaders worked hard and, after five years, were offered the opportunity to buy the land and houses they'd built and occupied. They did so, bringing the program to fruition by eliminating the need for it.

The Homesteads Tower, once the project's administration building, is now a museum open to the public and supported by visitor donations.

Directions: The center of the community is at the junction of US 127 and TN 68 southeast of Crossville.

Activities: Looking at photos, documents, and artifacts of the 1930s and 1940s, and furniture made by former residents.

Facilities: Museum.

Dates: Open year-round.

Fees: None.

Closest town: Crossville, about 3 miles.

For more information: Cumberland Homesteads Tower Museum, 96 Highway 68, Crossville, TN 38555. Phone (931) 456-9663.

🌿 CUMBERLAND MOUNTAIN STATE PARK

[Fig. 15(5)] A short distance down US 127 from the Homesteads Tower is the 1,720-acre Cumberland Mountain State Park, once part of the Cumberland Homesteads. The beautiful seven-arch dam made of Crab Orchard Stone built by the CCC reflected in 50-acre Byrd Lake is a top contender for the most photographed view in a Tennessee state park.

The dam forms the bridge leading into the park and you drive across it to reach the Cumberland Mountain Restaurant, which has good food and a nice view of Byrd Lake and the dam. The restaurant serves lunch and dinner daily except during the Christmas holidays. Behind the restaurant is a wide path leading down to the lake that's just right for an easy after-meal walk.

The park has 147 campsites with electric and water hookups available on a first-come first-serve basis. A group lodge and 37 cabins ranging from rustic to modern are available. The park features a broad variety of wildflowers in the spring. Fishing is a popular pastime if you have a valid Tennessee fishing license. There are also several day-use hiking and nature trails as well as a 10-mile overnight backpacking trail.

Directions: From I-40 at Crossville, take US 127 south for 8 miles to the park entrance.

Activities: Hiking, camping, picnicking, fishing, boating, swimming, golf, seasonal naturalist programs.

Facilities: Cabins, group lodge, campsites, camp store, seasonal boat rentals, picnic pavilions, Olympic-sized swimming pool, tennis courts, playgrounds, and hiking trails. Reservations for cabins and the group lodge can be made up to one year in advance.

Dates: Open year-round. The pool is open Memorial Day through Labor Day.

Fees: There is a charge for cabins and camping.

Closest town: Crossville, 8 miles.

For more information: Cumberland Mountain State Park, 24 Office Drive, Crossville, TN 38555. Phone (931) 484-6138.

PIONEER LOOP TRAIL

[Fig. 15(4)] Beginning at the parking area near Lake Byrd dam, this is a fairly level trail that follows the shoreline of Byrd Lake and Byrd Creek through a forest of hemlock, pine, and rhododendron. In the springtime there is an impressive display of wildflowers.

Crossing the footbridge at the head of the lake and returning to the dam cuts off 3 miles of this trek. Hikers who continue will enjoy a less-used path that provides solitude in the forest.

Trail: 5 miles.

Elevation: Change, 60 feet.

Degree of difficulty: Easy.

Surface and Blaze: Forest floor.

OZONE FALLS STATE NATURAL AREA

[Fig. 15(6)] The community of Ozone was a stop on the Walton Road favored by travelers after the long climb up the eastern escarpment of the plateau. In the community is Ozone Falls State Natural Area under the management of the Cumberland Mountain State Park. It is dominated by old-growth forests and contains Ozone Falls, which drops 110 feet into a deep gorge. Care is required when walking to the waterfall because of a number of open areas along the drop-off. The falls was first named McNair Falls after the man who owned a gristmill on the creek, but in 1896 when someone declared that the falls created a stimulating effect on the air, it became Ozone Falls.

Directions: The state natural area is at Ozone on US 70 between Crab Orchard and Rockwood.

Activities: 0.5-mile round-trip hike to falls, rappelling, and rock climbing.

Facilities: None.

Dates: Open year-round.

Fees: None.

Closest town: Crab Orchard, 5 miles.

For more information: Cumberland Mountain State Park, Rt. 8 Box 322, Crossville, TN 38555. Phone (931) 484-6138.

GRASSY COVE

[Fig. 15(7)] Grassy Cove, a National Natural Landmark, is a 3,000-acre valley with many caves. None of the caves are developed for commercial use and all are on private property.

This unusual depression in the plateau was formed by the same overthrust system that created the Sequatchie Valley. The hard sandstone cap was eliminated, and the subsequent erosion exposed the limestone base. Because of this, the valley is one of the prime farmland areas on the plateau, producing many agricultural crops and grazing land for cattle.

John Ford, a Revolutionary War veteran who was a member of a party crossing the plateau, discovered the remote cove in 1801. Ford secured a land grant and was joined by other settlers in establishing a farming community in the cove.

Directions: 7 miles southeast of the Cumberland Homesteads on TN 68.

Activities: Scenic views of a wide valley with karst geology.

Facilities: None.

Fees: None.

Closest town: Crossville, 10 miles.

For more information: Greater Cumberland County Chamber of Commerce, PO Box 453, Crossville, TN 38557. Phone (931) 484-8444.

CRAB ORCHARD

[Fig. 15(13)] Settlers heading west along the Walton Road found Crab Orchard a pleasant place to make a stop. Stands of crab apple trees grew on the mountainsides, explaining the name of the community that was established here. In 1827, the widely known Crab Orchard Inn was built, and it was operated for nearly a century. Crab Orchard is the place where Crab Orchard Sandstone was discovered.

Directions: It is located on US 70 just off I-40 between Crossville and Rockwood.

Activities: Visit quarry sites of Crab Orchard Sandstone.

Facilities: None.

Fees: None.

Dates: Open year-round.

For more information: Greater Cumberland County Chamber of Commerce, PO Box 453, Crossville, TN 38557. (931) 484-8444.

Historic Lower Cumberland Plateau

▨ BEERSHEBA SPRINGS

[Fig. 17] Beersheba [pronounced BUR-shuh-buh] Springs was one of the most popular resort areas in the South in the late 1800s. Today it continues to fascinate visitors. The area has some beautiful antebellum homes, and many of them are open during the Arts and Crafts Fair held on the Methodist Assembly grounds in August.

The famous resort at the western edge of the plateau is named for Beersheba Cain, allegedly the first white person to ever drink from the mineral spring for which the community became known. She discovered the spring while she and her husband, John, were traveling across the plateau. John Cain was so impressed by the scenic beauty of the location that he purchased land along the top edge of the bluff that provides a panoramic view of the Collins River valley.

Later, after Alfred Paine and George R. Smartt built the Smartt Tavern, the Tennessee General Assembly incorporated Beersheba Springs as a summer resort under Smartt's management. In 1850, after John Armfield purchased the tavern, more buildings, homes, and guesthouses were built. A second story was added to the tavern, and it became known as the Beersheba Springs Hotel and was a stagecoach stop. The coachman would sound a horn at the base of the mountain, and by the time the coach arrived, food and rooms would be ready. The Civil War caused the hotel to go bankrupt, and over the years it changed hands a number of times.

The old hotel and guest cottages, most of which have a breathtaking view, were purchased in 1941 by the Tennessee Conference of the United Methodist Church to serve as a retreat. In 1980 the Beersheba Springs Historic District, consisting of 220 acres and 55 structures, was placed on the National Register of Historic Places.

Directions: Beersheba Springs is on TN 56 between McMinnville and Altamont.

Activities: A self-guided driving tour of 54 structures and the old Beersheba Springs Hotel in the Beersheba Springs Historic District, and scenic views of the Savage Gulf.

Facilities: None.

Fees: None.

Dates: Open year-round.

For more information: Grundy County Chamber of Commerce, HCR 76, Box 578, Gruetli-Laager, 37339. (931) 779-3238.

▨ GRUETLI-LAAGER

[Fig. 17] Much like the other colonies that were established on the plateau by other ethnic groups, this small community near Tracy City was settled by Swiss immigrants who left Switzerland during the country's major depression of the mid-1800s. Representatives of the Swiss Immigration Society and the Swiss Republic traveled to America seeking a place to locate a colony and came to the plateau on the recommendation of President Andrew Johnson.

Impressed by what they saw, they returned to their country and obtained the money to purchase a tract of land across the canyon from Beersheba Springs. Originally called Gruetli, the colony eventually merged with the nearby community of Laager, another Swiss colony. Although the venture was not successful, some residents of Swiss ancestry remain, and a local Swiss Historical Society works to preserve the heritage of the two communities.

Directions: Gruetli-Laager is on TN 399 east of TN 56 between Tracy City and Monteagle.

For more information: Grundy County Chamber of Commerce, HCR 76, Box 578, Gruetli-Laager, 37339. Phone (931) 779-3238.

TRACY CITY

[Fig. 18] The names Tracy City and Baggenstoss are virtually synonymous, because the Swiss-German family of John and Louise Baggenstoss were principally responsible for the community's success. The couple came to the area in 1880, attracted by the Gruetli colony (*see* page 89). In 1902 they established the Baggenstoss Bakery, now the Dutch Maid Bakery, Tennessee's oldest family-operated bakery and the attraction for which Tracy City is best known.

Old World recipe breads and famous applesauce fruitcakes are baked year-round and the shop is as much a museum as a bakery. Many appliances were new during the 1920s and now the parts have to be special made to repair them. If you're wondering why a Swiss man called his bakery Dutch, it was a mistake. The name Swiss Bakery was taken so Baggenstoss applied for Deutsche Bakery, but a bureaucratic mistake spelled it Dutch.

The six sons of John and Louise ran the bakeshop for many years. One of the brothers, Hermann, became well known throughout the state for his conservation efforts and was the major force in the creation of the South Cumberland State Recreation Area.

The other notable spot to visit in Tracy City is Mountain Lake Glassworks on Lake Road. Here you can see hand-blown glassware, pottery, bronze castings, and fine crafts.

Directions: To reach Tracy City from I-24 take US 41 east just southeast of Monteagle.

Activities: Visit the Dutch Maid Bakery and its museum of appliances made in the 1920s.

Facilities: Bakery and museum.

Fees: None.

Dates: Open year-round.

For more information: Grundy County Chamber of Commerce, HCR 76, Box 578, Gruetli-Laager, 37339. Phone (931) 779-3238. Dutch Maid Bakery, 111 Main Street, Tracy City, TN 37387. Phone (931) 592-3171.

MONTEAGLE

[Fig. 19] Monteagle sits 2,100 feet high and is considered the gateway to the southern Cumberland Plateau.

From its beginning, Monteagle has been the location of various theological and educational institutes. It was founded around 1870 by John Moffat, a Scotsman who retired from a career of leading a nationwide temperance crusade, and named for Lord Monteagle, an English friend. Moffat donated land for the establishment of the Fairmount School for Girls, dedicated to providing educational opportunities for women of the region.

He was also instrumental in creating the Moffat Collegiate and Normal Institute for training teachers, which eventually became the nondenominational Monteagle Sunday School Assembly. The assembly was a part of the Chatauqua movement that established summer retreats for the purpose of training Sunday school teachers. The appeal of the mountain environment soon led to the development of a summer resort. Chatauqua was a religious movement that began in 1874 on the shores of Lake Chatauqua in northern New York.

Today, The Monteagle Assembly is still a place where Sunday school teachers and others spend the summer in a religious environment attending classes and concerts, and engaging in other uplifting activities. This facility is the only one of its kind. In 1982 the Assembly was placed on the National Register of Historic Places.

Monteagle is also home to the Monteagle Wine Cellars. Located on Monteagle Mountain, this winery is dedicated to continuing and expanding the rich heritage of wine-making in the area. It offers a tasting room and retail shop where visitors can enjoy wines produced from some of the world's best-known grape varieties.

Directions: Monteagle is on US 41 just north of I-24 between Manchester and Chattanooga. To reach the winery, take Exit 134, turn left, and go 300 yards.

Facilities: Driving tour of the Monteagle Assembly. Winery.

Fees: There is a charge to enter the Monteagle Assembly during the summer. Monteagle Wine Cellars: None.

Dates: Monteagle Assembly is open year-round. Winery is open year-round, hours vary seasonally.

For more information: Grundy County Chamber of Commerce, HCR 76, Box 578, Gruetli-Laager, 37339. Phone (931) 779-3238. Monteagle Wine Cellars, Highway 41A/64, PO Box 638, Monteagle, TN 37356. Phone (800) 556-WINE.

SEWANEE

[Fig. 19] Sewanee is a few miles from Monteagle and is the location of the Domain of the University of the South, owned by 28 Episcopal dioceses in 12 states. The Episcopal school was founded in 1857 by Bishops Leonidas Polk and James Oey of the Episcopal Church. Polk, the bishop of Arkansas and Louisiana, sought to create a southern school that would match the great universities of North America

Fall Creek Falls State Resort Park

The park takes its name from Fall Creek Falls, which, at 256 feet, is the highest waterfall east of the Rocky Mountains.

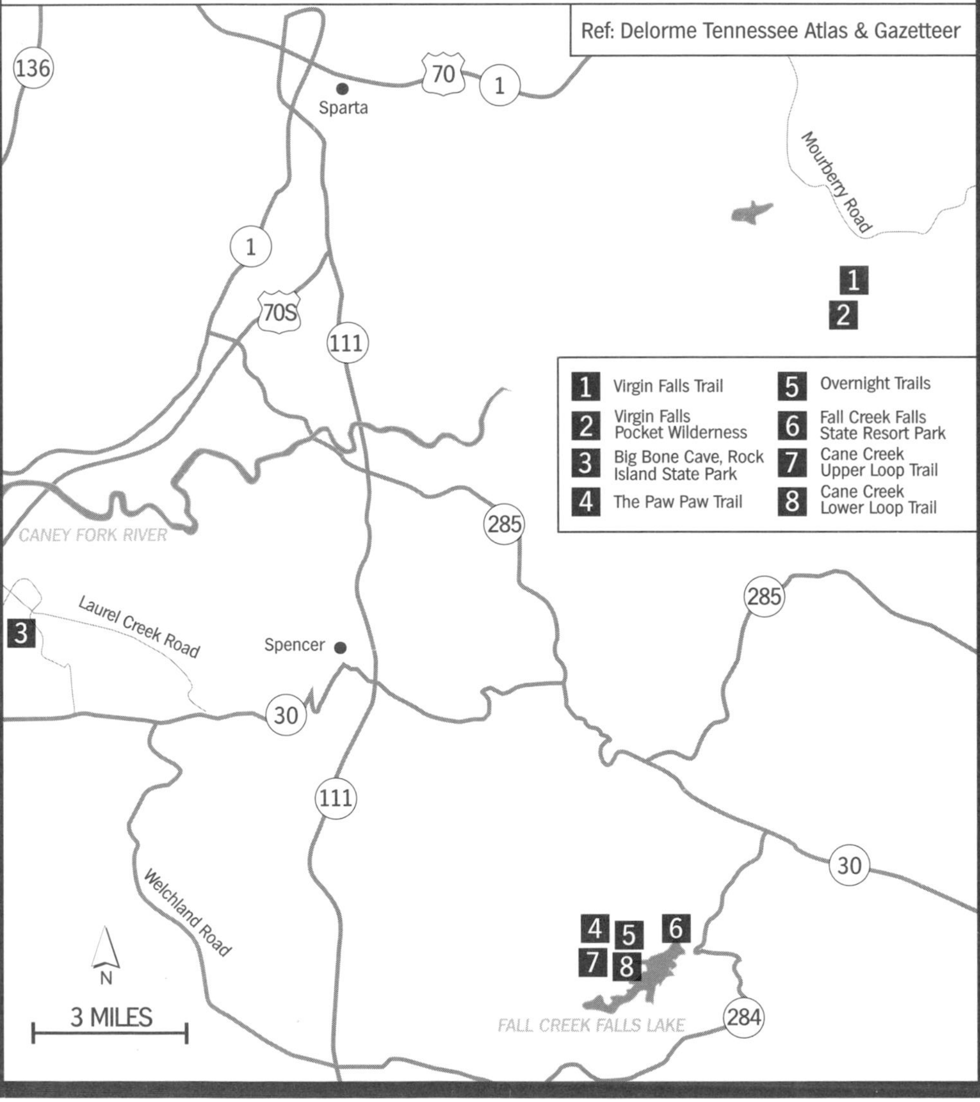

Ref: Delorme Tennessee Atlas & Gazetteer

136

70 | 1

Sparta

Mourberry Road

1

70S

111

1
2

1	Virgin Falls Trail	**5**	Overnight Trails
2	Virgin Falls Pocket Wilderness	**6**	Fall Creek Falls State Resort Park
3	Big Bone Cave, Rock Island State Park	**7**	Cane Creek Upper Loop Trail
4	The Paw Paw Trail	**8**	Cane Creek Lower Loop Trail

285

CANEY FORK RIVER

Laurel Creek Road

285

3

Spencer

30

111

30

Welchland Road

N

3 MILES

4 5 6
7 8

FALL CREEK FALLS LAKE

284

and Europe. The original charter for what became known as the Domain was for 10,000 acres, 5,000 of which were donated by the Sewanee Mining Company along with an enormous amount of building supplies and transportation facilities.

Built of Tennessee sandstone quarried from the property, it is said to look like a quaint English village. Civil War battles destroyed the school's buildings, but the school was re-established after the conflict and became a university that is now known as Sewanee. The university produces the respected literary journal, the *Sewanee Review*.

Directions: Sewanee is located on US 41A/64 east of Monteagle.

Activities: Visit the campus of the University of the South to see the All's Saints Chapel, the Shapard Tower with its 56-bell carillon, and the Heritage Room museum.

Facilities: Campus and museum.

Fees: None.

Dates: The campus is open year-round, and the museum is open when school is in session.

For more information: University of the South, 735 University Avenue, Sewanee, TN 37383. Phone (931) 598-1286. Franklin County Chamber of Commerce, PO Box 280, Winchester 37398. Phone (931) 967-6788.

Fall Creek Falls State Resort Park

[Fig. 16] Fall Creek Falls is one of Tennessee's best-known and most popular parks, and for very good reason. The 20,000-acre park has beautiful and spectacular features, including waterfalls, streams, gorges, hardwood and evergreen forests, and a broad offering of recreational facilities and activities. More than 200 species of blooming wildflowers attract visitors each spring. The brilliance of maple, dogwood, sourwood, and hickory also bring visitors back in the fall. A nature center is part of the park and is located approximately 1 mile from the north entrance at the four-way stop. Inside the nature center are exhibits and videos.

The park takes its name from Fall Creek Falls, which, at 256 feet, is the highest waterfall east of the Rocky Mountains. Other falls are Piney Creek, Cane Creek (the waterfall seen in the movie *The Jungle Book*), Cane Creek Cascades, Rockhouse Creek, and Coon Creek. The deep, moist gorges have rhododendron and laurel thickets and plant species similar to those found in southern Canada.

The National Park Service bought the land in 1935 and it was developed by the CCC during the Depression. Tennessee took possession of the land in 1944, turning it into a state park in 1972. Visitors will enjoy many outdoor

FLAME AZALEA
(Rhododendron calendulaceum)

activities including hiking along 30 miles of trails.

Directions: Traveling eastbound on I-40, exit south on TN 111 at Cookeville, and continue on TN 111 to the park. Traveling westbound on I-40, exit south on TN 127 west of Crossville, then go east on TN 30 at Pikeville.

Activities: Hiking, biking, horseback riding, golfing, tennis, swimming, fishing, boating, backpacking, picnicking, nature programs, and playground activities.

Facilities: Inn, restaurant and snack bar, gift shop and general store, cabins, campsites, group lodges, bathhouses, nature center, Olympic-sized swimming pool, championship golf course, hiking/biking/horse and motor nature trails, recreation hall, horse rentals.

Dates: Open year-round.

Fees: There is a charge for camping, golf, boat rentals, bicycle rental, and horseback riding.

Closest town: Spencer, approximately 10 miles.

For more information: Fall Creek Falls State Resort Park, Route 3, Pikeville, TN 37367. Phone (423) 881-3297. (Note: Because of the park's popularity, lodging reservations often must be made a year in advance.)

THE PAW PAW TRAIL

[Fig. 16(4)] The Paw Paw Trail passes through pine-oak forest in the higher elevations and rhododendron in the lower portions. It has short side trails leading to the base of Cane Creek Falls and to the east rim of the Cane Creek Gorge overlooking Cane Creek Falls.

The trail leaves the parking lot at the nature center with a quick rocky descent to Rockhouse Creek and then climbs to the pine-oak forest with a holly understory before returning by a connecting trail to the nature center.

Trail: Approximately 5 miles, a loop.

Elevation: Change of 200 feet to base of the falls.

Degree of difficulty: Moderate.

Surface and Blaze: Forest floor and orange blaze.

OVERNIGHT TRAILS

[Fig. 16(5)] Use of two overnight trails, the Cane Creek Upper Loop and Cane Creek Lower Loop, requires registration at the nature center. A parking area is provided for the users of the trails. Each loop must be traveled in a clockwise fashion, and there are two primitive campsites on each trail.

CANE CREEK LOWER LOOP TRAIL

[Fig. 16(8)] This trail encircles all of the gorges within the park boundary, staying mostly on top of the plateau, and provides access to Fall Creek Falls, Piney Falls, and Cane Creek Cascade on a route that offers great scenic views and opportunities to see a variety of wildflowers, and bird and animal life.

The strenuous part of the trail descends into Cane Creek Gulf about 3.5 miles along the hike. The 800-foot drop takes place in 0.8 mile with the 800-foot ascent taking only 0.7 mile. There is a campsite at the top of the climb. From the camp the trail goes along a road for a short distance and crosses two wooden bridges and a suspension bridge near the nature center.

Trail: 13 miles.

Elevation: Begins at 1,820 feet and ends at 800 feet.

Degree of difficulty: Strenuous.

Surface and Blaze: Rock and forest floor.

CANE CREEK UPPER LOOP TRAIL

[Fig. 16(7)] Generally following the gently rolling uplands of the top of the plateau, this trail isn't as well traveled as its counterpart (*see* above). Along the way there are extensive patches of blueberries (*Vaccinium corymbosum*) and large fern beds. The sighting of deer and ruffed grouse is not uncommon.

Trail: 14 miles.

Elevation: Change of 240 feet.

Degree of difficulty: Strenuous.

Surface and Blaze: Forest floor and white blaze.

RIVER OTTER
(*Lutra canadensis*)
Sociable animals, river otters wrestle, play tag, and roll around riverbanks and in water. Their streamlined bodies, webbed toes, and eyes and ears that can be closed underwater make them well suited for life in and around water.

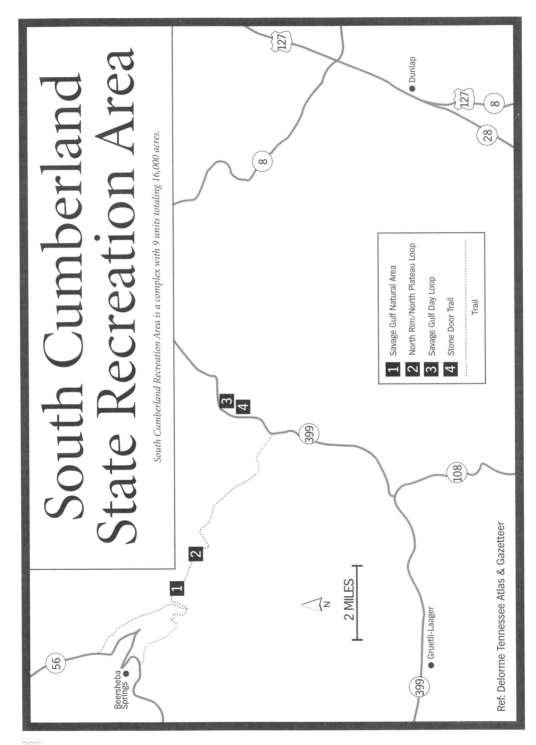

South Cumberland State Recreation Area

South Cumberland Recreation Area is a complex with 9 units totaling 16,000 acres.

1	Savage Gulf Natural Area
2	North Rim/North Plateau Loop
3	Savage Gulf Day Loop
4	Stone Door Trail
....	Trail

N

2 MILES

Ref: Delorme Tennessee Atlas & Gazetteer

South Cumberland State Recreation Area

[Fig. 17] Unlike the other natural areas and state parks on the plateau, the South Cumberland State Recreation Area (SCRA) isn't a single entity. Instead, it's a complex with 9 units totaling 16,000 acres spread over a 100-square-mile area that includes some of the region's most spectacular attractions.

The SCRA visitor center is primarily a hub at which to become familiar with the location of the other features. The center provides maps, directions, and other information. Hiking, backpacking, and primitive camping are the main attractions in this area. All camping requires a permit but the permit is free.

Surrounding the visitor center is the South Cumberland State Park, which offers visitors a variety of activities and amenities. Be sure to watch the 15-minute video about the 9-unit park system while at the visitor center. There are no camping facilities at the visitor center.

Contact the park for a list of monthly events including guided hikes.

Directions: The visitor center is on US 41 between Tracy City and Monteagle. All units of the SCRA are open year-round, but not all have ranger stations.

Activities: Hiking, basketball, baseball, picnicking, museum tour, tennis.

Facilities: Picnic areas, nature trails, museum, tennis courts, restrooms, and a large lawn for group activities, recreational equipment, baseball field, basketball court.

Fees: None.

Dates: Usually closed Thanksgiving and Christmas. Call before visiting.

Closest town: Monteagle.

For more information: South Cumberland Recreation Area, Rt. 1, Box 2196, Monteagle, TN 37356. Phone (931) 924-2980.

SAVAGE GULF NATURAL AREA

[Fig. 17(1)] "Savage" in the name Savage Gulf is often misinterpreted to mean wild, ferocious, and uncivilized, and many have been puzzled by the term "gulf." While this gulf, a local term for gorge, is a rugged wilderness, the Savage Gulf get its name from Samuel Savage, an early settler in the area.

The Big Creek from the west, the Collins River from the south, and the Savage Creek from the east, each about 5 miles long, carved their own gorges then joined to form a wide, steep valley. The deepest point is 800 feet below the Cumberland Plateau rim.

The 14,500-acre Savage Gulf area also includes 500 acres of virgin forest and 55 miles of trails, offering visitors the opportunity to see and explore some of the plateau's most rugged and primitive surroundings. There is no road into the gulf.

Robert Brandt says in his book *Middle Tennessee On Foot* that there are 680 plant species here, representing almost one-third of all the plants in the state, and that most of the common mammals of the eastern United States are found here, too.

The late Hermann Baggenstoss recognized the need to preserve some of the land that attracted the Swiss immigrants from whom he was descended. As chairman of the

Grundy County Conservation Board, Baggenstoss and his board worked diligently in the 1960s and 1970s to establish the South Cumberland Recreation Area (SCRA) to preserve this wild area. Selective timber harvest occurred throughout the south Cumberland region, except for 500 acres within Savage Gulf. Sam Werner, from Switzerland, once owned the land that included the virgin forest, and in the mid-1960s Sam Werner III joined the effort to encourage the state to buy the Savage Gulf. By 1978, the SCRA was established with the aid of Tennessee Valley Authority, the Savage Gulf Preservation League, The Nature Conservancy, many individuals, and other organizations.

The 500-acre virgin tract of mixed mesophytic forest is described as one of the best in the eastern United States and is listed as a National Natural Landmark.

Directions: There are two entrances to the area, Savage Gulf and Stone Door, with ranger stations at both locations. The Savage Gulf Entrance can be reached by traveling south from Spencer on TN 111 and turning on TN 399, or north from Dunlap on TN 8, turning on TN 399. The entrance is 5.5 miles on the right. To reach the Stone Door entrance, from Beersheba Springs on TN 56 turn east at the state park sign. Bear right 0.1 mile at fork, and continue to Stone Door entrance.

Activities: Hiking, camping, rock climbing/rappelling, and picnicking.

Facilities: Ranger stations and picnic areas.

Fees: None.

Closest town: Beersheba Springs, 1 mile from Stone Door entrance. Palmer, 5 miles from Savage Gulf entrance.

For more information: South Cumberland State Recreation Area, Rt. 1, Box 2196, Monteagle, TN 37356. Phone (931) 924-2980.

SAVAGE GULF DAY LOOP

[Fig. 17(3)] Mixed forests and wildflowers are seen on this hike that passes Savage Falls Overlook and Rattlesnake Point, both of which present views of Savage Gulf. The trail begins at the ranger station on the eastern side of the Savage Gulf off TN 399 and crosses a suspension bridge over Boyd Branch shortly beyond the trailhead. Savage Falls Overlook spur at 1.5 miles goes left off the trail to see a 30-foot vertical drop waterfall. At 2 miles along the Savage Gulf Day Loop is a sensational view of the gulf from Rattlesnake Point.

Trail: 4.2 miles, loop.

Elevation: 1,800 feet.

Degree of difficulty: Easy.

Surface and Blaze: Forest floor. White blaze.

NORTH RIM/NORTH PLATEAU LOOP

[Fig. 17(2)] The portion of the trail that follows the rim of Savage Gulf offers more than a dozen overlooks, many that offer spectacular views of the deep gorges. Meadow Creek, Loose Rock (on a spur trail), Quartz Pebble, Jumpin' Water, Yellow Bluff, and Trail Edge overlooks are the most notable. The trail also passes over the tallest bluff in Savage Gulf, a waterfall, streams, hardwood forests, a backwoods campsite, and an old railroad bed. The trail begins 2.2 miles along the Savage Day Loop.

Trail: 13 miles, loop.
Elevation: 1,830 feet. Change, 240 feet.
Degree of difficulty: Easy.
Surface and Blaze: Forest floor, white blaze.

STONE DOOR TRAIL

[Fig. 17(4)] One of the best views of Savage Gulf is from the overlook adjacent to the Great Stone Door at the end of this hike. The Stone Door is a crevice in the bluff that provided access to the plateau for the Chickamauga Trace Indian Trail. The Chickamauga Trace Indian Trail, also called the Chickamauga Path, ran from north Georgia to Kentucky. The Stone Door Trail begins at the Stone Door Ranger Station.

AMERICAN MOUNTAIN ASH
(Sorbus americana)

Trail: 1 mile, one-way.
Elevation: 1,800 feet. No change.
Degree of difficulty: Easy.
Surface: Paved, wheelchair accessible for 0.2 mile. Forest floor 0.8 mile. No blaze.

GRUNDY FOREST STATE NATURAL AREA

[Fig. 18(4)] Grundy Forest State Natural Area is a 237-acre natural area containing the Grundy Forest Day Loop that leads to the 12.5-mile Fiery Gizzard Trail, one of the most popular overnight backpacking trails in the South Cumberland complex.

The citizens of Tracy City donated this area in 1935 asking that the tract become a state forest suitable for accommodating the Civilian Conservation Corps Camp S-67. There is a parking lot next to the CCC-built picnic shelter, where the trailhead for the Grundy Day Loop Trail is also located.

Directions: Go west on TN 56 from Tracy City 1 mile, and turn left (south) at the sign for the natural area.
Activities: Hiking and primitive camping.
Facilities: Picnic shelter, pit toilet.
Dates: Open year-round.
Fees: None.
Closest town: Tracy City, 3 miles.
For more information: South Cumberland State Recreation Area, Rt. 1, Box 2196, Monteagle, TN 37356. Phone (931) 924-2980.

GRUNDY FOREST DAY LOOP

[Fig. 18(5)] The trailhead is at the parking lot and CCC picnic shelter just south off US 41 southeast of Tracy City. This pleasant hike provides an introduction to the Fiery Gizzard area, as well as views of waterfalls and cascades and the junction of Big and Little Fiery Gizzard creeks. The Fiery Gizzard trail begins 0.7 mile along the loop.

The hike begins as a sandy path that passes by a 15-foot cascade and then the trail passes through a marshy area via a bridge. The trail descends to the Fiery Gizzard Creek surrounded

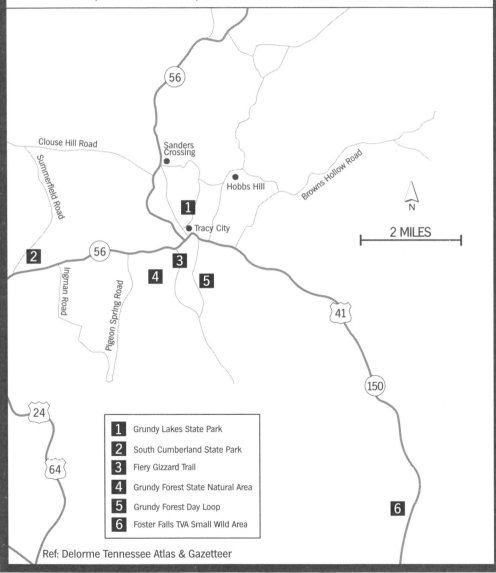

Grundy Lakes State Park

Grundy Lakes State Park is a day-use area whose main attraction is the historic coke ovens.

Clouse Hill Road

Summerfield Road

Sanders Crossing

Hobbs Hill

Browns Hollow Road

1 Tracy City

2

Ingman Road

Pigeon Spring Road

3

4

5

41

150

24

64

N

2 MILES

1	Grundy Lakes State Park
2	South Cumberland State Park
3	Fiery Gizzard Trail
4	Grundy Forest State Natural Area
5	Grundy Forest Day Loop
6	Foster Falls TVA Small Wild Area

6

Ref: Delorme Tennessee Atlas & Gazetteer

by hemlock and rhododendron and reaches Hanes Hole Falls at the 1-mile point. Beyond is the junction of the Little Fiery Gizzard with the Big Fiery Gizzard Creek, the modest 9-foot Blue Hole Falls, and the ascension to Cave Spring Rockhouse where there is a 500-year-old hemlock..

HOODED WARBLER
(Wilsonia citrina)
The hooded warbler's nest is an impressive combination of bark, plant fibers, down, grass, and spiderweb.

Trail: 2 miles, loop.
Elevation: 1,800 feet. Change, 500 feet.
Degree of difficulty: Easy to moderate.
Surface and Blaze: Rock, boardwalk, and forest floor. Blazes on trees.

FIERY GIZZARD TRAIL

[Fig. 18(3)] Hikers find this long trail that begins at Grundy Forest Natural Area and terminates at the Foster Falls TVA Wild Area both difficult and rewarding. The trail offers an exceptional variety of features that include many scenic views, rock formations, wildflower displays, waterfalls, swimming holes, and two campsites. A permit from the SCRA visitor center is required for camping.

Several stories tell how Fiery Gizzard got its name, the one most often cited being that David Crockett burned his tongue on a hot turkey gizzard while he camped along the creek. Kelly Roark, in her book *Hiking Tennessee*, offers another possibility: An Indian chief, wishing to get the attention of the white men attending a peace conference, threw a turkey gizzard into the fire.

One mile along the trail is Chimney Rock, a 20-foot-tall column. At 2 miles is another rock feature called the Fruit Bowl, which consists of house-sized boulders. A short spur trail to Raven Point provides another grand view of the gulf at mile 3.7. It's 1 mile to the Perpendicular Creek crossing and another mile to a small waterfall where there are remnants of a moonshine still. At about 10 miles is the descent into and out of Laurel Gorge. After the ascent is the Laurel Gorge Overlook, giving you another view of where you've been. At about 12 miles you arrive at 60-foot Foster Falls.

Trail: 12.5 miles, one-way.
Elevation: Begins at 1,720 feet and ends at 1,700 feet.
Degree of difficulty: Strenuous.
Surface and Blaze: Rock and forest floor. White blaze.

GRUNDY LAKES STATE PARK

[Fig. 18(1)] Grundy Lakes State Park is a day-use area whose main attraction is the historic coke ovens. These beehive-shaped ovens, many of which are still intact, were built in 1883 and used for making coke from the coal mined nearby. This is one of the sites that was involved in the miners' rebellion against convict labor in the 1890s. The ovens are on the National Historic Register.

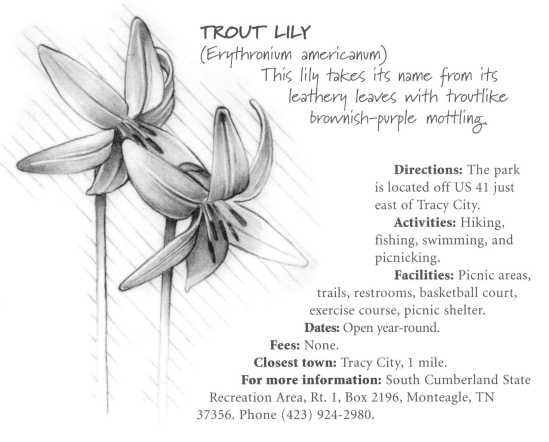

TROUT LILY
(*Erythronium americanum*)
This lily takes its name from its leathery leaves with troutlike brownish-purple mottling.

Directions: The park is located off US 41 just east of Tracy City.

Activities: Hiking, fishing, swimming, and picnicking.

Facilities: Picnic areas, trails, restrooms, basketball court, exercise course, picnic shelter.

Dates: Open year-round.

Fees: None.

Closest town: Tracy City, 1 mile.

For more information: South Cumberland State Recreation Area, Rt. 1, Box 2196, Monteagle, TN 37356. Phone (423) 924-2980.

🌾 FOSTER FALLS TVA SMALL WILD AREA

[Fig. 18(6)] This area is managed jointly by TVA and Tennessee State Parks and offers picnic facilities and seasonal overnight camping. The waterfall for which it is named is 60 feet tall and marks the southern end of the Fiery Gizzard Trail. Hemlocks, mountain laurels, and azaleas grow above the falls along a sandstone overlook.

Directions: Foster Falls is off US 41 about 6.5 miles south of Grundy Lakes State Park (*see* page 101).

Activities: Camping, picnicking, climbing, rappelling, and hiking.

Facilities: Hiking trails, picnic area, water, showers, and campsites.

Dates: The wild area is open year-round, and the campground is open mid-Apr. to mid-Oct.

Fees: There is a charge for camping.

Closest town: Tracy City, 7 miles.

For more information: South Cumberland State Recreation Area, Rt. 1, Box 2196, Monteagle, TN 37356. Phone (931) 924-2980.

🌾 SEWANEE NATURAL BRIDGE STATE NATURAL AREA

[Fig. 19(2)] The University of the South donated the 1.5-acre area in which the

Highbush blueberry (Vaccinium corymbosum) *provides fruit for animals and human mountain travelers.*

bridge is located to the state. After walking a gravel and dirt path to the top, visitors can walk across the bridge. The sandstone bridge is 27 feet high and 50 feet long. According to Russ Manning in his book *The Historic Cumberland Plateau*, a spring at the base of the bridge eroded the unusual formation. But there is only a seep spring present today.

Directions: Take TN 56 south for 3 miles from Sewanee, turn left (east) at a sign pointing to the site on an unnumbered road.

Activities: Scenic viewing.

Facilities: None.

Dates: Open year-round.

Fees: None.

Closest town: Sewanee, 3 miles.

For more information: South Cumberland State Recreation Area, Rt. 1, Box 2196, Monteagle, TN 37356. Phone (931) 924-2980.

CARTER STATE NATURAL AREA

[Fig. 19(3)] The main feature of this natural area is Lost Cove Cave via the Buggytop Trail. The entrance to the cave is 100 feet wide and 80 feet high and is considered "one of the most impressive cave openings in the state," according to

Hawkins Cove State Natural Area

This 244-acre Hawkins Cove State Natural Area is the newest unit in the SCRA, and it was set aside mainly to protect the rare Cumberland rosinweed (Silphium brachiatum).

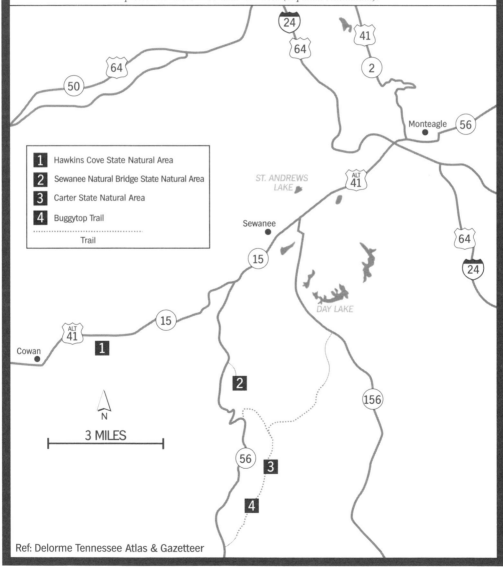

1 Hawkins Cove State Natural Area
2 Sewanee Natural Bridge State Natural Area
3 Carter State Natural Area
4 Buggytop Trail
.... Trail

N

3 MILES

Ref: Delorme Tennessee Atlas & Gazetteer

Caves of Tennessee by Thomas Barr. The cave is open for exploration, and SCRA naturalists conduct tours. The 2-mile trail to the cave is difficult but worth the effort. The trailhead is a few miles south of Sewanee on TN 56. There is no camping allowed in this area.

Directions: Take TN 56 south for 6 miles from Sewanee, turn left (east) into the parking area.

Activities: Hiking and cave touring.

Facilities: None.

Dates: Open year-round.

Fees: None.

Closest town: Sewanee, 6 miles.

For more information: South Cumberland State Recreation Area, Rt. 1, Box 2196, Monteagle, TN 37356. Phone (931) 924-2980.

OPOSSUM
(Didelphis virginiana)
The opossum is North America's only marsupial (pouched animal).

HAWKINS COVE STATE NATURAL AREA

[Fig. 19(1)] This 244-acre area is the newest unit in the SCRA, and it was set aside mainly to protect the rare Cumberland rosinweed (*Silphium brachiatum*). The Cumberland rosinweed is a member of the sunflower family (*Asteraceae*). It takes its name rosinweed because it exudes a resinous sap.

The site is undeveloped, although trails and day-use facilities are planned.

Directions: The area is 6 miles southwest of Sewanee via US 41A and south of the highway.

Activities: Hunting.

Facilities: None.

Dates: Open year-round.

Fees: None.

Closest town: Sewanee, 6 miles.

For more information: South Cumberland State Recreation Area, Rt. 1, Box 2196, Monteagle, TN 37356. Phone (931) 924-2980.

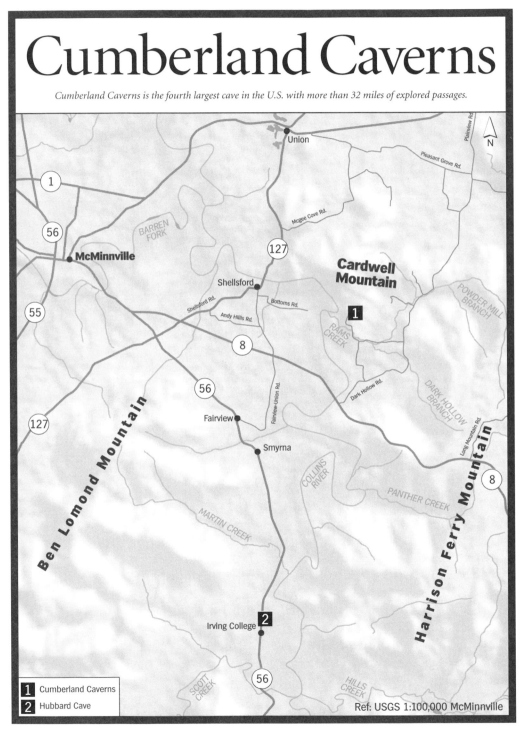

Cumberland Caverns

Cumberland Caverns is the fourth largest cave in the U.S. with more than 32 miles of explored passages.

Union

Plainview Rd
Pleasant Grove Rd.

1

56

Mcgee Cove Rd.

BARREN FORK

127

McMinnville

Cardwell Mountain

Shellsford

POWDER MILL BRANCH

55

Bottoms Rd.

1

Shellsford Rd.
Andy Hillis Rd.

RAMS CREEK

8

DARK HOLLOW BRANCH

Dark Hollow Rd.

56

Fairview-Union Rd.

127

Fairview

Long Mountain Rd.

Ben Lomond Mountain

Smyrna

8

COLLINS RIVER

PANTHER CREEK

Harrison Ferry Mountain

MARTIN CREEK

2

Irving College

SCOTT CREEK

56

HILLS CREEK

1 Cumberland Caverns
2 Hubbard Cave

Ref: USGS 1:100,000 McMinnville

N

Caves and Caverns

CUMBERLAND CAVERNS

[Fig. 20(1)] The western edge of the plateau has several outliers, portions of the main structure that have been detached by erosion, and Cumberland Caverns is located on one of these geologic islands. Cumberland Caverns is the second largest cave system in the country, with 32 miles of passageways, and it is the most extensively mapped cave in Tennessee.

As with all caves, water dissolves and erodes rock to carve an underground hole. The water follows the path of least resistance and sometimes flows uphill or downhill depending on where cracks or fractures allow it to flow. The stream that helped carve out the Cumberland Caverns still flows, in fact it forms a 60-foot waterfall in the Waterfall Room. The Hall of the Mountain King is one of the largest rooms in a cavern east of the Mississippi. It extends 600 feet with a 140-foot-high ceiling and is 140 feet wide, and all of it is more than 300 feet below ground level. There is also an underground dining room for groups.

Cumberland Caverns is commercially operated, and tours provide visitors the chance to see a wide variety of formations: stalactites, stalagmites, helectites, columns, flowstone, cave coral, gypsum flowers, and other features. Also part of the tour is a dramatization of the creation of the cave in sound and light.

Directions: To reach the caverns from McMinnville, take TN 56 south to TN 8 and travel southeast for 7 miles and follow the signs.

Activities: Guided cave touring, overnight spelunking, picnicking, hiking, and gem stone panning.

Facilities: Picnic area, hiking trails, and primitive camping

Dates: The caverns are open daily from May–Oct. and by appointment from Nov.–Apr.

Fees: There is a charge for the guided tour and spelunking.

Closest town: McMinnville, 7 miles.

For more information: Cumberland Caverns, 1437 Cumberland Caverns Road, McMinnville, TN 37110. Phone (931) 668-4396.

HUBBARD CAVE

[Fig. 20(2)] This cave is also know as Bat Cave because of the hundreds of thousands of gray bats (*Myotis grisescens*) that use it as a hibernaculum. The 50 acres that include Hubbard Cave are on the western wall of the plateau and are owned by The Nature Conservancy. To protect the bat population, a gate blocks one of the three entrances. Like many of the caves in the region, it was mined for saltpeter during the Civil War, and some evidence of this activity is still present near the entrance used by people who explore the cave. Because of the bat population, visitation isn't encouraged and only guided tours are offered.

Directions: Hubbard Cave can be reached off TN 56 south of McMinnville, near

SPRING PEEPER
(Hyla crucifer)
This treefrog is identified
by an X on its back.

the community of Irving College.

Activities: Field trips are available through The Nature Conservancy.

Facilities: None.

Fees: There is a charge for field trips.

Dates: Open for guided field trips only and advance reservations are required. Two to three tours are scheduled each summer.

For more information: The Nature Conservancy, 50 Vantage Way, Suite 250, Nashville, TN 37228. Phone (615) 255-0303.

BIG BONE CAVE

[Fig. 16(3)] Big Bone Cave is another of the caverns on one of the western outliers, located in the Big Bone Cave State Natural Area near the town of Rock Island.

The cave was an important source of the saltpeter used for making gunpowder during the Civil War and the War of 1812. It got its name after miners discovered the bones of a giant Pleistocene ground sloth (*Megalonyx jeffersoni*) here in 1811. The bones of a jaguar, or American leopard (*Felis onca*), were also found.

Radon gas is in the cave, and it is open for tours by appointment only. Appointments can be made by calling Rock Island State Park, phone (931) 686-2471. Rock Island State Park is not on the plateau, but is in charge of conducting tours of Big Bone Cave.

Directions: Go to Rock Island State Park for directions.

Activities: Cave touring by appointment only.

Facilities: None.

Fees: None.

Closest town: Rock Island, 5 miles.

For more information: Rock Island State Park, 82 Beach Road, Rock Island, TN 38581. Phone (931) 686-2471.

Bowaters Pocket Wilderness Areas

The Southern Division of Bowaters, Inc., a company that owns more than 350,000 acres of timberlands in Tennessee, began establishing pocket wilderness areas within its holdings in 1970. There are seven sites, all designated as state natural areas.

For more information: Bowater Newsprint and Directory Division, Calhoun Woodlands Operations, 5020 Highway 11 South, Calhoun, TN 37309. Phone (423) 336-7301.

VIRGIN FALLS POCKET WILDERNESS

[Fig. 16(2)] This 317-acre parcel of land owned by the Southern Division of Bowaters, Inc. was the first pocket wilderness area the company opened in Tennessee. The main attractions in the area are the waterfalls that plunge from considerable heights: Big Branch Falls, Sheep Cave Falls, Big Laurel Falls, and Virgin Falls.

The sensational Virgin Falls emerges from a cave and drops 110 feet. Virgin Falls is located on the western edge of the plateau 8 miles south of DeRossett off US 70 between Crossville and Sparta.

Directions: From Sparta, go east on US 70 approximately 11 miles to Eastland Road. Turn right on Eastland Road and travel 5.9 miles to Scott Gulf Road. Turn right on Scott Gulf Road and go 2 miles to the parking area and trailhead for the Virgin Falls Trail.

Activities: Hiking.

Facilities: None.

Dates: Open year-round

Fees: None.

Closest town: DeRossett, 8 miles.

For more information: Bowater Newsprint and Directory Division, Calhoun Woodlands Operations, 5020 Highway 11 South, Calhoun, TN 37309. Phone (423) 336-7301.

VIRGIN FALLS TRAIL

[Fig. 16(1)] This scenic trail offers hikers a wide variety of features, including three waterfalls, caves, an overlook that provides a spectacular view of the Caney Fork River, and moist valleys with many wildflowers. For day hikers it is recommended that eight hours be allowed for the trip. There is a camping area for backpackers at an area near Virgin Falls.

Maps are available at the trailhead and it is requested you take one and fill out the questionnaire to help Bowater judge the use of the area. The first part of the trail passes through a second-growth forest, descending to the modest, fan-shaped cascade of Big Branch Falls. Beyond the waterfall the trail becomes more rugged while descending 160 feet to Big Laurel Creek. Care should be used when crossing the creek when the water is high. A spur loop trail leads to an overlook with views of the Caney Fork River, Scott's Gulf, and Scott's Pinnacle. Back on the main trail, the next feature is Big Laurel Falls with a 40-foot drop. The creek disappears into a cave below the falls. When the trail forks, take the right fork to hike a loop trail past Sheep Cave and reach Virgin Falls, which flows from an underground stream to drop 110 feet and disappear into another cave. Spelunkers explore the caves during dry weather. Both hikers and spelunkers must be careful. The area is slick and rescue is a long time coming to this remote spot.

Trail: 4 miles, one-way.

Elevation: Begins at 1,700 feet and ends at 950 feet.

Degree of difficulty: Strenuous.

Surface and Blaze: Forest floor and white and blue blazes.

▒ LAUREL-SNOW POCKET WILDERNESS AREA

[Fig. 15(11)] The 710-acre site takes its name from two waterfalls: Laurel Falls and Snow Falls. Laurel Falls drops 80 feet, and the smaller Snow Falls only drops 12 feet but the water richochets off rocks at a 45-degree angle. Southeast of Snow Falls and southwest of Laurel Falls are Buzzard Point and Snake Head Point, respectively, two overlooks providing panoramic perspectives of the wilderness.

Directions: In Dayton, turn west off US 27 just north of the Rhea County Hospital on Walnut Grove Road and follow the signs to the Pocket Wilderness parking area and trailhead.

Activities: Hiking.

Facilities: None.

Fees: None.

Closest town: Dayton, 3 miles.

For more information: Bowater Newsprint and Directory Division, Calhoun Woodlands Operations, 5020 Highway 11 South, Calhoun, TN 37309. Phone (423) 336-7301.

LAUREL-SNOW TRAIL

[Fig. 15(12)] The Laurel-Snow Trail was the first National Recreation Trail in Tennessee, and it has many interesting features. It follows an old railroad bed, passes an abandoned mine shaft, and crosses a bridge over Laurel Creek. The trail forks, the east leg leading to Laurel Falls and Snake Head Point, and the west leg to Buzzard Point and Snow Falls.

Trail: 10.5 miles, round-trip.

Elevation: Begin and end at 850 feet with a high point of 1,700 feet.

Degree of difficulty: Strenuous.

Surface and Blaze: Rock and forest floor.

▒ STINGING FORK POCKET WILDERNESS

[Fig. 15(9)] The 104-acre Stinging Fork Pocket Wilderness is another of Bowater's small backcountry contributions to the public. One of the major attractions is a fan-shaped waterfall that drops 30 feet on Stinging Fork Creek. It also contains Stinging Fork Trail dedicated in 1976 as a State Recreational Trail.

Directions: Take Shut-In-Gap Road off TN 68 just 1 mile north of Spring City. Continue 5 miles on Shut-In-Gap Road to the pocket wilderness and trailhead.

Activities: Hiking and picnicking.

Facilities: Picnic area.

Fees: None.

Closest town: Spring City, 6 miles.

For more information: Bowater Newsprint and Directory Division, Calhoun Woodlands Operations, 5020 Highway 11 South, Calhoun, TN 37309. Phone (423) 336-7301.

STINGING FORK TRAIL

[Fig. 15(9)] Stinging Fork Trail, created in 1969, was the first trail on Bowater property, according to Evan Means in *Hiking Tennessee Trails*. This trail is picturesque, passing through a pine forest and on through stands of laurel and patches of blueberries. A spur trail leads to Indian Head Point where an overlook provides a view of the rugged Stinging Fork Gorge, and the trail passes within a short distance of the 30-foot-high Stinging Fork Falls and cascades.

Trail: 3-mile loop.

Elevation: Change of 300 feet.

Degree of difficulty: Moderate.

Surface and Blaze: Rock and forest floor, and blue blaze.

TWIN ROCKS NATURE TRAIL

[Fig. 15(8)] The trail leads to Twin Rocks, which overlooks the Tennessee Valley and the Soak Creek and Piney River gorges. This trail begins at the Piney River Picnic Area. Take Shut-In-Gap Road off TN 68 just north of Spring City to reach the picnic area.

Trail: 2.5 miles one-way.

Elevation: Change, 510 feet.

Degree of difficulty: Moderate.

Surface and Blaze: Forest floor.

PINEY RIVER TRAIL

PILEATED WOODPECKER
(Dryocopus pileatus)

[Fig. 15(10)] A National Recreation Trail, the Piney River Trail offers hikers a fascinating array of features, including steel and suspension bridges, an old railroad bed, waterfalls and cascades, an old mine tipple, hardwood forest, and a rock house. The trailhead also begins at the Piney River Picnic Area (*see* directions above). The trail follows the Piney River, crossing it on a 100-foot suspension bridge, walking along an old narrow-gauge Dinky railroad bed, crossing another bridge, then following Duskin Creek and crossing three more bridges before reaching the end of the trail. Materials for the bridges were flown in by helicopter to prevent harming the area by building a road.

Trail: 10 miles one-way.

Elevation: Begins at 850 feet and ends at 1,100 feet.

Degree of difficulty: Easy–moderate.

Surface and Blaze: Rock and forest floor. Green and blue blazes.

NORTH CHICKAMAUGA POCKET WILDERNESS AREA

[Fig. 21(2)] Opened in 1993, this 1,100-acre wilderness is named for North Chicka-

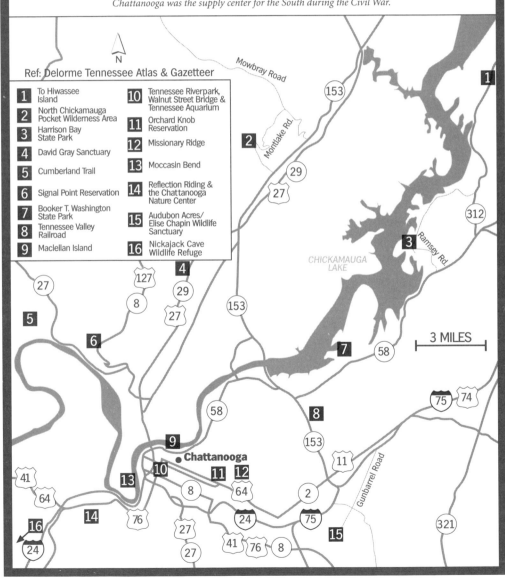

Chickamauga and Chattanooga Area

Chattanooga was the supply center for the South during the Civil War.

Ref: Delorme Tennessee Atlas & Gazetteer

1. To Hiwassee Island
2. North Chickamauga Pocket Wilderness Area
3. Harrison Bay State Park
4. David Gray Sanctuary
5. Cumberland Trail
6. Signal Point Reservation
7. Booker T. Washington State Park
8. Tennessee Valley Railroad
9. Maclellan Island
10. Tennessee Riverpark, Walnut Street Bridge & Tennessee Aquarium
11. Orchard Knob Reservation
12. Missionary Ridge
13. Moccasin Bend
14. Reflection Riding & the Chattanooga Nature Center
15. Audubon Acres/ Elise Chapin Wildlife Sanctuary
16. Nickajack Cave Wildlife Refuge

CHICKAMAUGA LAKE

3 MILES

Chattanooga

mauga Creek. Two easy trails, Hogskin Branch Loop, a 1.5-mile round-trip hike, and the 7.8-mile round-trip Stevenson Branch Trail take you by overlooks, waterfalls, wildflowers, picnic tables, and a camping area. The North Chickamauga Pocket Wilderness Area is within the Chickamauga Gulch, a gorge about 600 feet deep.

Directions: From Chattanooga, go north on US 27 to the intersection with TN 153. At the junction of TN 153 and US 27, TN 153 becomes Dayton Pike. Continue on Dayton Pike 3 miles to the intersection with Montlake Road. Turn left on Montlake Road and go 1 mile to the pocket wilderness sign and access road. Turn left (west) on the access road, and continue to the parking and picnic areas and trailhead.

Activities: Hiking, fishing, picnicking.

Facilities: Paved trails, boat launch, and picnic area.

Fees: None.

Closest town: Chattanooga, 2 miles.

For more information: Bowater Newsprint and Directory Division, Calhoun Woodlands Operations, 5020 Highway 11 South, Calhoun, TN 37309. Phone (423) 336-7301.

Chickamauga Lake

HARRISON BAY STATE PARK

[Fig. 21(3)] With 1,200 acres and nearly 40 miles of shoreline along Chickamauga Lake, Harrison Bay is one of the largest and most popular state park camping areas in the state. It is named for a large bay off the lake's main channel. The park was one of the demonstration areas Tennessee Valley Authority developed during the 1930s.

Directions: Take TN 58 north from Chattanooga. It is 15 miles to the park entrance.

Activities: Swimming, fishing, boating, picnicking, tennis, volleyball, planned programs, and camping.

Facilities: Campsites, group camp, RV hookups, bathhouses, swimming pool, nature trail, marina, boat-launching ramp, camp store, restaurant, tennis court.

Dates: Open year-round.

Fees: There is a charge for camping.

Closest town: Chattanooga, 8 miles.

For more information: Harrison Bay State Park, 8411 Harrison Bay Road, Harrison, TN 37341. Phone (423) 344-6214.

BOOKER T. WASHINGTON STATE PARK

[Fig. 21(7)] This park, also on the shores of Chickamauga Lake, is named for Booker Taliaferro Washington, a former slave who secured an education and went on to become the president of the Tuskegee Institute, a black organization for higher education. The park is mainly for day use, although there is a youth group camp and a group lodge for longer stays.

Directions: The park is on Champion Road off TN 58 just north of the Chattanooga city limits.

Activities: Swimming, fishing, picnicking, and field games.

Facilities: Boat-launching ramp, volleyball court, basketball court, bath house, playground, group camp, and lodge.

Fees: There is a charge for group camp and lodge and for swimming.

Closest town: Chattanooga, 10 miles.

For more information: Booker T. Washington State Park, 5801 Champion Road, Chattanooga, TN 37416. Phone (423) 894-4955.

▓ HIWASSEE ISLAND SANDHILL CRANES

[Fig. 21(1)] Hiwassee Island on Chickamauga Lake, one of the waterfowl refuges managed by the Tennessee Wildlife Resources Agency (TWRA), is the largest migrational stop for sandhill cranes (*Grus canadensis*) in eastern North America. A small number of the big wading birds have traditionally rested and refueled at this location while on their way between the northern U.S. and Florida. However, instead of the fewer than a dozen birds that showed up less than 10 years ago, the population is now estimated to be between 3,000 and 4,000. Also, instead of continuing on their journey, many of the cranes now remain for the entire winter, eating the corn provided by the TWRA. The Hiwassee Refuge is normally closed to visitors, but each February the Chattanooga Chapter of the Tennessee Ornithological Society and the TWRA conduct a sandhill crane viewing weekend for bird watchers.

For more information: Tennessee Wildlife Resources Agency, 218 Genesis Road, Crossville, TN 38555. Phone (931) 484-9571.

Chattanooga

Chattanooga is located at the southern end of the Great Valley of Tennessee. By the mid-1800s, it was one of the South's most important transportation centers, with railroads connecting Charleston, Savannah, Atlanta, and Knoxville; major roads running north to Knoxville and beyond, south to Atlanta, and west to Nashville; and barge traffic on the Tennessee River from Knoxville, down through Alabama, and on to Kentucky.

It also became the supply center for the South during the Civil War, and the battles that ensued between the Confederate and Union forces for control of the city were some of the fiercest and most decisive of the war.

The Civil War struggle for control of Chattanooga, and thus the state of Tennessee, began in the fall of 1863 when Confederate forces under Gen. Braxton Bragg were forced to retreat from Chattanooga into North Georgia by Union troops commanded by Maj. Gen. William S. Rosencrans. In the meantime, Bragg's army had been nearly doubled by reinforcements, and he mounted an offensive that resulted in the Battle of Chickamauga, the bloodiest two-day battle of the war, during which more than 37,000 casualties were suffered by the Union. Union forces were pushed out of North Georgia, and when Rosencrans abandoned Lookout Mountain, Bragg quickly seized it. With his troops also lined up on Missionary Ridge and Orchard Knob, the Confederates were prepared to starve the Union troops trapped in Chattanooga.

The tide began to turn when President Lincoln gave Gen. Ulysses S. Grant command forces to go to the aid of troops entrenched in Chattanooga. Shortly after Grant arrived on the scene, a new supply route was established by capturing Browns Ferry, a river crossing. Once Browns Ferry was in the hands of the Union army, goods began flowing freely.

The battles for Chattanooga began when Union troops attacked the defenses at Orchard Knob, a low hill in front of Missionary Ridge. The Confederate defenders were routed, and the stage was set for an attack on the main ridge. Before this could occur, Lookout Mountain had to be captured, and on the rainy, misty morning of November 24, Grant ordered Maj. Gen. Joseph Hooker with his three brigades to take the mountain. What resulted was the famous Battle Above the Clouds, during which the Union forces overran the Confederate defenses and took control of Lookout Mountain. Next came a pincer movement engineered by Grant. He had Gen. William Tecumseh Sherman attack Bragg's Missionary Ridge fortifications from the north, while Hooker advanced from the south. The Confederate troops on Missionary Ridge were then overwhelmed by troops under Maj. Gen. George H. Thomas, who charged up the 500-foot hill in a spontaneous attack. The Union forces were victorious, and the Confederates were forced to retreat back into Georgia.

The Battle of Lookout Mountain and the Battle of Missionary Ridge essentially broke the spirit of the Confederate army, and with Chattanooga firmly in its control, the Union army was free to strike into the deep South. In the spring of 1864, Sherman launched his infamous March to the Sea that was the death knell for the Confederacy.

Today, more than a century after the Civil War, Chattanooga is one of Tennessee's most vital and energized cities, with an exciting and varied combination of historic sites, environmental wonders, premier outdoor experiences, and activities that makes it one of the South's most popular tourist destinations.

For more information: Chattanooga Convention and Visitors Bureau, 1001 Market Street, Chattanooga, TN 37402. Phone (423) 756-8687.

TENNESSEE RIVERPARK

[Fig. 21(10)] Still under development, the Tennessee Riverpark will eventually form a 22-mile greenway and already offers visitors a number of features and activities, including fishing piers, picnic areas, a snack bar, restrooms, playgrounds, and boat launching ramps.

The most interesting experience offered is the 10-mile Riverwalk, a paved sidewalk that begins at Ross's Landing in downtown Chattanooga and extends to Chickamauga Dam. Along the way, this walking tour passes by seven sites that are on the National Register of Historic Places.

Directions: Begins across the street from the Tennessee Aquarium at Ross's Landing and follows the river upstream.

Activities: Walking, fishing, picnicking, and sight-seeing.

Facilities: Paved walkway, picnic areas, and fishing piers, snack bar, restrooms, playgrounds, boat-launching ramp.

Fees: None.

Closest town: Chattanooga.

For more information: Chattanooga Convention and Visitors Bureau, 1001 Market Street, Chattanooga, TN 37402. Phone (423) 756-8687.

WALNUT STREET BRIDGE

[Fig. 21(10)] Walnut Street Bridge was renovated from a condemned, multipurpose bridge to become the longest pedestrian bridge in the world. The 2,370-foot bridge in downtown Chattanooga reopened in 1993. Built in 1891, the old truss bridge became the first multiuse structure to span the Tennessee River, and for almost three decades it served as the only way to cross the river.

The bridge was a busy thoroughfare for many decades, but it was closed nearly 100 years after its construction on the advice of engineers who feared its collapse. Today, following a $4 million renovation, the bridge is stronger that the original, and it is a part of the Tennessee Riverpark.

The Walnut Street Bridge provides pedestrians access to many of the major attractions on either side of the river.

For more information: Chattanooga Convention and Visitors Bureau, 1001 Market Street, Chattanooga, TN 37402. Phone (423) 756-8687.

TENNESSEE AQUARIUM

[Fig. 21(10)] This $45 million freshwater life center, which stands as tall as a 12-story building, was created to celebrate the life-giving forces of rivers and was funded as an educational facility to provide enjoyment, understanding, and conservation efforts.

The exhibits begin with the Tennessee River's source in the Appalachian highlands, then display habitats ranging all the way to the Gulf of Mexico where saltwater tanks contain ocean species. Included is a Rivers of the World exhibit that allows visitors to stand on the banks of the world's great rivers: North America's Tennessee and Mississippi, South American's Amazon, Africa's Zaire, Japan's Shimanto, and Siberia's Yenisey.

More than 40 exhibits, 22 tanks, two living forests, and a 60-foot canyon display 7,000 kinds of fish, birds, amphibians, reptiles, mammals, and other living creatures.

Directions: Take I-24 to downtown Chattanooga to US Highway 27 North, Exit 1-C. Take a right onto Fourth Street. Turn left at the second stoplight onto Broad Street. Go two blocks and see aquarium.

Activities: Visiting Tennessee Aquarium and IMAX 3D Theater.

Facilities: Aquariums, gift shop, IMAX 3D Theater.

Fees: There is an admission charge.

For more information: Tennessee Aquarium, PO Box 11048, Chattanooga, TN 37401-2048. Phone (800) 262-0695.

BROAD-WINGED KATYDID
(Microcentrum rhombifolium)
Heard more often than seen, these insects are named for their shrill song.

MOCCASIN BEND

[Fig. 21(13)] The lower portion of Moccasin Bend in the Tennessee River at Chattanooga is a National Historic Landmark due to its archeological and historical significance. The river bend was a trade center for the Indians who controlled the region for thousands of years, and excavations have indicated that early Spanish explorers, possibly including Hernando De Soto, visited the area. There are also Civil War earthworks at the site.

A study is underway to determine if Moccasin Bend will become part of the National Military Park or remain in the hands of the city, county, and state under the protectorship of Friends of Moccasin Bend. Its future is uncertain at this writing and there are no archeological sites open to the public.

Directions: Go north from Chattanooga on US 27 and take the first road west after crossing the river, and then turn left (south) on Moccasin Bend Road.

Activities: None.

Facilities: None.

Dates: Open year-round

Fees: None.

Closest town: Chattanooga, 1 mile.

For more information: Bob Davenport, The Trust for Public Land, Design Center/ Miller Plaza, Chattanooga, TN 37402. Phone (423) 265-5229.

ORCHARD KNOB RESERVATION

[Fig. 21(11)] This is the hill from which Grant and Thomas launched the attack on Missionary Ridge that eventually routed the Confederate troops and put Union forces back in control of Chattanooga. The reservation is on Orchard Knob Avenue, and several state monuments and a number of cannon commemorate the battle.

Directions: At Orchard Knob Avenue and East Third Street.

For more information: Chattanooga Convention and Visitors Bureau, 1001 Market Street, Chattanooga, TN 37402. Phone (423) 756-8687.

MISSIONARY RIDGE

[Fig. 21(12)] Following the Battle of Chickamauga, Confederate troops occupied

Missionary Ridge as one of the key parts of the battle line that surrounded Union forces in Chattanooga. During the battle for the city, Union troops attacked and captured the ridge, ending the blockade imposed by Bragg's army.

There are numerous plaques, monuments, and Civil War cannons sitting among the elegant homes along Crest Drive. There is limited parking at the Bragg and Sherman reservations.

Directions: Follow Crest Road from Glass Street.

For more information: Chattanooga Convention and Visitors Bureau, 1001 Market Street, Chattanooga, TN 37402. (423) 756-8687.

SIGNAL POINT RESERVATION

[Fig. 21(6)] Signal Point on Signal Mountain, across the Tennessee River from Lookout Mountain, was the site used by the U.S. Signal Corps during the siege of Chattanooga. Signal Point Overlook provides a panoramic view of the Tennessee River gorge.

Directions: Take US 127 north to the town of Signal Mountain and follow signs to the Signal Point parking area.

For more information: Chattanooga Convention and Visitors Bureau, 1001 Market Street, Chattanooga, TN 37402. Phone (423) 756-8687.

CUMBERLAND TRAIL

[Fig. 21(5)] Near the Signal Point overlook is the trailhead for section 9 of the Cumberland Trail. From this point the trail travels through the Prentice Cooper State Forest; along bluff tops; into ravines lush with Eastern hemlocks (*Tsuga canadensis*), rhododendron, and laurel thickets, and a great variety of wildflowers and deciduous trees. There are two primitive campsites located in the first 11 miles, and hikers are warned against attempting to complete the entire trip in one day due to conditions along the route. The trail terminates at an overlook and fire tower near TN 27.

Trail: 13 miles.

Degree of difficulty: Strenuous.

Surface and Blaze: Forest floor.

For more information: Tennessee Division of Forestry, PO Box 160, Hixson, TN 37347. Phone (423) 658-5551.

TENNESSEE VALLEY RAILROAD

[Fig. 21(8)] The Tennessee Valley Railroad (TVR) and Museum was formed in 1961 by a group of Chattanoogans who wanted to preserve the city's railroad heritage. Today, an impressive collection of classic pieces from railroad history have been brought together to make the largest operating historic railroad in the South.

The TVR owns 40 acres that include four railroad bridges and a tunnel through Missionary Ridge. Included in the collection is a steam engine built in 1911; a 1917 office car, complete with three bedrooms and four bathrooms; Dining Car 3158, built in 1926 and still capable of serving full meals; Encore River, a 1954 stainless steel Pullman sleeping car; and a 1929 wooden caboose which saw service on both the Florida East Coast Railroad and the Nashville, Chattanooga, and St. Louis Railroad.

During the summer the Downtown Arrow Train makes weekend runs between the museum and the Chattanooga Choo-Choo/Holiday Inn. Longer excursions into North Georgia are regularly available, as well as the Pops in the Park Excursion in conjunction with the Chattanooga Symphony's outdoor summer event.

Directions: Take Exit 4 off I-75 and go north on TN 153 to Jersey Pike Exit. From there follow the signs.

For more information: Chattanooga Convention and Visitors Bureau, 1001 Market Street, Chattanooga, TN 37402. Phone (423) 756-8687.

CHATTANOOGA AUDUBON SOCIETY AREAS

Noted Chattanooga naturalist Robert Sparks Walker created the Chattanooga Audubon Society (CAS) in 1944, which currently owns and operates three sanctuaries in the area.

AUDUBON ACRES/ELISE CHAPIN WILDLIFE SANCTUARY

[Fig. 21(15)] This is a 120-acre sanctuary in the city's East Brainerd area that features a rich diversity of plant and animal life, an aviary, and 10 miles of hiking trails. Once the home of both Woodland Indians and Cherokee Indians, it is listed on the National Register of Historic Places.

Directions: Take Exit 3A off I-75 and go right at the second traffic light onto Gunbarrell Road. Gunbarrell Road dead-ends into Audubon Acres.

Facilities: Trails, summer lecture programs, Cherokee cabin built in the 1700s, guided tours on request, Walker Hall may be rented for special events, and the new Interpretive Center/Museum.

Fees: There is a charge for admission.

Dates: Open year-round.

For more information: Chattanooga Audubon Society, 900 North Sanctuary Road, Chattanooga, TN 37421. Phone (423) 892-1499.

MACLELLAN ISLAND

[Fig. 21(9)] The 18-acre Maclellan Island is in the middle of the Tennessee River in downtown Chattanooga. Formerly inhabited by Indians, and later by European settlers, the island is rich in plant and animal life. Bird watchers can see great blue herons (*Ardea herodias*), ospreys, several kinds of migrating warblers, ducks, geese, and wading birds. Squirrels, rabbits, foxes, raccoons, and opossums (*Didelphis virginiana*) also inhabit the island. Two footpaths allow a tour of the sanctuary.

Get to the island via a boat service available at Ross's Landing from May to October. Tours are available during the remainder of the year by calling the society for an appointment.

Directions: Maclellan Island is located in the middle of the Tennessee River off downtown Chattanooga with access available only by water craft. It is visible from the Walnut Street Bridge and the Veterans Bridge.

Activities: Wildlife viewing, and a guide is required.

Facilities: None.

Fees: There is a charge for the watercraft.

Dates: Open year-round.

For more information: Chattanooga Audubon Society, 900 North Sanctuary Road, Chattanooga, TN 37421. Phone (423) 892-1499.

DAVID GRAY SANCTUARY

[Fig. 21(4)] The 460-acre David Gray Sanctuary is also known as Audubon Mountain because of its popularity as a hawk-watching location. There are trails throughout the sanctuary that wind through hemlock and hardwood forests, laurel and rhododendron thickets, and wildflower niches. An observation platform on Walden Ridge provides a sweeping view of the valley and surrounding area.

Directions: Contact the Chattanooga Audubon Society to arrange for a guide and directions.

Activities: Viewing wildlife and wildflowers, and hiking.

Facilities: Observation platform.

Fees: There is an admission charge, and a guide is required to enter the area.

Dates: Open year-round.

For more information: Chattanooga Audubon Society, 900 North Sanctuary Road, Chattanooga, TN 37421. (423) 892-1499.

REFLECTION RIDING AND THE CHATTANOOGA NATURE CENTER

[Fig. 21(14)] On the western slope of Lookout Mountain and along Lookout Creek are Reflection Riding and the Chattanooga Nature Center. The Nature Center is an environmental education facility with nature exhibits and a rehabilitation center for injured wildlife. Reflection Riding is a 300-acre nature preserve that adjoins Lookout Mountain National Park. A wide variety of trees, scrubs, and wildflowers are maintained in an English landscape.

The drive along Lookout Creek is delightful. It is a serene change from the bustle of the city. The park contains more than 1,000 species of plants, with more than 300 wildflowers identified.

The Great Indian Warpath that ran from Alabama to New York remains in its original condition within the park. It is thought that De Soto and his men traveled the Great Indian Warpath in 1540. Also, the 1807 Old Federal Road that ran from Augusta, Georgia to Nashville, the first road through the Cherokee Nation, is preserved here. There are markers throughout the park noting history that took place here and noting Cherokee Chief Walking Stick's log cabin, one of the oldest structures in the state.

Directions: Go west from Chattanooga on US 11 and turn southwest on Garden Road.

Activities: Walking, wildlife viewing, and driving tour.

Facilities: A 300-acre botanical garden, wetland walkway, wildlife dioramas and exhibits, and wildlife hospital.

Dates: Open year-round.

Fees: There is a charge for admission.

Closest town: Chattanooga, 3 miles.

For more information: Reflection Riding, 400 Garden Road, Chattanooga, TN 37419. Phone (423) 821-1660.

NICKAJACK CAVE WILDLIFE REFUGE

[Fig. 21(16)] This cave is not as much of an attraction as the creatures who roost here. Visitors will want to come to this site on an evening between late April and early September. That's when more than 100,000 federally endangered gray bats leave the cave and take to the sky. The bats emerge from their maternity roost nightly like a black veil unfurling, a show that lasts approximately 45 minutes.

Pregnant female bats arrive each spring and find just the right conditions for giving birth in Nickajack Cave. Warm air is trapped in pockets in the cave ceiling, creating an incubator-like temperature. Each night, gray bats feed on mosquitoes, moths, and beetles, with this colony consuming 274,000 pounds of insects annually. The cliff swallows visitors will see flying around in front of the cave feed on the same insects during the day. These birds build their jug-like mud nests in the twilight zone (the zone where light from the outside still penetrates the cave darkness), sharing the bats' habitat and food source but on a different schedule. The young gray bats are very vulnerable to human disturbance, so the Tennessee Valley Authority has fenced in the cave. Visitors stand on a viewing platform a safe distance away. This site is so biologically important, it became Tennessee's first non-game wildlife refuge in 1992, and today it is managed solely for the protection of the bats.

Nickajack Cave is adjacent to Maple View Recreation Area, which is operated by the City of New Hope. The cave is managed jointly by the Tennessee Valley Authority and the Tennessee Wildlife Resources Agency, and there are strict penalties for harassing the bats.

Directions: From Chattanooga, take I-24 west to the Haletown/New Hope Exit #161 and turn left onto Route 156 south. Travel 5 miles and turn left into Maple View Recreation Area. A 0.2-mile trail leads from the parking area to the cave entrance.

Activities: Seasonal viewing of bats. At the recreation area, boating, swimming, fishing, and picnicking.

Facilities: Viewing platform at Nickajack Cave. At the recreation area, there is a boat ramp, swimming beach, restroom, and picnic areas.

Dates: Bats can be seen each evening between late Apr. and early Sept.

Fees: There is a small charge for parking.

Closest town: Chattanooga, approximately 15 miles.

For more information: Tennessee Valley Authority, Chickamauga/Nickajack Land Management Office, 4833 Highway 58, Chattanooga, TN 37416. Phone (423) 954-3811. Or, Tennessee Wildlife Resources Agency, Region III, 216 Penfield Street, Crossville, TN 38555. Phone (800) 262-6704.

HIGHBUSH BLACKBERRY
(Rubus allegheniensis)

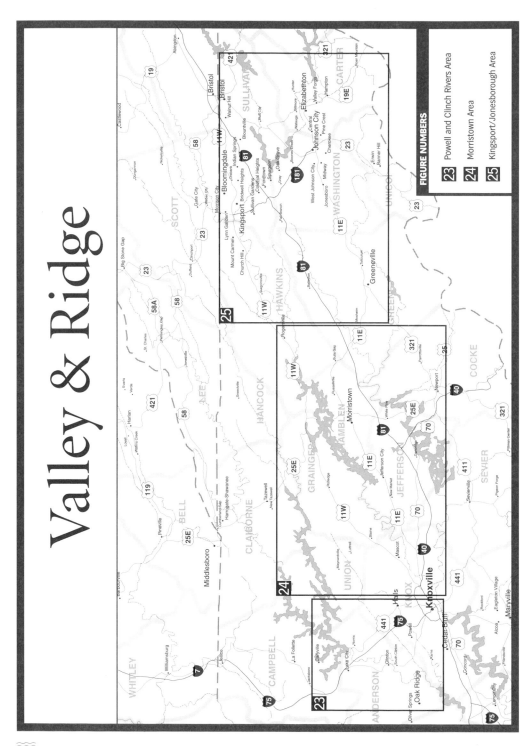

Valley & Ridge

Valley and Ridge

Adjacent to the western side of the Unaka Mountains is the 40-mile-wide Valley and Ridge province. Tennessee's section of this province is often referred to as the Valley of East Tennessee because of its unusual topography. Essentially, it is a low-lying area between the Unaka Mountains and the Cumberland Plateau that runs diagonally across eastern Tennessee from Virginia to Georgia.

The extensive drainage system includes many streams and rivers that converge to form the mainstream Tennessee River. Along many of these rivers, the Tennessee Valley Authority has built dams to produce electrical power and control flooding. The vast system of reservoirs the dams impound provides the public with a wide variety of recreational opportunities.

After North America and Africa drifted apart during the Jurassic Period of the Mesozoic Era, opening the area that is now the Atlantic Ocean, the last overthrust of

[*Above:* Trout fishing is popular in the Tennessee mountains]

the Allegheny orogeny left deformed rock from the Unaka Range to the Cumberland Plateau. Erosion, the ever-present process, began sculpting eastern Tennessee again.

Approximately 2,500 square miles of the Valley and Ridge province is made up mostly of sediments from the Paleozoic Era. Originally these were parallel layers of sandstones, conglomerates, shales, and limestones, but nearly all the rock was folded or faulted. The jumble of rock left between the Unakas and the Cumberland Plateau is about 1,000 feet above sea level and runs from Virginia to Georgia. It roughly forms a line from Chattanooga to Bristol on the east, and along the Cumberland Plateau on the west. It has undergone the same thrust faulting and erosion as the Unakas.

Hard metamorphic strata and softer sedimentary strata folded like an accordion when the Unakas were lifted. The softer rock, limestone and shales wore away sooner, forming valleys and leaving the harder sandstones and conglomerates as ridges.

Clinch Mountain, Powell Mountain, and Bays Mountain are the prominent ridges in the north. The highest point in the series is 3,097 feet at Bays Mountain. The highest and longest ridge in the south is Whiteoak Mountain between Chattanooga and Cleveland. Whiteoak Mountain rises to 1,495 feet elevation.

The streams of the Valley and Ridge closely follow the areas where the softer rocks were exposed during the thrust faulting. The softer rock eroded forming the valleys and streambeds. Where streams are found running perpendicular to the orientation of the valleys and ridges rock fractures let water through, and the water eventually eroded through a ridge to let a stream form.

The flora of the Valley and Ridge is unusually varied, but there are some communities of species that remain somewhat constant. For example, the forests of the ridges contain mesophytic species such as red oak, white oak, red maple, scarlet oak, chestnut oak, mockernut hickory, pignut hickory, sweet birch, cucumbertree, serviceberry, striped maple, mountain holly, witch hazel, and a few others. Bear oak (*Qurcus illicifolia*) may dominate the windswept slopes of the Valley and Ridge, and the valley floors are usually populated by oaks.

The ravines and coves are where hemlock and other mesic species, including basswood, buckeye, beech, white ash, magnolias, spicebush (*Lindera benzoin*), pawpaw (*Asimina triloba*), bitternut hickory, and yellow birch are found. The Tennessee River valley running through the southern Valley and Ridge contains mostly mixed mesophytic forests of oaks, hickories, maples, and ash, with some hemlocks and pines.

Because the area is dominated by limestone and underground streams, caves and caverns are numerous in the Valley and Ridge. Since the Cambrian Period, in the Appalachians west of the Blue Ridge, underground water has found breaks and crevices in limestone, enlarged these weaknesses, and formed tunnels miles long and hundreds of feet deep. The result is a system of caves, primarily stretching from Pennsylvania to Tennessee, that is home to land and water species adapted to this unique environment. In the older northern Appalachians, caves don't form because the rock is harder and underground reservoirs do not accumulate.

In the cool, dark cave world, stalactites extend from the ceiling, and stalagmites reach up from the floor. When a stalactite and a stalagmite meet, a column is formed. In Appalachian caves, most cave life is concentrated in the zone where light from the outside still penetrates, called the twilight zone. Animals in this zone include cave crickets with excessively long antennae to receive stimuli, and other insects such as midges and beetles. Joining the insects are grandaddy longlegs, salamanders, wood frogs, and, in caves with streams, crayfish and fish.

When it comes to mammals, no other is as famous for residing in caves as bats. In the caves of the Appalachians there are several species of bats, some that are permanent residents and others that hibernate in caves for the winter. When they are resting, bats hang head down from cave ceilings or crowd into small crevices, and they are not only found in the twilight zone. Bats stretch back into the dark recesses of caves.

Another mammal that calls caves home is the Allegheny woodrat (*Neotoma magister*). With a long hairy tail, huge eyes, and a yellowish brown body, this rodent nests here, dragging food like magnolia seed pods in to eat.

CERULEAN WARBLER
(*Dendroica cerulea*)
Observing this warbler can be difficult because it usually feeds high in trees.

People have reported seeing blind, white fish in Appalachian caves. While ichthyologists are still investigating which fish are present, there may be cavefishes here, belonging to the family Amblyopsidae. These fish are lightly pigmented and have greatly reduced eyes or no eyes at all. Their sensory systems are elaborately developed, and some members of the family are strictly cave dwelling while others are not.

Cavefishes found in Tennessee are the spring cavefish (*Forbesichtys agassizi*) and southern cavefish (*Typhlichthys subterraneus*). While the spring cavefish is not strictly a cave dweller, is generally colored dark gray to black, and is found in western Tennessee, the southern cavefish may be responsible for rumors of blind, white fishes in the caves of eastern Tennessee. Wild specimens of this species are white, occurring with no pigments, and have a highly evolved sensory system on their heads and along the sides of their bodies. This sensory system allows the fish to exist in a subterranean world of darkness. Growing to a maximum length of 3.5 inches, its principal food items are copepods, amphipods, and isopods. The southern cavefish has been placed on the protected species list of Tennessee fishes.

Ichthyologists know this species exists in western Tennessee but are not sure whether or not the southern cavefish lives in the caves of eastern Tennessee. The blind, white fishes spotted here may be cave-inhabiting sculpins, a species in which scientists have reported albinism.

Powell and Clinch Rivers Area

The Upper Clinch River has one of the most diverse fish faunas in North America.

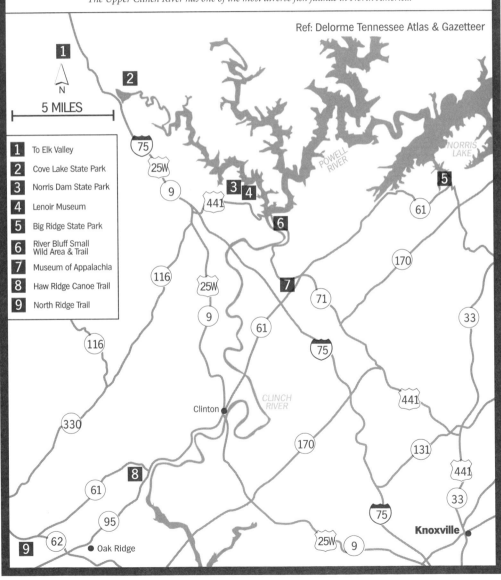

Ref: Delorme Tennessee Atlas & Gazetteer

1   To Elk Valley
2   Cove Lake State Park
3   Norris Dam State Park
4   Lenoir Museum
5   Big Ridge State Park
6   River Bluff Small
    Wild Area & Trail
7   Museum of Appalachia
8   Haw Ridge Canoe Trail
9   North Ridge Trail

Powell and Clinch Rivers Area

🏵 POWELL RIVER

[Fig. 23] Between the Cumberland Plateau and Powell Mountain is a long, fairly broad valley carved out by the Powell River. The river has its origin near Big Stone Gap, Virginia, another of the smaller niches in the plateau wall that eventually became a migration and trade route. The Wilderness Road ran alongside a portion of the river in Virginia, and US 58 generally follows the route of the old road. The mountain, valley, and river are named for Ambrose Powell, who accompanied Thomas Walker on his exploration of the area.

The Powell is one of the finest remote float streams in the state, winding through sparsely populated and beautiful country that offers excellent fishing for smallmouth bass and rock bass, as well as bird and wildlife viewing. From Olinger Bridge near Bales Ford to the bridge on US 25E, there are 115 miles of water, so float trips can be of whatever length desired. The river is rated Class I–II, which is suitable for beginners and novices.

In Tennessee there are access points at the bridges on US 25E and TN 63 and at numerous locations along local paved and gravel roads. The Powell River is one of the major tributaries of Norris Lake, and it flows into the reservoir near the town of Speedwell on TN 63.

For more information: Clinch-Powell RC & D Council, Route 2, PO Box 379, Rutledge, TN 37861. Phone (423) 828-5927.

🏵 CLINCH RIVER

[Fig. 23] The Clinch River, flowing through a long, narrow valley between Powell Mountain and Copper Ridge, also comes into Tennessee from Virginia, entering near the town of Kyles Ford less than 1 mile from the state line at the junction of TN 70 and TN 33. From this point to the US 25E bridge, there are 50 miles of Class I water that flow through pastoral and woodland country flanked by low mountains. Throughout its length it is well-removed from main routes of travel. The only access points on paved roads other than at Kyles Ford are at the US 25E bridge between Tazewell and Harrogate and at a bridge near the junction of TN 31 and TN 66. The Clinch is noted for its biological diversity. The Upper Clinch River holds one of the most diverse fish faunas in North America.

The Clinch River valley supports 382 species of wildlife, and the river provides good fishing for a number of species, including smallmouth bass, rock bass, crappie (*Pomoxis annularis,*) white bass (*Roccus chrysops,*) and walleye. It is an excellent float stream, with Class I and II water suitable for beginner and novice canoeists or boaters. With well over 50 miles of river available, two- and three-day trips are possible. The Clinch is the other main tributary of Norris Lake, and it flows into the lake a short distance southwest of Thorn Hill.

For more information: Clinch-Powell RC & D Council, Route 2, PO Box 379, Rutledge, TN 37861. Phone (423) 828-5927.

✳ ▦ COVE LAKE STATE PARK

[Fig. 23(2)] Cove Lake and its nearby sister parks, Big Ridge and Norris, were established in the 1930s as recreational demonstration areas by the Tennessee Valley Authority, the National Park Service, and the Civilian Conservation Corps (CCC). Cove Lake State Park is located on an arm of Norris Lake, whose water level is controlled by a subsidiary dam. The entire park is within the city limits of Caryville.

Cove Lake has limited facilities, but its restaurant with a spectacular view of the lake and the hundreds of Canada geese that winter here is a favorite meeting place for groups and families. Before funding was withdrawn by the state, Cove Lake was the location of the Cumberland Trail Office.

Directions: Take I-75 north from Knoxville for 30 miles, and take Exit 134. Take a right and go through a traffic light. The state park is 0.5 mile down on the left.

Activities: Hiking, biking, swimming, fishing, boating, tennis, softball, volleyball, horseshoes, and other playground activities.

Facilities: Camping, bathhouses, swimming pool, picnicking, boat ramp, hiking and biking trails, restaurant, recreation lodge, summer recreation and naturalist programs. Recreation equipment is available free at the boat dock.

Dates: Open year-round.

Fees: There is a charge for camping.

For more information: Superintendent's Office, Cove Lake State Park, 110 Cove Lake Lane, Caryville, TN 37714-9629. Phone (423) 566-9701.

✳ ▦ NORRIS DAM STATE PARK

[Fig. 23(3)] The 4,500-acre Norris Dam State Park lies on both sides of Norris Dam, built in the mid-1930s as the Tennessee Valley Authority's (TVA) first project in a reservoir system that became known as The Great Lakes of the South. The western part of the park was initially a TVA recreation demonstration area and is the site of most of the park's facilities. The eastern part was added later, and eventually the entire park was deeded to the state.

Naturalists are particularly fond of the park because of the trails that pass through stands of virgin forests with an enormous profusion of wildflowers and songbirds, as well as caves, bluffs, and scenic views. There is a fairly extensive system of trails, most of which are less than 1 mile in length.

One of these, the High Point Trail system, connects with the Norris city watershed trail system, which consists of 20 miles of interconnecting trails.

Access to four trails is on the eastern side of Norris Dam just north of the picnic area and ranger station.

Directions: Going north from Knoxville on I-75, take Exit 128 onto US 441 South at Lake City, and go south on US 441 for 2.5 miles. Turn at sign for park entrance.

Activities: Swimming, boating, water skiing, fishing, hiking, volleyball, tennis, summer nature programs, picnicking, and camping.

Facilities: Boat ramps, marina, cabins, laundromat, restaurant, snack bar, boat rentals, bathhouses, hiking trails, campground.

Dates: Open year-round.

Fees: There is a charge for camping.

Closest Town: Lake City, 2.5 miles.

For more information: Superintendent's Office, Norris Dam State Park, 125 Village Green Circle, Lake City, TN 37769. Phone (423) 426-7461.

The Coal Creek Wars

In the late 1800s coal companies working the rich deposits in the northeastern parts of the plateau began leasing convicts from state prisons to supplement the regular work force. Using the prisoners reduced costs, and the prisoners could be worked longer hours and treated more harshly without repercussions. Yet a backlash came from the miners themselves, who mounted a revolt against the prisoner-lease system. The revolt broke out at Briceville, near Coal Creek, which is now Lake City.

The revolt then spread to Oliver Springs and Tracy City, at which time the state militia was sent in to put down the insurrections. The militia effort succeeded, but the revolt resulted in the legislature putting an end to the convict leasing system in 1896. Convicts from Brushy Mountain State Prison legally worked the state-owned mines on the plateau until the mines closed in the 1950s.

LENOIR MUSEUM

[Fig. 23(4)] The Lenoir Museum is a part of Norris Dam State Park. It features a collection of more than 1,000 pioneer items and photographs of the construction of Norris Dam and the town of Norris. There is also an eighteenth-century threshing barn and a grist mill that operates during the summer months.

Directions: At the junction of US 441 and Clear Creek Road about 1 mile from Norris Dam.

Facilities: Museum and picnic areas by the gristmill.

Dates: Open year-round. Open weekends only Nov. 15–Apr. 15.

Fees: None.

Closest Town: Norris, 7 miles.

For more information: Superintendent's Office, Norris Dam State Park, Route 1, Box 500, Lake City, TN 37769. Phone (423) 426-7461.

RIVER BLUFF SMALL WILD AREA

[Fig. 23(6)] Adjacent to Norris Dam State Park to the south and along both banks of the Clinch River below the dam is the Tennessee Valley Authority's 300-acre River Bluff Small Wild Area. This unique ecosystem contains old-growth, deciduous forest, 40-year-old pines (*Pinus* sp.), more than 100 species of wildflowers, a wide variety of songbirds, and steep bluffs overlooking the Clinch River.

Hundreds of people visit here in the last days of March and through April to see the wildflowers, and the main attraction is the trout lilies (*Erythronium americanum*). Several acres of yellow trout lilies bloom the last part of March or the first part of April. Folklore claims that trout don't bite until the trout lily blooms. Among the other wildflowers are Dutchman's breeches (*Dicentra cucullaria*), bloodroot (*Sanguinaria canadensis*), toothwort (*Dentaria laciniata*), toadshade (*Trillium erectum*), twinleaf (*Jeffersonia diphylla*), and celandine poppy (*Stylophorum diphyllum*).

An orchard of Oriental chestnut (*Castanea mollissima*) was planted in the 1930s to replace the loss of the American chestnut (*C. dentata*). The imported chestnut makes poor lumber, but it does provide mast for some of the wildlife. About 40 percent of the forest in the River Bluff Small Wild Area contained the doomed chestnut trees.

The steep bluffs along the Clinch River are kept moist and cool by the water discharged through Norris Dam. The water is drained from the bottom of Norris Lake where the water is cold, and creates clouds of mist along the river.

Directions: Going north from Knoxville on I-75, take Exit 122 (Norris/Clinton). Turn right on Hwy. 61, travel past the Museum of Appalachia, and turn north on Hwy. 441 toward Norris Dam. Travel 6 miles, cross Norris Dam, take the second left, and follow the signs.

Activities: Wildflowers and wildlife watching and hiking.

Facilities: None.

Dates: Open year-round

Fees: None.

Closest Town: Norris, 7 miles.

For more information: Judith P. Bartlow, TVA, 17 Ridgeway Road, Norris, TN 37828. Phone (423) 632-1592.

RIVER BLUFF TRAIL

[Fig. 23(6)] Walk from the parking lot south along the Clinch River. The trail splits to form a loop trail.

The trail has several segments. First is the chestnut orchard and shortleaf pines (*Pinus echinata*). In the second segment the trail drops and goes through a mature mesophytic forest. The trail begins a gradual climb to a higher area with oak (*Quercus* sp.), hickories (*Carya* sp.), red cedar (*Juniperus siliciola*), and pines with an understory of redbud (*Ceris canadensis*), blueberry (*Vaccinium* sp.), and dogwoods (*Cornus* sp.). Many stumps from chestnut trees can be seen here. A switchback leads to the beginning of the trail.

Trail: 3.1 miles.

Elevation: Change, 260 feet.

Degree of Difficulty: Easy with some steep grades.

Blaze: Signed.

CLINCH RIVER BELOW NORRIS DAM

[Fig. 23] When TVA gave the land that would become Norris Dam State Park to the state, it retained control of a 13-mile stretch of the Clinch River below Norris

Dam. This is a prime river float that goes to the headwaters of Melton Hill Dam and is popular with both boaters and fishermen.

The Clinch tail water has a large population of rainbow trout and brown trout, with rainbows of up to 6 pounds and brown trout of more than 10 pounds commonly taken. The state record brown trout, 28 pounds, 12 ounces, was caught there in 1988. Angling success for wading fishermen is most likely when water isn't being released from the dam, while float fishermen do well when the water levels are higher.

There are 11 points of public access on the 13-mile stretch. The canoe access points are Birdsong, Miller Island, Peach Orchard, Highway 61 bridge, Eagle Bend, Highway 25W, Lost Bottom, Gibbs Ferry, Melton Lake Park/Oak Ridge Marina, Bull Run, and Solway Park. The Birdsong, Miller Island, and Peach Orchard access points are above I-75 near Norris Dam. The Highway 61 bridge, Eagle Bend, Highway 25W, Lost Bottom, and Gibbs Ferry access points are near Clinton. The others are east of Oak Ridge. Ask the Anderson County Tourism Council for its brochure, The Ultimate Waterway—Norris Lake, which contains a map of Norris Lake and Clinch River canoe access points.

For more information: Anderson County Tourism Council, PO Box 147, Clinton, TN 37717. Phone (800) 524-3602 or (423) 457-4542.

MUSEUM OF APPALACHIA

[Fig. 23(7)] The Museum of Appalachia is a few miles south of the Lenoir Museum off US 441 on TN 61. John Rice Irwin's Museum of Appalachia is a full reproduction of a pioneer village, complete with more than 30 log structures and a three-story Hall of Fame dedicated to the men, women, and children of Appalachia. There are also demonstrations of many pioneer activities, including weaving and spinning, the making of Kentucky rifles, spring plowing, and many others. There is an annual Homecoming Week each October with nonstop festivities.

Directions: East of Clinton 6 miles on TN 61.

Facilities: Store, museums, gift shop, restaurant, and 65-acre farm.

Dates: Open year-round.

Fees: There is an admission charge to the museums and farm.

Closest Town: Norris, 1 mile.

For more information: Museum of Appalachia, Box 1189, Norris, TN 37828. Phone (423) 494-7680 or 494-0514.

BIG RIDGE STATE PARK

[Fig. 23(5)] Big Ridge is another of the early TVA demonstration areas, and it is a spot ideally suited for those

COPPERHEAD
(*Agkistrodon contortrix*)

who are looking for places off main routes of travel. Located on the shores of Norris Lake, the 3,687-acre park is situated in a heavily forested area with prominent parallel hills and valleys typical of this part of the Valley and Ridge region.

The Big Ridge trails are considered to be some of the best in the state park system, and the area offers a great diversity of wildlife and wildflowers.

Directions: Driving north from Knoxville on I-75, go east from the Clinton/Norris interchange on TN 61 approximately 10 miles to the entrance to the park.

Activities: Hiking, swimming, boating (canoes, paddleboats, and rowboats for rent at Big Ridge Lake), water-skiing, fishing, picnicking.

Facilities: Cabins, campsites, bathhouses, picnic sites, snack bar, boat-launching ramp, swimming beach, hiking trails, tennis and volleyball courts, and children's playground.

Dates: Open year-round. Swimming, boat rental, and snack bar open during summer only.

Fees: There is a charge for camping.

Closest Town: Norris, 17 miles.

For more information: Superintendent's Office, Big Ridge State Park, 1015 Big Ridge Park Road, Maynardville, TN 37807. Phone (423) 992-5523.

Oak Ridge

The historic significance of Oak Ridge is monumental: in 1943 scientists involved in the top-secret "Manhattan Project" at this obscure rural location created the technology that led to the production of the first atomic bomb. It was a discovery that eventually affected every human being on the planet in one way or another.

Yet until the bombs were dropped on Japan in 1945, Oak Ridge didn't exist. It was a city behind a fence that was not on any map. Throughout the war it remained a maximum-security operation.

Today, Oak Ridge is a vibrant city and the home of the Department of Energy's Oak Ridge National Laboratory, a multipurpose, multiuse facility for basic science research and development in energy resources, environmental quality, educational foundations, and economic competitiveness, and the American Museum of Science and Energy, a center for exploration of science, technology, and Oak Ridge history. Oak Ridge is also the headquarters for the Tennessee Citizens for Wilderness Planning (TCWP), the

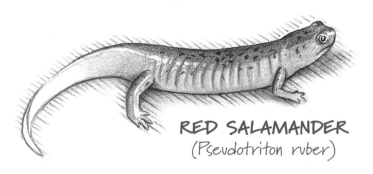

RED SALAMANDER
(Pseudotriton ruber)

organization that spearheaded the crusade that led to the establishment of the Big South Fork National River and Recreation Area (*see* page 26). Subsequently the TCWP has contributed to efforts that led to the abandonment of a plan to build another highway across the Great Smoky Mountains National Park; to the passage of the Tennessee Scenic Rivers Act; to the inclusion of the Obed River in the National Wild and Scenic Rivers system; and to the passage of the Tennessee Natural Areas Preservation Act and the Tennessee Trails System Act.

VIRGINIA CREEPER
(Parthenocissus quinquefolia)
A cousin of grapes, the Virginia creeper climbs and sprawls as it grows up to 150 feet high.

Directions: Oak Ridge is 15 miles west of Knoxville on TN 62.

Activities: Tour the American Museum of Science and Energy, the historic World War II Manhattan Project sites, and the University of Tennessee Arboretum.

Facilities: The American Museum of Science and Energy offers interactive exhibits, live demonstrations, and audiovisuals on fossil fuels, alternative energy sources, and the World War II Manhattan Project. Manhattan Project sites include the Graphite Reactor, a National Historic Landmark, and nature trails in the arboretum.

Fees: None.

Dates: Open year-round.

For more information: Oak Ridge Convention and Visitors Bureau, 302 South Tulane Avenue, Oak Ridge, TN 37830-6726. Phone (800) 887-3429.

NORTH RIDGE TRAIL

[Fig. 23(9)] This trail, built and maintained by the TCWP, is a National Recreation Trail and one of the first inside a city. It is located on public greenbelt lands on the city's northern border. There are eight access points. The westernmost access is about 1.4 miles west of Illinois Avenue (TN 62) on West Outer Drive. The easternmost access is on the extension of Endicott Lane that runs north off East Outer Drive. The entire trail is north of the West Outer Drive and the East Outer Drive.

The trail features hardwood forest, streams, and rock formations.

Trail: 7.5 miles.

Elevation: Change, 150 feet.

Difficulty: Moderate.

Surface and Blaze: Mixed surfaces (asphalt, concrete, dirt) with white blaze.

HAW RIDGE CANOE TRAIL

[Fig. 23(8)] This is a 4-mile loop in a flatwater area in Melton Hill Reservoir that follows

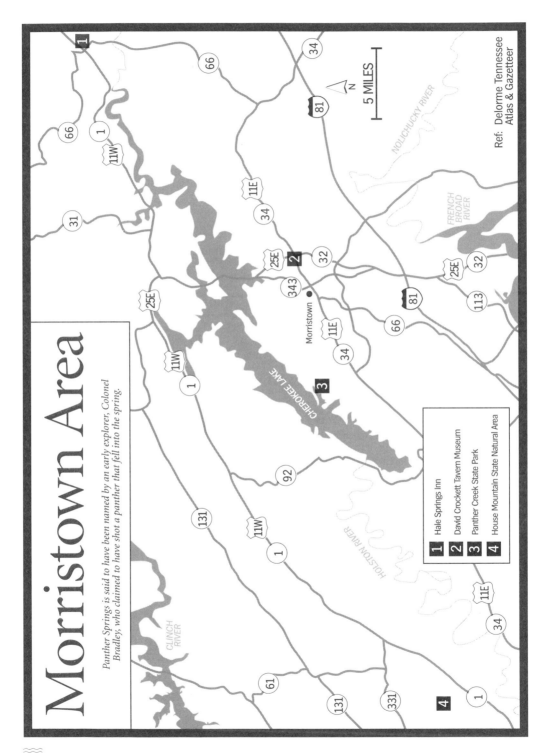

Morristown Area

Panther Springs is said to have been named by an early explorer, Colonel Bradley, who claimed to have shot a panther that fell into the spring.

Ref: Delorme Tennessee Atlas & Gazetteer

CHEROKEE LAKE

Morristown

NOLICHUCKY RIVER

FRENCH BROAD RIVER

HOLSTON RIVER

CLINCH RIVER

N
5 MILES

1 Hale Springs Inn
2 David Crockett Tavern Museum
3 Panther Creek State Park
4 House Mountain State Natural Area

the shoreline and coves, offering a view of a variety of shorebirds, duck, geese, ospreys (*Pandion haliaetus*), kingfishers (*Megaceryle alcyon*), and muskrats (*Ondatra zibethicus*).

Directions: Access is in Solway Park near Solway Bridge on TN 62. Take the second entrance to the park after passing the boat-launching ramp.

State Lands

HOUSE MOUNTAIN STATE NATURAL AREA

[Fig. 24(4)] The 500-acre House Mountain area was acquired in 1986 by the Trust for Public Land, then purchased in 1987 by the Department of Environment and Conservation. The north side of the 2,100-foot-high mountain, the highest point in Knox County, is still privately owned. The public area offers views of the Great Smoky Mountains, the Cumberland Mountains, and the beautiful farmlands and hills surrounding the mountain. The House Mountain area is still largely undeveloped with no buildings, restrooms, or water supply, and the park is for day use only. There is a system of trails that range from easy to strenuous. Call the natural area to request trail descriptions and a map.

Directions: From Knoxville, take TN 11W north from I-40 and travel approximately 10 miles to Idumea Road. Turn left and go 0.5 mile and turn left on Hogskin Road. The parking area is 0.7 mile ahead on the right.

Activities: Hiking.

Facilities: 5 miles of hiking trails.

Dates: Open Tuesday through Sunday, year-round.

Fees: None.

Closest Town: Knoxville, 10 miles.

For more information: House Mountain State Natural Area, PO Box 109, Corryton, TN 37721. Phone (423) 933-6851.

TIGER SWALLOWTAIL
(*Papilio glaucus*)
This butterfly takes its name from its yellow wings with black tigerlike stripes.

PANTHER CREEK STATE PARK

[Fig. 24(3)] Located on the shores of Cherokee Lake, a TVA reservoir, Panther Creek State Park offers a variety of recreational activities. Panther Springs, which creates Panther Creek, is said to have been named by an early explorer, Colonel Bradley, who claimed to have shot a panther that fell into the spring.

Development of the state park began in 1965 when the state purchased 122 acres for a day-use area. The state owns 1,435 acres.

Directions: Panther Creek is accessible from US 11E between Knoxville and Morristown. A sign directs travelers to the park.

Activities: Hiking, fishing, swimming, boating, playground sports, biking, horseback riding.

Facilities: Campsites, bathhouses, swimming pool, playground with recreational equipment, boat-launching ramp, hiking and horse trails, tennis courts, sand volleyball, and laundry. Some facilities are only available seasonally.

Dates: Open year-round.

Fees: There is a charge for camping.

Closest Town: Jefferson City, 8 miles.

For more information: Superintendent's Office, Panther Creek State Park, 2010 Panther Creek Park Road, Morristown, TN 37814. Phone (423) 587-7046.

WARRIOR PATH STATE PARK

[Fig. 25(5)] The park gets its name for its proximity to the old Cherokee trading and war path. The 950-acre area was first purchased by TVA in 1952 and later turned over to the state. Situated within a few miles of three major cities, Kingsport, Bristol, and Johnson City, Warrior Path receives lots of attention, but it has facilities capable of handling large amounts of traffic. Situated on the shores of Fort Patrick Henry Lake, the reservoir offers additional recreational opportunities. Nearly 9 miles of trails wind through the park, making hikes of various lengths possible. All trails are easy to moderate.

Directions: The park is located 2 miles southeast of Kingsport and accessible on TN 36. From I-81, exit on TN 36, go north to Hemlock Road and turn right to reach the park entrance.

Activities: Hiking, biking, horseback riding, swimming, fishing, boating, water-skiing, golfing, tennis.

Facilities: Campsites, camp store, snack bar, recreation center, bathhouses, boat-launching ramp, marina and boat cruises (seasonal), golf course, Olympic-size swimming pool (seasonal), picnic area, playgrounds, tennis courts, hiking trails.

Dates: Open year-round.

Fees: There is a charge for camping.

Closest Town: Kingsport, 2 miles.

For more information: Warrior Path State Park, POB 5026, Kingsport, TN 37663. Phone (423) 239-8531.

Rogersville

HALE SPRINGS INN

[Fig. 24(1)] Hale Springs Inn at Rutledge was built from 1824 through 1825 on what was then a major stage route from upper eastern Tennessee to Knoxville. Over the years the inn hosted U.S. Presidents Andrew Jackson, Andrew Johnson, and James K. Polk.

Originally called McKinney's Tavern after the man who built it, the inn became a Union headquarters during the Civil War. A few years later the name was changed to Hale Springs Hotel, and it served as a stopover for tourists going to nearby Hale Springs Resort, a famous mineral springs. The inn was fully restored in 1982 and is on the National Register of Historic Places, listed as the oldest continually run inn in Tennessee.

Directions: Downtown Rogersville on West Main Street.

Activities: Self-guided tour, restaurant, and lodging.

Facilities: Three-story inn.

Dates: Open year-round except Christmas day and night.

Fees: There is a charge for lodging but the tour is free.

Closest Town: Rogersville.

For more information: Hale Springs Inn, 110 West Main Street, Rogersville, TN 37857. Phone (423) 272-5171.

EBBING AND FLOWING SPRINGS

[Fig. 25(7)] Called Sinking Spring in a land grant given a Union officer for distinguished service, it is now known as Ebbing and Flowing Spring, one of only two known springs in the world to exhibit tidal characteristics. During a period of 2 hours and 47 minutes, the flow ranges from an indiscernible trickle to 500 gallons per minute. Unlike thermal springs that produce warm water, the water in Ebbing and Flowing Spring maintains a constant temperature of 34 degrees Fahrenheit.

This phenomenon is not understood, but it generated much speculation. The spring was credited with having extraordinary powers in matters of the heart. Local legend claimed that any couple drinking from the spring at the peak of its flow would marry within the year. Several other springs in the vicinity were believed to possess medicinal properties.

The spring is privately owned by descendants of Thomas Amis (pronounced Amy), but is open to the public.

Directions: From Rogersville's town square, travel east 1.1 miles on Main Street to Burem Road, bearing right at Amis Historical House. Turn left on Ebbing and Flowing Spring Road and go 2.3 miles. Ruins of a stone mill are 0.1 mile on the right, and the spring is 0.4 mile beyond.

Activities: See the spring. Drink at your own risk.

Facilities: None.

Fees: None.

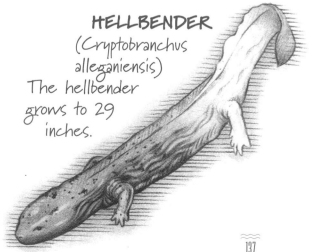

HELLBENDER
(Cryptobranchus alleganiensis)
The hellbender grows to 29 inches.

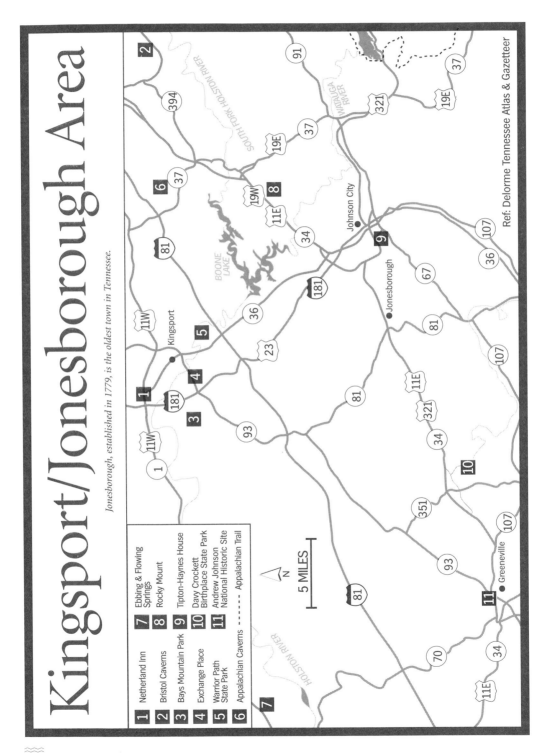

Kingsport/Jonesborough Area

Jonesborough, established in 1779, is the oldest town in Tennessee.

Ref: Delorme Tennessee Atlas & Gazetteer

Legend:

1. Netherland Inn
2. Bristol Caverns
3. Bays Mountain Park
4. Exchange Place
5. Warrior Path State Park
6. Appalachian Caverns
7. Ebbing & Flowing Springs
8. Rocky Mount
9. Tipton-Haynes House
10. Davy Crockett Birthplace State Park
11. Andrew Johnson National Historic Site
- - - - - Appalachian Trail

5 MILES

N

Dates: Open year-round.

For more information: Rogersville/Hawkins County Chamber of Commerce, 107 East Main Street, Rogersville, TN 37857. Phone (423) 272-2186.

Kingsport

BAYS MOUNTAIN PARK AND PLANETARIUM

[Fig. 25(3)] This 3,000-acre nature preserve atop Bays Mountain, which is owned and operated by the city of Kingsport, offers visitors a variety of outdoor experiences. There are animals exhibited in their natural habitat, including bobcats (*Felis rufus*,) river otters (*Lutra canadensis*,) beavers (*Castor canadensis*), gray wolves (*Canis lupus*), and gray and red foxes (*Urocyon cinereoargenteus* and *Vulpes vulpes*). There is also a 44-acre lake, a planetarium and observatory, an interpretive nature center, a saltwater tidal pool and marine aquarium, a farmstead museum, and 25 miles of interconnecting trails that permit walks as short as a few hundred yards up to 4.8 miles. By following all of the trails, a day-long hike is possible.

The park features a wide range of activities that include programs about various kinds of wildlife, such as reptiles, amphibians, and birds; stargazing; spring wildflower walks; barge cruises and canoe tours on the lake; and moonlight hikes. Special educational programs are also arranged for students from schools in the area.

Directions: If traveling north on I-81, take Exit 52 and at the light turn left on Meadow View Parkway, which will turn into Reservoir Road. Travel 2 to 3 miles to the sign for Bays Mountain Park.

Activities: Mountain biking, hiking, nature programs, barge rides, wildlife viewing.

Facilities: Lake, visitor center, artificial cave, planetarium, nature interpretive center, museum, and aquarium.

Dates: Open year-round.

Fees: There is a charge for parking and all nature and planetarium programs.

Closest Town: Kingsport, 7 miles.

For more information: Bays Mountain Park, 853 Bays Mountain Park Road, Kingsport, TN 37660. Phone (423) 229-9447.

NETHERLAND INN

[Fig. 25(1)] The historic Netherland Inn on the banks of the Holston River at Kingsport was built in 1802 by William King as a boat yard from which to ship his salt. It was sold in 1818 at a sheriff's sale to Richard Netherland, who immediately established the beautiful three-story building as an inn and tavern on the Old Stage Road. Since the road was the main route to western Kentucky and middle Tennessee, Netherland obtained a contract with the stage line to provide the services of his inn to stagecoaches, mail coaches, ox carts, and river traffic. Presidents Andrew Jackson, Andrew Johnson, and James K. Polk visited the Netherland Inn.

RUFOUS-SIDED TOWHEE
(Pipilo erythrophthalmus)

The inn was sold in 1906 and became a boarding house, then in 1968 it was purchased by the Netherland Inn Association to be preserved as a historic house museum.

Directions: Go 2 miles west past the I-181 interchange on 11W, and turn left (south) on Big Elm Road. Turn left (east) from Big Elm Road onto Netherland Inn Road and go to the inn.

Activities: Tour of inn, picnicking.
Facilities: Inn and picnic area.
Dates: Open May–Oct.
Fees: There is a charge for guided tours.
Closest Town: Kingsport.

For more information: Kingsport Chamber of Commerce, PO Box 1403, Kingsport, TN 37662. Phone (423) 392-8820 or (800) 743-5282.

EXCHANGE PLACE

[Fig. 25(4)] This 1816 frontier homestead was once the center of a 2,000-acre plantation that also served as a stop on the Great Stage Road. Its name was acquired because it was a place where travelers could exchange Virginia currency for Tennessee currency, or vice versa, and where tired horses could be replaced by fresh ones.

The main building, as well as several others, has been restored by the Netherland Inn Association, which received the buildings, 7.5 acres of land, and a generous amount of money as a gift from the heirs of one of the previous owners. The homestead is listed on the National Register of Historic Places.

Directions: Turn east on Memorial Boulevard from I-81 at Exit 66, then right on TN 93. A short distance ahead, turn right on Orebank Road that leads to the site.

Activities: Guided tour of the house and outbuildings.
Dates: Open May–Oct.
Fees: There is a charge for guided tours.
Closest Town: Kingsport.

For more information: Kingsport Convention and Visitors Bureau, POB 1403, Kingsport, TN 37662. Phone (423) 288-6071.

Historic Sites

DAVY CROCKETT BIRTHPLACE

[Fig. 25(10)] The Davy Crockett Birthplace State Historic Park in Greene County is a 103-

acre historic park located near Limestone, Tennessee on the Nolichucky River. This park is a monument to Crockett who was born here August 17, 1786. At the park is a limestone marker and a cabin on the spot where he was born and a visitor center with a museum.

There are numerous picnic sites throughout the park and two large picnic pavilions. Picnic shelters may be reserved by calling the park office. The Nolichucky River offers excellent fishing opportunities for several species including smallmouth and largemouth bass, catfish, crappie, and muskie. A state fishing permit is required.

Many groups and individuals use the park's large open areas for field games such as soccer, softball, and volleyball. A 0.25-mile trail leads the hiker across the Nolichucky River bluffs that overlook the falls where Crockett almost drowned as a small boy.

The park has a seasonal recreator/naturalist during the summer months who provides programs of interest to all ages. Programs include nature walks, films, games, crafts, and much more. A local civic organization hosts the annual Davy Crockett Celebration at the park. This event is usually held on the weekend closest to Crockett's birthday, August 17.

Directions: Take US 321/State 11E east from Greeneville for approximately 10 miles and watch for park signs. Turn right onto Old TN 34. Stay on Old TN 34 for about 1 mile, then turn right (south) on Davy Crockett Road and travel approximately 2 miles to Davy Crockett Birthplace State Historic Park.

Activities: Swimming, picnicking, camping, fishing, and hiking.

Facilities: Ball fields, swimming pool, picnic pavilions, picnic sites, children's playground, campground with 75 sites with water, electricity, dumping station, sewer, and bathhouse.

Dates: The pool is open in summer, and the park is open year-round.

Fees: There is a charge for swimming, camping, and picnic pavilions.

For more information: Davy Crockett State Historic Park, 1245 Davy Crockett Park Road, Limestone, TN 37681. Phone (423) 257-2167.

JONESBOROUGH

[Fig. 25] The General Assembly of the State of North Carolina established Jonesborough, the oldest town in Tennessee, in 1779 because North Carolina had authority over what is now called east Tennessee. Being separated by the Unaka Mountains, the settlers in the area did not recognize the authority of North Carolina and founded the State of Franklin. They elected John Sevier their governor and made Jonesborough the state's first capital.

In the 1780s, Jonesborough was simultaneously a seat of civilization and the edge of the Wild West. Its culture of long-ago lives indelibly along its streets. Andrew Jackson lived at the Christopher Taylor house on Main Street and practiced law here as a public prosecutor from 1788 to 1789. Taylor was a veteran of the French and Indian War and served as a major in the American Revolution.

Three United States presidents from Tennessee; Jackson, Polk, and Johnson, stayed at the Chester Inn on Main Street. One of the historic markers along West Main Street describes Jonesborough as the place of publication from 1819 to 1820 of the first periodicals in the United States devoted to the abolition of human slavery, *The Manumission Intelligencer* and *The Emancipator*.

Jonesborough is probably best known as the home for the National Storytelling Festival sponsored the first full weekend in October (including Friday) by the National Association for the Preservation and Perpetuation of Storytelling.

In 1969 Jonesborough became the first entire Tennessee town to be placed on the National Register of Historic Places. The Jonesborough-Washington County History Museum is inside the visitor center and displays changing exhibits addressing themes of unsung heroines of northeastern Tennessee and covering the history of Jonesborough and its citizenry. A walking tour brochure available at the visitor center describes the history and architecture of many of Jonesborough's oldest structures.

Directions: About 5 miles southeast of Johnson City on US 11E.

Facilities: Visitor center, museum, and national storytelling center.

Dates: Open year-round except for holidays.

Fees: There is a charge for museum admission.

For more information: Historic Jonesborough Visitor Center, 117 Boone Street, Jonesborough, TN 37659. Phone (423) 753-1012.

ANDREW JOHNSON NATIONAL HISTORIC SITE & LOST STATE OF FRANKLIN CAPITOL

[Fig. 25 (11)] About 25 miles southeast of Jonesborough on US 11E is Greeneville, which claims it's the second oldest town in Tennessee. It was named for Revolutionary War hero Gen. Nathanael Greene in 1783 by the authority of the State of North Carolina. It began with a 300-acre tract of land owned by Robert Kerr centered on the Big Spring behind the present site of the library on Main Street. In 1784, North Carolina ceded its western lands to the central government created by the Articles of Confederation.

By December 1784, a group of citizens of the Washington District in what is now east Tennessee, decided that because they were now without the protection of North Carolina, their interests were best served by the creation of a new state, named for Benjamin Franklin. John Sevier was elected governor of the State of Franklin and established its first capital at Jonesborough. By the next year, the capital of the State of Franklin had been moved to the log courthouse in Greeneville.

In the meantime, North Carolina reconsidered its decision to cede these lands and rescinded the action. The North Carolina government wanted to re-establish its authority over the area. To further complicate the situation, there were factions who had remained loyal to the government of North Carolina. A Franklin Constitutional Convention was held November 14, 1785, but a bitter division arose over the type of constitution to be adopted. In May 1787, a North Carolina–type constitution was "permanently" adopted.

Several attempts to admit Franklin as the fourteenth state in the Union failed. The Franklin Legislature elected Evan Shelby to succeed John Sevier when his term expired in the fall of 1787, but he refused to serve. Without leadership, the movement toward statehood floundered and failed, and the State of Franklin quietly ceased to exist.

In 1789, North Carolina again ceded its western frontier, and the area was given the title Territory of the United States of America South of the River Ohio, commonly known as the Southwest Territory. William Blount was appointed governor and began to direct the territory toward statehood. On June 1, 1796, George Washington signed legislation making Tennessee the 16th state in the Union.

Today, the downtown Nathanael Greene Museum offers information about Greeneville's early history and men like John Sevier, Davy Crockett, and President Andrew Johnson. Greeneville was the home of Andrew Johnson, the 17th President of the United States and today is the site of the Andrew Johnson National Historic Site. Here you will find a visitors center, Andrew Johnson's tailor shop, two homes of the former president, (one furnished with Andrew Johnson memorabilia) and the National Cemetery. A true example of the American Dream, this man, who was an indentured servant in his early years, rose to hold the highest office in the land during our nation's darkest hours.

In 1861, Tennessee was divided over the issue of slavery, with east Tennessee being strongly pro-Union. A state convention called in February 1861 yielded results clearly favoring the Union. When the events at Fort Sumter prompted Lincoln to call for two Tennessee regiments to help put down the rebellion, another convention was called to decide whether or not the requested troops should be sent. This time the vote was strongly proseparationist. Tennessee seceded from the Union and ratified the Confederate Constitution in August 1861. Much of upper east Tennessee remained sympathetic to the Union cause. President Lincoln appointed former Governor Johnson military governor of Tennessee after the occupation of Nashville by Union forces in 1862. Johnson tried to force citizens to swear an oath of allegiance to the federal government, going so far as to imprison Confederate supporters who refused and to seize their properties within the state. President Lincoln selected Johnson for the vice presidency in 1864, and he assumed the presidency after Lincoln's assassination. Two of Johnson's homes and his tailor shop are open to the public. His first home is across the street from his tailor shop inside the visitor center. His shop became the place for local political activity and discussion that kindled his political ambitions. As he prospered, he moved his family to a home on Main Street. Johnson is buried a few blocks from his home in the Andrew Johnson National Cemetery.

Directions: Greeneville is on US 321, US 11E, and TN 107. The visitor center, tailor shop, and the first home are at the corner of Depot Street and College Street. The second home is 2 blocks south

COMMON FOXGLOVE
(Digitalis purpurea)
This is the source of digitalis, a drug used to treat heart disease.

and 1 block west on Main Street.

Dates: Open year-round except Thanksgiving, Christmas, and January 1.

Fees: There is a nominal fee charged to visit Johnson's second home on Main Street, but there is no charge to visit the visitor center and Johnson's first home.

For more information: Andrew Johnson NHS, PO Box 1088, Greeneville, TN 37744. Phone (423) 638-3551.

DAVID CROCKETT TAVERN MUSEUM

[Fig. 24(2)] Davy Crockett was young when his family moved the 50 miles from Limestone to Morristown. His father established a business where the replica tavern stands today. The original structure became a pest house for people ill with smallpox when the Crocketts moved out in 1811. In 1865 the house was burned to prevent the spread of disease.

Today the replica contains authentic furnishings. The main room served as a social room and dining room for people stopping for supper and to stay the night. Patrons slept upstairs in the loft on rope beds. Below the kitchen is the loom room with spinning wheels and a loom. The basement houses antiques in the Crockett Pioneer Museum.

Directions: From I-81, take Davy Crockett Parkway (US 25E) to US 11E, turn left (west), then turn right (north) on Morningside Drive. The tavern will be on your right.

Dates: Open May to Oct.

Fees: There is a charge for admission.

For more information: Crockett Tavern Museum, 2002 Morningside Drive, Morristown, TN 37814. Phone (423) 587-9900.

ROCKY MOUNT

[Fig. 25(8)] Built from 1770 to 1772 by William Cobb, Rocky Mount is a two-story, nine-room log structure of white oak. It was not a mansion by the standards of the day, but it was comfortable according to William Blount, who stayed with the Cobb family. He said it was commodious with glass windows and a fireplace.

It was in 1790 that North Carolina gave its western holding—the land that was to become Tennessee—to the new United States. Congress quickly organized these lands into the Southwest Territory. George Washington appointed William Blount governor and superintendent of Indian affairs of the Southwest Territory in 1790. Blount came to live with the Cobb family, which made Rocky Mount the site of the first territorial seat of government of the Southwest Territory.

Rocky Mount is one of the oldest buildings in the state and is the oldest original territorial capitol. It became the capitol of the Territory of the United States South of the River Ohio in 1790. In 1792 the capitol was moved to Knoxville as westward growth continued.

Cobb gave the house and farm to Henry Massengil Jr., his son-in-law, and it remained in the family until 1959 when the state bought it to restore and preserve. Rocky Mount is now the property of the State of Tennessee.

Directions: In the community of Piney Flats about 7 miles northeast of Johnson City on US 11E on the right (east).

Facilities: House, grounds, outbuildings, theater, weaving cabin, and the Massengil Museum of Overmountain History.

Date and hours: Open daily except weekends in Jan. and Feb., Thanksgiving, and Dec. 21 to Jan. 5.

Fees: There is a charge for admission.

For more information: Rocky Mount Museum, 200 Hyder Hill Road, Piney Flats, TN 37686. Phone (423) 538-7396.

RACCOON
(Procyon lotor)
The raccoon often appears to wash its food, resulting in its Latin name, "lotor," meaning "a washer."

TIPTON-HAYNES HOUSE

[Fig. 25(9)] The Tipton-Haynes Historic Site is along an old buffalo trail that was visited by Woodland Indians and later by the Cherokee. The trail became the Stage Road and Colonel John Tipton built the home along it in 1783. Original structures on the site today include the home, the law office, the corncrib, and the barn. The limestone cave and spring on the property are believed to have been occupied as early as the Woodland Indian period (1000 B.C. to about 900 A.D.) and were probably used by early explorers reaching the area as well.

The dispute that took place here between Tipton, a North Carolina magistrate, and John Sevier, the governor of the State of Franklin, became known as the Battle of the State of Franklin. According to Vicki Rozema in *Footsteps of the Cherokee*, slaves and property belonging to Sevier were seized by the sheriff as payment for North Carolina taxes in the winter of 1788. This situation developed, at least in part, because of the unusual political situation of the time. This area had been under the jurisdiction of North Carolina, which for various reasons first ceded the area to the newly established central government and then reversed its position.

When North Carolina ceded the land, the State of Franklin was created by east Tennessee pioneers who gained experience in self-government about 15 years earlier. The Franklinites, as they came to be called, elected John Sevier to be their first governor.

When news was received in the area that North Carolina had rescinded its land cession, the Franklinites refused North Carolina's demands that the state be dissolved. For a while there were parallel governments. One represented the State of North Carolina and the factions in the area loyal to it. The other represented the proposed State of Franklin and those loyal to it. The Franklin faction sent repeated envoys to Washington requesting recognition of the proposed new state, but their efforts failed. Of course, the Franklinites refused to acknowledge North Carolina's right to collect taxes from the citizens of what they considered another state.

The North Carolina sheriff took the confiscated persons and property to the home of another North Carolina loyalist, Magistrate John Tipton. When Sevier returned to his home and discovered what he considered the theft of his property, he marched with a group of men to John Tipton's home and demanded its return. A contingent of Tipton allies resisted, a fight ensued, and in the melee Sheriff Pugh was killed and two of Sevier's sons were captured. The dispute threatened to escalate, but intermediaries of both men were able to intervene. North Carolina Governor Caswell took a moderate stance, and the losses on both sides were kept to a minimum.

Directions: Take Exit 31 off I-181, go 1 mile south on South Roan Street, and the home is on the left (south) side of the street.

Dates: Open year-round, hours are seasonal.

Fees: There is a charge for admission.

For more information: Tipton-Haynes Historical Association, 2620 South Roan Street, Johnson City, TN 37601. Phone (423) 926-3631.

Caverns

APPALACHIAN CAVERNS

[Fig. 25(6)] Caverns in this area of Tennessee were formed by underground streams dissolving holes in the limestone formations. After a space in the rock appeared, water with dissolved minerals dripped from or ran over cavern surfaces. Over long periods of time, these dissolved minerals were deposited to produce a variety of formations. Butterfly onyx, helicitites (curved stalactite-like forms), anthodites (radiating clusters of acicular crystals), and other rare karst formations are found in Appalachian Caverns.

There is an hour-long 1-mile tour among rock formations of stalactites and stalagmites made of manganese, calcite, and limestone. The tour also goes through a large room 100 feet wide by 135 feet high that is 1,400 feet long.

In March, about 15,000 endangered gray bats (*Myotis griescens*) and hundreds of *Myotis pipistrol* and Virginia brown bats return to Appalachian Caverns. Bluegill, carp, catfish, and turtles inhabit the cave's stream called Linville Creek. The cave was explored during the 1800s and was inhabited by Native Americans beginning 15,000 years ago, judging by skeletons and artifacts found inside. A 4.5-acre underground lake and an expected 200 miles of the cavern system

MAYFLY
(Order Ephemeroptera)
The translation of the mayfly's Latin name is "living a day."

have yet to be explored.

Exploration continues, not only by the staff but also by those interested in spelunking. Special opportunities for those joining the Wild Tours, tours through less explored parts of the cave, include seeking uncharted rooms, rappelling, mud crawling, and discovering rock formations.

Directions: Blountville is southwest of Bristol and south of I-81 at Exit 69 on TN 37. Travel south of Blountville on TN 37 for about 1 mile, turn right (southwest) on Buncombe Road, go 1.5 miles, and turn left (south) on Cave Hill Road.

Activities: Cavern tour, picnicking, and spelunking.

Facilities: Picnic shelter, gift shop, and restrooms.

Dates: Open daily year-round except Thanksgiving, and Dec. 24 through Jan. 3.

Fees: There is a charge for admission.

Closest Town: Bristol, about 15 miles.

For more information: Appalachian Caverns, 420 Cave Hill Road, Blountville, TN 37617. Phone (423) 323-2337.

LITTLE
BROWN BAT
(Myotis lucifugus)

🦇 BRISTOL CAVERNS

[Fig. 25(2)] Bristol Caverns, off US 421, is 5 miles southeast of Bristol and 200 million years old. Local legend claims Indians used the caverns and the underground river through them as their attack and escape route. The cavern allowed the Indians to appear and vanish before the settlers' eyes.

A tour of the cavern goes along paved, lighted walkways that wind through the vaulted chambers along the river that carved Bristol Caverns. The 78-acre cave is filled with geological formations, a variety of stalactites and stalagmites ranging from tree-trunk size down to soda-straw size, columns reaching from floor to ceiling, and waterfalls made of rock. And a river still runs through it.

A new lighting system not only shows off the formations better but also is an aid to those taking pictures. Be sure to bring a flash for your camera.

Directions: Take US 421 southeast from Bristol for about 6 miles, turn left (east) on Bristol Caverns Highway (Highway 435) and follow the signs.

Activities: Cavern tour and picnicking.

Facilities: Gift shop, restrooms, and picnic tables.

Dates: Open year-round except Thanksgiving and Christmas. Hours are seasonal.

Fees: There is a charge for the tour.

Closest Town: Bristol, about 5 miles.

For more information: Bristol Caverns, PO Box 851, Bristol, TN 37621. Phone (423) 878-2011.

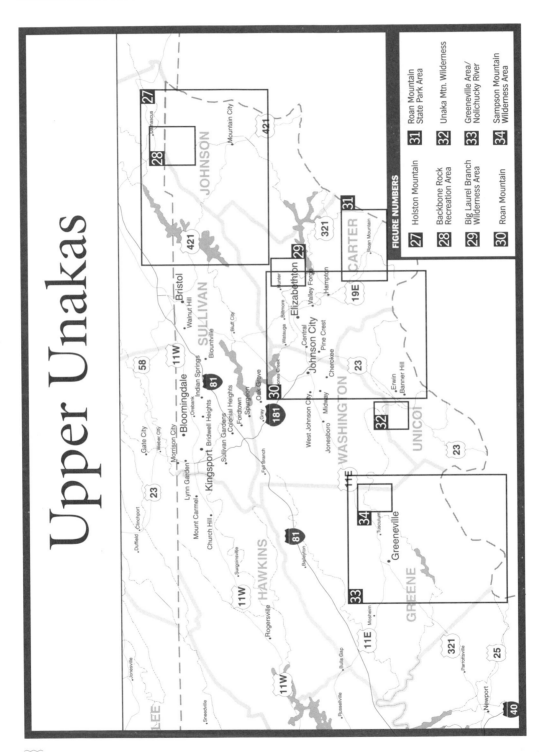

Upper Unakas

FIGURE NUMBERS

27 Holston Mountain

28 Backbone Rock Recreation Area

29 Big Laurel Branch Wilderness Area

30 Roan Mountain

31 Roan Mountain State Park Area

32 Unaka Mtn. Wilderness

33 Greeneville Area/ Nolichucky River

34 Sampson Mountain Wilderness Area

Upper Unakas

Throughout most of Tennessee, ancient rocks formed during the Precambrian Era over 1 billion years ago lie below the surface of sedimentary rock; however, in the Unaka Range the ancient rocks are exposed. About 600 million years ago, sediments collected in a sinking trough (geosyncline) on the Unakas' western side and formed the Ocoee Supergroup and Chilhowee Group that make up most of the present-day Unaka Range. A period of folding took place about 470 million years ago during the Ordovician Period, when the older rock was forced over the younger rock of the Ocoee and Chilhowee formations.

Eroded Precambrian rock and marine debris settled into another geosyncline between the Devonian and the Triassic periods, forming new layers of sedimentary rock. In the final phase of the formation of the Unakas, these strata were pushed into mountains during the Alleghanian orogeny, when North America collided with Africa 290 million

[*Above:* A view of the 14,500-acre Roan Mountain]

years ago. Many thousands of feet of rock folded like a rug pushed from one end. The pressure generated great heat, melting and fusing the rock of the Unakas into what is called metamorphic rock.

The Unaka Range runs along Tennessee's border with North Carolina and has three divisions: the Upper Unakas, the Great Smoky Mountains, and the Lower Unakas. Tennessee's Upper Unakas are sandwiched between the North Carolina border on the east and the Tennessee cities of Bristol, Elizabethton, Johnson City, Greeneville, and Newport on the west. Virginia is the northern border, and the Great Smoky Mountains form the southern line of demarcation.

The Unakas include the Cherokee National Forest (CNF), which is divided into the northern CNF, which is in the Upper Unakas, and the southern CNF in the Lower Unakas. The CNF covers more than 633,000 acres in 10 east Tennessee counties from Bristol to Chattanooga.

The northern and southern divisions of the CNF are subdivided into ranger districts. In the northern CNF, there are two ranger districts: the Watauga and the Nolichucky/ Unaka ranger districts. In the southern CNF, there are currently three districts: the Tellico, Hiwassee, and Ocoee ranger districts.

At this writing, plans are underway to change the southern CNF districts from three districts into two. Since the southern district's plans have not been completed, this book will treat the CNF as five distinct districts, two in the northern CNF and three in the southern portion.

In the northern CNF there are four designated wilderness areas and five scenic areas, as well as 169 miles of protected area along the Appalachian Trail. Scenic drives ranging from short outings to all-day trips are possible on the northern CNF's 650 miles of roads. All seasons have much to offer those looking at landscapes and panoramic vistas. Outdoor enthusiasts find hiking, camping, fishing, hunting, whitewater rafting, canoeing, picnicking, biking, horseback riding, swimming, and wildlife viewing among the many opportunities in the CNF.

In the northern CNF, there are 74 hiking trails covering 391 miles and ranging in difficulty from easy to extremely strenuous. CNF maps designate trails with numbers instead of names. For example the Appalachian Trail is Trail #1, and the Holston Mountain Trail is Trail #44. Hereafter, the text will give the name of a trail with its number in parenthesis. Loop and one-way trails are available to hikers with no permits or check-ins required, but for safety, leave detailed hiking plans with someone.

Six whitewater streams can add excitement to a CNF visit. Commercial outfitters will rent you gear or you can strike out on your own, if you are experienced, to float the Pigeon, French Broad, and Nolichucky rivers. South Holston, Watauga, Tellico, Chilhowee, Calderwood, Ocoee, Indian Boundary, and McKamy lakes provide opportunities for fishing, boating, and swimming.

A wilderness area in a national forest is defined by the National Wilderness Preservation Act of 1964 as an area of undeveloped, federally owned land that is designated by Congress and has the following characteristics: (1) Primarily the forces of nature affect it, where man is a visitor who does not remain. It may contain ecological, geological, or other features of scientific, educational, scenic, or historical value. (2) It possesses outstanding opportunities for solitude or a primitive and unconfined type of recreation. (3) It is an area large enough so that continued use will not change its unspoiled, natural condition.

For protection, certain uses of wilderness areas are not encouraged. Trapping, hunting, and fishing are allowed during their seasons; however, they must be done in a way that is consistent with the wilderness character. Only nonmotorized and nonmechanical methods of travel are permissible, except in an emergency. Emergency categories include removal of deceased persons, law enforcement involving serious crime or fugitive pursuit, health and safety, and fire suppression.

Wilderness areas require the practice of "leave no trace." Leave no trace means exactly that—if you took it in, take it out, and if you didn't take it in, don't take it out. Call (800) 332-4100 for more information and educational materials on leave no trace practices.

Scenic areas are areas of another type within national forests. Guidelines for managing scenic areas are less restrictive than management guidelines for wilderness areas. Scenic areas possess unusual recreation and scientific values, and timber may be cut to enhance vistas, remove hazards, and remove diseased trees.

Fraser fir (*Abies fraseri*), Eastern hemlock (*Tsuga canadensis*), red spruce (*Picea rubens*), table mountain pine (*Pinus pungens*), chestnut oak (*Quercus prinus*), scarlet oak (*Quercus coccinea*), white oak (*Quercus alba*), yellow-poplar (*Liriodendron tulipifera*), sugar maple (*Acer saccharum*), yellow birch (*Betula alleghaniensis*), northern red oak (*Quercus rubra*), hickories (*Carya* sp.), Virginia pine (*Pinus virginiana*), pitch pine (*Pinus rigida*), white pine (*Pinus strobus*), sweet gum (*Liquidamber styraciflua*), sycamore (*Plantanus occidentalis*), black cherry (*Prunus serotina*), and beech (*Fagus grandifolia*) commonly compose the forests of the Upper Unakas. Some stands of scarlet oak over 100 years old can be see in the Pond Mountain Wilderness Area (*see* page 166). Extensive logging occurred between 1913 and 1927 throughout the Upper Unakas, but some timber stands date back to 1861.

Black bear (*Ursus americanus*), bobcat (*Felis rufus*), white-tailed deer (*Odocoileus virginianus*), ruffed grouse (*Bonasa umbellus*), turkey (*Meleagris gallopavo*), gray squirrel (*Sciurus carolinensis*), largemouth bass (*Micropterus salmoides*), brown trout (*Salmo trutta*), brook trout (*Salvelinus fontinalis*), rainbow trout (*Salmo gairdneri*), bream (*Lepomis* sp.), and catfish (*Ictalurus* sp.) are game animals found in the Cherokee National Forest in the Upper Unakas. To see red foxes (*Vulpes vulpes*), turkey, wild hogs, and bears you need patience and

BLACK BEAR
(Ursus americanus)
This bear grows to 300 pounds.

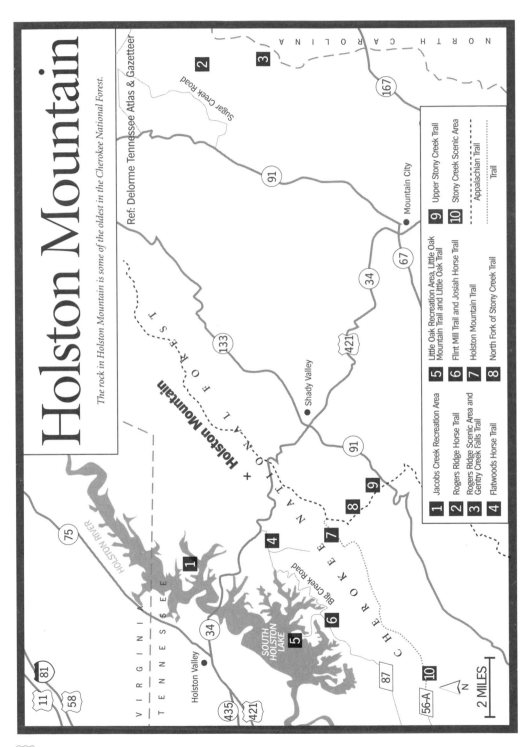

Holston Mountain

The rock in Holston Mountain is some of the oldest in the Cherokee National Forest.

Ref: Delorme Tennessee Atlas & Gazetteer

+ Holston Mountain

HOLSTON RIVER

SOUTH HOLSTON LAKE

CHEROKEE NATIONAL FOREST

VIRGINIA
TENNESSEE

Holston Valley

Shady Valley

Mountain City

Sugar Creek Road

Big Creek Road

NORTH CAROLINA

1 Jacobs Creek Recreation Area

2 Rogers Ridge Horse Trail

3 Rogers Ridge Scenic Area and Gentry Creek Falls Trail

4 Flatwoods Horse Trail

5 Little Oak Recreation Area, Little Oak Mountain Trail and Little Oak Trail

6 Flint Mill Trail and Josiah Horse Trail

7 Holston Mountain Trail

8 North Fork of Stony Creek Trail

9 Upper Stony Creek Trail

10 Stony Creek Scenic Area

- - - Appalachian Trail

······· Trail

2 MILES

N

perseverance, for these are elusive and reclusive animals. The mountains are marginal territories for deer, but they are present and less elusive than most big game animals. Chances are excellent you will see some of the 23 species of reptiles, 32 amphibians, 43 mammals, 140 fish, and 150 birds in the northern CNF.

Auto Tours

Majestic vistas, spring flowers, wildlife, fall colors, rivers, lakes, and heritage resources that can be seen without leaving the automobile make pleasure driving through the northern CNF the most popular recreational activity. The following are premier drives.

Trailing Arbutus

The trailing arbutus (*Epigea repens*) blooms from February to June with white or sometimes pink, exquisitely sweet, fragrant flowers. Trailing arbutus is also called mayflower, but there is a disagreement about how it got that name. Some say it came from England on the *Mayflower*, and others contend that it was the first spring flower the newly landed Pilgrims saw in this country. Indians used the trailing arbutus as an astringent. White pioneers considered it a diuretic, but don't use it because it can cause harm if ingested. Its beauty has caused people to try transplanting, which this low-growing, evergreen shrub does not tolerate well.

Northwest of Elizabethton on US 19E at Keenburg, Flatwoods Road (Forest Road 87) runs northeastward along southern South Holston Lake. Turn left (west) on FR 87G to get a better view of the lake from the Little Oak Recreation Area. From the recreation area continue northeast on FR 87 to US 421. Turn left (west) to go to Bristol or turn right to go to Shady Valley and Elizabethton.

Unaka Mountain offers one of the best views in the state from Unaka Overlook and Beauty Spot. Take TN 395 east from Main Street in Erwin and go 10 miles. Turn left (northeast) on FR 230 for the Auto Tour on the Tennessee/North Carolina border to TN 107, and turn left (west) on TN 107 to go to Unicoi. The Auto Tour is truly mountainous driving with switchbacks and is rough for low-riding passenger cars. The tour takes you around Unaka Mountain Scenic and Wilderness areas.

Roan Mountain is east of Elizabethton on 19E. In the town of Roan Mountain turn right (south) on TN 143 for a pleasant drive into Roan Mountain State Park, to the state line at Carvers Gap, then up the peak to the Roan High Knob.

US 321 southeast from Elizabethton goes along the southern shore of Watauga Lake, past Cardens Bluff and Watauga Point. Take TN 67 north from US 321 to drive along Doe Creek between Doe Mountain and Iron Mountain to Mountain City.

The southern end of the northern CNF contains a scenic drive along the French Broad River. From Greeneville take TN 70 south across Nolichucky Dam, turn right on TN 107 which travels through Houston Valley, then turn right on US 25/70 and travel along the French Broad River to Newport.

Watauga Ranger District of Cherokee National Forest

The Watauga Ranger District (approximately 170,000 acres) is mountainous, with elevations ranging from 1,500 feet in the river valleys to 4,321 feet on Holston Mountain, 4,880 feet on Rogers Ridge, and 4,329 feet on Pond Mountain. This district contains two wilderness areas, two scenic areas, developed campgrounds, 177 campsites, 181 miles of trails, including 20 miles of horse trails, 300 miles of U.S. Forest Service roads, seven developed picnic areas, three developed swimming areas, four boat ramps, and two shooting ranges. All this falls within the four northeastern counties of Tennessee: Carter, Johnson, Sullivan, and Unicoi.

The headquarters for the Watauga Ranger District is at 4400 Unicoi Drive in Unicoi about 0.5 mile east of Exit 23 of US 19/23. This office should be your first stop for information, maps, and knowledge of any recent changes within the district. For instance, damage from a flood in early 1998 may have lingering effects, such as closures of some areas.

Three lakes offer excellent rainbow trout and smallmouth fishing. South Holston Lake (7,580 acres in Tennessee and Virginia) also contains walleye, white bass, crappie, largemouth bass, sauger, catfish, and bream. Watauga Lake (6,430 acres) and Wilbur Lake (72 acres) contain lake trout, walleye, white bass, catfish, bream, crappie, and largemouth bass. Watauga Lake holds the state record for lake trout: 20 pounds and 0.79 ounces.

The Watauga Ranger District, along with the rest of the CNF, is part of the Cherokee Wildlife Management Area and is managed cooperatively by the U.S. Forest Service and Tennessee Wildlife Resources Agency for fishing and hunting, as well as wildlife viewing. During the hunting season several gated roads are opened to hunters, but these change each year.

In the Watauga District, the Tennessee Wildlife Resources Agency (TWRA) stocks Laurel Creek, Gentry Creek, and Beaverdam Creek. Other streams stocked by TWRA in Johnson and Carter counties include Buffalo Creek, Watauga River, Simerly Creek, Laurel Fork Creek, Doe River, Big Stoney Creek, Upper Roan Creek, Laurel Bloomery Creek, and Forge Creek. These creeks are on both national forest and private land.

The U.S. Forest Service began buying land from willing sellers in this area back in 1913. The Watauga Ranger District, founded that year, was part of the White Top National Forest until 1920 when it became part of the Unaka National Forest. It became what it is today, part of the Cherokee National Forest, in 1936.

For more information: Watauga Ranger District, PO Box 400, Unicoi, TN 37692. Phone (423) 735-1500.

ROGERS RIDGE SCENIC AREA

[Fig. 27(3)] The Rogers Ridge Scenic Area (3,865 acres) is in the northeastern corner of

Johnson County and is bordered by North Carolina and Virginia to the east and Virginia to the north. It offers vistas of several popular mountains in the southern highlands: Grandfather and Roan to the south in North Carolina, and Whitetop and Mount Rogers to the north in Virginia. Also, Rogers Ridge Scenic Area's Gentry Creek Falls and balds are touted as the loveliest in the southern highlands.

Within the scenic area are many wildflowers including Appalachian twayblade (*Listera smallii*), rock bells (*Aquilegia canadensis*), Robbins ragwort (*Senecio schweinitzianus*), and rattlesnake root (*Prenanthes altissima*). Here and throughout the CNF, deer and turkey sightings abound.

CAROLINA SILVERBELL

(*Halesia carolina*) Carolina silverbell takes its name from its delicate white flowers that dangle like bells from its twigs in spring.

Balds like the ones in Rogers Ridge Scenic Area are large grassy areas that appear in stark contrast to their surrounding environs. They are treeless areas ranging in size from a few acres to many. Controversy abounds as to how balds came to exist, and there are many theories. Some claim these are naturally occurring spaces caused by wind, ice, storms, or other natural calamities. Others say they were man-made. Indians may have burned the areas so grass could grow to be used for grazing game animals and to improve hunting. Early settlers may have cleared the areas for cattle. According to one theory, balds may be the result of animals instead of man. Before man inhabited the region, mastodons, ground sloths, and later bison and elk may have grazed and cleared the areas. There may be more than one reason for the various balds. These open spaces provide opportunities for wildlife viewing, hiking, camping, and enjoying the unobstructed views.

Directions: From Mountain City go north on TN 91 about 10 miles, turn right (east) on Gentry Creek Road (FR 123). At the junction of FR 123 and Sugar Creek Road, FR 123 leads east to the southern end of the scenic area.

Activities: Hiking, hunting, horseback riding, camping.

Facilities: None.

Fees: None.

Closest town: Mountain City, about 10 miles.

For more information: Watauga Ranger District, PO Box 400, Unicoi, TN 37692. Phone (423) 735-1500.

ROGERS RIDGE HORSE TRAIL

[Fig. 27(2)] The Rogers Ridge Scenic Area features the Rogers Ridge Horse Trail (#192). This is the main trail in the area. The Rogers Ridge Horse Trail climbs and follows Rogers Ridge to the intersection with old Dry Branch Road. The trail follows Dry Branch Road for 2.1 miles into a series of balds that offer spectacular views of Tennessee, Virginia, and North

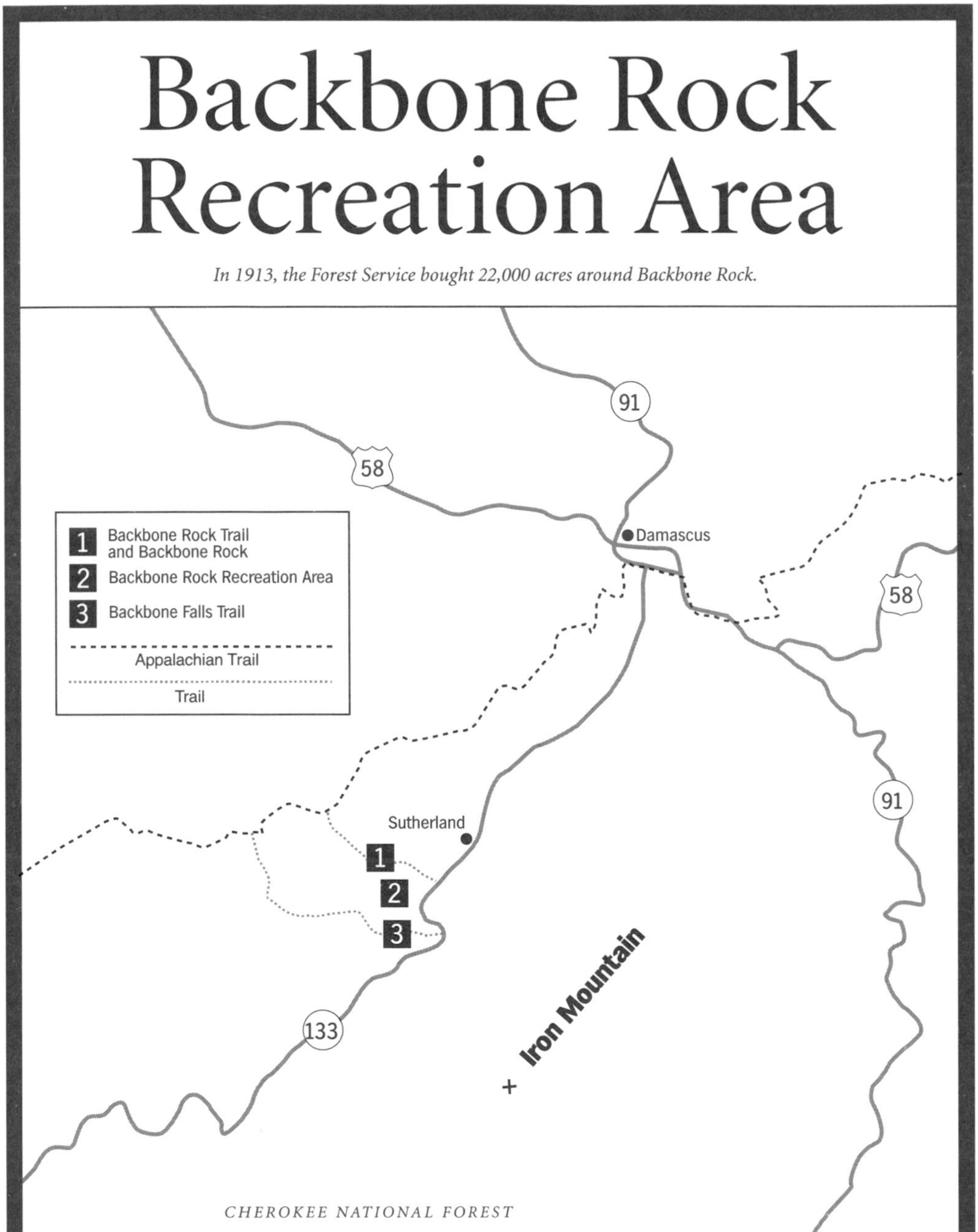

Backbone Rock Recreation Area

In 1913, the Forest Service bought 22,000 acres around Backbone Rock.

91

58

Damascus

58

1 Backbone Rock Trail
and Backbone Rock

2 Backbone Rock Recreation Area

3 Backbone Falls Trail

- - - - Appalachian Trail

.... Trail

91

Sutherland

1

2

3

133

Iron Mountain

+

CHEROKEE NATIONAL FOREST

N

1 MILE

Ref: Delorme Tennessee Atlas & Gazetteer

Carolina, and it then ends at the hitching rails near the Mount Rogers United States Geological Survey benchmark. The trail does not connect with roads on private land at the Tennessee/North Carolina/Virginia border.

There is a marvelous view and plenty of camping available in the meadow east of the high point on Rogers Ridge, elevation 4,880 feet. The springs feeding the headwaters of Gentry Creek are about 200 yards south-southeast of the camping area.

Directions: From Laurel Bloomery take FR 123 (east) to large, signed parking area. Trailhead is on the north side of the road.

Trail: 5.8 miles, one-way.

Elevation: Begins at 2,680 and ends at 4,640 feet.

Degree of difficulty: Moderate to strenuous.

Blaze: Vertical yellow slash and metal horse-and-rider symbol.

Table Mountain Pine

One of the pine trees on the Appalachian Mountain ridges is the slow-growing table mountain pine (*Pinus pungens*). It rarely reaches 60 feet in height. It inhabits dry, rocky areas between 2,700 feet and 4,000 feet. It is sometimes called hickory pine because of its tough, hickory-like branches.

GENTRY CREEK FALLS TRAIL

[Fig. 27(3)] Reaching Gentry Creek Falls requires a 4.6-mile round-trip hike that climbs 1,200 feet. A good trail deteriorates to a primitive trail after a point. The 15 creek crossings on this trail can be dangerous during high water. The waterfall is an attractive, two-tiered, 40-foot, double horsetail-shaped falls.

Directions: From Laurel Bloomery take FR 123 (east), and continue about 1 mile beyond the Rogers Ridge Horse Trail trailhead to the beginning of the Gentry Creek Falls Trail.

Trail: 2.3 miles, one-way.

Elevation: Begins at 2,800 and ends at 4,020 feet.

Degree of difficulty: Moderate to strenuous.

Blaze: Blue.

BACKBONE ROCK RECREATION AREA

[Fig. 28] The Backbone Rock Recreation Area has four major features that attract visitors: the trout stream, the trails, the falls, and Backbone Rock. Backbone Rock Recreation Area is known for the unique rock formation located where Beaverdam Creek flows past a spur ridge of Holston Mountain. The spur ends sharply at a large bend in the creek and is named Backbone because it resembles a spine. The spine is a wall of sandstone about 50 feet thick that rises nearly a hundred feet and runs for several hundred feet. A tunnel was drilled 22 feet through Backbone Rock in 1901 to allow a railroad to operate, creating what was called the "shortest tunnel in the world." After the timber was harvested, the railroad was abandoned and later became TN 133 that now runs through the tunnel.

In 1913, the Forest Service bought 22,000 acres around Backbone Rock, and during the early 1920s, people began using it for recreation. The Civilian Conservation Corps (CCC) built a picnic and camping area here in the 1930s. All 11 campsites in the area were reworked during 1994 and 1995 to accommodate camping equipment from tents to RVs. The U.S. Forest Service also completely restored two CCC-era picnic pavilions and made general improvements to the area.

Some stands of white pine in the Backbone Rock Recreation Area were planted after logging was completed. Wildflowers are another attraction when they bloom along the creek bottom. Early saxifrage (*Saxifraga virginiensis*) and grass-of-parnassus (*Parnassia asarifolia*) are two notables. On the Backbone Rock Trail (*see* page 159), about 250 feet before it intersects the AT, is a colony of the rare shinleaf (*Pyrola elliptica*) that blooms in June.

Beaverdam Creek flows through public land, but only for 6 miles. One of many access points to the public stream is at the TN 133 bridge north of Crandull. The highway and the stream run parallel for about 6 miles northeast into Virginia.

Tennessee's trout streams contain rainbow and brown trout that were introduced during the early part of the 1900s when improper logging practices destroyed the habitat of the brook trout. Restoration of the brook trout and its habitat has been successful in the higher elevations. The brook trout in the tributaries of Beaverdam are wild, not stocked, fish that have survived.

Beaverdam Creek is a very popular stream, and wild rainbows and browns can be caught here. There are also abundant trout in the CNF section of the creek. The upper part of Beaverdam and its tributaries in the CNF are wild trout streams with special regulations: three trout limit, single hook, and artificial lures, flies, etc. only.

Directions: Go north from Shady Valley on TN 133 for 9 miles, turn left at sign into Backbone Rock Recreation Area.

Activities: Picnicking, hiking, camping, swimming (no designated area), and fishing.

Facilities: Picnic pavilions and tables, drinking water, toilets, 11 campsites, and hiking trails.

Dates: Open May to Oct.

Fees: There is a fee for camping and day use. Pavilions may be reserved in advance for a fee.

Closest town: Shady Valley, 9 miles south on TN 133. Damascus, VA, 5 miles north via TN 133.

For more information: Watauga Ranger District, PO Box 400, Unicoi, TN 37692. Phone (423) 735-1500.

BACKBONE FALLS TRAIL

[Fig. 28(3)] The Backbone Falls Trail (#198), a short loop trail, begins and ends in the parking lot at the south end

GOLDEN-CROWNED KINGLET
(Regulus satrapa)
A restless, flitting movement and a high, thin "ssst" identify the kinglet.

of the recreation area. It is an easy walk with CCC-era rockwork and steep drop-offs. Adult supervision of children is recommended. The trail passes Backbone Falls 0.1 mile from the parking lot. This falls is small with a horsetail form.

Trail: 0.38 mile, loop.

Degree of difficulty: Easy.

BACKBONE ROCK TRAIL

[Fig. 28(1)] The Backbone Rock Trail (#53), a 2.36-mile hike, begins at the parking area on TN 133 and climbs many steps to the top of Backbone Rock. One spur of this trail veers over the top of the rock with a solid path and steep drop-offs and leads to the picnic area on the south side of TN 133. The main trail continues to the crest of Holston Mountain where it intersects the AT (#1).

Trail: 2.36 miles, one-way.

Degree of difficulty: Easy.

Blaze: Blue.

HOLSTON MOUNTAIN

[Fig. 27] Holston Mountain, running 30 miles from Elizabethton to Damascus, Virginia, is part of the Upper Unaka Mountains.

The rock in this mountain is some of the oldest in the CNF. Ancient metamorphic rock (schist and gneiss) and igneous rock (granite and gabbro) form the basement complex.

The mountain is crisscrossed with trails for hiking and horses. Three of the trails are in the Stony Creek Scenic Area (*see* page 162) and are described in that section. The others are described here in order from the northern part of Holston Mountain to the southern end.

FLINT MILL TRAIL

[Fig. 27(6)] The Flint Mill Trail (#49) leaves FR 87 just south of the junction with FR 87A and FR 87D, and it heads south, climbing Holston Mountain. It passes the Flatwoods Horse Trail (#46) and goes by the touted Flint Rock that provides a 180-degree vista of Holston Valley and South Holston Lake before intersecting with the Holston Mountain Trail (#44) (*see* page 162). This is a very steep trail leading to the main ridge of Holston Mountain. Flint Rock is 1 mile up the trail. At 1.3 miles the trail crosses a stream and a small bog. A bog is an area where the groundwater rises to the surface, causing it to be saturated. It is a good idea to walk around these soft, waterlogged areas. This bog zone supports yellow lady's slipper (*Cypripedium ciliaris*), pink lady's slipper (*Cypripedium acaule*), yellow fringed orchid (*Habenaria ciliaris*), whorled pogonia (*Isotria medeoloides*), adder's tongue (*Erythronium americanum*), and twayblade orchid (*Liparis lilifolia*). Continue through the hardwoods to the intersection with the Holston Mountain Trail.

Directions: From the eastern end of South Holston Lake Bridge on US 421 go east 3.9 miles, turn right (south) on Camp Tom Howard Road (FR 87). Continue past Little Oak Recreation Area, just beyond the junction with FR 87A and FR 87, stay on FR 87 to the left (east), and park along the road. It is 14.2 miles from the Holston Lake Bridge to the trailhead.

Trail: 1.4 miles, one-way.

Elevation: Begins at 2,120 feet and ends at 3,880 feet.

Degree of difficulty: Moderate to strenuous.

Blaze: Blue.

FLATWOODS HORSE TRAIL

[Fig. 27(4)] The Flatwoods Horse Trail (#46) runs from FR 87B southwest. This trail includes 8.32 miles of gated roads (FR 87A and 87B) and 5.43 miles of trail. Small sections are rocky, but the grade is gentle. The trail follows the base of Holston Mountain. Josiah Horse Trail (#45) spurs off to the east (*see* below) to FR 87. Take this spur for a shorter ride or continue on the Flatwoods Trail to the end where it intersects with FR 87. Parking is available at both ends of the trail.

Directions: From Bristol take US 421 southeast for 12 miles to Camp Tom Howard Road (also known as Flatwoods Road and FR 87), turn right (southwest) and go 1 mile to the junction of FR 87 and FR 87B, the trailhead. The southern end of the trail is on the eastern side of FR 87 about 1 mile south of the FR 87 and FR 87D junction.

Trail: 13.75 miles, one-way.

Degree of difficulty: Easy.

Blaze: Yellow.

JOSIAH HORSE TRAIL

[Fig. 27(6)] The Josiah Horse Trail (#45) leaves FR 87, just south of Little Oak Recreation Area, and heads south for 0.76 mile. It ends where it intersects with the Flatwoods Horse Trail.

Directions: From Bristol take US 421 southeast for 12 miles to Camp Tom Howard Road and turn right (south). Continue for 8 miles to Three Rocks, a grassy area at the junction of FR 87 and FR 87G. The trailhead is 1 mile farther on FR 87.

Trail: 0.76 mile, one-way.

Degree of difficulty: Moderate.

Blaze: Yellow.

⬛ JACOBS CREEK RECREATION AREA

[Fig. 27(1)] Jacobs Creek Recreation Area, on the eastern shore of South Holston Lake, offers camping, fishing, swimming, picnicking, and hiking.

The Jacobs Trail (#604), an easy, one-way foot trail, follows the shoreline of the lake for 0.3 mile, beginning at the turn-around near Camping Loop C and ending on the main road between Camping Loops A and B.

Directions: East of South Holston Lake on US 421, turn north on Denton Valley Road (County Road 32), then turn left (west) on FR 337.

Activities: Camping, picnicking, swimming, fishing, and hiking.

Facilities: Restrooms, bathroom and shower house, 29 campsites, and picnic tables.

Dates: Open seasonally.

Fees: There are charges for day use and overnight use.

Closest town: Shady Valley is 6 miles east on US 421. Bristol is 12 miles west on US 421.

For more information: Watauga Ranger District, PO Box 400, Unicoi, TN 37692. Phone (423) 735-1500.

LITTLE OAK RECREATION AREA

[Fig. 27(5)] The Little Oak Recreation Area is on a peninsula jutting from the eastern shore of South Holston Lake. Bird watchers may want to stay at this popular recreation area to look for bald eagles (*Haliaetus leucocephalus*). More than two dozen eagles have been hacked on South Holston Lake under the Bald Eagle Hacking Program. Hacking is a term from falconry meaning gradual reintroduction to the wild. Eagles from 7 weeks old to 13 weeks old are kept in cages to imprint an area on them so the birds return there after they are sexually mature.

Wildflower Photo Tips

Photographing wildflowers requires special equipment. A 35mm single lens reflex (SLR) camera is ideal for this purpose. When photographing wildflowers, the sturdy support provided by a tripod is needed. A flash is often required for taking good shots. A through the lens (TTL) flash eliminates exposure guesswork. Other items to consider are extension tubes for closer focusing, teleconverters for increasing the focal length, and a special lens, such as a zoom, a zoom and/or fixed macro, or a two-element close-up lens.

Adult eagles have a wingspan of 7.5 feet, dark brown plumage, and large heads. Young birds are nearly black without the white head, neck, and tail characteristic of adults. Binoculars will help you see details of the birds better, and cameras with at least a 200mm lens are needed to photograph eagles best.

Directions: East of South Holston Lake on US 421, turn south on FR 87 (Camp Tom Howard Road). Go about 8 miles and turn right (west) on FR 87G at the sign.

Activities: Camping, hiking, fishing, and boating.

Facilities: 72 campsites, amphitheater, hiking trails, picnicking for campers, and toilets.

Dates: Open seasonally.

Fees: There is a charge for camping.

Closest town: Bristol, about 15 miles west on US 421.

For more information: Watauga Ranger District, PO Box 400, Unicoi, TN 37692. Phone (423) 735-1500.

LITTLE OAK MOUNTAIN TRAIL

[Fig. 27(5)] The Little Oak Mountain Trail (#601) is an interpretive loop trail with a spur to a scenic view of the lake and a climb to the crest of Little Oak Mountain. This walk offers you opportunities to view wildlife and take some scenic photos.

Directions: The trail begins at the pay station near the entrance to the recreation area.

Trail: 1.37 miles, loop trail.

Degree of difficulty: Easy to moderate.

Blaze: Trail signs.

LITTLE OAK TRAIL

[Fig. 27(5)] The Little Oak Trail (#52) is an easy interpretive walk around the edge of Little

EASTERN HEMLOCK
(Tsuga canadensis)
Long-lived hemlocks develop slowly in the shade.

Oak Recreation Area along the shore of South Holston Lake. The trail begins at the entrance station, meanders through the campgrounds, passes Little Oak Amphitheater, travels to the lake's edge, and ends on the north side of the peninsula. Take a fishing pole on this walk to try your luck at catching bream, bass, and catfish.

Trail: 1.38 miles, one-way.
Degree of difficulty: Easy.
Blaze: Trail signs.

STONY CREEK SCENIC AREA

[Fig. 27(10)] Stony Creek Scenic Area (formerly Flint Mill Scenic Area) lies on Holston Mountain in Carter and Sullivan counties just southwest of Shady Valley. This scenic area stands midway along the length of Holston Mountain. Bound by FR 87B to the northwest, TN 91 to the southeast, and by a line parallel to the AT to the northeast, the scenic area contains 3,920 protected acres with outstanding natural features.

One of the attractions in this area is Rich Knob, elevation 4,247 feet, which is on the AT just above Double Springs Shelter. Flint Rock offers an excellent view of the South Holston Valley, and Stony Creek has several small falls and pools. The steep northwestern slopes of Holston Mountain are covered with fire-dependent pine species such as table mountain pine, whereas the less steep southeastern slopes are covered with cove and upland hardwoods.

Three trails traverse the scenic area: Holston Mountain Trail (#44), North Fork of Stony Creek Trail (#42), and Upper Stony Creek Trail (#197).

Directions: From Elizabethton, go 12 miles northeast on TN 91, turn left (northwest) on Panhandle Road (FR 56), and go for 4.2 miles. Park here and follow FR 56A east on foot—FR 56A is closed to vehicles. Or go about 6 miles south of Shady Valley on TN 91 to FR 56.

Activities: Hiking, hunting, horseback riding, camping.
Dates: Open year-round.
Facilities: None.
Fees: None.
Closest town: Shady Valley, about 10 miles northeast on TN 91.
For more information: Watauga Ranger District, PO Box 400, Unicoi, TN 37692. Phone (423) 735-1500.

HOLSTON MOUNTAIN TRAIL

[Fig. 27(7)] The Holston Mountain Trail (#44) is reached by hiking from Low Gap on US

421 southwest 3.4 miles along the AT to the Double Springs Shelter where the AT turns south toward TN 91. The Holston Mountain Trail continues southwest along the crest of Holston Mountain to Holston High Knob at an elevation of 4,140 feet. These two trails were the same until 1954 when the AT's course was altered to

Yellownose or Rock Vole

The yellownose vole, or rock vole (*Microtus chrotorrhinus*), lives at the southern end of its range in the southern Appalachian Mountains. This rarely seen, secretive forest creature lives in moist areas where it can dine on moss, grasses, berries, underground fungi, and some caterpillars. This mammal is listed by the Tennessee Wildlife Resources Agency as one that is in need of management because it is so rare in the state.

avoid the wide valley-crossing to the south. From the diverging trails at Double Springs Shelter, it is 8.3 miles to Holston High Knob and the Holston Mountain Communications Tower. Then it is an additional 1.2 miles along FR 56A to the trailhead at the junction with FR 56. The Holston Mountain Trail intersects with the Flint Mill Trail (#49) (*see* page 159).

Trail: 9.5 miles, one-way.

Elevation: Begins at 4,150 feet and ends at 4,080 feet.

Degree of difficulty: Moderate.

Blaze: Blue.

NORTH FORK OF STONY CREEK TRAIL

[Fig. 27(8)] The North Fork of Stony Creek Trail (#42) follows the North Fork of Stony Creek to a 40-foot horseshoe waterfall. There is no formal right-of-way or easement across 600 feet of private land at the trailhead; you need to get the land-owner's permission to cross it. The waterfall is about 1.6 miles from the trailhead and is considered the most picturesque in the Stony Creek Scenic Area.

Directions: Go north of Elizabethton for 18 miles on TN 91, turn left (northwest) on Mose Stout Road, and the trail begins at the end of the right fork of Mose Stout Road. Ask at the nearest house for information and permission.

Trail: 3.2 miles, one-way.

Elevation: Begins at 2,420 feet and ends at 4,080 feet.

Degree of difficulty: Strenuous.

Blaze: None.

UPPER STONY CREEK TRAIL

[Fig. 27(9)] The Upper Stony Creek Trail (#197) follows the Upper Stony Creek through the Stony Creek Scenic Area, and it climbs the Old Road Ridge and ends at the intersection with the AT south of Double Springs Shelter. During periods of high water, the many creek crossings may become dangerous. This trail is not maintained and is considered challenging.

Directions: Go north of Elizabethton for 19 miles on TN 91 to the foot of Cross Mountain. The trailhead is on the left (northwest) side of the road just inside the CNF boundary but has limited parking.

Big Laurel Branch Wilderness Area

Big Laurel Branch Wilderness Area was designated by U.S. Congress in 1986.

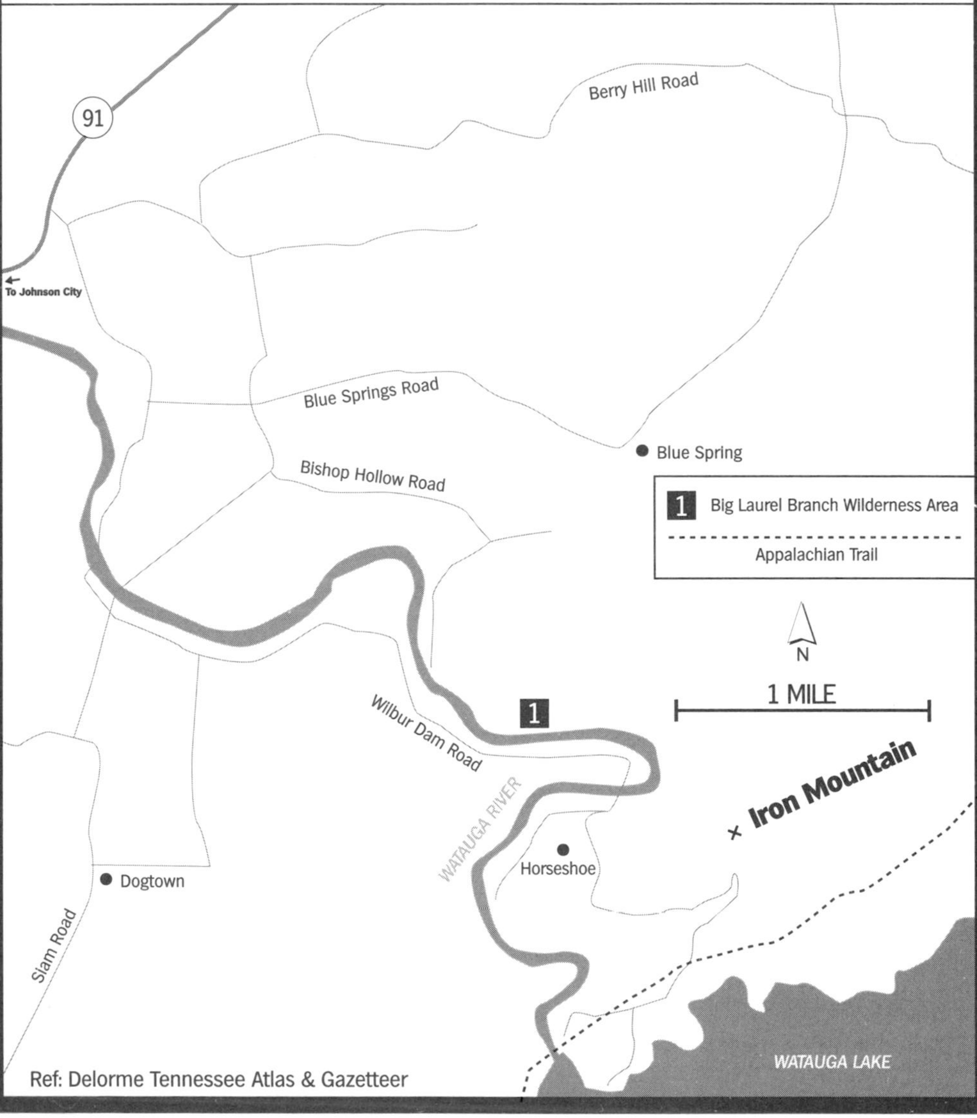

Berry Hill Road

91

← To Johnson City

Blue Springs Road

Bishop Hollow Road

● Blue Spring

| 1 | Big Laurel Branch Wilderness Area |
| - - - - - - - - - | Appalachian Trail |

N

1 MILE

Wilbur Dam Road

1

WATAUGA RIVER

× **Iron Mountain**

● Dogtown

Horseshoe ●

Siam Road

WATAUGA LAKE

Ref: Delorme Tennessee Atlas & Gazetteer

Trail: 2.54 miles, one-way.
Elevation: Begins at 2,759 feet and ends at 3,880 feet.
Degree of difficulty: Strenuous.
Blaze: None.

BOG TURTLE
(Clemmys muhlenbergi)
This turtle is only 4
inches long.

BIG LAUREL BRANCH WILDERNESS AREA

[Fig. 29] U.S. Congress designated Big Laurel Branch Wilderness in 1986. Big Laurel Branch Wilderness Area, bound by Watauga Lake to the south, stretches northeast to cover 6,251 acres at the southern end of Iron Mountain in Carter and Johnson counties. It is transversed by the AT, the principal trail in the wilderness.

In 1963, bulldozers built firebreaks for a fire burning nearly 3,000 acres along the Iron Mountain crest. Today, the scars of the breaks and the fire have grown over. Big Laurel Branch Wilderness is completely covered with trees. Carolina hemlocks can be found in large stands, but most of the trees are mixed hardwoods. Grand views of Watauga and Wilbur lakes are seen from the top of the bluffs along the Appalachian Trail (AT). At a point about 1,000 feet above the lakes, boats appear as bathtub toys. This is very rugged country with no maintained trails.

Directions: From Elizabethton take US 321 south 0.5 mile to Siam Road, turn left (east) on Siam Road, follow the Watauga River upstream, cross Wilbur Lake, and follow the road to Wilbur Dam. The wilderness area is on the north side of the road.

Activities: Hiking, camping, and hunting.
Facilities: None.
Dates: Open year-round.
Fees: None.
Closest town: Elizabethton, about 6 miles east.
For more information: Watauga Ranger District, PO Box 400, Unicoi, TN 37692. Phone (423) 735-1500.

APPALACHIAN TRAIL

[Fig. 29] Of the 150 miles of the Appalachian Trail within the northern CNF, 5.8 miles of the trail are within the Big Laurel Branch Wilderness Area. In the Watauga Lake area, the AT (#1) runs along the crest of Iron Mountain providing sensational vistas. The AT leads to the parallel crests at the southern end of Iron Mountain containing Big Laurel Valley and Little Laurel Valley, with no maintained trails leading into Big Laurel Valley. From Watauga Lake it is a steep walk on the AT to the crest of Iron Mountain, 1,400 feet elevation. Big Laurel Branch is one of many streams cutting into the rugged terrain.

About 13 miles along the AT from Watauga Dam Road look for an 8-foot monument. This is the grave of a mountain man. The cracked plaque reads, "Uncle Nick Grindstaff—

born Dec. 26, 1851—died July 22, 1923—lived alone, suffered alone, and died alone." He was a hermit, taking to the hills at age 26 to live the rest of his life on Iron Mountain.

The AT in the wilderness area is rated Opportunity Class AT, which limits group size to a maximum of 10 people, limits organized groups to a maximum of 2, prohibits commercial outfitter/guide activities, and insists hikers practice leave no trace visiting. The CNF strives to limit the number of visible campsites to one or less per mile of trail within the wilderness area.

Directions: From Elizabethton take US 321 south 0.5 mile to Siam Road, turn left (east) on Siam Road, follow the Watauga River upstream, cross Wilbur Lake, and follow the road toward Watauga Dam. The trailhead is on the east side of the road before reaching Watauga Dam.

Trail: 15.6 miles from Watauga Dam to TN 91 at the Carter/Johnson county line.

Elevation: Begins at 2,240 feet and ends at 3,459 feet.

Degree of difficulty: Strenuous.

Blaze: White.

▓ POND MOUNTAIN WILDERNESS AREA

[Fig. 30(23)] Pond Mountain Wilderness Area, bound by Watauga Lake to the north, Dennis Cove Road (also called County Road 50, FR 50, and Laurel Fork Road) to the south, and FR 39 on the east, covers 6,668 acres in the Watauga District. Elevation ranges from a high of 4,329 feet on top of Pond Mountain to 1,900 feet at Laurel Fork Creek. U.S. Congress designated Pond Mountain Wilderness in 1986, incorporating the former Watauga Scenic Area.

Wilderness is managed to preserve its exceptional natural qualities. It is a place where humans are visitors, and natural physical and biological forces are allowed to proceed unrestricted by human activities. This is a place to find solitude and enjoy primitive and unconfined recreation.

This rough region has cliffs up to 200 feet high in the spectacular Laurel Fork Gorge and some old-growth forests that were inaccessible to loggers. In addition to the old-growth forest of scarlet oaks more than 100 years old found in the gorge, there are some cove hardwoods, but upland hardwoods make up the majority of the forests in the Pond Mountain Wilderness. Flame azalea (*Rhododendron calendulaceum*), mountain laurel (*Kalmia latifloia*), rhododendron (*Rhododendron maximum*), maple, beech, and hemlock are common here. The railroad bed that ran to Dennis Cove and was used for logging during the first two decades of the 1900s is now part of the AT that passes through the gorge. Birth dates of some timber stands range from 1861 to 1944.

Potato Top, a projection covered with trees and difficult to see if you aren't looking for it, got its name because it looks like a potato hill. It and Buckle Rock, a 150-foot-high cliff so named for its folded rock strata, are two popular features in the Laurel Fork Gorge. The slopes of Black Mountain to the south rise 1,000 feet from the gorge.

Directions: East of Hampton about 1 mile on US 321 the road splits, with US 321 going north of the wilderness (south side of Watauga Lake) and FR 50 going south along the border.

Activities: Hiking, camping, and hunting.

Facilities: None.

Dates: Open year-round.

Fees: None.

Closest town: Hampton, about 2 miles west.

For more information: Watauga Ranger District, PO Box 400, Unicoi, TN 37692. Phone 423-735-1500.

LAUREL FORK FALLS

[Fig. 30(24)] The most popular scenic feature in the Pond Mountain Wilderness Area is Laurel Falls on Laurel Fork Creek. The segmented waterfall drops 45 to 55 feet and is probably the best known falls in this area. There is a large pool at the bottom suitable for swimming to those who enjoy cold mountain water. Laurel Fork Creek is also a good stream for fishing for wild rainbow and brown trout.

Upstream from Laurel Falls are Middle Laurel Falls (15- to 20-foot drop) and Upper Laurel Falls (15- to 25-foot drop). Between the Middle Laurel Falls and Upper Laurel Falls are Lower Dennis Cove Falls (10-foot drop) and Dennis Cove Falls (20- to 30-foot drop).

Dennis Cove Recreation Area, 5 miles east of Hampton on Dennis Cove Road, is a popular starting place for hiking to the waterfalls. After parking at the recreation area, go 0.8 mile west along Dennis Cove Road to where the AT crosses the road. There is a small parking area where the AT crosses the road but there is plenty of room to park at the recreation area. Follow the AT's white blazes to Laurel Falls.

Directions: From Elizabethton, go southeast on US 321 through Hampton, continue for 0.8 mile, turn right (south) on FR 50 (Dennis Cove Road) to reach a parking area at the Dennis Cove Recreation Area or to reach the Laurel Falls parking area on the AT.

Fees: There is a per-vehicle use fee at Dennis Cove Recreation Area.

Trail: 1.3 miles, one-way.

Degree of difficulty: Moderate to strenuous.

Blaze: White.

Solomon's Seal

False solomon's seal (*Smilacina racemosa*) and solomon's seal (*Polygonatum biflorum*), both in the lily family (*Liliaceae*), produce similar stems and leaves, but the false solomon's seal flowers are on top of the leaves, and solomon's seal flowers are under the leaves. The false solomon's seal makes a showier flower than the true solomon's seal.

The age of a solomon's seal can be determined by counting the root scars; one is produced each year. Some plants have been found with 50 scars. The round root scar looks like the seal of King Solomon of the tenth century B.C., hence the name. Indians pulverized the root of solomon's seal to make flour and pickled the roots. Crushed roots were used to reduce or remove the black and blue from a bruise. A tea made from the leaves was drunk as a contraceptive.

GARTER SNAKE
(Thamnophis sirtalis)
Garter snakes have three stripes, one on back and one on each side. They're often found near water.

POND MOUNTAIN TRAIL

[Fig. 30(25)] The Pond Mountain Trail (#40) is the only trail traversing the Pond Mountain Wilderness Area through its widest north/south dimension. The trail begins on US 321, entering the Pond Mountain Wilderness at the powerline crossing east of the Watauga Point Recreation Area (*see* page 169). It rises to the crest of Pond Mountain (4,329 feet elevation) via a 4.5-mile trail and then descends to Dennis Cove along Rough Ridge. The initial climb is very steep, but the 1,800-foot rise in 1.5 miles offers a good view of the lake. Locals say, "It's as steep as a mule's face." Care is required to stay on this primitive trail because some turns are not marked. Maintenance of this trail conforms to the standard that only allows primitive, nonmechanized tools; therefore, it may be more primal than nonwilderness trails. Portions of this trail are rocky. The trail ends at FR 50 on the southern side of the wilderness east of Dennis Cove.

The Pond Mountain Trail is rated Opportunity Class II, which requires limiting group size to a maximum of six people, limiting organized groups to a maximum of two, prohibiting commercial outfitter/guide activities, and practicing leave no trace visiting.

Directions: From Hampton take TN 67 east for 5.5 miles. Trailhead is on the south side of TN 67, about 0.5 mile east of Watauga Point Recreation Area. Roadside parking is available on the north side of the road. Access to the southern end of the trail is on FR 50, near its junction with FR 50F.

Trail: 4.5 miles, one-way.
Elevation: Begins at 1,968 feet and ends at 3,280 feet.
Degree of difficulty: Strenuous.
Blaze: Yellow.

CARDENS BLUFF RECREATION AREA

[Fig. 30(26)] Along US 321, bordering the Pond Mountain Wilderness Area, are several recreation areas. Cardens Bluff Recreation Area on the south shore of Watauga Lake, north of the Pond Mountain Wilderness Area, is for single camping units only. No group or double sites are available. This camping facility, on a peninsula jutting into Watauga Lake, is a gated recreation area. Hiking and fishing are available to campers.

Directions: From Hampton take US 321 east for 4 miles to entrance on north side of road.
Activities: Camping, fishing, boating, and hiking.
Facilities: 43 campsites, trailer space, drinking water, and restrooms.
Dates: Open seasonally.

Fees: There is a charge for camping.

Closest town: Hampton is 4 miles west on US 321.

For more information: Watauga Ranger District, PO Box 400, Unicoi, TN 37692. Phone (423) 735-1500.

CARDENS BLUFF TRAIL

[Fig. 30(27)] The Cardens Bluff Trail (#55) is an easy hike along and above the shoreline of Watauga Lake for about half the length of the campground. The trail begins beyond the host campsite (#5) at the apex of a curve just beyond the parking area, and it ends on the west side of the peninsula near the restrooms. The walk offers good views and ample opportunities to fish.

Trail: 0.69 mile, one-way.

Degree of difficulty: Easy.

WATAUGA POINT RECREATION AREA

[Fig. 30(28)] The Watauga Point Recreation Area is a day-use area only for picnicking, fishing, swimming, and hiking on the south shore of Watauga Lake.

The Watauga Point Trail (#59), an easy loop trail that is 0.41 mile long, begins at the parking lot on the right (east) near the entrance and follows the contours of the lake above the shoreline. The trail is gravel and offers some good views of the lake.

Directions: From Hampton take US 321 east for 6.5 miles to the entrance on the north side of the road.

Activities: Hiking, fishing, swimming, and picnicking.

Facilities: Restrooms, picnic tables, and drinking fountains.

Dates: Open seasonally.

Fees: There is a charge for day use.

Closest town: Hampton is 6.5 miles west on US 321.

For more information: Watauga Ranger District, PO Box 400, Unicoi, TN 37692. Phone (423) 735-1500.

MOUNTAIN BICYCLE TRAILS

There are no trails designated for bicycles in the Watauga Ranger District, but bikes are allowed on some trails and roads. All forest roads (FR) open to motorized vehicles are open to bicycles, and all gated forest roads closed to motorized vehicles are open to bicycles unless signs specify they are closed to bicycles. Horse trails are open to bicycles.

No bicycles are allowed on the AT or blue-blazed foot trails (with some signed exceptions). There are more than 200 miles of forest roads in Carter, Johnson, and Sullivan counties, ranging from high-standard gravel to primitive.

In the Watauga Ranger District, the following roads are suggested routes for bicycles:

Denton Valley Road (FR 32), 18 miles long in Sullivan County, is a paved and gravel road.

Flatwoods Road (FR 87 and old 87), 22 miles long, runs along the southeastern edge of South Holston Lake from the Virginia border south to near Biltmore, north of Elizabethton.

Forest Road 87A (3.9 miles long) and **87B** (5.3 miles long) in Sullivan County are gated gravel roads and are extensions of the Flatwoods Horse Trail.

McQueens Knob Road (FR 69), 5.4 miles long in Johnson and Sullivan counties, is a gravel road.

Pine Mountain Road (FR 4002), 5.4 miles long, and **Dogwood Bench Road** (FR 4431), 7.6 miles long, in Sullivan County are managed as gated closed roads.

For more information: Maps are available from the Watauga Ranger District, PO Box 400, Unicoi, TN 37692. Phone (423) 735-1500.

DOE RIVER GORGE SCENIC AREA

[Fig. 30(30)] The 1,783-acre Doe River Gorge Scenic Area lies south of Hampton and was designated in 1988, but the bottom of the gorge including the old railroad bed is privately owned. The trails leading into the gorge cross private land. The CNF boundary begins at an elevation of about 2,000 feet.

In 1868 workers began constructing a narrow-gage railroad to connect Johnson City, Tennessee, with Cranberry Iron Works near Elk Park, North Carolina. Completion in 1882 required hand-digging five tunnels and constructing trestles high over the Doe River. Laborers dug the tunnels with the aid of pack mules that had to be lifted over the ridges with pulleys because the cliffs of the gorge were too steep for the mules to climb.

The original purpose of the railroad was to haul iron ore from North Carolina to the furnaces in Johnson City. This line, East Tennessee and Western North Carolina, served many social functions as well. Isolated areas were connected to towns. The men who operated the train served as delivery men to people along the way, hauling items small and large and stopping to hand deliver them. Seven days a week the train ran, but it ran on a loose schedule. Anyone could hail the train, and it would stop to pick up passengers, to take orders or deliver goods, or to carry on a conversation. The line also hauled timber, supplies, and freight.

It is said some young ladies on their way to camp in North Carolina dubbed the line "the tweetsie" from the sound of the train's whistle. The name stuck, and is used today for an amusement park between Boone and Blowing Rock, North Carolina.

This 34-mile railroad suffered floods during the years of operation. Water roaring through the gorge washed out 39 places in 1901, and sections of the line were washed out again in 1904. Abandonment began then, but the railroad continued to operate, although less frequently, until 1975. During the early 1940s, the train operated three days a week, and by 1950 an abandonment request was filed and granted. A section of the line in the lower end of the gorge was rebuilt and operated by the Doe River Railroad Company for tourists until 1975.

On private land, the old railroad bed is the trail used in the lower end of the gorge, but the trail ends at an old trestle that is unsafe to walk. Permission and signing a release is required before hiking the trail. Hikers have fallen to their deaths from the rotten trestles. Do not attempt to cross one!

Directions: Southeast of Hampton on US 19E is Doe River Road, about 1 mile south of Hampton on the left (east) off US 19E. It leads 0.5 mile to a church camp where you need to get permission to park and sign a release form to trek into the gorge.

BUTTERFLY WEED
(Asclepias tuberosa)
This plant is often found in home gardens because its bright orange, star-shaped flowers attract butterflies.

Activities: Hiking.

Facilities: None.

Dates: Open year-round.

Fees: None.

Closest town: Hampton, about 1 mile north.

For more information: Christian Camp and Conference Center, PO Box 791, Elizabethton, TN 37643. Phone (423) 928-8936.

DOE RIVER GORGE TRAIL

[Fig. 30(31)] The Doe River Gorge Trail (not a CNF trail) is on private land, but it is worth getting permission to see the wildflowers blooming along it in May. Dogwood (*Cornus florida*), rhododendron, jack-in-the-pulpit (*Arisaeme triphyllum*), fire pink (*Silene virginica*), and bleeding hearts (*Dicentra cucullaria*) will make your heart glad in the spring. The steep and shadowed gorge delays blooming. Due to the high humidity held between the steep cliffs, lush is the word most often used to describe this rain forest–like gorge. Anglers enjoy trout fishing, and swimmers love the clear, cool pools.

From the trailhead, enter a 200-foot tunnel dug by the railroad builders. About 0.7 mile along the trail is a camping spot near the Doe River. Farther along there is a 0.9-mile-long tunnel that leads to a sensational view of the Doe River. At the end of the tunnel, climb to the top of the rocks on the left (north) to get a good view of the ridgeline several hundred feet away. There you can see exposed folded rock strata.

Trail: 2.4 miles, one-way.

Elevation: Begins at 1,960 feet and ends at 2,200 feet.

Degree of difficulty: Easy.

FORK MOUNTAIN TRAIL

[Fig. 30(32)] The Fork Mountain Trail (not a CNF trail) begins on private land across from the Fork Mountain Free Will Baptist Church parking lot, but hikers have been heretofore welcomed to walk on the trail. An old road is the trail that passes through new forest growth of sourwood (*Oxydendrum arboreum*) and maple in an area that was clear-cut in the 1970s. Farther along is an older forest of hardwoods that have grown since timber was cut in the early 1900s. A peak of 3,560 feet is

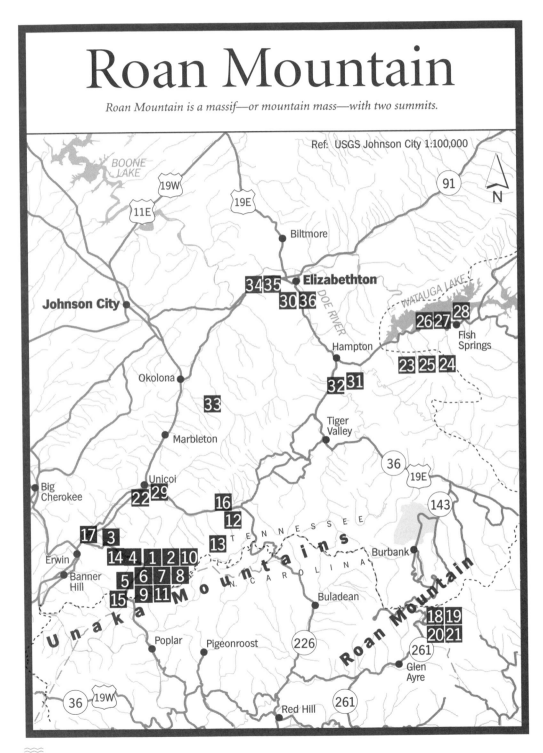

Roan Mountain

Roan Mountain is a massif—or mountain mass—with two summits.

Ref: USGS Johnson City 1:100,000

1	Unaka Mountain Wilderness Area	**21**	The Cloudland Trail
2	Unaka Mountain Scenic Area	**22**	Watauga Ranger District H.Q.
3	Unaka Mountain Auto Tour	**23**	Pond Mountain Wilderness Area
4	Rock Creek Recreation Area	**24**	Laurel Fork Falls
5	Rock Creek Falls Trail	**25**	Pond Mountain Trail
6	Rock Creek Bicycle Trail	**26**	Cardens Bluff Recreation Area
7	Hemlock Forest Trail	**27**	Cardens Bluff Trail
8	Indian Grave Gap	**28**	Watauga Point Recreation Area
9	Beauty Spot	**29**	Unaka Ranger District H.Q.
10	Beauty Spot Gap/Unaka Mountain Wilderness Area	**30**	Doe River Gorge Scenic Area
11	Unaka Mountain Overlook	**31**	Doe River Gorge Trail
12	Spruce Forests	**32**	Fork Mountain Trail
13	White Pine Plantation	**33**	The Laurels
14	Clear Fork Creek	**34**	Sycamore Shoals
15	Bell Cemetery At Limestone Cove	**35**	Sycamore Shoals State Historic Park
16	Limestone Cove Recreation Area	**36**	Doe River Covered Bridge
17	Erwin National Fish Hatchery and Unicoi Heritage Museum		Roan Mountain State Park
18	Highlands of Roan Mountain	- - - - - - - - - - -	Appalachian Trail
19	Twin Springs Picnic Area		
20	Roan High Knob and Carver's Gap		

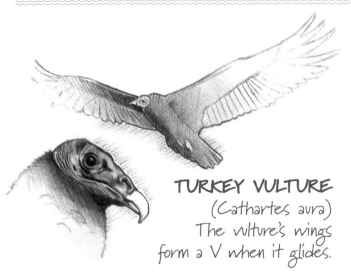

TURKEY VULTURE
(Cathartes aura)
The vulture's wings
form a V when it glides.

reached about 1.2 miles along the road, and after the peak, the road dwindles to a trail.

In about another 500 feet the trail divides. The left trail leads steeply to the saddle between the two peaks of Fork Mountain, hence the mountain's name. The right trail leads through mountain laurel and rock outcroppings, ascends sharply to the other peak at an elevation of 3,615 feet, and offers a grand view. During the leafless seasons, the rim of Doe River Gorge is visible to the north, and Strawberry Mountain is visible to the south.

Directions: Bear Gage Road (County Road 5307) leaves US 19E about 6 miles east from Hampton. It leads north to the southern end of Doe River Gorge Scenic Area. When Bear Gage Road divides, bear left onto Fork Mountain Road for 0.8 mile to the Fork Mountain Free Will Baptist Church. The trailhead is across the road from the parking lot.

Trail: 1.5 miles, one-way.

Degree of difficulty: Moderate.

Elevation: Begins at 2,600 feet and ends at 3,615 feet.

Blaze: None.

THE LAURELS

[Fig. 30(33)] The Laurels is a picnic area built by the Civilian Conservation Corps during the 1930s. This is a beautiful site with two pavilions, rockwork, and footbridges over Dry Creek.

Directions: From Unicoi, take TN 107 southeast. Turn left (northeast) on Scioto Creek Road, and go 6 miles. Turn left (west) on TN 361, then take the first left (southwest) on FR 362 to The Laurels.

Activities: Picnicking and walking.

Facilities: Drinking water, picnicking pavilions, and sanitary facilities.

Dates: Open May to early Oct.

Fees: There is a day-use fee. Pavilions may also be reserved in advance for a fee.

Closest town: Unicoi, about 6 miles northwest.

For more information: Watauga Ranger District, PO Box 400, Unicoi, TN 37692. Phone (423) 735-1500.

Nolichucky/Unaka Ranger District Of Cherokee National Forest

[Fig. 30(29)] The Nolichucky/Unaka Ranger District headquarters in Greeneville should be your first stop for information and maps of the district. A rack contains brochures, maps, and other useful information about the area. This is the southernmost of the two ranger districts of the northern Cherokee National Forest (CNF).

SCARLET TANAGER
(Piranga olivacea)

This bird has a distinctive "chick-kurr" call.

There are about 170,000 acres in the Nolichucky/Unaka Ranger District located in Cocke, Greene, Unicoi, and Carter counties. Primitive camping is allowed anywhere in the district year-round unless areas are otherwise designated. There are over 250 miles of trails, including 30 miles of horse trails and 24 miles of trails for ATVs and motorcycles. There are two designated swimming areas, 13 picnic areas, fishing opportunities on the Nolichucky River, French Broad River, and other streams, and hunting in the Cherokee Wildlife Management Area. Allen Branch Pond is a barrier-free fishing pond with a 0.25-mile interpretive trail. Black bear, white-tailed deer, ruffed grouse, and wild turkey are the most popular game species. To be safe, check with the Nolichucky/Unaka Ranger District before hiking during bear season in November and December—the time of organized hunts with dogs.

Stocked trout streams in Greene County are Horse, Paint, Middle Camp, and Cove creeks. In Cocke County the trout streams are Gulf Fork and Trail Fork creeks. Special regulations apply on many trout streams, and these may change from year to year. For a current issue of regulations, be sure to check with the Tennessee Wildlife Resources Agency, 6032 W. Andrew Johnson Highway, Talbott, TN 37877. Phone (423) 587-7037 or (800) 332-0900.

Possibly the most popular water sport in this part of the forest is whitewater rafting on the Nolichucky, Pigeon, and French Broad rivers (*see* Appendix XX for a list of guides and outfitters). The Nolichucky/Unaka Ranger District maintains the French Broad Boating Site on TN 25, 5 miles east of Del Rio. This site provides carry-down access to the river.

Songbirds in this ranger district include the tufted titmouse (*Parus bicolor*), red-eyed vireo (*Vireo olivaceus*), acadian flycatcher (*Empidinax virescens*), and blackburnian warbler (*Dendroica fusca*). The pine vole (*Microtus pinetorum*), muskrat (*Odontra zibethicus*), red fox (*Vulpes vulpes*), gray squirrel (*Sciurus carolinensis*), fox squirrel (*Sciurus niger*), southern flying squirrel (*Glaucomys volans*), northern flying squirrel (Glaucomys *sabrinus*), queen snake (*Regina septvittata*), spotted salamander (*Ambystoma maculatum*), slender glass lizard (*Ophisaurus attenuatus*), and painted turtle (*Chrysemus picta*) are among the rich fauna living in this district.

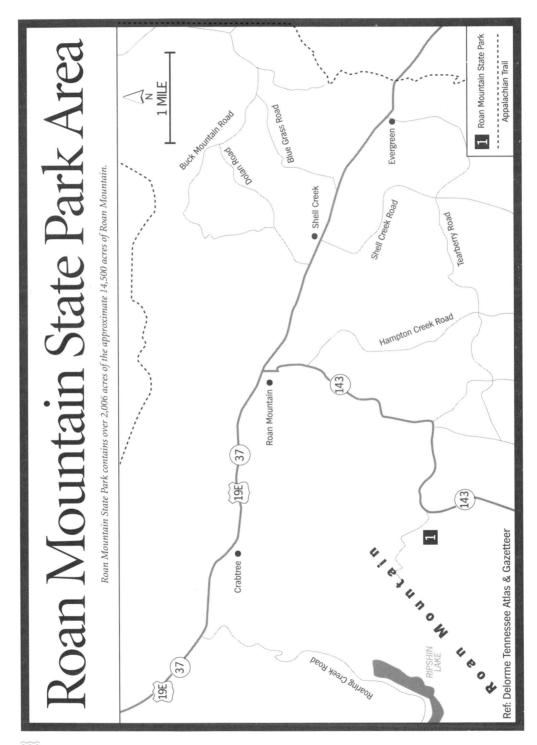

Roan Mountain State Park Area

Roan Mountain State Park contains over 2,006 acres of the approximate 14,500 acres of Roan Mountain.

N
1 MILE

Buck Mountain Road

Dolan Road

Blue Grass Road

Shell Creek Road

Tearberry Road

Evergreen

Shell Creek

Hampton Creek Road

143

37

19E

Roan Mountain

Crabtree

143

1

Roan Mountain

Roaring Creek Road

RIPSHIN LAKE

37

19E

Roan Mountain State Park

Appalachian Trail

Ref: Delorme Tennessee Atlas & Gazetteer

As with the fauna, the Nolichucky/Unaka Ranger District contains much the same flora as the other ranger district in the northern Cherokee National Forest: trillium, pink and yellow lady's slippers, foamflowers, solomon's seal (*Polygonatum biflorum*), hemlocks, oaks, pines, buckeye, mountain laurel, rhododendron, and flame azaleas.

For more information: Nolichucky/Unaka Ranger District, 124 Austin Street, Suite 3, Greeneville, TN 37745. Phone (423) 638-4109.

ROAN MOUNTAIN STATE PARK

[Fig. 31] Roan Mountain, known locally as The Roan, is one of the best-known mountains in the Unakas, and the state park, located just under the mountain's 6,285-foot peak, is one of Tennessee's most visited.

The park contains 2,006 acres of the approximate 14,500 acres of Roan Mountain, and efforts are under way to acquire more acreage to protect the unique features found at this location. In the state park and the portion administered by the U.S. Forest Service, The Roan boasts over 600 acres of Catawba rhododendron, the largest rhododendron garden in the United States, and there are 10 miles of grassy balds stretching from Carver's Gap on Roan Mountain north to Big Hump Mountain, which also display the beauty of the blooming rhododendrons in June. Roan Mountain is one of the very few areas east of the Rocky Mountains where igneous, or volcanic rocks are found. The rocks are called Roan Mountain Gneiss.

Upland slopes of The Roan are covered with oak, hickory, hemlock, black birch (*Betula lenta*), and yellow buckeye (*Aesculus flava*), with Fraser fir and red spruce at the highest elevations. There are more than 180 species of wildflowers in evidence from spring to fall. Deer, foxes, bobcats, skunks, owls, chipmunks (*Tamias striatus*), and an occasional bear may be seen, as well as an abundance of songbirds.

Roan Mountain is one of the only cross-country skiing state parks in the South, with three trails that total 8.5 miles designated for cross-country skiing. There is no ski lodge or lift, and skiers must bring their own equipment.

Camping is permitted in the campgrounds only. There are no backcountry campsites in Roan Mountain State Park.

Directions: Roan Mountain State Park is near the village of Roan Mountain on US 19E between Hampton, TN, and Elk Park, NC.

Activities: Hiking, camping, cross-country skiing, picnicking, swimming, naturalist programs, and guided hiking tours.

LEAST SHREW
(*Cryptotis parva*)
This mammal is also known as the "bee" shrew because it sometimes nests in beehives and feeds on bees and their larvae.

Facilities: Cabins, campgrounds (87 sites with water and electricity, 20 tent sites), restaurant, swimming pool, playground, tennis, volleyball, and basketball courts. There are 6 trails within the park, some interconnected, that range in length from 0.5 mile to 4.5 miles.

Dates: Open year-round, hours are seasonal.

Fees: There is a charge for cabins, swimming, and camping.

Closest town: Roan Mountain, 2 miles north.

For more information: Roan Mountain State Park, 527 Highway 143, Roan Mountain, TN 37687. Phone (423) 772-3303.

HIGHLANDS OF ROAN MOUNTAIN

[Fig. 30(18)] "This management area on Roan Mountain contains some of the most unique flora and fauna in the eastern United States. Much national attention has been directed to identifying and classifying these unique features as well as being recognized for its outstanding scenic qualities of high mountain balds, rhododendron gardens, and spruce-fir timber types…This area is unsuitable for timber production," says the CNF 1988 Management Plan for this area.

Roan Mountain forms an independent portion of the Unaka Range called the Roan Mountain Massif. It contains more than 300 species of plants, some rare and endangered, and wildlife, some at their northern and southern limits.

The balds in this area attract visitors in the spring to see wildflowers bloom. Flowers here include white fringed phacelia (*Phacelia purshii*), mayapples (*Podophyllum peltatum*), white and purple violets (*Viola primulifolia* and *V. papilionacea*), trout lilies (*Erythronium americanum*), hawkweed (*Hieracium* sp.), ragwort (*Senecio* sp.), flame azaleas (*Rhododendron calendulaceum*), and extensive areas of Catawba rhododendron, which are considered the most beautiful in the world. Gray's lily (*Lilium grayi*), Blue Ridge goldenrod (*Solidago spithimaca*), Roan Mountain bluet (*Houstonia purpurea* var. *montana*), and spreading avens (*Geum radiatum*) are among the rare plants living on the massif.

A yellow birch tree (*Betula alleghaniensis*) found in the hardwood forest was determined to be 385 years old. Dwarf beeches near the edge of a bald were dated at 250 years old but are only 12 inches in diameter. They grow so slowly because they are in a marginal area with harsh conditions. Two other unique species in the area are the dwarfed yellow buckeye and table mountain pine (*Pinus pungens*). Also, very old lichens grow among the rocks. Growing at a rate of 0.063 of an inch every quarter-century, some are reported to be centuries old.

The 18-mile Highlands of Roan ridge, influenced by topography, altitude, latitude, and the glaciers, is home to an unusual mix of wildlife. The last ice age forced some animals, such as the Appalachian cottontail (*Sylvilagus obscurus*) and the Southern bog lemming (*Synaptomys cooperi*), south from their former habitats. The warming period that followed the last glaciation made this area hospitable to some animals that were living farther south, and they migrated north. Some of these animals were the opossum and southern flying squirrel (*Glaucomys volans*). These new migrants found their niche among the local populations of bears, bobcats, skunks, foxes, owls, and mice and remain here today.

There are trails on the Highlands of Roan Ridge, which is partially in North Carolina, with the AT being the most popular. The 17 miles of the AT that traverse this area are considered the most beautiful of all 2,100 miles of the AT from Georgia to Maine. In the U.S. Forest Service Composite Plan for the Highlands of Roan it says, "There is no other area…that offers such extensive panoramic views of the high mountain country of the southern Appalachians. Unique is not, at least in this sense, misleading."

The AT crosses the Highlands of Roan, the high and grassy Round and Jane balds, and five mountain peaks above 5,400 feet elevation, including Roan High Knob (elevation 6,285 feet), Little Hump Mountain (elevation 5,549 feet), and Big Hump Mountain (elevation 5,587 feet).

DWARF GINSENG
(Panax trifolius)
Believed by some to be an aphrodisiac, ginseng has been overcollected.

Directions: Take TN 143 south from the town of Roan Mountain about 8.5 miles through Roan Mountain State Park to the area called the Highlands of Roan.

Activities: Picnicking, hiking, camping.

Facilities: Picnic tables, vault toilet.

Dates: Open from May to early Oct.

Fees: None at Carvers Gap trailhead.

Closest town: Roan Mountain, about 8.5 miles north.

For more information: Nolichucky/Unaka Ranger District, 124 Austin Street, Suite 3, Greeneville, TN 37745. Phone (423) 638-4109.

TWIN SPRINGS PICNIC AREA

[Fig. 30(19)] The Twin Springs Picnic Area offers a secluded spot in the woods for a picnic away from the highly visited Roan Mountain State Park.

Directions: Take TN 143 south from the town of Roan Mountain about 8.5 miles through Roan Mountain State Park to Twin Springs Picnic Area. The picnic area is alongside TN 143 about 1 mile after you enter the CNF.

Activities: Picnicking.

Facilities: Picnic tables, vault toilet, and a pavilion.

Dates: Open from May to early Oct.

Fees: None for day use. Pavilion may be reserved in advance for a fee.

Closest town: Roan Mountain, about 8.5 miles north.

For more information: Nolichucky/Unaka Ranger District, 124 Austin Street, Suite 3, Greeneville, TN 37745. Phone (423) 638-4109.

ROAN HIGH KNOB AND CARVER'S GAP

[Fig. 30(20)] Roan High Knob and Carver's Gap are beyond Roan Mountain State Park on TN 143. Carver's Gap is 8 miles from the park and is an obvious gap. The Tennessee/North Carolina border and the AT pass through here, and hikers may access the AT here. There is a

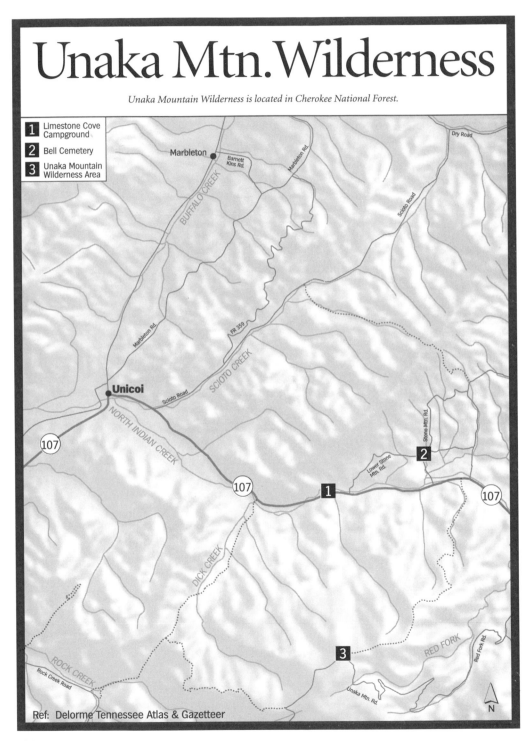

Unaka Mtn. Wilderness

Unaka Mountain Wilderness is located in Cherokee National Forest.

1 Limestone Cove Campground
2 Bell Cemetery
3 Unaka Mountain Wilderness Area

Marbleton

Barnett Kins Rd.

Marbleton Rd.

Dry Road

BUFFALO CREEK

Scioto Road

Marbleton Rd.

FR 359

SCIOTO CREEK

Unicoi

Scioto Road

NORTH INDIAN CREEK

Stone Mtn. Rd.

107

2

Lower Stone Mtn. Rd.

107

1

107

DICK CREEK

RED FORK

3

Red Fork Rd.

ROCK CREEK

Rock Creek Road

Unaka Mtn. Rd.

N

Ref: Delorme Tennessee Atlas & Gazetteer

lovely picnic area across the state line in North Carolina's Pisgah National Forest.

You may want to see the Rhododendron Gardens in North Carolina's Pisgah National Forest. From Carver's Gap, turn right on FR 130 toward Roan High Knob and the dense area of rhododendrons. At the end of FR 130 are picnic tables, restrooms, a parking lot, and an information station (open during the rhododendron bloom in May and June). From the parking lot, the Cloudland Trail (*see* below) begins to the southwest and passes parallel to the road.

Directions: From Roan Mountain State Park go 8 miles south on TN 143 to Carver's Gap at the TN/NC state line.

Activities: Hiking and picnicking.

Facilities: Sanitary facilities at Carvers Gap. Picnic tables, sanitary facilities at Rhododendron Gardens.

Dates: Open year-round, except when closed for snow.

Fees: None at Carvers Gap. There is a day-use fee for recreation areas off FR 130.

Closest town: Roan Mountain, about 10 miles north.

For more information: Pisgah National Forest, Appalachian Ranger District, POB 128, Burnsville, NC 28714. (704) 682-6146.

THE CLOUDLAND TRAIL

[Fig. 30(21)] The Cloudland Trail in North Carolina begins at the parking lot at the end of the paved road FR 130, and leads to a marker where the Cloudland Hotel once stood. In 1885, John Thomas Wilder, a Union general, built a three-story, 166-room hotel here at an elevation of 6,150 feet. The hotel had only four baths. The hotel straddles the Tennessee/North Carolina border. It was so designed to accommodate the drinking of alcohol in the Tennessee end of the hotel. North Carolina was dry at the time.

Railroad tracks were laid from valleys in Tennessee and North Carolina over the mountain to get building materials to the site. Cables connected railroad cars on opposite sides of the mountain; a weighted car on top would go down the mountain, thereby pulling up the car loaded with supplies from the opposite bottom. Supplies were sent up from both states. The hotel was abandoned in 1910.

Directions: From Roan Mountain State Park go 8 miles south on TN 143 to Carver's Gap at the TN/NC state line, turn right (south) on FR 130 and follow it to the end of the paved road. The trailhead is in the parking lot.

Trail: 0.3 mile, one-way.

Elevation: Hotel site is at 6,150 feet.

Degree of difficulty: Easy.

▨ UNAKA MOUNTAIN WILDERNESS AREA

[Fig. 32, Fig. 30(1)] The Unaka Mountain Wilderness Area consists of 4,700 acres in Unicoi County, with its highest point at 4,840 feet at Overlook and its lowest point at 2,600 feet at Timber Trail Branch. The wilderness area is on the north side of Unaka Mountain. The mountain peaks at 5,180 feet and gives its name to the quartzite, Unaka Mountain Quartzite, found on the peak. Its geology is similar to that of the Unaka Range. Unaka Mountain, like most of the CNF, was logged during the early 1900s. Scars from fires in 1925 have healed nicely, and the fire scars of 1978 are well into the healing process.

Of the many waterfalls in the area, Rock Creek Falls is pretty and accessible, but reaching it requires four creek fordings and crossing water up to 2 feet high or more during wet seasons. Large Eastern hemlocks, heath balds, dense upland hardwoods, red spruce at higher elevations, and ridges with spectacular views make trekking through this wilderness a delightful experience. Fraser's sedge (*Dichromena* sp.), Mitchell's St. John's wort (*Hypericum* sp.), rattlesnake root, gentian (*Gentiana* sp.), and mountain mint (*Pycanthemum incanum*) are some of the plants on Unaka Mountain. Wildlife includes bear, deer, grouse, fox, birds, and reptiles common to the CNF.

Directions: Take TN 395 east from Erwin 3 miles to the Rock Creek Recreation Area. Continue on TN 395 around the Unaka Mountain Scenic Area to FR 230 that runs along the wilderness area. Wilderness trailhead parking for Rock Creek Falls is also available in Rock Creek Recreation Area.

Activities: Primitive camping, hunting, fishing.

Facilities: None.

Dates: Open year-round, depending on weather.

Fees: None. There is a per day vehicle use fee in the Rock Creek Recreation Area.

Closest town: Erwin, about 3 miles.

For more information: Nolichucky/Unaka Ranger District, 124 Austin Street, Suite 3, Greeneville, TN 37745. Phone (423) 638-4109.

UNAKA MOUNTAIN SCENIC AREA

[Fig. 30(2)] The Unaka Mountain Scenic Area contains 910 acres. It is contiguous with the Unaka Mountain Wilderness Area at the southwestern end of the wilderness and shares the same flora, fauna, geology, and history.

Directions: Take TN 395 east from Erwin 3 miles to the Rock Creek Recreation Area. Continue on TN 395 to the scenic area.

Activities: Primitive camping, hunting, fishing.

Facilities: None.

Dates: Open year-round, depending on weather.

Fees: None.

Closest town: Erwin, about 3 miles.

For more information: Nolichucky/Unaka Ranger District, 124 Austin Street, Suite 3, Greeneville, TN 37745. Phone (423) 638-4109.

UNAKA MOUNTAIN AUTO TOUR

[Fig. 30(3)] This automobile tour is a 30-mile loop from Erwin through Unicoi County and around the Unaka Scenic and Wilderness areas with stops along the way. Beginning in Erwin, drive north on Main Street and turn right (southeast) on TN 395 (Rock Creek Road) toward the Rock Creek Recreation Area.

The following 14 listings are on the auto tour loop.

Directions: Take TN 395 east from Erwin 3 miles to the Rock Creek Recreation Area, continue on TN 395 around the scenic area to FR 230 that runs along the wilderness area. This auto tour is not appropriate for low-clearance passenger vehicles.

Activities: Camping, hunting, fishing, picnicking, hiking, horseback riding.

Facilities: Picnic tables, drinking water, sanitary facilities, grills, and campsites are available at Rock Creek and Limestone Cove recreation areas.

Dates: Auto route is open year-round, depending on weather. Recreation areas are closed seasonally.

SOUTHERN FLYING SQUIRREL

(Glaucomys volans)
This squirrel doesn't fly but glides through the air.

Fees: There is a charge in recreation areas for camping and day use.

Closest town: Erwin, about 3 miles.

For more information: Nolichucky/Unaka Ranger District, 124 Austin Street, Suite 3, Greeneville, TN 37745. Phone (423) 638-4109.

ROCK CREEK RECREATION AREA

[Fig. 30(4)] Rock Creek Recreation Area at the foot of Unaka Mountain has camping accommodations in a beautiful cove. The Civilian Conservation Corps (CCC) began this as a day-use area in the 1930s, and it was expanded to include camping in the 1960s.

Today, camping and picnicking are available on a first-come first-serve basis. Visitors come here to enjoy the clear, cool water of the swimming area. This area puts campers in a great location to explore Unaka Mountain with the added convenience of nearby Erwin.

Directions: About 3 miles southeast of Erwin on TN 395 (Rock Creek Road).

Activities: Camping, hiking, picnicking, bicycling, swimming.

Facilities: 36 camping sites, some with electrical hookups, that can accommodate RVs 35 feet long. Showers, toilets, grills, lantern posts, hiking trails, bicycle trails, amphitheater, and picnic tables.

Dates: Open May to early Oct.

Fees: There is a charge for camping and day use.

Closest town: Erwin, about 3 miles northwest.

For more information: Nolichucky/Unaka Ranger District, 124 Austin Street, Suite 3, Greeneville, TN 37745. Phone (423) 638-4109.

ROCK CREEK FALLS TRAIL

[Fig. 30(5)] The Rock Creek Falls Trail (#148) begins above Loop C in Rock Creek Recreation Area and travels to Rock Creek Falls. One of the outstanding falls in the area,

BOBCAT
(Lynx rufus)
The bobcat is the most common wild feline in North America. A solitary animal, the bobcat's preys are usually rabbits and mice.

Rock Creek Falls is a tiered falls that drops about 50 feet from overhanging cliffs.

The trail is a wilderness trail that requires fording four creeks and crossing water at least 2 feet high during wet seasons.

Trail: 1.5 miles, one-way.
Degree of difficulty: Moderate.
Blaze: Signed.

ROCK CREEK BICYCLE TRAIL
[Fig. 30(6)] Rock Creek Bicycle Trail (#178), an easy trail for all ages, begins opposite Loop B in Rock Creek Recreation Area and ends at Loop C.

Trail: 0.84 mile, one-way.
Degree of difficulty: Easy.
Blaze: Signed.

HEMLOCK FOREST TRAIL
[Fig. 30(7)] Hemlock Forest Trail (#179) is a short loop trail beginning at Rock Creek Recreation Area amphitheater. This is an easy walk through a charming woodland setting.

Trail: 0.37 mile, one-way.
Degree of difficulty: Easy.
Blaze: Signed.

INDIAN GRAVE GAP
[Fig. 30(8)] From Rock Creek Recreation Area, drive south 3 miles to Indian Grave Gap. TN 395 becomes FR 230. According to local history, this area takes its name from a battle fought here in the 1700s between Indians and settlers. According to the legend, some of the Indians were buried near here, but no evidence has been found.

On the ridgetop it is possible to put one foot in the Pisgah National Forest, North Carolina, while keeping one foot in the Cherokee National Forest, Tennessee. From here the famous Appalachian Trail that runs from Maine to Georgia follows the ridgetop.

This is a scenic viewing area.

BEAUTY SPOT
[Fig. 30(9)] Beauty Spot is about 2 miles farther along FR 230. Grassy openings like this are called balds due to their lack of trees. No one knows exactly what causes balds, but theories include over-grazing by cattle in the eighteenth century, severe forest fires, and feeding buffalo herds in the seventeenth and eighteenth centuries that may have trampled existing vegetation. Beauty Spot's grassy bald is mowed to prevent shrubs like huckleberry (*Vaccinium arboreum*), hawthorn (*Crataegus* sp.), and laurel from encroaching and covering the bald.

The grassy meadows here provide habitat for a variety of animals including deer, rabbits, voles, mice, hawks, owls, foxes, grouse, and many species of songbirds. This is one of the best places to take panoramic photos, as are the next two stops.

This is a scenic viewing and wildlife viewing area.

BEAUTY SPOT GAP

[Fig. 30(10)] Beauty Spot Gap, about 5 miles farther along the drive at an elevation of 4,500 feet, attracts many visitors who come to see wildflowers. Updrafts of wind along the steep mountainside bring thousands of seeds to this area on this side of Unaka Mountain. This area is a microclimate with much fog. The rich and moist soil provides an ideal habitat for trillium, spiderwort (*tradescantia virginiana*), coreopsis (*Coreopsis* sp.), whorled loosestrife (*Lysimachia quadrifolia*), bluebead lily (*Clintonia borealis*), and many other wildflowers.

Near here is believed to be an old silver mine. Many people have searched unsuccessfully for the lost mine that a prospector worked. He traveled on foot through the villages below the mountain en route to his secret mine. It is said that he always returned with some silver. If the mine has been rediscovered, it has been kept a secret.

This is a scenic viewing area.

UNAKA MOUNTAIN OVERLOOK

[Fig. 30(11)] Continue for 3.5 miles to the Unaka Mountain Overlook. The elevation here is nearly 1 mile high. Look 28 miles to the southeast to see Mount Mitchell in North Carolina, the highest mountain east of the Mississippi at 6,684 feet. To the right is Erwin where this tour began. Below is Beauty Spot Gap and farther out lies Beauty Spot.

This is a scenic viewing area.

SPRUCE FORESTS

[Fig. 30(12)] For the next 2 miles, the drive passes through a spruce forest. Many evergreens on Unaka Mountain are red spruce. Spruce forests are dense, and sunlight cannot penetrate them. As a result little groundcover grows here, and the forest is usually cool and moist. These conditions create habitat for unique wildlife species including the lungless Appalachian salamander (*Plethodon jordani*). Instead of laying their eggs in water like most amphibians, they use the moist forest floor. The forest also provides habitat for endangered species such as the northern flying squirrel (*Glaucomys sabrinus*).

WHITE PINE PLANTATION

[Fig. 30(13)] Continue for 3.5 miles to see a white pine plantation on the north side of the road. The CCC planted the white pines in the 1930s. A fire burned this area in 1925 destroying most of the trees and vegetation. The replanting efforts were successful, and the area is once again a productive forest. The remains of an old railroad grade are visible to the left of the curve. The railroad was constructed in the early 1900s to haul logs from here to sawmills in the valleys below. There are no fences, and this is a pretty place to walk through the trees.

This is a scenic viewing and wildlife viewing area, and there are no trails here.

CLEAR FORK CREEK

[Fig. 30(14)] Another 1.4 miles ahead is Clear Fork Creek. The U.S. Forest Service and the Tennessee Wildlife Resources Agency joined forces to enhance brook trout habitat by building fish barriers (waterfalls) like the one here. They help the native brook trout by

Greeneville Area/ Nolichucky River

The Nolichucky River winds through a gorge that is 2,600 feet deep.

Ref: Delorme Tennessee Atlas & Gazetteer

To Johnson City

34

321

11E

172

93

351

70

34

321

107

Tusculum

11E

Greeneville

35

321

350

351

107

70

NOLICHUCKY RIVER

Horse Creek Road

DAVY CROCKETT LAKE

Old Jonesborough Road

Greystone Road

2

3

331

4

5

88

6

7

8

9

351

70

10

1	Nolichucky Ranger District of Cherokee National Forest Headquarters	**6**	Old Forge Recreation Area	
2	Bald Mountain Ridge Scenic Area	**7**	Petes Branch Falls	
3	Horse Creek Recreation Area	**8**	Marguerite Falls and Marguerite Falls Trail	
4	Horse Creek Trail	**9**	Little Jennings Creek Trail and Round Knob Picnic Area	
5	Jennings Creek Trail	**10**	Paint Creek Recreation Area & Corridor	

- - - - - - Appalachian Trail
.... Trail

N

2 MILES

keeping nonnative rainbow trout from traveling upstream to where brook trout live. Rainbows, a highly competitive fish, compete for food and habitat of brook trout, a less competitive fish that prefers the cooler, upper sections of mountain streams.

This is pretty creek, but not exceptional. The main features here are the fish barriers and a rare flower, the large round-leaved orchid (*Platanthera orbiculata*). There are no trails here.

BELL CEMETERY AT LIMESTONE COVE

[Fig. 30(15)] From Clear Fork Creek continue to TN 107 and turn left (west). Just beyond the county road entering from the right (north) is Bell Cemetery in the community of Limestone Cove. This is a Civil War cemetery. The area is known for its Civil War history and for being the place where Andrew Jackson first entered Tennessee. He rode through Limestone Cove on his way to the state's first town, Jonesborough, to establish his law practice. This is a good place to see deer, bear, and turkey.

LIMESTONE COVE RECREATION AREA

[Fig. 30(16)] About 1.5 miles farther down TN 107 is Limestone Cove Recreation Area. It offers primitive camping at the northern end of Unaka Mountain, east of the town of Unicoi. This 18-unit campground was built in the 1960s and offers a relaxed atmosphere. Playing in the creek and fishing for rainbow and brown trout are favorite activities of children and adults alike.

Activities: Camping, picnicking, and fishing.

Facilities: 18 campsites, grills, lantern posts, and vault toilets. Day-use area features a trail, pier, and old railroad grade.

Dates: Open May to early Oct.

Fees: There is a charge for day use and camping.

Closest town: Unicoi, 3 miles west.

For more information: Nolichucky/Unaka Ranger District, 124 Austin Street, Suite 3, Greeneville, TN 37745. Phone (423) 638-4109.

ERWIN NATIONAL FISH HATCHERY AND UNICOI HERITAGE MUSEUM

[Fig. 30(17)] Continue on TN 107 for about 7 miles through the town of Unicoi to the Erwin National Fish Hatchery and Unicoi Heritage Museum. Congress made provisions for this fish hatchery in 1894, and it was established in 1897. The U.S. Fish and Wildlife Service operates it. Several strains of rainbow trout and fertilized eggs are produced here, and the hatchery supplies brood trout and eggs to other hatcheries, research facilities, and other countries. Brood fish weigh between 3 and 6 pounds. More than 18 million eggs are shipped each year. Viewing is allowed in a few raceways and indoor tanks. There are nature trails that go by ponds on the 30-acre area.

Streams stocked with trout in the Nolichucky/Unaka Ranger District include South and North Indian, Coffee Ridge, Rocky Fork, Spivey, and Clarks creeks.

The Unicoi County Heritage Museum, once scheduled to be razed, was saved through the efforts of concerned citizens. This beautiful Victorian-style house built in 1903, once the home of the superintendent of the hatchery, is used to display artifacts and exhibits that interpret local

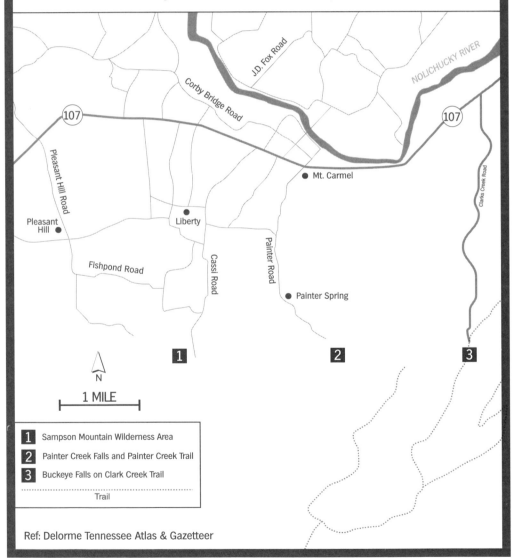

Sampson Mountain Wilderness Area

The Sampson Mountain Wilderness Area consists of 8,319 acres.

N

1 MILE

1 Sampson Mountain Wilderness Area

2 Painter Creek Falls and Painter Creek Trail

3 Buckeye Falls on Clark Creek Trail

Trail

Ref: Delorme Tennessee Atlas & Gazetteer

history from Indian times, through the Civil War, to the beginning of the twentieth century. Next door is Erwin City Park with swimming pool, tennis courts, and ball parks.

Directions: North of Erwin about 1 mile on TN 107 on the left (west).

Activities: Guided hatchery tour, museum, picnicking, and wildlife viewing.

Facilities: Picnic tables and nature trail.

Dates: Visitor center and picnic pavilion open daily, year-round. Tours on request. Museum is open May to Oct.

Fees: None.

For more information: Erwin Fish Hatchery, 750 Johnson City Highway, Erwin, TN 37650. Phone (423) 743-4712.

NOLICHUCKY RIVER

[Fig. 33] The Nolichucky River's churning whitewater winds through one of the deepest gorges in the eastern United States. The gorge is 2,600 feet deep. Its steep slopes and rising cliffs provide spectacular scenery. A railroad track lies along the southern side of the river, but there are no maintained trails in the gorge. Hikers are welcome to explore on their own, and there is good smallmouth bass fishing here.

U.S.A. Raft (*see* Appendix C), a commercial rafting company on the river, is one of the outfitters that operates where the road ends after turning right (south) at the Nolichucky Bridge. The company offers shuttle service, cabins, and camping. Rafters are shuttled to Poplar, North Carolina, for a day-long trip down the Nolichucky River.

Directions: From TN 181 (1923), take Exit 15 (Jackson Love Exit), turn east, and take the first right onto TN 1923 (before the old church). Go 0.75 mile, and turn left at the Chestoa Recreation Area sign onto River Road. At the next stop sign, turn left. Cross the bridge, take an immediate right onto Jones Branch Road, and continue 1.25 miles to U.S.A. Raft.

Activities: Fishing, wading, rafting, canoeing, kayaking, inner-tubing, swimming, hiking, biking. Camping at an independently run campground.

Facilities: Cabins, campgrounds, bunkhouse, volleyball court, hot showers, and picnic tables.

Dates: Access to the river open year-round but whitewater rafting limited to Mar. to Oct. Camping open Apr. to Oct.

Fees: There is a charge for water craft rentals, cabins, and camping.

Closest town: Erwin, about 5 miles northeast.

For more information: U.S.A. Raft/Nolichucky Campground, Box 2 Jones Branch Road, Erwin, TN 37650. Phone (800) USA-RAFT or (423) 743-7111.

SAMPSON MOUNTAIN WILDERNESS AREA

[Fig. 34] The Sampson Mountain Wilderness Area consists of 8,319 acres in Unicoi, Greene, and Washington counties, in the Nolichucky/Unaka District, with its highest elevation of 4,060 feet on Sampson Mountain and its lowest elevation of 1,780 feet on Cassi Creek. Scenic views and Buckeye Falls are the drawing cards to this wilderness.

Buckeye Falls, about 700 feet, is touted as the tallest waterfall in the eastern United States. Painter Creek Falls is an impressive 200-foot waterfall but is difficult to reach. Neither of these are true waterfalls but are cascades. A cascade is a series of small waterfalls whereas a waterfall is one vertical drop.

Timber dating to 1800 exists in the wilderness area, and in fact, there are 536 acres of trees here that are over 100 years old. But much of the area was logged prior to National Forest wilderness designation in 1986. Much of the timber was cut in the 1930s, and fires since then have left scars. Scars from the large fire of 1952 have healed, but scars from the 1981 fire that burned 1,600 acres along Painter Creek are still healing. No timber harvesting is allowed in wilderness areas.

Among the second-growth timber are wildflowers including showy orchids (*Galearis spectabilis*), foamflowers (*Tiarella cordifolia*), yellow lady's slipper (*Cypripedium calceolus*), bloodroot (*Sanguinaria canadensis*), alumroot (*Heuchera villosa*), and a species listed as threatened in Tennessee, turkeybeard (*Xerophyllum asphodeloides*).

Directions: From Erwin, take TN 81 to TN 107 and on to County Road 25, Clarks Creek Road. Turn left on Clarks Creek Road until it dead-ends at the trailhead for the wilderness. Access is also available from Horse Creek Recreation Area (*see* page 191).

Activities: Camping, hiking, hunting, fishing.

Facilities: None.

Dates: Open year-round.

Fees: None at trailhead on Clarks Creek Road. There is a day-use fee at Horse Creek Recreation Area.

Closest town: Erwin, about 19 miles.

For more information: Nolichucky/Unaka Ranger District, 124 Austin Street, Suite 3, Greeneville, TN 37745. Phone (423) 638-4109.

BUCKEYE FALLS ON CLARK CREEK TRAIL

[Fig. 34(3)] Buckeye Falls is reached by hiking along the Clark Creek Trail (no Forest Service number) with its trailhead at the end of Clarks Creek Road (County Road 25) at a barrier. Walk along Clark Creek. You will see a sign marking the wilderness area. Continue along the creek and look for arrows, "BF," or other markings on rocks and trees. The last 0.4 mile is described as grueling.

This waterfall is cited as a 500- to 700-foot falls, but Buckeye Falls is actually a cascade with a horsetail form. During dry weather there is no falls, and in winter there are several hundred feet of walls of ice down the cliffs.

Trail: 3.8 miles, one-way.

Elevation: Begins at 1,840 feet and ends at 3,000 feet.

Degree of difficulty: Strenuous.

Blaze: "BF" and arrows.

PAINTER CREEK FALLS AND PAINTER CREEK TRAIL

[Fig. 34(2)] The Painter Creek Trail (no Forest Service number) only goes for 1.1 miles, but Painter Creek Falls is another 1.25 miles farther upstream. The trail beyond the mile mark has stretches that are difficult to maneuver due to thick rhododendron. Switching from one side of the stream to the other makes walking easier in places. The trail ascends steeply at the 200-foot falls. If you want to continue upstream, the right side of the falls appears to be the best route, but be very careful. At least two people who have fallen here have died.

Painter Creek Road turns south off TN 107 leading into the wilderness area. There is a small parking area just before the road ends at a gate blocking vehicles from entering the wilderness area. The parking area is on private land and permission must be obtained to park there. Walk along the road beyond the gate for 0.2 mile, and then turn left on the trail.

HIGHBUSH
BLUEBERRY
(Vaccinium corymbosum)

Trail: 2.35 miles, one-way.

Elevation: Begins at 1,760 feet and ends at 2,400 feet at the foot of the falls.

Degree of difficulty: Strenuous.

Blaze: None.

HORSE CREEK RECREATION AREA

[Fig. 33(3)] Horse Creek Recreation Area, one of the most popular of the recreation areas in the Nolichucky/Unaka Ranger District, offers fishing, swimming, picnicking, and camping. At an elevation of 1,720 feet, the area is nestled into a hardwood cove on Horse Creek.

This recreation area is popular with swimmers, picnickers, and campers. A mountain stream feeds the swimming hole. There is one 0.2-mile trail in the recreation area, but several longer ones are nearby.

From May 1 to September 30, Horse Creek is under special fishing regulations. Only disabled persons, children 12 and under, and senior citizens (65 years old or older) are allowed to fish for a two fish limit. Upstream from the recreation area at the junction of Squibb Creek and Horse Creek, fishing is open to all.

Directions: From Greeneville take TN 107 east through Tusculum, and turn right on County Road 2519, the county road becomes FR 94. Horse Creek Recreation Area is 2.8 miles from TN 107.

Activities: Camping, picnicking, swimming, and fishing.

Facilities: There are 15 campsites (3 are trailer sites), drinking water, sanitary facilities, grills, picnic tables, and pavilion.

Dates: Open May 15 to Dec. 15.

Fees: There is a charge for camping and day use. Pavilion may be reserved in advance for a fee.

Closest town: Greeneville is about 10 miles northwest.

For more information: Nolichucky/Unaka Ranger District, 124 Austin Street, Suite 3, Greeneville, TN 37745. Phone (423) 638-4109.

▓▓ BALD MOUNTAIN RIDGE SCENIC AREA

[Fig. 33(2)] Bald Mountain Ridge Scenic Area, 8,653 acres in Greene County in the Nolichucky/Unaka Ranger District, is southwest of and adjacent to the Sampson Mountain Wilderness Area. Bald Mountain Ridge Scenic Area has been one of the most popular area in the Nolichucky/Unaka District for a long time with the locals, and its popularity is growing. It has 14 trails and balds on Cold Spring Mountain. Nearby recreation areas, Horse Creek and Old Forge, offer picnicking, swimming, and camping.

Greystone Mountain rises to 3,240 feet, Round Knob ascends to 3,280 feet, and Bald Mountain reaches 3,000 feet, providing some spectacular views. Another source for scenic views is Blackstack Cliffs on the Appalachian Trail (AT) between Jones Meadow and Big Butt, which soars to 4,838 feet. Photographs from these peaks taken with a 200mm lens or larger can rekindle memories of your visit for years to come.

Even though this scenic area has many trails, they are not hiked often; therefore, anyone seeking a wilderness experience can find it here. Hiking along these trails is not easy because many are not marked or maintained. In fact, hikers should have topographic maps of the area with them due to the rugged terrain. Of the 14 trails totaling about 29 miles (not including the AT) in the Bald Mountain Scenic Area, one of the most scenic and shortest, the 0.6-mile Marguerite Falls Trail (#189) (see page 195), leads to one of the best waterfalls in the area, Marguerite Falls. The longest trail, the Horse Creek Trail (#94) (see page 193), leading to the top of Cold Spring Mountain, runs 4.7 miles and is open to four-wheeling.

Mountain bicycles may use forest trails designated for that purpose, all forest development roads, and areas behind gated forest roads that are closed to motorists. The Doctor's Ridge Trail (#194), Poplar Cove Trail (#22), Cowbell Hollow Trail (#24), and Cold Spring Mountain Road (FR 5094) are the most popular mountain bicycling routes in Bald Mountain Ridge Scenic Area. FR 5094 accommodates ATVs and other off-road vehicles. Street-legal motorcycles and four-wheel-drive vehicles are allowed on open forest roads, but they must be equipped with spark arresters. Unlicensed motorcycles, four-wheel-drive vehicles, and three- and four-wheelers are not allowed on forest roads. These policies are enforced to prevent resource damage, to minimize conflict with other forest users and resources, and to comply with Tennessee state law. Horses and bicycles may be ridden on many roads, both open and closed to motorists.

Timber companies denuded this area in the pre-1930s, but the forest has recovered. The high ridges, such as Round Knob, are covered in oak forests. Cove hardwoods fill the hollows. Blueberry, rhododendron, and flame azalea abound on the southern slopes of Reynolds Ridge, Green Ridge, and Greystone Mountain. The thick vegetation is home to game animals and other forest wildlife. There are more than 200 acres of open land for wildlife that are closed to vehicles.

Directions: There are many access points into Bald Mountain Scenic Area. See directions in trail descriptions that follow.

Activities: Hiking, hunting, horseback riding, camping, fishing, picnicking, swimming, biking.

Facilities: Hiking trails, ATV trails, bicycle trails, horse trails. Picnic tables, sanitary facilities, drinking water, campsites, and trailer spaces are available in nearby recreation areas.

Dates: Open year-round. Recreation areas are closed seasonally.

Fees: There is a charge for camping and day use in recreation areas.

Closest town: Greeneville.

For more information: Nolichucky/Unaka Ranger District, 124 Austin Street, Suite 3, Greeneville, TN 37745. Phone (423) 638-4109.

HORSE CREEK TRAIL

[Fig. 33(4)] Horse Creek Trail is also FR 94, which is open to four-wheel-drive vehicles, off-road vehicles, three- and four-wheelers, and motorcycles. Because it is extremely rough, you may choose to bike, hike, or ride a horse instead of hiking. The trail begins at the end of the paved road at Horse Creek Recreation Area and ends at the parking area near the top of Cold Spring Mountain for a distance of about 4.75 miles. There is a day-use fee at Horse Creek Recreation Area.

At the end of Horse Creek Trail is a junction with the AT, which provides access to Big Butt Mountain and other trails in the Bald Mountain Ridge Scenic Area. (Remember the AT is a trail for foot travel only.) The views from Big Butt, a grassy bald, are worth the walk and the bald is a good place to camp.

At the junction with the AT, a right (southwest) turn leads to the Sarvis Cove Trail (#14) in 0.2 mile and the grassy bald on Cold Spring Mountain. The balds on Cold Spring Mountain are good examples of typical grassy balds found in the southeastern United States, and offer views of the Appalachian Mountains to the southwest. These balds are also good camping sites.

The Sarvis Cove Trail (#14), a trail roughly following Sarvis Creek, is a good way to return to the Horse Creek Recreation Area. Although the trail is not managed, it has yellow, sometimes difficult to see, blazes. The Sarvis Cove Trail is 2.9 miles long to where it joins the Poplar Cove Trail (#22), a hiking and horse trail that is 2.8 miles long. The Poplar Cove Trail goes downhill from an elevation of 4,560 feet via a dozen switchbacks and through dense hemlock forests to rejoin the Horse Creek Trail just above the Horse Creek Recreation Area. Along Sarvis Creek are a small waterfall and cascades. Wildflowers make a splash in the spring under the hemlocks, rhododendrons, and mature hardwoods. The forest becomes

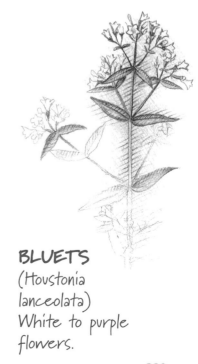

BLUETS
(Houstonia lanceolata)
White to purple flowers.

193

younger farther down the mountain.

Trail: 2.4 miles, one-way.

Elevation: Begins at 1,800 feet and ends at 4,550 feet.

Degree of difficulty: Easy to moderate.

Blaze: Yellow.

PETES BRANCH FALLS

[Fig. 33(7)] Petes Branch Falls is only worth the walk following a recent rain or during a wet season. But use caution after a heavy downpour because there are several fords to negotiate. The double, fan-tailed waterfalls drop 45 feet through a quartzite cleft in an impressive bluff. Mature poplar, hemlock, and buckeye surround the area.

Directions: Take the Horse Creek Trail (FR 94) (*see* page 193) to spur road 94B. Look for a backcountry parking area. Cross the creek to the Petes Branch Trail, and the falls are 0.6 mile up the branch.

Trail: 1.7 miles, one-way.

Elevation: Begins at 2,160 feet and ends at 2,600 feet.

Degree of difficulty: Moderate.

Blaze: None.

JENNINGS CREEK AND COWBELL HOLLOW TRAILS

[Fig. 33(5)] The easy and wide Jennings Creek Trail (#21) begins at the south end of the Old Forge Recreation Area (*see* page 195), crosses Jennings Creek, and passes by the swimming hole at the bottom of a falls. Look for a carved stone that says it's 2 miles to Round Knob Picnic Area to the right, but stay on this trail. When returning, you will come back along the trail to the right, which is the Little Jennings Creek Trail.

During the last of April and first of May, wild iris, foamflower, and white trillium bloom abundantly about 0.7 mile along the trail. Buckeye, poplar, hemlock, dogwood, and sugar maple shelter the creek and trail.

The Jennings Creek Trail leads to the Cowbell Hollow Trail (#24) that climbs 1.4 miles from the creek up Round Knob. Mountain bikers looking for a challenge may also use the Cowbell Hollow Trail. At the beginning of the trail the forest is much like that along Jennings Creek, and then as the altitude increases, the forest changes to red maple, oak, pine, rhododendron, and mountain laurel with an understory of wintergreen, trailing arbutus, and galax.

Trail: 3.1 miles, one-way.

Elevation: Begins at 1,920 feet and ends at 2,280 feet.

Degree of difficulty: Easy to moderate.

Blaze: Yellow.

THE LITTLE JENNINGS CREEK TRAIL AND ROUND KNOB PICNIC AREA

[Fig. 33(9)] Cowbell Hollow Trail ends at Round Knob Picnic Area where there are picnic tables, toilets, and a large pavilion with a stone fireplace. The Civilian Conservation Corps built the shelter during the 1930s. From here it is 2.1 miles back to the Old Forge Recreation Area down the Little Jennings Creek Trail (#195), also called the Round Knob Branch Trail. Round Knob is at an elevation of 3,280 feet, and the northwesterly walk back to the Old Forge Recreation Area is mostly downhill to 1,920 feet elevation where the trail joins the Jennings Creek Trail. The Little Jennings Creek Trail is also a horse and bike trail.

Those looking for wildflowers will enjoy a spring hike to see wild iris, trillium, showy orchids (*Galearis spectabilis*), jack-in-the-pulpit (*Arisaema triphyllum*), false solomon's seal, solomon's seal, and wild ginger (*Asarum canadense*).

Heart leaf, another name for wild ginger, blooms from April through May. Its heart-shaped leaves hide the brown flower called little brown jugs or little pig's feet. Indians boiled the root, claiming the tea was an oral contraceptive. Pioneer women used it as an analgesic to ease the pains of childbirth. The plant has proven to contain chemicals that are effective antibiotics. When the root is cooked with sugar, it is used as an alternative for ginger.

Trail: 1.9 miles, one-way.
Elevation: Begins at 3,100 feet and ends at 1,920 feet.
Degree of difficulty: Easy.

MARGUERITE FALLS AND MARGUERITE FALLS TRAIL

[Fig. 33(8)] Marguerite Falls, one of the most outstanding features in the Nolichucky/Unaka Ranger District, is fan-shaped and drops about 50 feet, cascading over stair-step rocks. The Marguerite Falls Trail (#198) rises about 500 feet through hardwoods and a gorge with sandstone cliffs, and just before reaching the falls, it offers a good view of Cathedral Rock—an impressive projection from the cliffs.

The Tennessee Wildlife Resources Agency, Trout Unlimited, and the U.S. Forest Service are working to restore brook trout in this stream, the West Fork of Dry Creek.

Directions: From Greeneville take TN 107 east through Tusculum, turn right on TN 351 and then left at TN 350 (Greystone Road). After about 5 miles, look for directional signs and turn right onto Shelton Mission Road. In 2.7 miles, turn left on FR 5099, a 0.5-mile road providing access to trailhead parking for the Marguerite Falls Trail, Phillips Hollow Trail, and Bullen Hollow Trail. Take the right-hand trail and bear to the left at the first split onto the Marguerite Falls Trail. The creek requires four fordings in the next 0.6-mile walk. Glen Falls, an 8-foot falls, is another 0.1 mile farther upstream. This waterfall makes a splendid photo opportunity.

Trail: 0.6 mile, one-way.
Elevation: Begins at 2,000 feet and ends at 2,500 feet.
Degree of difficulty: Moderate to strenuous.
Blaze: Blue.

OLD FORGE RECREATION AREA

[Fig. 33(6)] Old Forge Recreation Area offers a lovely 5-mile walk on the Jennings Creek Trail Complex (Jennings Creek Trail [#21], Cowbell Hollow Trail [#24], and Little Jennings Creek Trail [#195]) (*see* page 194) to see wildflowers in spring and to Round Knob. On a 1.5-mile hike along the pretty Jennings Creek Trail (#21) are trailing arbutus, several violets, iris, and trillium that attract wildflower-seekers in the spring. Horseback riders and mountain bikers are welcome to use this trail too.

Directions: From Greeneville take TN 107 east through Tusculum, turn right on County Road 2519 (Horse Creek Road). Old Forge Road (FR 331) enters from the right. Turn right (southwest) following the FR 331 for about 3 miles to Old Forge Recreation Area.

Activities: Camping, hiking, picnicking, horseback riding, swimming, trout fishing, and hunting.

Facilities: Tent camping, toilets, water, hiking, horse trails.

Dates: Open May to Oct.

Fees: There is a charge for camping and day use.

Closest town: Greeneville is about 10 miles northwest.

For more information: Nolichucky/Unaka Ranger District, 124 Austin Street, Suite 3, Greeneville, TN 37745. Phone (423) 638-4109.

PAINT CREEK RECREATION AREA AND CORRIDOR

[Fig. 33(10)] The Paint Creek Corridor is a 5-mile stretch between the Paint Creek Campground in the Paint Creek Recreation Area and the French Broad River. While scenic driving is a popular activity along FR 41, the road running along the corridor, bicycling and horseback riding are becoming more common.

At one end of the corridor is Paint Creek Recreation Area, nestled in a mountain cove along Paint Creek and featuring campsites shaded by rhododendron, hemlock, and laurel that offer streamside views.

Paint Creek provides two interesting falls that you can drive to, Kelley Falls and Dudley Falls. Swimming, wading, and fishing for stocked and wild trout are popular activities at Paint Creek.

Kelley Falls drops about 20 feet over the face of bedrock spanning about 50 feet, forming a block, or rectangular-shaped falls. Get to these falls by driving 0.5 mile from Moses Bend Picnic Area along Paint Creek on FR 41 and parking at the turnout. Kelley Falls is a short walk downstream.

Dudley Falls drops from a constricted width in Paint Creek about 12 feet into a punchbowl. This pool is suitable for swimming, but warning signs are posted to keep daredevils from jumping from the cliffs. Get to this waterfall by driving 2.5 miles from Moses Bend Picnic Area on FR 41 and parking in the signed lot.

Directions: From Greeneville take TN 107 south across Nolichucky Dam. At Rollins Chapel Road turn left (east), also look for the Paint Creek sign. Continue 0.4 mile, then turn right (south) onto FR 31 to go to the Paint Creek Recreation Area. Turn right (south) off FR 31 onto FR 41 to reach the Moses Bend Picnic Area and other recreation areas along the 5-mile corridor.

Activities: Camping, hiking, picnicking, trout fishing, hunting, and bicycling.

Facilities: RV and tent camping, toilets, and water in Paint Creek Recreation Area. Picnic tables and toilets along the corridor.

Dates: Recreation areas open May to Oct. Corridor is open year-round.

Fees: There is a charge for camping in Paint Creek Recreation Area and for day-use along the Paint Creek Corridor.

Closest town: Greeneville is about 10 miles northwest.

For more information: Nolichucky/Unaka Ranger District, 124 Austin Street, Suite 3, Greeneville, TN 37745. Phone (423) 638-4109.

ROUND MOUNTAIN CAMPGROUND

[Fig. 44(20)] Hikers and campers are attracted to this scenic site near the top of Round Mountain. In the summertime it is a naturally air-conditioned spot to pitch a tent or park a trailer. At 3,100 feet it is one of the highest campgrounds in the CNF. Altitude, dense vegetation of rhododendrons, and a small mountain stream lower temperatures.

Hikers come here because the Appalachian Trail (AT) is nearby. The Walnut Mountain Trail (#135) runs 2.07 miles along the AT between this campground and the Walnut Mountain shelter. The popular 7-mile AT hike between Lemon Gap and Max Patch is only 10 miles away. This scenic stretch of trail features spectacular high-elevation vistas and outstanding wildflower displays in spring and summer.

This is a remote campground accessed by a winding, narrow, two-lane gravel road. All camping is on a first-come first-served basis.

Directions: From Newport, travel south on TN 25/70 approximately 11 miles. Turn right onto TN 107, and follow camping symbols to the campground.

Activities: Camping. Hiking nearby.

Facilities: 12 campsites (some are trailer sites) and 2 picnic sites. Each campsite has a picnic table, fire ring, and lantern post. Campground features a hand-pumped water well and toilets.

Dates: Usually open from mid-Apr. to mid-Dec.

Fees: There is a charge for camping and day use.

Closest town: Newport, approximately 11 miles.

For more information: Nolichucky/Unaka Ranger District, 124 Austin Street, Suite 3, Greeneville, TN 37745. Phone (423) 638-4109.

EASTERN MOLE
(Scalopus aquaticus)
Spending most of its life underground, the mole feeds on earthworms and insect larvae in its passageway of tunnels 10 inches below the surface.

Historic Sites in the Upper Unaka Mountains

SYCAMORE SHOALS

[Fig. 30(34)] As settlers began coming into the area from Virginia and across the mountains from North Carolina, they established the first permanent American settlement outside the original 13 colonies at Sycamore Shoals (now Elizabethton). Soon afterward, in 1772, the settlers compiled the Articles of the Watauga Association, the first majority-rule system of American democratic government, and five members were elected to "govern and direct for the common good of the people."

As more pioneers arrived at Sycamore Shoals, it became the hub of the frontier, with trails connecting it with Bristol; Rocky Mount, the first territorial capital; and settlements in North Carolina and South Carolina.

In 1775, the Transylvania Purchase, the largest real estate transaction in United States history, took place at Sycamore Shoals. The Transylvania Company, led by Richard Henderson of North Carolina, purchased over 20 million acres of land from the Cherokee Indians, all the lands of the Cumberland River watershed and extending to the Kentucky River. The price was 2,000 pounds, along with 8,000 pounds of goods. Twelve hundred Indians spent weeks at Sycamore Shoals in counsel before signing the deed over the objections of Chief Dragging Canoe.

After the Transylvania Purchase, Dragging Canoe was determined to drive the whites from Cherokee lands. During the Revolutionary War, English agents, whose plan called for the Indians to attack the settlers from the rear while the English attacked them from the sea, aided him. A band of warriors laid siege to Fort Watauga, which had been built as a refuge. Most of the settlers had fled, but Lt. Col. John Carter, Capt. James Robertson (founder of Nashville in 1779), and Lt. John Sevier (Tennessee's first governor in 1796) held the fort two weeks until the Indians departed.

On September 25, 1780, the Overmountain Men, 1,100 strong, assembled at Sycamore Shoals in preparation for their march over the mountain in search of the Tory militia under the command of British Maj. Patrick Ferguson. Eleven days later, the Overmountain Men, under the command of Col. John Sevier and Col. Isaac Shelby, met and defeated Ferguson's army at the Battle of King's Mountain. The victory was a critical link in the chain of events that led to the eventual surrender of the British forces and an end to the Revolutionary War.

Directions: Sycamore Shoals was renamed Elizabethton. The historic area is on US 321/TN 91 in the northwestern part of the city of Elizabethton toward Johnson City, on the south side of the Watauga River.

For more information: Sycamore Shoals State Historic Park, 1651 W. Elk Avenue, Elizabethton, TN 37643. Phone (423) 543-5808.

SYCAMORE SHOALS STATE HISTORIC PARK

[Fig. 30(35)] Sycamore Shoals is a day-use area that has a visitor center with an interpretative facility, information, historic displays, and a theater open daily from daylight to dark year-round. There is also a reconstruction of Fort Watauga and a short scenic trail leading from the fort to the historic shoals. This is also the beginning of the Overmountain Victory National Historic Trail, which follows the route of the volunteer army on its march to face Maj. Patrick Ferguson's troops. The entire trail, except a 2-mile section in Tennessee on Roan Mountain, follows roads and highways.

Directions: On US 321/TN 67 in the northwestern part of the city of Elizabethton toward Johnson City, on the south side of the Watauga River.

Activities: Walking trail, picnicking, video of Overmountain People, and outdoor drama in July called *Wataugans*.

Facilities: Visitor center, museum, theater, gift shop, amphitheater, bookstore, and picnic area.

Fees: There is a charge for the drama.

Dates: Open year-round.

For more information: Sycamore Shoals State Historic Park, 1651 W. Elk Avenue, Elizabethton, TN 37643. Phone (423) 543-5808.

DOE RIVER COVERED BRIDGE

[Fig. 30(36)] The Doe River Covered Bridge, built in 1882, is believed to be the oldest such bridge in the state that remains in use. Made of oak planks, hand-forged nails, and threaded spikes, it is called the Queen of the South, and it remains the most admired and photographed historic structure in Carter County. The bridge withstood the Great May Flood of 1901 that destroyed all other bridges along the Doe River and provided people on the east side fleeing the rising water their only escape route. The structure has been termed an engineering feat and is listed in the Historic Engineering Record. It is one of two bridges in the state identified by a Tennessee Historical Commission marker and is also included in the National Register of Historic Sites.

Directions: The bridge is located just off US 19E in downtown Elizabethton.

For more information: Elizabethton/Carter County Chamber of Commerce Tourism Council, 500 19 E Bypass, Elizabethton, TN 37643. Phone (800) 347-0208.

Galax

Galax (*Galax aphylla*) only grows in the southern Appalachian Mountains and is vital to the florist industry as long-lasting greenery. The leaves are shiny green and distinctively shaped. Its stalk flower looks something like the foamflower, composed of many small white flowers, and blooms from May to July and from August to October.

YELLOW BUCKEYE
(Aesculus octandra)
Growing as tall as 90 feet, the yellow buckeye has 4—6 inch leaves and yellow flowers.

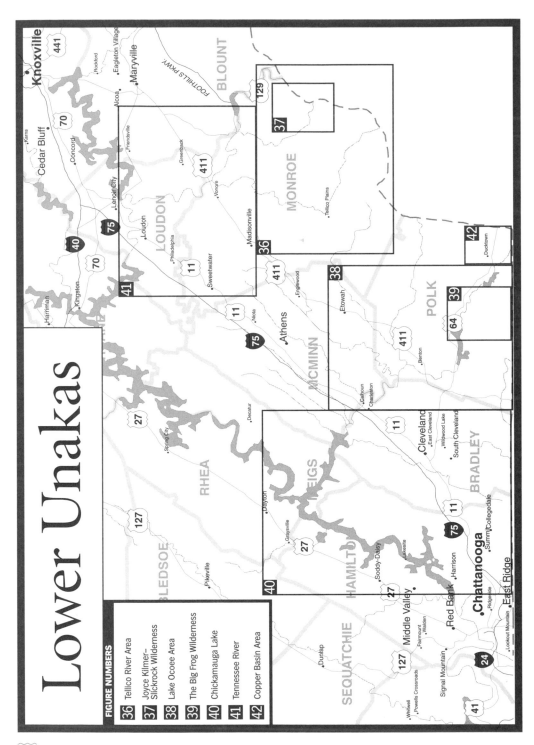

Lower Unakas

FIGURE NUMBERS

36	Tellico River Area
37	Joyce Kilmer–Slickrock Wilderness
38	Lake Ocoee Area
39	The Big Frog Wilderness
40	Chickamauga Lake
41	Tennessee River
42	Copper Basin Area

Lower Unaka
Mountains

S ince 1891, the federal government has set aside land for forest reserves, but in 1911, Congress passed the Weeks Law that allowed the purchase of land for national forests. The Weeks Law was perhaps more important to the eastern United States than to the West because growing populations in the East had already claimed most of the land. The goals of national forest laws—to protect watersheds and provide timber for the increasing population—were established by the Forest Management Act of 1897.

The Cherokee National Forest (CNF), like most southern national forests, once belonged to large timber companies. Much of the land was scarred from cutting and repeated wildfires. During the early days of the national forests in Tennessee, lands were purchased for two national forests. The lands in the northeastern part of the state became the Unaka National Forest that included land in North Carolina and Virginia. The lands in southeastern Tennessee became the Cherokee National Forest,

[*Above:* A view of the Appalachian Mountains on a clear day]

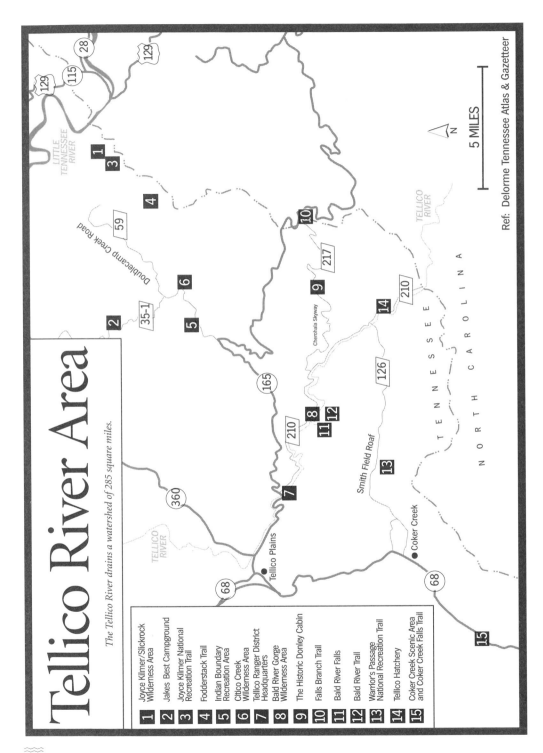

Tellico River Area

The Tellico River drains a watershed of 285 square miles.

1. Joyce Kilmer/Slickrock Wilderness Area
2. Jakes Best Campground
3. Joyce Kilmer National Recreation Trail
4. Fodderstack Trail
5. Indian Boundary Recreation Area
6. Citico Creek Wilderness Area
7. Tellico Ranger District Headquarters
8. Bald River Gorge Wilderness Area
9. The Historic Donley Cabin
10. Falls Branch Trail
11. Bald River Falls
12. Bald River Trail
13. Warrior's Passage National Recreation Trail
14. Tellico Hatchery
15. Coker Creek Scenic Area and Coker Creek Falls Trail

Ref: Delorme Tennessee Atlas & Gazetteer

5 MILES

to be covered here, and included land in Alabama, Georgia, and North Carolina.

President Woodrow Wilson, on June 14, 1920, officially proclaimed the two national forests be combined into one and called the Cherokee National Forest. In 1936, the national forests were reorganized by state lines. That gave Tennessee its present day form of the CNF. Separated from the Great Smoky Mountains National Park (GSMNP), the 633,000 acres of the CNF were separated into the northern and southern divisions. The southern division contains three ranger districts—(from north to south) Tellico, Hiwassee, and Ocoee—all named for the rivers flowing through them. These districts total 304,000 acres of timberland and watersheds.

Much of the early work of the United States Department of Agriculture's Forest Service concentrated on fire-fighting and acquisition of land. In the 1930s, the Civilian Conservation Corps built many recreation areas in the CNF.

The CNF takes its name from the Cherokee Indians who lived here before European settlers claimed the land for their own. Since 1960 when Congress passed the Multiple Use-Sustained Yield Act, the Forest Service has officially managed national forests for multiple purposes, including water, timber, wildlife, soil, minerals, cultural resources, wilderness, and outdoor recreation.

The Lower Unakas are sometimes referred to as the Unicoi Mountains. The geology of the Lower Unaka Mountains is similar to the Upper Unakas, and the flora and fauna are essentially the same in the southern division as in the northern one.

For more information: Forest Supervisor's Office, 2800 North Ocoee Street, Cleveland, TN 37320. (423) 476-9700.

Tellico Ranger District

Headquarters for the Tellico Ranger District is about 5 miles east of Tellico Plains just off the Cherohala Skyway on Forest Road (FR) 210, which runs along the Tellico River. Nestled at the end of a Forest Road (look for the headquarters sign) in an idyllic setting is a historic CCC complex converted into offices for this district. This is a good starting point for gathering information about the area. Friendly personnel, maps, brochures, and books will make your visit more rewarding.

The Cherohala Skyway, a 52-mile scenic highway, connects Tellico Plains, Tennessee with Robbinsville, North Carolina. "Cherohala" is a combination of the names of the two national forests—the Cherokee and Nantahala—that the highway links. The skyway, one of only 20 Federal Highway Administration Scenic Byways in the nation, begins at an elevation of 900 feet just east of Tellico Plains and follows the Tellico River gorge for 5 miles. Then it rises with the Unaka Mountains to an elevation of 5,390 feet at Santeetlah Gap before descending toward Robbinsville. Twenty-two miles east of Tellico Plains is the highest major bridge in the southeastern United States. It is 700 feet long at an elevation of 4,000 feet. The 26-mile mark is near where the Trail of Tears that forced thousands of Cherokee Indians to Oklahoma began.

The Tellico Ranger District contains 123,372 acres in Monroe County with its highest peak, Haw Knob, reaching 5,472 feet above sea level. Although there are many undeveloped areas available for camping, there are eight developed campgrounds. Hikers may trek 150 miles on 29 trails, and equestrians have access to 31 miles along 8 trails. If touring by automobile is more appealing, the Cherohala Skyway is a unique drive providing many grand vistas with parking at prominent overlooks. The Tellico River Road (FR 210), North River Road (FR 217), and Citico Creek Road (FR 35) are the other popular scenic routes.

Be sure to take your camera and plenty of film to capture the spectacular scenes from river bottom to mountaintops. Some of the best places to shoot on the Cherohala Skyway are Lake View in Tennessee, and Sugar Cove and Hooper Bald in North Carolina. A 200mm lens or larger will help bring the distant mountains and valleys closer for a deeper appreciation later.

Bald River Falls will also make you glad you had a camera. Here is a good place to try different filters for special effects and to use different shutter speeds to create a milky, silky effect with the falling water. Early morning would be the time to snap a misty shot.

Anglers enjoy 38 miles of stocked rainbow and brown trout waters with 19 miles managed for brook trout. Indian Boundary Lake offers 96 acres of warm-water fishing, with species including blue catfish (*Ictalurus furcatus*), largemouth bass (*Micropterus salmoides*), smallmouth bass (*Micropterus dolomieu*), bluegill (*Lepomis macrochirus*), and redbreasted sunfish (*Lepomis auritus*).

Hunters of big and small game are welcomed in the Tellico Ranger District. About 50 permanent forest openings are maintained for wildlife. Bear, boar, deer, turkey, grouse, squirrel, and raccoon are the sought-after species. The boar are reported to have been imported from the German Hartz Mountains to stock a preserve in North Carolina—but they didn't stay there. Today they are referred to as Russian, or "Rooshian" boar, and the escapees' descendants populate these mountains.

The seepage salamander (*Desmognathus aeneus*), masked shrew (*Sorex cinereus*), star-nosed mole (*Conylura cristata*), ginseng (*Panax quinquefolius*), huckleberry (*Gaylussacia ursina*), and hedge nettle (*Stachys* sp.) are a few other animals and plants found in the Tellico District.

No complete botanical surveys have been conducted, but some areas have been studied. Citico Creek Wilderness Area has 536 vascular plant species and 70 species of trees. Vascular plants include most flowering plants, conifers, ferns, and club mosses.

Today's forests in the Tellico Ranger District are thought to closely resemble ancient ones consisting of cove hardwoods in coves or valleys below 4,500 feet elevation. Dominant species include yellow-poplar, yellow birch, Eastern hemlock, silverbells, buckeye, basswood, sugar maple, Southern yellow pine, and white pine. Doghobble (*Leucothoe axillaris*), rhododendron, wild hydrangea (*Hydrangea arborescens*), and strawberry bush (*Euonymus americanus*) are shrubs found in the understory.

The Tellico Ranger District contains many of the spring wildflowers found throughout the Unaka Mountains. Blue cohosh (*Caulophyllum thalictroides*), squirrelcorn (*Dicentra canadensis*), umbrella-leaf, (*Diphylleia cymosa*) sharp-lobed hepatica (*Hepatica acutiloba*), bishop's cap (*Mitella diphylla*), and bloodroot (*Sanguinaria canadensis*) are among these.

About 19 percent (23,659 acres) of the Tellico Ranger District is in the National Wilderness Preservation System to maintain naturalness and solitude. While hiking, camping, hunting, fishing, and riding horses (in designated areas) is allowed, no motorized vehicles or equipment, bicycles, or other wheeled carriers are.

For more information: Tellico Ranger Office, U.S. Forest Service, 250 Ranger Station Road, Tellico Plains, TN 37385. Phone (423) 253-2520.

Yellowfin Madtom

The yellowfin madtom (*Noturus flavipinnin*) is known to exist in only three stream reaches: Citico Creek in the Tellico Ranger District of the CNF; the Powell River in Hancock and Claiborne counties, Tennessee; and Copper Creek in Scott and Russell counties, Virginia. Attempts are under way to re-establish a population in Abrams Creek in the Great Smoky Mountains National Park.

The small catfish grows to 4.5 inches long and has a yellowish tinge on the paler parts of its body. This secretive fish is seldom seen by most people visiting a stream because it hides under flat rocks and undercut banks. It feeds at night on aquatic insects.

TELLICO RIVER

[Fig. 36] Originating in the Snowbird Mountains of North Carolina, the Tellico River drains a watershed of 285 square miles, taking its water 53 miles to the Little Tennessee River at Tellico Lake. Many streams feed the river, with Sycamore Creek, North River, and Bald River among the major contributors. There are many especially scenic views along the river.

When the water is low in the Tellico River it is not suitable for navigation within the Tellico Ranger District, but when the water is high, it provides canoeists and kayakers ample opportunity to run the river and be challenged by rapids up to Class V.

Rivers were historically used as routes through the rough mountain terrain. The Tellico River was in use as a corridor for at least 12,000 years. Native Americans used this area, the *te-li-quo*, which is Cherokee for plains, for hunting game and gathering food. For the last 2,000 years it served for agriculture.

The Tellico River is lined with sites showing signs of use by Indians. Cherokee Indians lived and farmed the land along the river until 1819 when a boundary was established giving whites the land downstream from river-mile 34. The two groups lived together until 1838 when the Cherokee were forced by the whites to move to Oklahoma.

With more land opened to the settlers, they began subsistence farming, harvesting some timber, and raising livestock on the open range. Cattle, pigs, and sheep grazed on

Copperhead

Although the bite of a copperhead is painful, it is rarely lethal. Copperheads' dens are usually among rocks, where they hibernate from late October until April. In summer they may migrate as far as 0.4 mile to lower elevations. Copperheads kill their prey by injecting them with venom through their fangs that rotate about 90 degrees from the roof of their mouth. Copperheads shed these hypodermic injectors about once a month. Several new fangs are lined up behind the functioning ones as replacements. Their venom is about six times weaker than a rattlesnake's, but copperheads bite more people.

land after it was cleared by fire and grasses grew there. Remnants of old farmsteads can be found throughout the area today.

After the Civil War, the Tellico River area became the target of timber companies. Babcock Timber Company acquired the area and hauled out timber from the late 1800s until the late 1920s. Remnants of the logging operation exist today. In fact, FR 120—the Tellico River Road—was one of the logging railroad beds. Some old splash dams can be found along the river.

After the denuding of the forests, erosion became a serious problem. The Weeks Act of 1911 gave the federal government authority to purchase private lands east of the Mississippi River and establish national forests in the region to manage the natural resources of the southern Appalachian Mountains. The Tellico River area was only one small area that suffered over-logging and erosion.

In 1920, the Tellico River corridor became part of the Cherokee National Forest and the Nantahala National Forest. Within a decade the area was ironically blessed by the Great Depression. Civilian Conservation Corps members found work all along the Tellico River, and, like the Indians before them, their work is evident today. One of the CCC efforts still functioning is the Tellico Ranger Station, which was the first CCC camp constructed in Tennessee and among the first 50 built in the United States.

The Forest Service has managed, maintained, and improved the Tellico Ranger District since taking over in the 1920s.

Directions: Going east from Tellico Plains the river runs along the highway. Turn right into the Tellico Ranger District following the river. Access points can be found where bridges cross the river along FR 210 and at the various parking areas along the river.

Activities: Fishing, primitive camping, hiking, canoeing, kayaking, horseback riding, and picnicking.

Facilities: Hiking trails and picnic tables.

Dates: Open year-round.

Fees: There is a charge for camping in some areas.

Closest town: Tellico Plains, about 4 miles from the ranger district.

For more information: Tellico Ranger Office, U.S. Forest Service, 250 Ranger Station Road, Tellico Plains, TN 37385. Phone (423) 253-2520.

THE HISTORIC DONLEY CABIN

[Fig. 36(9)] According to legend, a man named Hughes built a one-room cabin in this remote part of the South during the 1860s to hide from being asked to be a soldier in the Civil War. After the war, there was an addition to the one-room cabin. Construction continued until its log style included Swiss, German, and English designs. The fireplace is the oldest part of the cabin.

STONEFLY NYMPH
(Family Perlidae)

Jack Donley purchased the cabin and some adjacent land after the war. The pioneer became fairly well known: Donley Mountain and Donley Branch bear his name. He lived until 1941, and his descendants maintained possession of the cabin until 1994.

Today, the pioneer cabin is restored, and it can be rented for a three-night maximum through the Tellico Ranger District.

Directions: From Tellico Plains go east on Cherohala Skyway about 4 miles, turn right on FR 210, and continue for 12 miles. Turn left (north) on FR 217 and continue for about 6 miles to the cabin.

Activities: Rental cabin and hiking.

Dates: Open year-round.

Fees: There is a rental charge.

Closest town: Tellico Plains, about 20 miles.

For more information: Tellico Ranger Office, U.S. Forest Service, 250 Ranger Station Road, Tellico Plains, TN 37385. Phone (423) 253-2520.

CITICO CREEK WILDERNESS AREA

[Fig. 36(6)] The Tellico Ranger District contains three wilderness areas: the Joyce Kilmer/Slickrock Wilderness designated in 1975, and the Citico Creek Wilderness and the Bald River Gorge Wilderness designated in 1984.

Citico Creek Wilderness Area is north of the Cherohala Skyway on the North Carolina border. Fodderstack Trail (#95) runs from the north at Salt Spring Mountain south to and along the Tennessee/North Carolina border, forming the dividing line between the Joyce Kilmer/Slickrock Wilderness Area and Citico Creek Wilderness Area. The Unicoi Mountains and steep ridges running along Citico Creek Wilderness Area's western side create steep slopes with rugged terrain covered in oaks and pine.

Citico Creek Wilderness Area, 16,226 acres in Monroe County, is the largest wilderness area in the CNF with about 58 miles of trails. Citico, derived from the Cherokee word *sitiku*, means "a place of clean fishing water."

The timber in this area was cut in the early 1900s except for about 400 acres of hemlock and hardwoods in the Jefferys Hell section in the southern end of Citico Creek Wilderness Area. A fire, in 1925, destroyed half of what would later become the Citico Creek Wilderness area, many of the structures needed to harvest timber, and the timber-

Pileated Woodpecker

The pileated woodpecker, also called a logcock, is reclusive. It is more often heard than seen. It has a wingspan of 30 inches and flies with a swooping, undulating motion. Its size and red topknot make identification easy. It nests in holes in large trees and is a beneficial bird because it eats carpenter ants, caterpillars, cockroaches, and other wood-destroying insects but rarely eats berries.

carrying railroad. The operation was deemed too expensive to reconstruct for the remaining, nearly unreachable 400 acres. Today hikers can take Falls Branch Trail (#87) and Jefferys Hell Trail (#196) for a walk through the old-growth forest of hemlock and poplar.

Jefferys Hell was named, as one story has it, for a man who went looking for his lost dogs and became lost himself. The story doesn't say if he found his dogs, but it claims he lost his life. Legend has it that before he went into the dense rhododendron and mountain laurel growth he said, "I'll find them if I have to go to hell for them."

Another account is that Jeffery wandered from camp among the uninhabited wild mountains of steep cliffs, ravines, and dense, tangled growths of rhododendron and doghobble. After two days without food, he came out at the headwaters of the Tellico River and was asked where he had been. His answer was, "I don't know, but I have been in hell."

Directions: To get to the Citico Creek Wilderness from Tellico Plains go east on Cherohala Skyway for about 16 miles to FR 345. Turn left (northeast) on FR 345 and continue to the junction with FR 35-I. Turn right (east) on FR 35-I and continue for about 3 miles to the Citico Corridor Area.

Activities: Hiking, hunting, fishing, camping, horseback riding.

Facilities: None.

Dates: Open year-round.

Fees: None.

Closest town: Tellico Plains, about 20 miles.

For more information: Tellico Ranger Office, U.S. Forest Service, 250 Ranger Station Road, Tellico Plains, TN 37385. Phone (423) 253-2520.

FALLS BRANCH TRAIL

[Fig. 36(10)] The Falls Branch Trail (#87), a short, easy hike, leads to the 80-foot waterfall on Falls Branch at the southern end of Citico Wilderness Area. This scenic trail runs north from the Cherohala Skyway at Rattlesnake Rock parking lot. This trail is marked at the western end of the parking lot. The trail passes through the old-growth hemlock and hardwoods saved by the fire of 1925. A springtime hike will treat you to blooming wildflowers.

The trail follows the stream down to the falls. There are several good views of the falls, but do not climb them. They are slick with moss and dangerous.

This is considered one of the prettiest waterfalls in the southern CNF, dropping about 30 feet, cascading down a large escarpment for several feet, then plummeting about 30 feet more in a horsetail shape. The falls looks like angel hair when the flow is light but is dramatic when the flow is heavy.

Directions: Go east from Tellico Plains on the Cherohala Skyway about 25 miles to Rattlesnake Rock observation site parking lot on the north side of the skyway.

Trail: 1.3 miles, one-way.

Elevation: Begins at 3,960 feet and ends at 3,520 feet.

Degree of difficulty: Easy–moderate.

Blaze: White.

FODDERSTACK TRAIL

[Fig. 36(4)] The Fodderstack Trail (#95), the longest trail in the area, runs along the divide between the Citico Creek Wilderness Area and the Joyce Kilmer/Slickrock Wilderness Area, and gives hikers access to other trails into both wildernesses. Beginning at Farr Gap where you can see into the Joyce Kilmer/Slickrock Wilderness Area, the hike passes close to the Little Fodderstack, the Big Fodderstack, and the Rockstack. These three rises offer good views, but the best view of the countryside is from Bob Stratton Bald in North Carolina via the Stratton Bald Trail

PERSISTENT TRILLIUM
(*Trillium persistens*)
A rare flower, it grows under or near rhododendrons.

(#54), which leads east where the Fodderstack Trail heads southwest at the southern edge of the wilderness area. The hike is 0.4 mile.

The Bob Stratton Bald rises to 5,261 feet with views of the Great Smoky Mountains National Park to the north and the Slickrock Creek valley. Campsites in the grass and spring water on the southeastern side make this an excellent resting spot before returning to the Fodderstack Trail and finishing the hike to Cold Spring Gap on the Cherohala Skyway.

Fodderstack is also a horse trail with several campsites but no potable water. Horses can drink form several streams.

Directions: From Tellico Plains go east on Cherohala Skyway for about 16 miles to FR 35 leading to Indian Boundary Lake, continue on FR 35 for about 6 miles and turn right on Doublecamp Road, continue for 6.7 miles to the parking area. A short way up the road is Farr Gap and the trailhead.

Trail: 10.5 miles, one-way.

Elevation: Begins at 2,800 feet and ends at 4,400 feet.

Degree of difficulty: Strenuous.

Blaze: White.

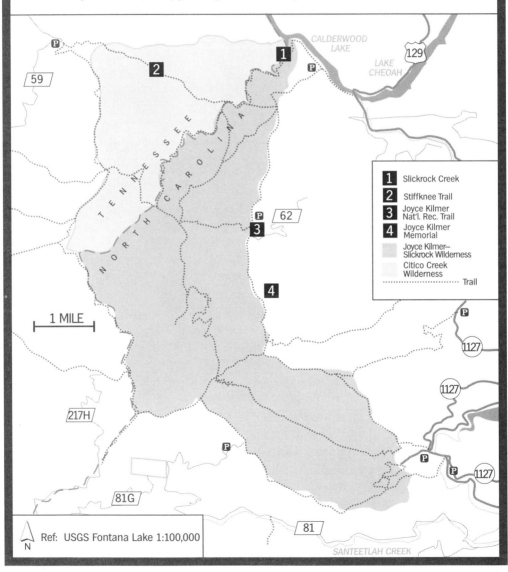

Joyce Kilmer–Slickrock Wilderness

The U.S. Forest Service purchased 13,055 acres in the Little Santeetlah basin from Gennett Lumber Company in 1935 for $28 an acre, thereby preserving what is now the Joyce Kilmer–Slickrock Wilderness.

1 Slickrock Creek

2 Stiffknee Trail

3 Joyce Kilmer Nat'l. Rec. Trail

4 Joyce Kilmer Memorial

Joyce Kilmer–Slickrock Wilderness

Citico Creek Wilderness

········· Trail

1 MILE

Ref: USGS Fontana Lake 1:100,000

N

JOYCE KILMER/SLICKROCK WILDERNESS AREA

[Fig. 36(1), Fig. 37] The Joyce Kilmer/Slickrock Wilderness Area contains 17,013 total acres in Tennessee and North Carolina with 3,881 acres in the Tellico District. The Joyce Kilmer Memorial Forest within the Nantahala National Forest in North Carolina is a 3,840-acre preserve named for the poet who wrote "Trees." A well-worn trail from the trailhead shelter, which has the poem framed on one of its walls, leads through trees 400 years old, 150 feet tall, and 20 feet around.

Kilmer, killed in 1918 during a World War I reconnaissance mission in France, wrote his famous poem about the white oak trees on the campus of Rutgers College, which he attended from 1904 to 1906. Veterans of Foreign Wars asked the federal government for a memorial to Kilmer. This led to the Forest Service being asked to locate a section of virgin forest to fulfill the veterans' wish.

In 1935, such a tract was located but the price was high—seven times more than the going rate. At $28 per acre, 13,055 acres were purchased from Gennett Lumber Company in Little Santeetlah basin. The virgin forest had been spared the saw because the Lakes Calderwood and Santeetlah flooded the railroad tracks used to haul out trees. The timber company went bankrupt before another way to move the logs was ready. As fire saved some trees in the Citico Creek Wilderness Area, water saved the trees that became a tribute to the poet and *Croix de Guerre* soldier on July 30, 1936, exactly 18 years after his death.

Directions: To get to Joyce Kilmer/Slickrock Wilderness Area go east from Tellico Plains on the Cherohala Skyway to FR 81. Turn left (northeast) on FR 81, continue to where the road T-bones with NC 143, then turn left (north) on NC 143, continue about 3.5 miles, and turn left (west) into the wilderness area.

Activities: Hiking, hunting, fishing, camping, picnicking, horseback riding.

Facilities: None.

Dates: Open year-round.

Fees: None.

Closest town: Robbinsville, NC, about 17 miles.

For more information: Cheoah Ranger Station, Route 1, Box 16A, Robbinsville, NC 28771. Phone (704) 479-6431.

JOYCE KILMER NATIONAL RECREATION TRAIL

[Fig. 36(3), Fig. 37(3)] The Joyce Kilmer National Recreation Trail offers two loops (shaped like a figure eight) through the forest. The loop nearer the parking lot is 1.25 miles long and the upper trail is 0.75 mile long. Pay attention to the warning about falling limbs, called widow-makers. Poplar trees typically lose their lower limbs and some of the old trees are dying. Clearing them is prohibited. Also note the large rock with a plaque honoring Kilmer located across the trail from the shelter.

Along the trail, in addition to the huge poplar and hemlocks, are red maple, beech, red oak, yellow birch, and Carolina silverbell (*Halesia carolina*). Wildflowers include trilliums, violets, galax, crested dwarf iris (*Iris cristata*), and jack-in-the-pulpit among the

Why Leaves Change Color

It is not fully understood why leaves change color, but a complex interaction of chemicals, temperatures, photoperiod, and moisture are involved. During shorter photoperiods trees release a kind of hormone that restricts the flow of sap to the leaves, causing them to change color. The leaf's green color comes from chlorophyll, which is eventually used by the leaf but not replaced. This allows the other colors that were masked by the green to show. Browns, yellows, oranges, and similar colors become outstanding. Reds and purples, not present before the change in the photoperiod, develop in the sap of the leaf cells. Red, purple, and their combinations depend on the breakdown of sugars in the presence of bright light as the level of phosphate in the leaf dwindles. The brighter the light during this period the more brilliant the colors.

nearly ubiquitous ferns. Wildlife is same as in the CNF but songbirds love these woods. Wood thrushes (*Hylocichla musteline*) supply one of the prettiest songs in the forest. Other songs come from ovenbirds (*Seiurus aurocapillus*), golden-crowned kinglets (*Regulus satrapa*), brown creepers (*Certhia familiaris*), and scarlet tanagers (*Piranga olivacea*).

Trail: 0.75-mile and 1.25-mile loop trails.

Degree of difficulty: Easy.

Blaze: Signed.

CAMPING AREAS

There are three notable camping areas in the Tellico District and several smaller ones. The three detailed here are unique among all the camping grounds, providing more activities and facilities.

INDIAN BOUNDARY RECREATION AREA

[Fig. 36(5)] The Indian Boundary Recreation Area is the largest and most popular campground in this district. The Indian Boundary Lake is the focal point of the campground during the summer when it is open for swimming. The lake is open to fishing all year but no gasoline motors are allowed to operate in the lake. Hikers use the campground as a base camp to take advantage of nearby trails.

Directions: Go east from Tellico Plains on the Cherohala Skyway for about 16 miles, turn left on FR 345 and follow signs to the campground and lake.

Activities: Camping, picnicking, swimming, fishing, biking, boating, horseback riding, and hiking.

Facilities: Water, sanitary facilities, bathhouses, electricity at some sites, launch ramp, and fishing pier with handicap access.

Dates: Camping from Apr.–Sept., and boating and fishing year-round.

Fees: There is a charge for camping, picnicking, and swimming.

Closest town: Tellico Plains, about 17 miles west.

For more information: Tellico Ranger Office, U.S. Forest Service, 250 Ranger Station Road, Tellico Plains, TN 37385. Phone (423) 253-2520 or (800) 289-2267.

JAKES BEST CAMPGROUND

[Fig. 36(2)] Jakes Best Campground is north of Indian Boundary Lake on FR 35-1 (Citico Creek Road). This is a pack-it-in, pack-it-out area with trailer space but no electricity. This place attracts anglers, hunters, and hikers.

Directions: Go east from Tellico Plains on the Cherohala Skyway for about 16 miles, turn left on FR 345, turn right on FR 35-1 for about 8 miles.

Activities: Hiking, hunting, camping, and fishing.

Facilities: Sanitary facilities.

Dates: Open year-round.

Fees: There is a charge for camping.

Closest town: Tellico Plains, about 23 miles southwest.

For more information: Tellico Ranger Office, U.S. Forest Service, 250 Ranger Station Road, Tellico Plains, TN 37385. (423) 253-2520 or (800) 289-2267.

YOUNG BRANCH HORSE CAMP

[Fig. 41(4)] Young Branch Horse Camp is the northernmost camping area in the Tellico District. This unique campground is restricted to people with saddle, pack, and draft animals. There are special regulations for this area, and there is space for 25 animals and 35 people (seven campsites hold a maximum of five people each).

Directions: Go east from Tellico Plains on the Cherohala Skyway for about 16 miles, turn left on FR 345, turn right on FR 35-1 for about 12 miles.

Activities: Horseback riding, picnicking, camping, and fishing.

Facilities: Sanitary facilities and campsites.

Dates: Open year-round.

Fees: Fees are charged and reservations are required.

Closest town: Tellico Plains, about 29 miles southwest.

For more information: Tellico Ranger Office, U.S. Forest Service, 250 Ranger Station Road, Tellico Plains, TN 37385. Phone (423) 253-2520 or (800) 289-2267.

TELLICO HATCHERY

[Fig. 36(14)] It is listed on maps as the Pheasant Field Fish Hatchery, but its present name is the Tellico Hatchery. It is located on FR 210 at Sycamore Creek.

Originally this was a trout-rearing station, not a hatchery, built by the CCC between 1939 and 1941 with six circular pools inside a frame house. In the 1940s six raceways were added. In the 1960s the rearing station grew to become a hatchery. The raceways were rebuilt with the addition of a work station, a manager's residence, and a line of 16 raceways and earthen pools.

In 1991 it became a hatchery for southern and northern strains of brook trout and brown trout. The fish, about 9 inches long, come from the Dale Hollow Hatchery and are intensively managed for stocking in local waters: 12 miles of the Tellico River, 6 miles of the Citico Creek, a handicapped-accessible facility called Green Cove Pond, and a few small streams in Polk County. In 1991 the 16 raceways and earthen pools were removed and replaced with 28 modern raceways.

There is some natural reproduction of trout in the stocked waters but not enough to keep up with demand. All the trout streams are put-and-take. A daily permit helps fund the stocking program.

Southern brook trout restoration is in the research stage here. The upper end of Sycamore Creek was stocked with brook trout, and heavy rains washed some down among the browns and rainbows stocked several years ago in the lower section. Studies are under way to see how the less-competitive brook trout fares among the other trout.

Directions: Go east from Tellico Plains about 4 miles, turn right (southeast) on FR 210, and continue for about 12 miles to the hatchery at FR 61.

Activities: Hatchery tour.

Facilities: Water and sanitary facilities.

Dates: Open daily, year-round

Fees: None.

Closest town: Tellico Plains, about 17 miles.

For more information: Tellico Fish Hatchery, POB 265 Tellico Plains, TN 37385. Phone (423) 253-2661.

BALD RIVER GORGE WILDERNESS

[Fig. 36(8)] The Bald River Gorge Wilderness Area (3,887 acres) lies between FR 210 to the north and FR 126 to the south. The Basin Lead marks the eastern boundary but there is no discernible landmark denoting the western boundary. The gorge has steep slopes; clean, cold-water streams containing trout; beautiful wildflower displays in spring; gorgeous colored leaves in fall; and small and big game, as well as wildlife typical in the CNF.

The wilderness area, as in most sections of the Tellico Ranger District, was logged in the 1920s but experienced less agricultural use. Subsistence farming may have been conducted here before timber companies bought the land, but evidence is difficult to find, except at the head of Brookshire Creek near the North Carolina border.

Some logging continued into the 1960s, and during the 1980s clear-cut logging occurred south of Henderson Top near Maple Camp Lead and at the head of Bald River. Conservationists fought a long time to have the Bald River watershed protected. It took until 1984 to get the Bald River Gorge area protected, but today it is safe from logging.

Directions: Go east from Tellico Plains on the Cherohala Skyway about 5 miles, turn right on FR 210, and continue to the wilderness area.

Activities: Fishing and hiking.

Facilities: None.

Dates: Open year-round.

Fees: None.

Closest town: Tellico Plains, about 11 miles.

For more information: Tellico Ranger Office, U.S. Forest Service, 250 Ranger Station Road, Tellico Plains, TN 37385. (423) 253-2520.

BALD RIVER TRAIL

[Fig. 36(12)] Only one trail completely traverses the Bald River Wilderness Area, the Bald River Trail (#88). The Bald River Trail follows the Bald River upstream through a deciduous forest with some white pine, hemlock, doghobble, mountain laurel, and rhododendron. Along the trail are small camping areas, which see heavy use from spring through the fall. There are some nice views of the river and one good view of a large cascade. Cantrell parking area on FR 126 is the end of the trail.

Trail: 4.8 miles, one-way.

Elevation: Begins at 1,380 and ends at 1,860

Degree of difficulty: Easy–moderate.

Blaze: Signed.

BALD RIVER FALLS

[Fig. 36(11)] The Bald River Falls, lauded as the most impressive waterfall in eastern Tennessee and accessible by automobile, tumbles about 90 feet into a small plunge pool. This very attractive waterfall attracts so many visitors and photographers it may be difficult to find a parking space.

The waterfall is segmented, cascading across the wide rock rim, and then becoming a single stream before reaching the bottom. There is an excellent view from the nearby bridge.

Directions: Go east from Tellico Plains of the Cherohala Skyway about 5 miles. Turn right on FR 210, and continue for 6 miles.

Trail: A brief walk to the falls from the parking lot.

Degree of difficulty: Easy.

Blaze: Signed.

WARRIOR'S PASSAGE NATIONAL RECREATION TRAIL

[Fig. 36(13)] Before the settlers came, the Cherokee used the Warrior's Passage Trail. As with most trails, it was probably a game trail that Indians used, and through the years it became part of their road system connecting tribes and hunting grounds. White settlers and British soldiers improved the road and built a bridge over the

Eastern Wild Turkey

The Eastern wild turkey, the most numerous of the five turkey subspecies, was shunned by the Indians. Turkey numbers were high, and turkeys were easily hunted before the white settlers came. Some Indian tribes would not eat the bird because they thought any bird that was easily hunted was dim-witted, and they feared that dim-wittedness could be acquired by eating it.

Turkeys were trapped in the Ocoee Ranger District for repopulating other areas of the state. In fact, the Ocoee Ranger District is where the first cannon-propelled net was used in the state for capturing the bird. An open space near well-known turkey haunts would be baited with grain in front of the cannons. When the birds came to eat the grain, the cannons were triggered and a net flew over the birds and trapped them.

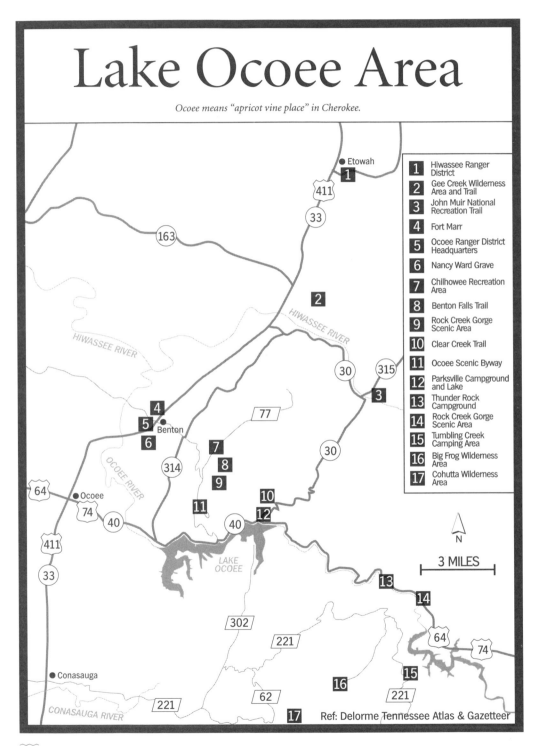

Lake Ocoee Area

Ocoee means "apricot vine place" in Cherokee.

1 Hiwassee Ranger District
2 Gee Creek Wilderness Area and Trail
3 John Muir National Recreation Trail
4 Fort Marr
5 Ocoee Ranger District Headquarters
6 Nancy Ward Grave
7 Chilhowee Recreation Area
8 Benton Falls Trail
9 Rock Creek Gorge Scenic Area
10 Clear Creek Trail
11 Ocoee Scenic Byway
12 Parksville Campground and Lake
13 Thunder Rock Campground
14 Rock Creek Gorge Scenic Area
15 Tumbling Creek Camping Area
16 Big Frog Wilderness Area
17 Cohutta Wilderness Area

3 MILES

Ref: Delorme Tennessee Atlas & Gazetteer

Tellico River. This trail connected with Fort Loudoun on the Little Tennessee River in the mid-1700s. Once a trail through the southern Appalachian Mountains, today a small 5-mile section remains in the Tellico Ranger District and is protected under the 1988 CNF Management Plan.

The trail is difficult to follow in places because blazes are sometimes hard to find and the trail is not maintained.

The prominent feature 0.8 mile off the trail on Waucheesi Mountain Road (FR 126C) is the Waucheesi tower at an elevation of 3,692 feet. Once a fire tower, it is now a microwave relay station. From this high point, you have a spectacular 360-degree view with the Bald River Gorge Wilderness to the northeast.

Trail: 5.3 miles, one-way.

Elevation: Begins at 1,600 feet and ends at 3,200 feet.

Degree of difficulty: Moderate–strenuous

Blaze: A vertical rectangle with a dot or line above and below the rectangle.

DUTCHMAN'S BREECHES
(Dicentra cucullaria)
White, waxy petals shaped like baggy trousers give this plant its humorous name.

Hiwassee Ranger District

[Fig. 38(1)] The Hiwassee Ranger District is known for its family float trips down the Hiwassee River; trout-fishing areas, including a trophy section; the scenic Coker Creek; hiking trails; and horse trails.

John Muir, founder of the Sierra Club, walked along the Hiwassee River in 1867. In 1972 the Youth Conservation Corps and the Senior Community Service Employment Program built the 19-mile John Muir National Recreation Trail. Those walking the trail have opportunities to see songbirds, grouse, turkey, and beaver (*Castor canadensis*). Raccoon, fox, deer, and boar may be present but show themselves only to stealthy hikers.

The Hiwassee Ranger Station has brochures, maps, and books about the area. The Hiwassee Ranger District (about 86,000 acres) has more privately owned lands interspersed among the Cherokee National Forest (CNF) lands than the other districts.

Ayuwasiu, the Cherokee name from which Hiwassee was derived, means "meadow at the foot of the hill."

For more information: Hiwassee Ranger District, Etowah, TN 37331. Phone (423) 263-5486.

HIWASSEE RIVER

This popular east Tennessee river's headwaters are in the northwestern slopes of the Blue Ridge Mountains along the Appalachian Trail in northern Georgia. The Hiwassee courses through North Carolina and then turns west into Tennessee. The Hiwassee River drains a mountainous watershed of 750,000 acres in the Cherokee National Forest, Nantahala National Forest, and Chattahoochee National Forest. Because these lands are forested, the water flowing through the Hiwassee Ranger District is of good quality.

Rocks exposed along the river were formed of sediments that were eroded from highland masses into shallow seas that covered this area 800 million years ago. These layers of sediments formed sandstones and shales that were metamorphosed into quartzites and slates with inclusions of gold, garnet, quartz ruby, emeralds, and other elements and minerals.

About 250 million years ago, a slow uplifting and folding formed the Appalachian Mountains. The Hiwassee River and its tributaries began carrying the materials washed from their slopes. Erosion by the young Hiwassee River carved the steep gorge the river runs through today.

Archaeological evidence testifies that ancient people lived in the Hiwassee Valley long before the Cherokees, Creeks, and other tribes came to the region. Hernando De Soto, the Spanish explorer, and his men were reported to have traveled along the Hiwassee River's banks in the summer of 1540. De Soto behaved as Cortez did in Mexico and as Pizarro did in Peru, ransacking villages in search of gold and taking supplies to sustain his quest.

Later, French and English explorers came, and then settlers. In 1835, the Cherokee were forced to surrender their homelands to the newcomers and, three years later, were removed. More Europeans moved into the area permanently.

This land along the Hiwassee River, under the stewardship of the Indians, was lush. Forests of chestnut, poplar, oaks, pines, and hundred of other trees flourished along with thousands of other plants species. This abundant vegetation provided food and cover for wildlife—bison (*Bison bison*), elk (*Cervus elaphus*), turkey, deer, bear, and mountain lion (*Felis concolor*), also called puma, panther, or cougar.

The Indians may have cultivated portions of the Hiwassee River valley as long as 3,000 years ago. The first Europeans to enter the area saw the valley used for agriculture but the mountains were unchanged.

By the late 1800s, this country, new to the whites, was hungry for building materials. By the 1920s these mountains were cleared of timber, and the Hiwassee River was again carrying materials from erosion. The Forest Service moved into the region to manage the natural resources of the southern Appalachian Mountains. Reforestation began, and we have those results to enjoy today.

Families delight in rafting, canoeing, and kayaking on the Hiwassee River. The 12-mile run from Appalachia Powerhouse to US 411 bridge provides exciting whitewater experiences. Most of the river is easy to navigate on Class I water. Class I means there are few obstructions, small waves, and easily manageable rapids. The river also has Class II and III waters. Class II rapids are still considered easy to manage, but Class III rapids have waves high enough to swamp an open canoe and require complex maneuvering.

There are commercial outfitters under special use permit with the Forest Service to provide services on the river (*see* Appendix C).

Directions: From Etowah go south 9 miles on US 411, turn left (east) on TN 30, and go 6 miles to Reliance. TN 30 runs along the river from the western edge of the CNF east to Reliance. There are outfitters in Reliance (*see* Appendix C).

Activities: Fishing, rafting, canoeing, kayaking, camping, and picnicking.

Facilities: Campgrounds, picnic tables, and outfitters.

Dates: Open year-round.

Fees: There is a charge for camping and rafting with an outfitter.

Closest town: Etowah, about 15 miles.

For more information: Hiwassee Ranger District, Etowah, TN 37331. Phone (423) 263-5486.

▓ GEE CREEK WILDERNESS AREA

[Fig. 38(2)] The Gee Creek Wilderness Area (2,573 acres) is located on the western edge of the Hiwassee Ranger District. It is bound on the west by Starr Mountain and on the east by Chestnut Mountain, and it lies about 9 miles southeast of Etowah. Gee Knob rises to 2,000 feet at the southeastern tip of the wilderness area.

The Gee Creek Wilderness Area's Starr Mountain was named for Caleb Starr. Caleb moved to Tennessee, then part of North Carolina, from Pennsylvania after the Revolutionary War. Starr married the granddaughter of Nancy Ward named Nancy Harlan. The Starrs, owners of Starr Mountain, grew wealthy raising livestock and amassing land that was under Cherokee jurisdiction.

James Starr, son of Caleb and Nancy, convinced President Andrew Jackson to give 640 acres to white settlers moving into the area. This, among other events, led to the federal government forcing the Cherokee to give up their homelands and move to Oklahoma. James Starr's plans went awry because the Starrs were part Cherokee and they too lost their lands to walk the Trail of Tears.

James Starr was killed for selling out the Cherokees. Another of Caleb's sons, Tom, became a murderous outlaw at the age of 19, revenging his brother's death. Caleb's grandson, Sam Starr became an outlaw riding with the infamous Younger gang. Sam's wife, Belle, also earned her place in history, becoming a better-known outlaw than all her relatives.

Gee Creek Wilderness Area became the CNF's first so designated area in 1975. Lying between two mountains, the gorge is surrounded by steep drops. The lower elevations contain rhododendron, hemlock, and poplar, and the higher elevations hold Virginia pine, red and white oaks, and hickory. The largest trees remaining in the area are in the Gee Creek gorge. Loggers took most of the timber from here within the last half-century.

Directions: Take US 411 south of Etowah for 7 miles, turn left (east) in Wetmore on TN 30, then turn left (north) on FR 2013, and continue about 1 mile to wilderness area.

White-Tailed Deer

White-tailed deer provided Indians and white settlers with meat and pelts until the mid-1800s. After 1850, white settler populations grew, and by the early 1890s, deer were virtually extinct not only in Tennessee but in most of the eastern United Sates. Restocking was tried off-and-on until the Tennessee Game and Fish Commission, known today as the Tennessee Wildlife Resources Agency, began a project in earnest in 1943. Before that, in 1937, 178 deer were trapped in Pisgah National Forest and released in the southern CNF, including the Ocoee Ranger District. The restocking programs were successful, and today hunters are depended on to keep growing deer populations in check.

Activities: Hiking.

Facilities: None.

Dates: Open year-round.

Fees: None.

Closest town: Etowah, about 9 miles.

For more information: Hiwassee Ranger District, Etowah, TN 37331. Phone (423) 263-5486.

GEE CREEK TRAIL

[Fig. 38(2)] Gee Creek flows south through the gorge into the Hiwassee River, and Gee Creek Trail (#191) follows it. The trail was originally a path anglers made to get to the trout-rich waters.

Hikers will enjoy viewing and photographing two waterfalls and the remnants of an old concrete flume that was used in iron mining from 1825 to 1860 by the Tennessee Copper Company.

About 1 mile down the trail is a hemlock-encircled campsite between the creek and a 150-foot cliff with another waterfall nearby. (No overnight camping is allowed because this wilderness area is too small.) Just above the campsite is one of the largest hemlocks remaining in the gorge. Here is where many hikers turn around because there are few features farther along, there are more creeks to cross, and the trail wanes. Hikers should be careful about getting off the trail and going up the canyon side to avoid crossing the creek. The ground is unstable and dangerous.

Directions: Take US 411 south of Etowah for 7 miles, turn left (east) in Wetmore on TN 30, then turn left (north) on FR 2013.

Trail: 1.9 miles, one-way.

Elevation: Begins at 920 feet and ends at 1,400 feet.

Degree of difficulty: Moderate. Upper stretches are difficult.

Blaze: None.

JOHN MUIR NATIONAL RECREATION TRAIL

[Fig. 38(3)] The John Muir National Recreation Trail (#152) follows the Hiwassee River upstream (east) from Childers Creek for 18.9 miles to FR 311 east of Coker Creek Scenic Area and TN 68. Muir walked along the north shore of the Hiwassee River in September of 1867, making a note in his journal on September 19 stating this was an impressive river with a fine forest, multiple falls, and forest walls as vine-draped and flowery as Eden.

Had he walked the banks in spring he would have seen many wildflowers in bloom, as hikers see today. Bloodroot, fire pink, trillium, trout lily, squaw root (*Conopholis americana*), bishop's cap, and wild ginger are among those in evidence.

The first 3 miles of the trail are easy going through a meadow, and then it passes between the river and high bluffs of metamorphic rocks consisting of quartz schist, mica schist, mica slate, and micaceous quartzite. The trail leads away from the river, where rhododendrons and hemlocks cover the bluffs, into a marshy area. At the end of the easy 3-mile section is Big Bend Recreation Area with water and sanitary facilities.

Big Bend takes its name from the sharp southerly bend in the river. The trophy trout section begins here and runs west to the L&N Bridge in Reliance.

Three miles farther is the Appalachia Powerhouse, which has drinking water and sanitary facilities. A suspension bridge hangs over the Hiwassee River. Although this is not part of the trail, it offers a good view of the river and its banks.

The trail continues along the river to the Narrows, where there are some interesting rock formations caused by erosion. In about 3 more miles the trail runs along the top of a bluff furnishing a spectacular view. Coker Creek joins the Hiwassee River just beyond the bluff. Primitive camping is allowed here near the Coker Creek/John Muir parking lot at the southern end of FR 22B.

The remaining 7 miles run along the river and through the forest of flame azalea, mountain laurel, and rhododendron that bloom in early summer. Many hikers forgo the last mile of the hike and stop at TN 68. The last difficult leg leaves TN 68 and ends at FR 311.

Directions: From Etowah go south 9 miles on US 411, turn left (east) on TN 30, go 6 miles to river bridge in Reliance next to Webb's Store, go over the bridge, take first right (east) on FR 108, and continue for 0.5 mile to parking lot.

Trail: 18.9 miles, one-way.

Elevation: Begins at 600 feet and ends at 1,100 feet.

Degree of difficulty: Ranges from easy to strenuous.

Blaze: John Muir Trail blue markers.

COKER CREEK SCENIC AREA

[Fig. 36(15)] To reach other interesting places and features in the eastern Hiwassee Ranger District, the route via TN 68 through Tellico Plains offers the best roads. Coker Creek Scenic Area is closer to Etowah as the crow flies than Tellico Plains, but the saying "you can't get there from here" applies unless you are willing to meander through the mountains on gravel roads.

Coker Creek Scenic Area (375 acres) is a small part of the Coker Creek valley, but it offers outstanding features including Coker Creek Falls; thick, lush forests of deciduous and evergreen trees with some old-growth hemlocks and white pine; wildflowers; and flocks of wild turkeys. Coker Creek flows into the Hiwassee River.

The community of Ironsburg near the headwaters of Coker Creek got its name from an ironworks built by the Cherokee before 1812. Carroll Ironworks later bought it from the Indians, and in the winter of 1863 General Sherman destroyed it.

Coker Creek was the site of a gold strike. When the discovery was made in 1820s, about the same time gold was found in northeast Georgia and more than two decades before the California strike, Coker Creek became a bustling place. Most of the mining ended by 1860, but visitors are welcome to shake a pan at local commercial mining establishments.

Directions: From Tellico Plains take TN 68 south for about 13 miles through the community of Coker Creek and look for Ironsburg Methodist Church. Turn right (west) past the church on FR 22 (Duckett Ridge Road), continue for 0.9 mile, and take the left (south) fork. Continue until you see the sign for Coker Creek Falls, then continue to Coker Creek/John Muir parking lot.

Activities: Hiking, picnicking, and primitive camping.

Facilities: Picnic sites.

Fees: None.

Dates: Open year-round

Closest town: Tellico Plains, about 17 miles.

For more information: Hiwassee Ranger District, Etowah, TN 37331. Phone (423) 263-5486.

COKER CREEK FALLS TRAIL

[Fig. 36(15)] Coker Creek Falls Trail (#183) begins at the northern end of the scenic area at the end of FR 2138. The roar of the waterfalls leaves no doubt as to which way to go. It is only 0.1 mile down the trail to the upper falls and about 100 feet farther to the main waterfall. The upper falls drops about 8 feet over a 35-foot width of the creek. Coker Creek Falls, the most spectacular of the series of waterfalls, cascades and drops about 20 feet in a block form.

Look for a spur path several yards downstream that leads south to Hidden Falls. Lower Coker Creek Falls, a short distance more downstream, drops about 10 feet in a tier form, and is the last significant waterfall along the creek.

The remainder of the trail goes along the creek, zigzags up a hill (follow the white blazes), descends, and ends at the Coker Creek Falls/John Muir parking lot, but don't stop. Continue following the creek to the Hiwassee River for a reward of scenic vistas, roaring rapids, clear pools, the large river, and metamorphic rock bluffs. The John Muir Trail (*see* page 220) crosses here.

Trail: 2.7 miles, one-way.

Elevation: Begins at 1,306 feet and ends at 940 feet.

Degree of difficulty: Easy.

Blaze: White.

YELLOW BIRCH
(Betula alleghaniensis)
The unique bark of the birch is thin and shreddy. This bark is flammable even when wet, so it is useful for campsites.

Ocoee Ranger District

[Fig. 38(5)] The Ocoee Ranger District (94,628 acres) is the southernmost ranger district in the Cherokee National Forest (CNF) in the extreme southeastern corner of Tennessee. This district offers camping, boating, fishing, hiking, biking, horseback riding, rafting, kayaking, picnicking, and swimming. The district contains Chilhowee Recreation Area, Rock Creek Gorge Scenic Area, Little Frog Wilderness Area, Big Frog Wilderness Area, and Cohutta Wilderness Area.

Ocoee means "apricot vine place" in Cherokee. It is thought the apricot vine refers to the passion flower plant (*Passiflora incarnata*), also called maypop. The globular fruit, when squeezed, may pop or it may not, hence, maypop. The seeds in the fruit are covered with a sweetish, fleshy pulp when ripe in late summer.

The Ocoee Scenic Byway was the first National Forest Byway in the nation. The route includes 19 miles of US Highway 64 and 7 miles of FR 77 going up Chilhowee Mountain in Polk County. This route was designed to take motorists through some of the most beautiful areas in east Tennessee. It includes natural beauty, many popular recreation spots, and the opportunity to view historic sites. Visitors can see over the Tennessee Valley to the Cumberland Plateau and to the Blue Ridge province. On a clear day, North Carolina and Georgia are visible, and the Ocoee Scenic Byway offers excellent views of nearby Sugarloaf Mountain. On Chilhowee Mountain visitors will find Chilhowee Recreation Area (*see* page 226) with campground, lake, swimming area, picnic grounds, and trails.

The Cherokee National Forest is rich with history. This area has been inhabited for over 12,000 years. The Cherokee Indians used to make their home here and the hills are filled with their history and culture. Much later, armies flowed through the valleys near here during the Civil War. A handful of Confederate soldiers were surprised by Union troops one night on Chilhowee Mountain. Their camping spot is marked next to the byway.

The scenic byway traces its way along parts of the Old Copper Road that used to follow some of the route of US 64. Horse-drawn wagons followed the road to transport a wealth of high-grade copper ore from Copperhill and Ducktown down the Ocoee River gorge to railway cars in Cleveland. It was not unusual for men working the wagons to spend the night at the Halfway House located near the mouth of Greasy Creek at Parksville Lake. The next day, they would complete the two-day journey from Copperhill to Cleveland. Parts of the old inn are under the waters of Parksville Lake.

For more information: Ocoee Ranger District, RT1, Box 348, Benton, TN 37307. Phone (423) 338-5201

▨ OCOEE RIVER

The Ocoee River originates from the Toccoa River that flows from the north Georgia mountains into Ocoee Lake Number Three. The river's name changes from

Toccoa River to Ocoee River at the state line near Copperhill.

As a free-flowing, whitewater river, it carved out the Ocoee Gorge. Today the water power is harnessed for hydroelectricity and recreation in the form of calm lakes. Whitewater occurs only when water is released through the dams. The eastern dam, Ocoee Dam Number Three, is between Big Frog and Little Frog wilderness areas; the middle dam, Ocoee Dam Number Two, is at Caney Creek; and the western dam, Ocoee Dam Number 1 (also called Parkville Dam), is at the western edge of the district, south of Benton near the junction of US 64 and TN 314.

There were no roads in the Ocoee River gorge at the time of the Cherokee Indian removal in 1838, and the basin (Copperhill area) was also inaccessible. This land had few white settlers and was the land no one wanted until copper was discovered here in 1843. This discovery marked the demise of the rich soil, lush forests with huge trees, and green rolling mountains.

John Caldwell moved to Ducktown in 1849 with the idea to build a 33-mile road connecting Cleveland with the copper-producing area. The Copper Road, completed in 1853, doomed the environment to exploitation and ruin for financial benefit. This exploitation did bring livelihoods to many people. In the 1930s, US 64 was built using the old Copper Road route, except for about a 2.5-mile stretch that moved away from the Ocoee River.

The Civil War ceased the operation except for some small amount of mining and smelting to benefit the Confederacy. By 1876 all the wood in the area had been cut to fuel the smelters, and wood had to imported from surrounding areas. Two years later mining and smelting stopped after producing 24 million pounds of copper. Fifty square miles of trees had been cleared for fuel. It was again the land no one wanted— raw, infertile dirt piles, appearing much like one imagines the moonscape to look.

In 1899, the Tennessee Copper Company started the Burra Burra mine and operated it until the last mine closed in 1987. In the 1930s government agencies and copper companies began to revegetate the 23,000 acres of polluted and eroded land. Today, most of the moonscape is green.

The Tennessee Electric Power Company looked upon the Ocoee River as a source of inexpensive hydroelectric power, and it began construction of the Parksville Dam south of Benton in 1910. The completion in 1911 gave the Ocoee River its first lake, Parksville Lake, also called Ocoee Lake. Parksville Dam is built on top of the Great Smokey Fault, where older rock was shoved over younger rock. This is the place the Blue Ridge province meets the Valley and Ridge province.

In 1912, construction began on Ocoee Dam Number Two at Caney Creek. Construction began in 1941 on Ocoee Dam Number Three, and the dam became operational in 1943. Ocoee Dam Number Three funnels water into a 2.5-mile tunnel cut through the rock on the western side of the river that goes downstream to Powerhouse Number Three. In 1939, the Tennessee Valley Authority (TVA) took control of the Ocoee system.

When a 5-mile wooden flume that carried water from the Ocoee Number Two Diversion Dam downstream to Powerhouse Number Two needed repair in 1976, the water was released into its natural river bed. This became the whitewater portion of the Ocoee River. The river ran wild, attracting whitewater rafters, kayakers, and canoeists. This area gained much attention, as word spread among whitewater enthusiasts.

This led to a confrontation between whitewater enthusiasts and TVA when the flume was repaired and operational. The whitewater area dried up. A compromise resulted in TVA releasing water at certain times to please those needing the swift water for their sport. The flume is on the National Register of Historic Places.

The Ocoee River was the site of the 1996 Olympic Slalom Canoe/Kayak events. The flow at the Ocoee Whitewater Center is about 1,400 cubic feet per second (cps). This is awesome power. Imagine 44 times that much water, 62,000 cps, moving through here. That was what the gauging station measured at Powerhouse Number Two on November 19, 1906 during a flood.

The Ocoee Whitewater Center is 1,500 feet long below Ocoee Dam Number Three. TVA releases water from the dam to generate the whitewater for sporting activities. Call TVA at (800) 238-2264, and when prompted, press 5 on a touch-tone phone for the Ocoee River dams release schedule.

Directions: From Benton take TN 314 south for about 7 miles. Turn left (east) on US 64 to follow the Ocoee River.

Activities: Rafting, canoeing, kayaking, camping, fishing, and picnicking.

Facilities: Outfitters, campgrounds, and picnic tables.

Dates: Open year-round.

Fees: There is a charge for camping and rafting with an outfitter.

Closest town: Benton, about 7 miles.

For more information: Ocoee Ranger District, RT1, Box 348, Benton, TN 37307. Phone (423) 338-5201

Purple Passion Flower

The purple passion flower is also known as *flor da las cinco llagas* (flower of five wounds). The Jesuits believe this is the flower that grew on the cross in a St. Francis of Assisi vision. Each part of the flower is said to represent the instruments of the Passion of Christ. Five petals and five sepals symbolize the 10 faithful apostles, not including Judas for his betrayal or Peter for denying knowing Jesus. The fringe stands for the crown of thorns, and the five stamens denote the five wounds. The ovary depicts the hammer and the three styles, the nails.

The fruit of the passion flower, or maypop, was believed by some Indians to cure insomnia, but when the Jesuits saw Indians eating the fruit, they interpreted it to mean the Indians were hungry for Christianity. The passion flower is the state flower of Tennessee.

SCENIC AUTOMOBILE ROUTES

[Fig. 38(11)] The first Forest Service scenic byway in the nation, Ocoee Scenic Byway, is located in Polk County on sections of US 64 and Forest Route FR 77 up Chilhowee Mountain in the southern Ocoee District. From Parksville go east on US 64 then turn left (north) on FR 77. This 26-mile, two-lane highway winds through scenic rock bluffs of the Ocoee River gorge and past the site of the 1996 Olympic canoe and kayak competition.

A side trip up Chilhowee Mountain is a 3-mile climb up FR 77 offering many opportunities to survey the valley lands, the Cumberland Mountains, and some of the north Georgia mountains.

TN 68 is another scenic drive through the southern Appalachian countryside. The drive passes along Coker Creek to the community of Coker Creek, then through Turtletown and Dogtown, then within view of Little Frog Mountain and Big Frog Mountain, and then to Ducktown. If towns with animal names aren't enough, TN 68 takes you to a town named after a mineral, Copperhill.

For more information: Ocoee Ranger District, RT 1, Box 348, Benton, TN 37307. Phone (423) 338-5201

▒ CHILHOWEE RECREATION AREA

[Fig. 38(7)] Chilhowee Recreation Area has the most developed areas in the CNF and is an excellent place for families. It offers just about all outdoor recreational activities. It has nine trails, including one that leads to magnificent Benton Falls and another that is a watchable wildlife trail, and Lake McCamy is available for fishing, swimming, and boating. McCamy was one of the early and best-known settlers in this area, and he helped build Benton Springs Road up Chilhowee Mountain.

The Chilhowee Trail Complex contains many interconnected trails: Azalea (2 miles), Arbutus (0.7 mile), Red Leaf (0.3 mile), Clear Creek (5.4 miles), Benton Falls (1.6 miles), Scenic Spur (1.7 miles), Clemmer (3 miles), Slickrock (5.1 miles), and Rimrock (4.5 miles). All trails welcome bikers except the Scenic Spur Trail.

The Arbutus Trail, in the campground area, is the watchable wildlife trail that goes through hardwood and white pine regeneration areas and through a grassy opening and tracking pits. This trail takes about 45 minutes to walk and shows how the different types and ages of forests provide habitats for a variety of plants and animals. Along the trail you can see animals from insects to white-tailed deer and birds. Depending on the season, summer tanagers (*Pirangra ruba*), black-throated green warblers (*Dendroica virens)*), golden-crowned kinglets (*Regulus satrapa*), pine warblers (*Dendroica pinus*), and Carolina chickadees (*Parus carolinensis*) visit the area.

The two tracking pits, also called bait stations, are baited to attract animals onto the sandy area so they will leave their tracks. It's fun to see how many animals visit the area and how many you can identify. Some of the critters that show up regularly include raccoon, opossum, gray fox (*Urocyon cineroargenteus*), and wild hog. Deer, turkey, rabbit, squirrel, mice, and a variety of birds may leave their tracks also.

Directions: From Benton take TN 314 east about 1 mile to the intersection with County Road 100, go east another mile to the junction with Oswald Dome Road (FR 77), turn left (north), then take the first right (east) into the recreation area. Or from the junction of FR 77 and US 64, go 7 miles north on FR 77 and turn right at the sign.

Activities: Camping, hiking, biking, fishing, swimming, picnicking, boating, and wildlife watching.

Facilities: 88 campsites, swimming area, hiking trails, bicycle trails, nonmotorized boating, dumping station, sanitary facilities, cold-water showers, picnic table, drinking water, and grills.

Dates: Reservations taken for May–Oct. 26 for camping. Some camping is available year-round.

Fees: There is a charge for camping.

Closest town: Benton, about 3 miles.

Seepage Salamander

Seepage salamander is the name of the species that used to be called the Cherokee salamander and the Alabama salamander. Tennessee is the northeastern edge of the seepage salamander's range. It is more common in North Carolina, Georgia, and Alabama. It has straight-edged, reddish-brown stripes in the northern part of its range and wavy-brown stripes in Alabama. It lives among leaf litter and eats springtails, beetle larvae, and mites.

For more information: Ocoee Ranger District, RT 1, Box 348D, Benton, TN 37307. Phone (423) 338-5201 or (800) 280-2267.

BENTON FALLS TRAIL

[Fig. 38(8)] Benton Falls Trail (#131) begins at McCamy Lake dam. The waterfall is about 1.5 miles down along the trail. Most of the trek is easy but there is a steep section where extra care is needed.

Benton Falls is fan shaped and tumbles from a rock ledge down the face of the rock onto another rock face. From top to bottom the water falls about 65 feet before entering a small plunge-pool. This is a worthwhile walk and be sure to carry a camera.

Trail: 1.6 miles, one-way.

Elevation: Begins at 1,880 feet and ends at 1,600 feet.

Degree of difficulty: Easy to moderate.

Blaze: Blue.

CLEAR CREEK TRAIL

[Fig. 38(10)] Clear Creek Trail (#79) starts at State Highway 30. From there it leads west and then south to the northern end of the Rock Creek Gorge Scenic Area to run along the eastern boundary of the scenic area. From midway down the scenic area the trail turns west and then southwest to finish on FR 30 near Parksville Lake.

Trail: 5.4 miles, one-way.

Elevation: Begins at 1,800 feet and ends at 880 feet.

Degree of difficulty: Moderately strenuous.

Blaze: None.

ROCK CREEK GORGE SCENIC AREA

[Fig. 38(9)] Just southwest of Chilhowee Recreation Area is the 220-acre Rock Creek Gorge Scenic Area. It was designated a scenic area in 1965 to protect this area because it had become too popular with tourists.

Rock Creek flows south through the gorge and has 11 waterfalls. One waterfall cascades over 175 feet of rock and another drops about 60 feet vertically from a ledge.

There is no road to Rock Creek Gorge Scenic Area. Benton Falls Trail (*see* page 227) and Clear Creek Trail (*see* page 227) lead from Chilhowee Recreation Area to the northern end of the scenic area.

Directions: From Benton take TN 314 east about 1 mile to the intersection with County Road 100. Go east another mile to the junction with Oswald Dome Road (FR 77), turn left (north) then take the first right (east) into the recreation area. Or from the junction of FR 77 and US 64, go 7 miles north on FR 77 and turn right at sign. Go to McCamy Lake dam to the Benton Falls trailhead. Take the trail to the scenic area.

Activities: Hiking, wildlife watching.

Facilities: None.

Dates: Open year-round.

Fees: None.

Closest town: Benton, about 3 miles.

For more information: Ocoee Ranger District, RT 1, Box 348D, Benton, TN 37307. Phone (423) 338-5201 or (800) 280-2267.

PARKSVILLE CAMPGROUND AND LAKE

[Fig. 38(12)] Parksville Campground and Lake offers another major family camping attraction, in addition to the Chilhowee Recreation area, in the Ocoee Ranger District. Although there are no listed trails in the camping area, many are nearby. The large Parksville Lake, also called Lake Ocoee, is just south of the campground across US 64.

Directions: From Benton take TN 314 south about 6 miles to US 64, turn left (east) on US 64, continue about 4 miles, and look for the campground road on the north side of the road.

Activities: Boating, camping, swimming, fishing, bicycling, hiking, and picnicking.

Facilities: 41 campsites (24 on first-come, first-served basis and 17 by reservation), drinking water, sanitary facilities, warm-water showers, picnic tables, electric hookups, and grills.

Dates: Reservations taken for May–Oct. 26 for camping. Some camping is available year-round.

Fees: There is a charge for camping.

Closest town: Benton, about 10 miles.

For more information: Ocoee Ranger District, RT 1, Box 348D, Benton, TN 37307. Phone (423) 338-5201 or (800) 280-2267.

THUNDER ROCK CAMPGROUND

[Fig. 38(13)] Thunder Rock Campground on the upper Ocoee River is near the put-in for whitewater sports and the Whitewater Center. This is a popular spot for those looking for whitewater action.

Directions: From Benton take TN 314 south for about 6 miles, turn left (east) on US 64, continue for about 11 miles, turn right (south) across bridge and follow the road around the powerhouse, and take the first right.

Activities: Whitewater rafting, canoeing, and kayaking, camping, bicycling, hiking, and picnicking.

Facilities: 42 campsites on first-come, first served basis, drinking water, sanitary facilities, picnic tables, and grills.

Dates: Open year-round.

Fees: There is a charge for camping.

Closest town: Benton, about 18 miles.

For more information: Ocoee Ranger District, RT 1, Box 348D, Benton, TN 37307. Phone (423) 338-5201 or (800) 280-2267.

🌿 LITTLE FROG WILDERNESS AREA

[Fig. 42(1)] Beautiful seems to be the best word to describe the 4,666-acre Little Frog Wilderness Area. Bound by US 64 to the south and the Ocoee/Hiwassee ranger districts boundary to the north, this wilderness takes its name from Little Frog Mountain, which provides the eastern boundary. The highest point in the wilderness area is 3,322 feet above sea level, but depending on which map you use, it has different names. Some call this high point Sassafras Knob, others label it Little Frog. The lowest point is near the Ocoee River which flows parallel to US 64 at Powerhouse Number Three.

SHOWY ORCHIS
(Orchis spectabilis)
Bees and dragonflies thrust tongues into the spur of this blossom for pollen.

Little Frog Wilderness, in spite of being located only 4 miles from the once lethal Copper Basin, fared well while much of the surrounding areas were damaged by the air pollution. This good fortune was attributed to the protection of Little Frog Mountain and prevailing winds. The area, however, did not escape logging during the time of the copper mining and smelting. It is now covered with second growth.

Rock Creek Trail (#125), the only trail in the area, goes through the prettiest and wildest part of the wilderness, Pressley Cove. Little Frog Mountain to the east and Dry Pond Lead to the west form the cove.

Directions: From Ducktown go west on US 64 for 5 miles. Little Frog Mountain Wilderness is north of the highway.

Activities: Primitive camping, hiking, and hunting.

Facilities: None.

Dates: Open year-round.

Fees: None.

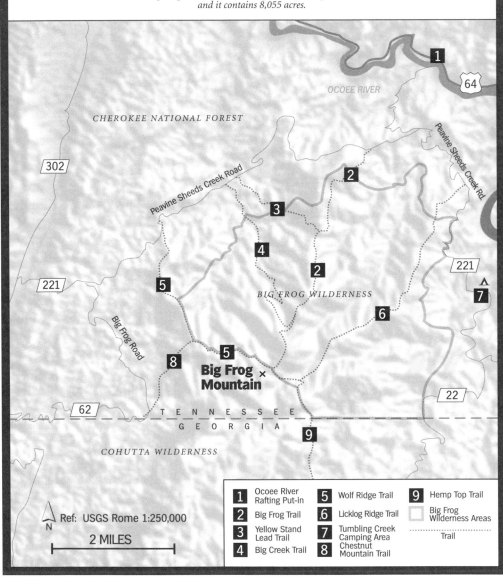

The Big Frog Wilderness

*The Big Frog Wilderness was designated by Congress in 1984,
and it contains 8,055 acres.*

OCOEE RIVER

64

CHEROKEE NATIONAL FOREST

302

Peavine Sheeds Creek Road

Peavine Sheeds Creek Rd

221

1

2

3

4

2

221

7

BIG FROG WILDERNESS

5

6

Big Frog Road

8   5

**Big Frog
Mountain** ×

22

62   T E N N E S S E E
G E O R G I A

9

COHUTTA WILDERNESS

N
Ref: USGS Rome 1:250,000

2 MILES

1	Ocoee River Rafting Put-In	5	Wolf Ridge Trail	9	Hemp Top Trail
2	Big Frog Trail	6	Licklog Ridge Trail		Big Frog Wilderness Areas
3	Yellow Stand Lead Trail	7	Tumbling Creek Camping Area		Trail
4	Big Creek Trail	8	Chestnut Mountain Trail		

Closest town: Ducktown, about 5 miles.

For more information: Ocoee Ranger District, RT 1, Box 348D, Benton, TN 37307. Phone (423) 338-5201.

ROCK CREEK TRAIL

[Fig. 42(2)] Rock Creek Trail (#125) leaves US 64 leading into the beautiful valley between two ridges. Flame azalea, rhododendron, mountain laurel, hemlock, trailing arbutus, redbud, toothwort (*Dentaria diphylla*), and crested dwarf iris are among the many plants along the winding trail. Several feeder creeks cross the trail. Look for the crested dwarf iris along the creek banks. A trek to the rhododendron thickets when they are in bloom is worthwhile. Occasionally, large hemlocks that escaped cutting loom overhead. If it's quiet, turkey, deer, a variety of birds, including the pileated woodpecker (*Dryocopus pileatus*), and other animals may come into view.

At 4 miles along the trail is the stunning, swift-running Rock Creek. It is here that this trail grants the feeling of peaceful isolation. Few other places revive the spirit like this.

Rock Creek is about 10 feet wide and usually less than 1 foot deep. The trail runs along the creek for a short distance, but long enough to pass a small waterfall about 5 feet high. Rock Creek Trail ends at the junction with Dry Pond Lead Trail. Instead of backtracking to the Rock Creek trailhead, turn left (south) for a 2-mile walk back to US 64 across from Powerhouse Number Three, which is 4 miles west of the Rock Creek trailhead via US 64.

Trail: 5.5 miles, one-way.

Elevation: Begins at 1,480 and ends at 1,880.

Degree of difficulty: Moderate.

Blaze: Signed.

BIG FROG WILDERNESS AREA AND COHUTTA WILDERNESS AREA

[Fig. 39] The Big Frog and Cohutta wilderness areas' combined total of 45,111 acres in Tennessee's Cherokee National Forest and Georgia's Chattahoochee National Forest makes this the largest wilderness tract in the eastern United States. Big Frog Wilderness Area contains 7,986 acres in Tennessee and 83 acres in Georgia, and Cohutta Wilderness Area contains 1,795 acres in Tennessee and 37,042 in Georgia.

In the Big Frog Wilderness Area, Big Frog Mountain reaches 4,224 feet elevation, the highest point in Polk County, and rules the Ocoee Ranger District's skyline. Looking at a map, Big Frog Wilderness forms a steep arch from the Georgia border, listing slightly to the east. The Tennessee portion of the Cohutta Wilderness Area is a small bump under Big Frogs' southwestern corner. Cohutta Wilderness Area has no trails but Big Frog Wilderness Area is crisscrossed with them.

The rarest type of trail found in the eastern United States, the perfect contour trail, follows a contour line, the imaginary line connecting points with the same elevation. In the Big Frog Wilderness Area, a perfect contour trail follows along a 50-degree slope on the Big Creek (#68)/Barkleggin (#67) Trails. The Civilian Conservation Corps (CCC) laid out this trail along the base of Big Frog Mountain using a surveyor's compass and stretching string lines. The CCC created most of the trails here in the 1930s.

Other trails in the Big Frog Wilderness Area, Licklog, Wolf Ridge, and The Big Frog, predate the CCC by 15 years or more. The Forest Service says that Big Frog Mountain's trails are among the best and most extensive in the CNF. The dozen trails totaling over 40 miles are marked and easy to follow. However, unlike other areas in the CNF, Big Frog Wilderness Area provides little water, requiring hikers to carry their own.

There are no roads in the wilderness areas but access is available via FR 221 and FR 62, which parallels the arc of these areas. Bear signs are common in the wilderness areas because of Tennessee Wildlife Resource Agency's re-introduction program initiated in the 1970s. Bears from the Great Smoky Mountain National Park (GSMNP) were imported into a 52,825-acre bear reserve. Old orange and black wildlife management area signs still exist in the area.

This area was also restocked with deer but their numbers remain low. Wild hogs, on the other hand, are well represented. Farmers used to give their domestic pigs free rein, allowing them to fend for themselves in the forests. These pigs were often marked, but some escaped the identifying brand. Russian hogs trapped in the GSMNP and released here bred with domestic stock. Their offspring look more like the black Russian parent with sharp, prominent tusks. Turkey and bobcats inhabit the area, as do timber rattlesnakes (*Crotalus horridus*) and copperheads (*Agkistrodon contortrix*).

Several plant studies conducted in the Big Frog Mountain area found, in addition to the usual trees and plants of the CNF, white pine and several rare plants: catchfly (*Silene noctiflora*), cow parsnip (*Heracleum maximum*), rattlesnake root (*Prenanthes alba*), and bush honeysuckle (*Diervilla sessilifolia*). A survey identified 479 species of plants with 22 being non-natives. Because humans are one of the major ways exotic species enter an area, this small number of non-native species indicates little human intrusion in this area. Unlike most of the Unaka Range that is considered to be in the Canadian zone for plants, the Ocoee District is not. But high annual rainfall and the mountainous terrain provide the habitat needed by Canadian zone flora.

Directions: From Ducktown take TN 68 south about 2 miles, turn right (west) on County Road 2326, and continue for about 5 miles, staying on the paved road until it T-bones with FR 122. Turn right (north) on FR 122, an improved dirt road. This road arcs over the wilderness area. At the northern tip of the arc the road becomes an improved gravel road running southwest, then south to the intersection with FR 62 (Big Frog Road) that runs west of Cohutta Wilderness Area to the Georgia border where it turns west, running just inside the Tennessee/Georgia state line, and rejoins FR 122.

Activities: Hiking and primitive camping.

Facilities: None.

Dates: Open year-round.

Fees: None.

Closest town: Ducktown, about 8 miles.

For more information: Ocoee Ranger District, RT 1, Box 348D, Benton, TN 37307. Phone (423) 338-5201.

TUMBLING CREEK CAMPING AREA

[Fig. 39(7)] The Tumbling Creek Camping Area is an isolated camping area just east of Big Frog Wilderness Area. Tumbling Creek runs into Ocoee Lake Number Three. This is a nice place for those looking to get away from it all, but this area is not recommended for trailers.

Directions: From Benton take TN 314 south for about 6 miles, turn left (east) on US 64, and continue for about 11 miles. Turn right (south) across the bridge, follow the road around the powerhouse for 2 miles, take the left fork (FR 221), and continue for 6 miles to the campsites.

Activities: Camping and picnicking.

Facilities: 8 campsites, drinking water, sanitary facilities, picnic tables, and grills.

Dates: Open year-round.

Fees: None.

Closest town: Benton, about 25 miles.

For more information: Ocoee Ranger District, RT 1, Box 348D, Benton, TN 37307. Phone (423) 338-5201.

CATAWBA RHODODENDRON
(Rhododendron catawbiense)
This shrub forms dense thickets on mountain slopes.

CONASAUGA RIVER CORRIDOR

Flowing from northern Georgia into Tennessee, the Conasauga River then weaves back and forth a couple of times across the border before heading west out of the Ocoee Ranger District and dipping back into Georgia. When the water level is high enough, it is an easy stream for canoeists. Its waters carry 22 fish species that have yet to be found anywhere else in Tennessee. The Trout Unlimited organization listed the Conasauga River among the best 100 trout streams in the nation.

Under the 1988 CNF Management Plan the Conasauga River is a protected corridor. This plan safeguards areas with high visual sensitivity and a high degree of public interest, and generally prohibits timber harvesting.

The river ranges from 50 to more than 100 feet wide with some rapids and slow pools. A few large hemlocks, small hardwoods, and pines grow along the banks. Steep escarpments on both sides sometimes shadow the river. Canoeists will need to concern themselves with rocks and rapids, but the view is wonderful. Bear, deer, wild hogs, and many small animals may be seen streamside. Signs of beaver are evident. Canoeists have said the Conasauga River is among the most beautiful rivers you could paddle.

Two major rapids lie between the put-in point on FR 62 and the take-out point on US 411. Scout these before attempting to float through them.

Chickamauga Lake

John Thomas Scopes was charged with violating a law banning the teaching of evolution in Tennessee.

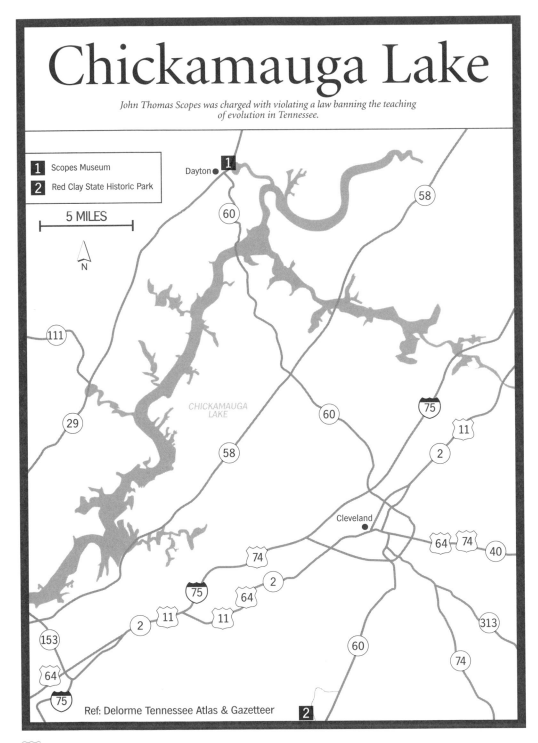

1 Scopes Museum

2 Red Clay State Historic Park

5 MILES

N

Dayton

1

60

58

111

29

CHICKAMAUGA LAKE

58

60

75

11

2

Cleveland

74

64 74

40

2

75

64

11

11

153

2

11

313

60

74

64

75

Ref: Delorme Tennessee Atlas & Gazetteer

2

Those willing to brave the cold water will find underwater viewing exceptional in the Conasauga River. A mask and snorkel are all you need to catch a glimpse of 65 fish species, including rainbow trout, brown trout, blue shiner (*Cyprinella caerulea*), amber darter (*Percina antesella*), Conasauga logperch (*Percina caprodes*), and an extraordinary community of mussels. The best underwater viewing is possible when it hasn't rained for several days.

Directions: From Cleveland go 8 miles east on US 64 to the community of Ocoee, turn right (south) on US 114, and continue for about 7 miles to the junction with County Road 221 (Ladds Springs Road). Turn left (east), continue to FR 221, and turn left (east) on FR 221, which runs roughly along the river until the intersection with FR 62. Take FR 62 to a spot near the Georgia state line for a canoe put-in point. The take-out point is 9 miles downstream north of the community of Conasauga on US 411 at the bridge.

Activities: Canoeing, bird and animal watching, hunting, hiking, and primitive camping.

Facilities: None.

Dates: Open year-round.

Fees: None.

Closest town: Cleveland, about 18 miles.

For more information: Ocoee Ranger District, RT 1, Box 348D, Benton, TN 37307. Phone (423) 338-5201.

Historic Sites in the Lower Unaka Mountains

SCOPES MUSEUM

[Fig. 40(1)] In July 1925, William Jennings Bryan and Clarence Darrow faced each other to settle a case involving a law banning the teaching of evolution in Tennessee. A teacher, John Thomas Scopes, was charged with violating this law. The trial became a media carnival and a historical event. The Scopes Evolution Trial became the Monkey Trial.

The law prohibiting the teaching of evolution passed the Tennessee legislature in March of 1925. It stated that it was unlawful for any public teacher "to teach any theory that denies the story of the divine creation of man as taught in the Bible, and to teach instead that man descended from a lower order of animals." The statute stated that "any teacher violating this section shall be guilty of a misdemeanor and fined not less than one hundred dollars ($100) and not more than five hundred dollars ($500) for each offense."

In the spring of 1925, Scopes was a 24-year-old science teacher at Rhea County High School in Dayton. Discussions took place in Dayton at Robinson's Drug Store where a small group conspired with Scopes to violate the Tennessee statute to provide a court test case. On the surface, this was a publicity stunt, but worldwide fascination with the case astonished the conspirators. The original drug store table where the decision was made on May 15 to make a test case is in the Scopes Museum in the basement of the Rhea County Courthouse in Dayton.

Chattanooga, aware that the publicity would be of economic value, tried to have the trial moved from Dayton to that city. The prosecution was headed by William Jennings Bryan, the most celebrated orator of his day. He was also a leader of the fundamentalist movement. Clarence Darrow, America's most famous criminal lawyer and an agnostic, came to Dayton after his success in the Chicago Loeb-Leopold murder trial of 1925 to defend Scopes. The American Civil Liberties Union contacted him for the job. It was the meeting of the fundamentalist and the liberal.

The media carnival began as hundreds of reporters came to town for the Monkey Trail. The Baltimore Sun sent several writers, including the famous and acrimonious H.L. Mencken. A new invention, the radio, was used to report the proceedings. Thousands of visitors swarmed Dayton daily to see the trial.

The trial lasted from July 10 to July 21 in one of the hottest and driest Tennessee summers. Emotions ran as high as the temperatures in the overcrowded courtroom, so the trial was relocated under the oak trees on the north side of the courthouse.

The trial was supposed to determine whether Scopes violated the Tennessee law while acting as a substitute biology teacher. Public interest, however, lay in academic freedom, science, evolution, and religion. Many people came to see the contest between Darrow and Bryan. Darrow began the questioning. During preliminary proceedings, Bryan was promised equal time for rebuttal, but the judge decided that enough verbal fireworks had taken place. The trial was cut short, depriving the audience of some anticipated theater.

The jury convicted Scopes, and Judge Raulston fined him $100. The Tennessee Supreme Court later overturned the conviction on the technicality that the jury, rather than the judge, should have set the fine.

Bryan died five days after the trial, Darrow returned to Chicago, and Scopes attended the University of Chicago to study geology, which led him into Louisiana's oil industry.

Directions: Dayton is on US 27 approximately 36 miles north of Chattanooga.

Activities: A self-guided tour of the Scopes Museum in the basement of the Rhea County Courthouse. Exhibits include clippings and photos of the trial.

Facilities: Museum.

Dates: Open year-round except weekends and holidays.

Fees: None.

Closest town: Dayton.

For more information: Rhea County Courthouse, 1475 Market Street, Dayton, TN 37321. Phone (423) 775-7801.

▨ LOST SEA

[Fig. 41(3)] The Lost Sea between Madisonville and Sweetwater claims to be America's largest underground lake. It is designated a Registered National Landmark and is listed in the *Guinness Book of Records*. An early known visitor to the cave was a saber-tooth tiger whose fossilized remains are now in the Museum of National History in New York City.

After a guided walk through the cavern's large rooms, a glass-bottomed boat ride takes visitors to see some of the largest rainbow trout in the United States living in the underground lake. The temperature remains at 58 degrees Fahrenheit year-round. Take a camera with a flash to snap shots of trout and of rare cave flowers, anthodites, and other rock formations.

Directions: Take TN 68 northwest from Madison-ville about 5 miles and look for a sign on the right (north) side of the road.

Activities: Cave touring and riding boat on under-ground lake.

Facilities: Restrooms.

Dates: Open year-round except Christmas.

Fees: There is a charge for admission.

Closest town: About 5 miles northwest of Madison-ville, and about 7 miles southeast of Sweetwater.

For more information: Lost Sea, 140 Lost Sea Road, Sweetwater, TN 37874. Phone (423) 337-6616.

CHRISTMAS
FERN
(Polystichum
acrostichoides)

FORT LOUDOUN STATE HISTORIC AREA

[Fig. 41(1)] During the French and Indian War (1754–1763) the British Colony of South Carolina felt threatened by the French. Governor James Glen ordered the building of a fort on the Little Tennessee River in 1746, but it wasn't until 1756 that construction began.

Fort Loudoun, named after John Campbell, the fourth Earl of Loudoun and British commander-in-chief in North America, helped solidify the Cherokee-British alliance against the French to assure that trade continued between the Indians and British. The command consisted of 90 British regulars and 120 South Carolina militiamen.

During the fort's four-year existence, that alliance deteriorated, and in 1760 the Cherokee captured the fort. On August 9 of that year, 180 men, 60 women, and children left the fort. The next morning, the Cherokee attacked them, killing all the officers except one and about 25 others. The remaining people were taken and sold as slaves to the Cherokees. People in South Carolina and Virginia eventually ransomed most of the British, allowing them to return to white settlements.

Directions: Take TN 360 southeast of Vonore about 2 miles and turn left (east) at the sign and continue about 1 mile to the fort.

Activities: Tour the museum and the fort.

Facilities: Restrooms.

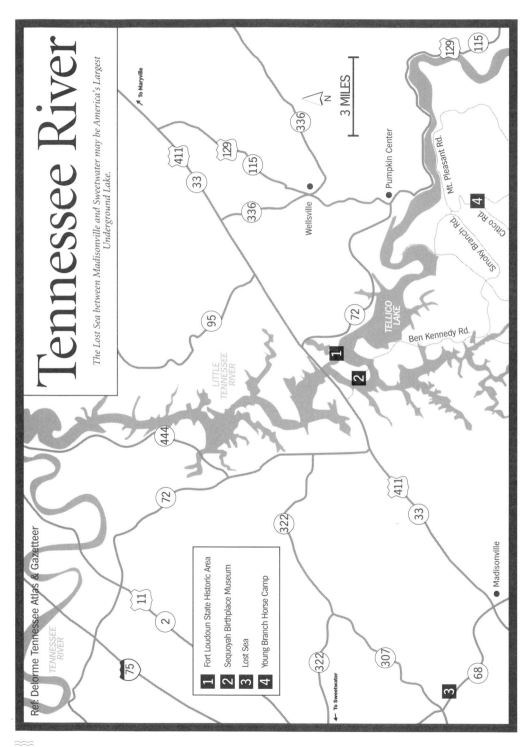

Tennessee River

The Lost Sea between Madisonville and Sweetwater may be America's Largest Underground Lake.

Ref: Delorme Tennessee Atlas & Gazetteer

1 Fort Loudoun State Historic Area
2 Sequoyah Birthplace Museum
3 Lost Sea
4 Young Branch Horse Camp

Dates: Open year-round except Thanksgiving, Christmas, and Jan. 1.

Closest town: Vonore, about 2 miles.

For more information: Fort Loudoun State Historic Area, 338 Fort Loudoun Road, Vonore, TN 37885. Phone (423) 884-6217.

SEQUOYAH BIRTHPLACE MUSEUM

[Fig. 41(2)] Located on the Eastern Band of Cherokee Indian's tribal lands across the road and a little south of Fort Loudoun is the Sequoyah Birthplace Museum. Near the museum, in the village of Tuskeegee, Sequoyah was born in 1776. The son of Nathaniel Gist, a hunting partner of Daniel Boone, and *Wut-teh*, daughter of a Cherokee Chief, Sequoyah (named George Gist) was born with a limp. Nathaniel Gist left the family when Sequoyah was a child.

Sequoyah later married a Cherokee, had a family, and became a silversmith. Although he was exposed to writing in his early life, he didn't learn the English alphabet, but he began playing with the idea of a Cherokee alphabet. This idea grew as he saw that Cherokee warriors could not write home as their allies, the British, did. Reading orders or recording events was not possible either. After the war, Sequoyah began working on a writing system for his people.

It took him 12 years, until 1821, to develop the Cherokee's written language. He created 85 symbols to represent the spoken language. Thousands of Indians became literate within a few months' time. The Bible and hymns were translated by 1825, and by 1828 the Cherokee were publishing their own newspaper, the *Phoenix*. This was the first bilingual newspaper in the nation. The Cherokee Nation awarded Sequoyah a lifetime pension and presented him with a medal for his accomplishment and contribution to his people.

The museum has several rooms of artifacts and a thorough accounting of Cherokee history and culture. There is also a gift shop with crafts and books.

Directions: Take TN 360 southeast of Vonore about 2 miles. Museum is on the right (west) side of the road.

Activities: Tour museum and burial wall.

Facilities: Gift shop and bookstore.

Dates: Open year-round except Thanksgiving, Christmas, and Jan. 1.

Fees: There is a charge for admission.

Closest town: Vonore, about 2 miles.

For more information: Sequoyah Birthplace Museum, POB 69, Vonore, TN 37885. Phone (423) 884-6246.

FORT MARR

[Fig. 38(4)] Fort Marr's blockhouse, all that remained of the fort built in 1814, was relocated from its original site on the Conasauga River to a park in Benton. This blockhouse is just one corner of the old fort.

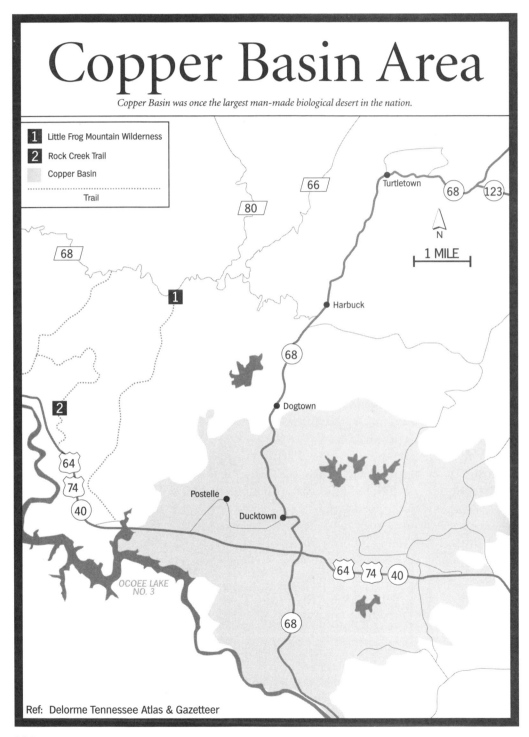

Copper Basin Area

Copper Basin was once the largest man-made biological desert in the nation.

1 Little Frog Mountain Wilderness
2 Rock Creek Trail
Copper Basin
Trail

66

80

68

Turtletown
68   123

N

1 MILE

1

Harbuck

68

2

Dogtown

64

74

Postelle

40

Ducktown

64   74   40

OCOEE LAKE
NO. 3

68

Ref: Delorme Tennessee Atlas & Gazetteer

Fort Marr was built to guard Andrew Jackson's shipping trains. It also protected the Cherokee from warring Creek Indians. Later it became a stockade to hold Cherokees before being they were forced on the Trail of Tears.

The blockhouse is in a park in Benton. The outside is available for viewing, but the inside of the blockhouse is not open to the public.

Directions: In the town of Benton on the east side of US 411.

Activities: Sight-seeing.

Dates: Open year-round.

Fees: None.

Closest town: Benton.

For more information: Tennessee Overhill Heritage Association, PO Box 143, Etowah, TN 37331. Phone (423) 263-7232.

NANCY WARD GRAVE

[Fig. 38(6)] Nancy Ward was a Cherokee Indian who tried to keep peace between her people and the whites. She warned the newcomers of impending Indian attacks, but the Indians held her in high esteem because of her service to her tribe. The chiefs called her Beloved Woman. She was also known as the Wild Rose of the Cherokee.

She spoke in council meetings and had the power to release condemned prisoners. When a white woman, Mrs. William Bean, mother of the first white child born in Tennessee, was taken from Fort Watauga to be burned, Nancy Ward released her.

Her grave rests on top of a mound under a red cedar tree (*Juniperus virginiana*). The graves next to hers belong to her son, Five Killer, and her brother, Long Fellow.

Directions: South of Benton on US 411 about 1 mile. Look for marker on east side of road.

Activities: Sight-seeing.

Facilities: None.

Dates: Open year-round.

Fees: None.

Closest town: Benton, about 1 mile.

For more information: Tennessee Overhill Heritage Association, POB 143, Etowah, TN 37331. Phone (423) 263-7232.

COPPER BASIN

[Fig. 42] Copper Basin was once the largest man-made biological desert in the nation. The sulfuric acid released during the smelting of copper ore killed nearly everything within 50 square miles and beyond. The acid fumes filled the basin and rained from the sky, giving the nation its first experience with acid rain. Various forms of pollution (heavy metals, acids, and waste materials) ran into streams carried by nearly 50 inches of annual rainfall. The Ocoee River (*see* page 223) downstream is just beginning to support aquatic forms of life again, and some stretches remain dead. Copper Basin

MOUNTAIN LAUREL
(Kalmia latifolia)

was a working mine from the 1850s until 1987.

Reclamation of the torturously eroded Copper Basin moonscape begun in the 1930s has taken root. The landscape is growing trees again after a century. More than 16 million trees, acid-resistant grasses and legumes, and lime and fertilizer were used to reduce soil erosion from 195 tons per year to 8 tons per year.

Visitors to the Ducktown Museum, in the middle of Copper Basin, can still see part of the moonscape. Three hundred acres at the Burra Burra mine site have been set aside as a memorial to devastation and are listed on the National Register of Historic Places. By contrast, the view from the museum includes many acres that have been reclaimed. The museum has exhibits on environmental law, mining in the basin, and the people who migrated to the basin.

Directions: US 64 and TN 68 intersect in the middle of Copper Basin. Ducktown is just north of the intersection.

Activities: Sight-seeing.
Facilities: Museum with history about the mining process and equipment.
Dates: Open year-round, Mon–Sat. Closed major holidays.
Fees: There is charge for admission.
Closest town: Ducktown.
For more information: Ducktown Basin Museum, POB 458, Ducktown, TN 37326. Phone (423) 496-5778.

RED CLAY STATE HISTORIC PARK

[Fig. 40(2)] Red Clay State Historic Park, located in the extreme southwestern corner of Bradley County, is dedicated to the preservation and interpretation of Cherokee history. It is a certified interpretive site on the Trail of Tears.

The park's 263 acres were used as cotton fields and pastureland, and there are forested ridges that average 200 feet or more above the valley floor in height. The site contains a natural landmark, the great council spring, or blue hole, which rises from beneath a limestone ledge to form a deep pool that flows into Mill Creek, a tributary of the Conasauga and Coosa river system. The spring was used by the Cherokee for their water supply during council meetings.

Red Clay served as the seat of Cherokee government from 1832 until the Indians' forced removal in 1838. Those years were filled with frustrating efforts to insure the future of the Cherokee. Chief John Ross led the fight to keep the Cherokees' eastern lands and to refuse the government's efforts to move his people to Oklahoma. Controversial treaties resulted in the Cherokee losing their lands and being removed.

Here is where the Trail of Tears began because this is where they learned of that loss.

By 1832, the State of Georgia had stripped the Cherokees of their political sovereignty and prevented them from meeting together. They were prohibited from holding council meetings in Georgia for any reason other than to sign treaties giving their land away. As a result, the Cherokee capital was moved from New Echota, Georgia to Red Clay, Tennessee.

Many of the Cherokee had adopted the Christian religion, and their political and judicial systems were similar to those of the United States. Sequoyah had developed a syllabary, making it possible to write the Cherokee language. In spite of the social and political advancements made by the Cherokee, Red Clay proved to be the Cherokees' last refuge before being moved westward.

The James F. Corn Interpretive Center, located near the park entrance, houses a theater, a resource reading room, artifacts, nineteenth-century documents emphasizing Cherokee history and culture, and exhibits. Replicas of a Cherokee farmstead and council house show how the area might have looked more than 160 years ago. The great council spring, located near the council house, is accessible by a paved trail designed to accommodate the handicapped. The council spring is about 15 feet deep and produces more than 504,000 gallons of water a day.

Directions: From Cleveland, go south on TN 60 for about 8 miles, turn right (west) on TN 317 for about 1 mile, turn left (south) on Blue Springs Road that leads to the park in about 2 miles.

Activities: Sight-seeing, hiking, and picnicking.

Facilities: Restrooms, a 500-seat amphitheater, a 50-seat theater, a 100-person picnic pavilion, outdoor picnic area with tables and grills, a self-guided nature trail, and a 2-mile loop trail.

Dates: Open year-round with seasonal hours.

Fees: None.

Closest town: Cleveland, 11 miles.

For more information: Red Clay State Historical Park, 1140 Red Clay Park Road S.W., Cleveland, TN 37311. Phone (423) 478-0339.

WILD TURKEY (Meleagris gallopavo) Turkeys can fly well for short distances but prefer to run.

Great Smoky Mountains Section

The state lines of Tennessee and North Carolina split the Great Smoky Mountains National Park down the middle.

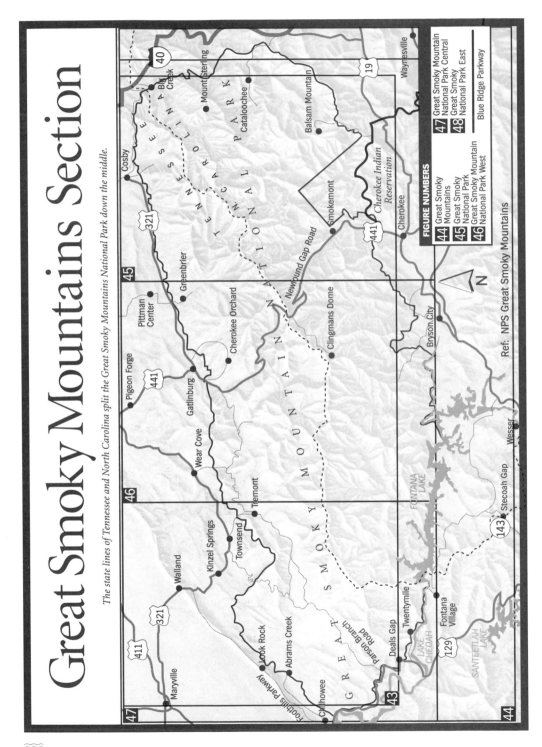

FIGURE NUMBERS

44 Great Smoky Mountains

45 Great Smoky National Park

46 Great Smoky Mountain National Park West

47 Great Smoky Mountain National Park Central

48 Great Smoky National Park East

Blue Ridge Parkway

Ref: NPS Great Smoky Mountains

Great Smoky Mountains National Park

The sprawling, 521,000-acre Great Smoky Mountains National Park (GSMNP) forms a saddle across the Unaka Mountains and separates the northern and southern portions of the Cherokee National Forest in Tennessee and the Pisgah National Forest and the Nantahala National Forest in North Carolina.

The total acreage in the 800-square-mile park is about evenly split, with 55 percent in North Carolina and 45 percent in Tennessee. The mountains are bisected by a single highway, the Newfound Gap Road, and are served by a few secondary roads that lead to campgrounds, trailheads, and scenic views. Large portions of the park remain roadless and retain an unspoiled quality.

Drained by more than 700 miles of trout streams and crisscrossed by more than 800 miles of hiking trails, the Great Smoky Mountains National Park, the most popular park in the United States, is visited by nearly 10 million people annually. In

[*Above:* The Chimney Tops rise 50 feet above the summit of Sugarland Mountain]

order to preserve the quality of outdoor experiences, some of the backcountry campsites have limited access and permits are required to use them.

Geologic History

The basement rock foundation of the Smokies was created about 1 billion years ago when great forces of heat and pressure changed sedimentary rock to metamorphic rock before the Cambrian Period of the Paleozoic Era. The next level of rock is the Ocoee Supergroup, sedimentary rock deposited more than 600 million years ago in the late Precambrian Era.

Four major faults, or breaks, distort the rock formations in the Smokies. The Great Smoky, Greenbrier, Gatlinburg, and Oconaluftee faults are believed to have resulted when North America collided with Africa about 290 million years ago during the Allegheny orogeny. This event created the compression that formed the Smokies by folding layers of sedimentary rock on top of crystalline bedrock like a giant accordion run amok.

One widely accepted theory postulates that the tremendous geologic forces that shaped the Smokies resulted from the widening of the bottom of the Atlantic Ocean. The plate tectonic theory explains this widening as the result of the movement of large sections of earth's crust known as plates. They drift on the mantle, the second of earth's layers. The molten portion of the mantle heats unevenly, creating convection currents that carry the plates toward each other at times, and away from each other during other periods.

When collisions occur between plates, the plates may buckle under the pressure, with the heavier plate sliding under the lighter plate, creating tremendous upheavals. Since their formation, the Smoky Mountains are believed to have traveled about 100 kilometers (61 miles) northwestward.

After tectonic and weathering events created the peaks, they began to be eroded by wind, rain, and temperature extremes. About 20,000 years ago, pre-Wisconsin glaciation reached a maximum extension, coming within 100 miles of Tennessee.

At times the frozen soil in the Smokies took on the characteristics of permafrost, permanently frozen subsoil. One theory suggests the boulder streams and boulderfields seen today resulted from the freeze-thaw cycles that split boulders from the bedrock of peaks. The boulders were gradually smoothed as they were moved downhill by gravity and running water.

As the glaciers retreated, cold-loving plants were limited to the higher elevations. Streams began to erode their way through the Smokies, creating the ridges separated by deep valleys that we see today.

NORTHERN RED OAK
(Quercus rubra)
Red oaks can be identified by tiny bristles on the tip of each leaf.

The History of Man in the Smokies

The earliest human inhabitants of this rugged and magnificent cluster of Appalachian Mountains were the Cherokee Indians. The traditional territory of the Cherokee included the Smokies and extended beyond to include much of what is now Tennessee, North Carolina, and north Georgia.

The Middle Cherokee were scattered through the mountains, while Valley Cherokee lived in the foothills to the south, and the most prosperous group, the Overhill Cherokee, lived beyond the mountains in eastern Tennessee.

It was a land of plenty, with streams and rivers teeming with fish and virgin forests populated with elk (*Cervus elphus*), bison (*Bison bison*), black bear (*Ursus americanus*), white-tailed deer (*Odocoileus virginianus*), wild turkey (*Meleagris gallopavo silvestris*), and many species of small game.

The Cherokee considered the Smokies a sacred place, the source of many legends, the home of magical creatures and enchanted lakes. Their name for these mountains was *Shaconage*, meaning mountains of blue smoke. The Smokies later became their refuge.

Their utopia was first interrupted by Spanish explorers who came to America in search of gold and other riches. Some historians believe Hernando De Soto visited the Smokies. The Spanish presence was temporary, but soon afterward fur traders followed game trails through this remote Cherokee country. They arrived as early as 1673, and by 1690 they had established trading posts. Early surveyors establishing the boundary of North Carolina and Tennessee called the peaks we now know as the Great Smoky Mountains, the Iron Mountains.

European migrants began sifting into the mountains and carving out small homesteads. Many of these settlers were of Scottish and English heritage, and they sought out the remote coves and hidden valleys to reside in and lead solitary lives. In 1821 white families moved to Cades Cove, the first area to be settled by whites in the Smokies. Settlers followed them to the Cataloochee Valley in 1836.

First, there were wars between the Cherokees and neighboring white settlers. Wars followed between whites and whites, and all the while the population in the mountains was growing as more immigrants entered the area.

The major blow to the natural resources was struck when several big timber and paper companies began clearing stands of virgin timber. In the 1880s, the first lumber companies reached the Smokies. Prior to that time, logging had been confined to harvesting black walnut (*Juglans nigra*), cherry (*Prunus* sp.), ash (*Fraxinus* sp.), yellow poplar (*Liriodendron tulipifera*), and oak (*Quercus* sp.) along streams and close to sawmills.

The earliest timber-related industry was the acquisition of tanbark for use in curing leather. Large chestnut, oak, and hemlock trees were felled and stripped of bark. The trees were often left to rot because it was too difficult to haul them to the sawmill.

The invention of the Shay locomotive in 1877 provided transportation well suited to steep grades and heavy loads. Soon selective harvesting of a renewable resource was replaced by large scale clear-cutting of every tree that was 12 inches in diameter and 4 feet above the ground.

In the late 1890s, a few farsighted people saw what was happening and began to talk about a public land preserve in the cool and healthful air of the southern Appalachians. A bill to bring this about was introduced in the North Carolina Legislature, but it failed.

The movement to save the Smokies gained momentum, and by the early 1900s, there was increasing pressure on Washington to create some kind of preserve. But at the same time, the lumber industry was gaining strength. In 1901, Col. W.B. Townsend purchased 86,000 acres, stretching from Tuckaleechee Cove near present-day Townsend to Clingmans Dome, for lumbering. In 1910, Parsons Pulp and Lumber Company purchased 25,000 acres from the Eastern Band of the Cherokee. In 1916, Champion Fiber and Paper Company purchased 92,000 acres, including 25,000 acres in Greenbrier Cove. Lumber towns grew up in Townsend, Smokemont, Greenbrier, Fontana, and Bryson City. Railroads were quickly built to areas being harvested, then dismantled and moved to the next location.

Many mountainsides, once blanketed with trees, appeared as a virtual moonscape. And even then, the lumbering continued. It took less than 40 years to essentially destroy the forests of the northwestern portion of the Smokies.

William P. Davis, a Knoxville businessman, and his wife helped organize the Smoky Mountain Conservation Association in 1923 to promote the development of a national park in the Smoky Mountains.

Although about 75 percent of the Smokies' forests had been logged by this time, at least 100,000 acres of old-growth forests remained. It was the largest remaining area of old-growth forest in the eastern United States and an area of unparalleled natural beauty.

A debate began over whether to designate the Smokies as a national forest or a national park. Because consumptive uses of renewable natural resources are permitted in national forests, while in national parks the scenery and natural resources are protected, the park concept won out with those who wanted to save the Smokies.

With the plan for a park adopted by members of the Southern Appalachian National Park Committee in 1924, competition escalated between two groups of supporters, one in Asheville, North Carolina, and the other in Knoxville, Tennessee, regarding its location. In order to prevent the movement from losing momentum, they agreed on a park in the heart of the Smokies, halfway between the two cities.

The situation in the Smokies was different from President Theodore Roosevelt creating the first national parks in the West. Yellowstone and Yosemite were simply carved out of land already owned by the federal government. In the Smokies hundreds of small farmers and a number of large lumber companies owned the land. The farmers didn't want to leave their family homesteads, and the large corporations didn't want to abandon their forest holdings, railroads, logging equipment, and the villages they established to house their workers.

In 1926, President Calvin Coolidge signed a bill establishing the Great Smoky Mountains National Park and the Shenandoah National Park, which allowed the

Department of the Interior to assume responsibility for the administration and protection of the park in the Smokies as soon as 150,000 acres of land had been purchased.

This posed a major problem because the federal government was not allowed to buy land for national park use. As a result, the groups of citizens in Tennessee and North Carolina who had banded together to pursue the park effort formed a funding coalition that grew to include thousands of individuals, corporations, associations, and even schoolchildren who pledged their pennies.

By 1928, $5 million had been raised, but with the cost of land rapidly escalating, the sum wasn't sufficient to buy all that was needed. The salvation of the crusade came when the Laura Spellman Rockefeller Memorial Fund donated an additional $5 million to assure completion of the purchases.

In all, there were 6,000 small farms, large tracts, and other miscellaneous parcels of land that had to be surveyed, appraised, argued over, and sometimes condemned in court. Also, in addition to their holdings, the timber companies had to be compensated for equipment and standing inventories. It was a lengthy and often painful process that displaced families from their ancestral homeplaces.

AMERICAN BEECH
(Fagus grandifolia)
This beech is identified by thin gray bark and papery leaves that may stay on all winter to twist and rustle in the wind.

By 1934, the states of Tennessee and North Carolina had transferred deeds for 300,000 acres to the federal government, at which time Congress authorized full development of public facilities. Workers building facilities were greatly aided by the Civilian Conservation Corps (CCC), an agency created during the Great Depression to provide young men with work and wages. The CCC developed roads, trails, campgrounds, and beautiful stone bridges and buildings between 1933 and 1942, when World War II shut the program down.

Standing at the Rockefeller Monument at Newfound Gap, President Franklin D. Roosevelt officially dedicated the Great Smoky Mountains National Park in September 1940.

Flora and Fauna

A study is now in progress to identify and categorize every living creature within the park's boundaries. It is estimated that between 40,000 and 70,000 multicellular species exist in the park. The project is expected to take 10 to 15 years to complete. Also, to assist in monitoring and classifying the unique inventory of rare plants,

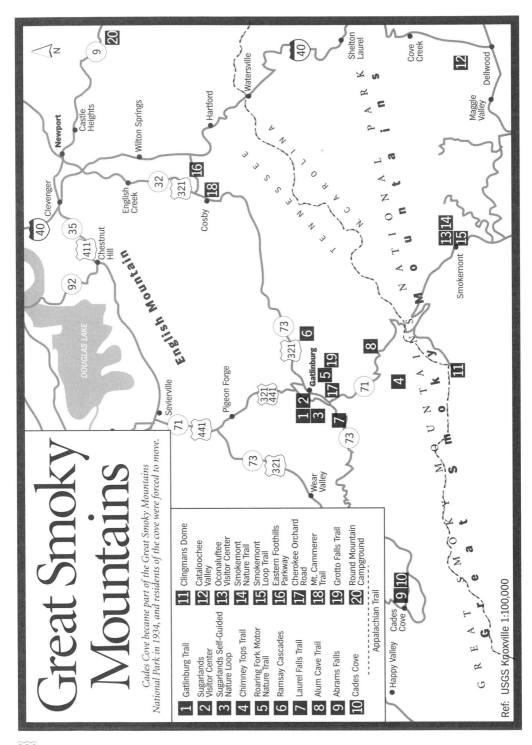

Great Smoky Mountains

Cades Cove became part of the Great Smoky Mountains National Park in 1934, and residents of the cove were forced to move.

1 Gatlinburg Trail	**11** Clingmans Dome
2 Sugarlands Visitor Center	**12** Cataloochee Valley
3 Sugarlands Self-Guided Nature Loop	**13** Oconaluftee Visitor Center
4 Chimney Tops Trail	**14** Smokemont Nature Trail
5 Roaring Fork Motor Nature Trail	**15** Smokemont Loop Trail
6 Ramsay Cascades	**16** Eastern Foothills Parkway
7 Laurel Falls Trail	**17** Cherokee Orchard Road
8 Alum Cave Trail	**18** Mt. Cammerer Trail
9 Abrams Falls	**19** Grotto Falls Trail
10 Cades Cove	**20** Round Mountain Campground
	- - - Appalachian Trail

• Happy Valley

Ref: USGS Knoxville 1:100,000

animals, and ecosystems in the park, the GSMNP, in cooperation with The Nature Conservancy, became the first park in the nation to set up a National Heritage Data Center.

Establishment of the park saved more than 100,000 acres of old-growth forest, including some of the largest stands in the eastern United States. The areas scarred by lumbering operations have regenerated, and much of the damage done to various flora and fauna species has been reversed. Because the GSMNP is so biologically diverse, the United Nations Educational, Scientific, and Cultural Organization (UNESCO) designated it as an International Biosphere Reserve in 1976.

Today the park is home to some 1,600 flowering plants, 130 kinds of trees (including the largest known examples of 15 species), 300 mosses and liverworts, 1,800 fungi, 50 ferns and fern allies, and 230 lichens.

The GSMNP is well known for its diverse wildflower displays beginning in early spring and continuing through the fall. With up to 100 inches of annual rainfall (depending on location), ideal conditions are created for many species.

An even greater variety of plant life stems from the varied ecosystems within the park. Generally, the higher elevations are wetter and cooler, but as the altitude decreases, factors like the direction and shape of a slope become increasingly important. Although the elevation may change very little, the flora dramatically changes as you move through the folds of moist valleys and dry ridges. The more convex the ridge slope, the drier the conditions. When you consider the changes in elevation and the variety in topography found here, you begin to understand the reason for the diversity within the plant community of the GSMNP.

Over the years more than 300 species of non-native plants have invaded or been introduced into the Smokies. Many are ornamental flowers, such as daffodils (*Narcissus* sp.), that decorate open areas around old homesteads and cause no problems. Other species are detrimental and are considered serious threats to native flora by park officials.

Plants high on the list of detrimental species are kudzu (*Pueraria lobata*), Oriental bittersweet (*Celastrus orbiculatus*), mimosa (*Albizzia julibrissin*), princess trees (*Paulownia tomentosa*), and wisteria (*Wisteria frutescens*), while Japanese honeysuckle (*Lonicera japonica*) and privet (*Ligustrum vulgare*) are also problematic.

Non-native insects and diseases have caused much of the past and continuing damage to park trees. The first to heavily impact both the forest and, indirectly, the wildlife population was the Chinese chestnut blight that arrived in the 1930s and eliminated the American chestnut (*Castanea dentata*).

Until the blight occurred, the chestnut was the most common canopy tree in the park, and its prolific and consistent mast was a main food source for many animals and birds. Since the blight, more problems have surfaced.

Dutch elm disease, a well-known fungus, is transmitted to the American elm (*Ulmus americana*), slippery elm (*U. ruba*), and winged elm (*U. alata)* in the park by the elm

Pollution in the Smokies

Despite its splendor, this highland paradise is far from worry free. Natural visibility from the highest peaks of the Smokies should be around 100 miles, but pollution has decreased it to an average of 20 miles. The man-made pollution results from fossil fuel burning in industrial and urban areas which releases sulfur dioxides and nitrogen oxides. About half of the nitrogen oxides released into the atmosphere come from automobile exhaust. Forty-five of the top 50 polluting power plants are east of the Mississippi, and air currents carry pollutants to the highest peaks of the Smokies, the first barrier to pollutants that have been carried from the industrialized Ohio and Tennessee river valleys in the jet stream. The rates of pollution at the higher elevations in the Smokies tend to be among the highest in the continental United States.

Nitrogen oxides and volatile organic compounds combine in the presence of sunlight to form ozone, which damages plant life and sometimes reaches levels hazardous to human health. In the presence of moisture, these substances become weak sulfuric and nitric acids, commonly known as acid rain. These acidic compounds threaten the plants and high-level streams within the park in the form of rain as well as clouds, which bathe the peaks in pollutants, particles, and gases.

bark beetle (*Scolytus multistriatus*). Since the late 1980s, hundreds of elms have died from the disease, mostly in the Little River drainage.

Butternut canker is believed to have been introduced into the U.S. about 30 years ago, but it went unnoticed in the park until the late 1980s when butternut (*Juglans cinera*) populations began plummeting. So far, no solutions to the problem have been discovered.

American holly (*Ilex opace*) trees have suffered defoliation and mortality in the park during the past decade, but no single agent has yet been identified as the cause of the problem.

American beech (*Fragus grandifolia*) trees have suffered a decline in the park, and in 1993 it was confirmed that the beech bark scale insect from Europe and the Nectaria fungus together cause beech bark disease. Large areas of New England have lost entire populations of beech trees, and park officials see the insect as a threat in the Smokies.

Dogwood anthracnose (*Discula destructiva*) was first found in Washington State in 1977, and shortly afterward it was found in the New York City area. It was found in Maryland in 1983 and in north Georgia in late 1987. It can kill all dogwoods (*Cornus* sp.) in large populations in just a few years. It has destroyed many trees in the park, where, ecologically, the flowering dogwood (*C. florida*) plays an important role. Its foliage, twigs, and fruit are higher in calcium than any other forest species, which makes it a prime soil builder. Migratory birds depend on its high protein fruit in the autumn, and the leaves and twigs are preferred by all herbivores, from deer to invertebrates.

During the past half-century, the balsam woolly adelgid, an insect from Europe, has devastated the once-magnificent stands of Fraser fir (*Abies fraseri*) in the park. The park contains 74 percent of all of the spruce-fir forest in the Southeast, and 91 percent of the mature trees in the park are dead. A related species, the hemlock woolly adelgid, is approaching the Smokies from the north and is capable of decimating stands of Eastern hemlock (*Tsuga canadensis*) trees. There is a ray of hope in the discovery of some small groups of mature Fraser fir found growing at high elevations. It is possible that some of these trees have a genetic resistance to the pests.

The European mountain ash sawfly (*Cimbex americana*) was first introduced to North America in Canada, and it has since spread throughout eastern U.S. forest regions. It defoliates American mountain ash (*Sorbus americana*) where it grows at high elevations along the crest of the Smokies.

The gypsy moth (*Lymantria dispar*) defoliates oak, maple (*Acer* sp.), beech, birch (*Betula* sp.), and other deciduous trees and poses a threat to the park. It has already done severe damage to forests to the North, and in eastern Tennessee, western North Carolina, and northern Georgia. Park officials are carefully monitoring the spread of this exotic and its presence in the park.

Fauna

Among the fauna found within the park are 50 mammals, 200 birds, 70 fish, and 80 reptiles and amphibians. The black bear attracts the most attention from visitors. White-tailed deer and wild turkeys are numerous, and along streams and rivers, it's not unusual to see river otters (*Lutra canadensis*) and mink (*Mustela vision*). Beaver (*Castor canadensis*) are being seen occasionally.

Groundhogs (*Marmota monax*), opossums (*Didelphis marsupialis*), cottontail rabbits (*Sylvilagus floridanus*), skunks (*Mephitis mephitis*), long-tailed weasels (*Mustela freneta*), gray (*Urocyon cinereoargenteus*) and red (*Vulpes fulva*) foxes, and bobcats (*Lynx rufus*) are commonly seen in coves and other open areas. The red wolf (*Canis rufus*) once roamed the Southeast, but is now one of the most endangered mammals on earth. In 1991, the U.S. Fish and Wildlife Service and Great Smoky Mountains National Park began an experimental red wolf recovery plan with a pair of red wolves obtained from captive breeding programs, but the restoration was not successful and was abandoned in 1998 for various reasons.

Gray squirrels (*Sciurus carolinensis*), fox squirrels (*Sciurus niger*), southern flying squirrels (*Glaucomys volans*), northern flying squirrels (*Glaucomys sabrinis*), and red squirrels (*Tamiasciurus hudsonicus*) are common throughout both the hardwood and coniferous forests. There are numerous members of the mouse family present as well as shrews and moles.

Other than the Eastern wild turkey, the birds visitors are most likely to see or hear include the dark-eyed junco (*Junco hyemalis*), crow (*Corvus brachyrhynchos*), raven (*Corvus corax*), red breasted nuthatch (*Sitta canadensis*), black-capped chickadee (*Parus atricapillus*), barred owl (*Strix varia*), Eastern phoebe (*Sayornis phoebe*), tufted titmouse (*Parus bicolor*), ruffed grouse (*Bonasa umbellus*), red-eyed vireo (*Vireo olivaceus*), Carolina wren (*Thyrothorus ludovicianus*), Carolina chickadee (*Parus carolinensis*), song sparrow (*Melospiza melodia*), veery (*Catharus fuscescens*), wood thrush (*Hylocichla mustelina*), golden-crowned kinglet (*Regulus satrapa*), Indigo bunting (*Passerina cyanea*), northern cardinal (*Cardinalis cardinalis*), rufous-sided towhee (*Pipilo erythrophthalmus*), scarlet tanager (*Piranga olivacea*), and American goldfinch (*Carduelis tristis*).

There are about 60 species of birds that reside within the park, and annual Christmas bird counts generally number about 65 species on an average day. During spring migrations, the numbers jump closer to 100 species per day. The peregrine falcon (*Falco peregrinis*) is back after an absence of about 50 years.

Snakes are not uncommon in the park, but nonpoisonous species by far outnumber the poisonous kind. The ones to avoid are the timber rattlesnake (*Crotalus horridus*) and the copperhead (*Agkistrodon contortrix mokasen*). Rattlers like rocky, warm slopes, and copperheads frequent rocky places and areas around old buildings. Rattlesnakes are seldom seen at the higher elevations, and copperheads usually are below the 2,500-foot level.

Fisheries

There is no place in the eastern U.S. that offers trout fishermen more opportunities than the GSMNP, because within it are well over 300 streams and rivers and more than 2,000 miles of water, 700 miles of which contain one or more species of trout.

All of this water is contained in what biologists have identified as 45 separate watersheds, with six major drainages: Little River, Little Pigeon River, Pigeon River, Oconaluftee River, Little Tennessee River, and Cades Cove.

Waterways within this broad array of streams include tiny branches that can be almost stepped across; larger, turbulent streams that hurtle down the steep slopes; gentle brooks that wind through placid meadowlands; and rivers with large volumes of water.

Some are quite remote, accessible only by lengthy treks into the backcountry, while others are just a few steps away from a paved road, so anglers have a wide variety of opportunities from which to choose.

The only trout native to the Smokies are brook trout (*Salvelinus fontinalis*), but extensive logging and clear-cutting destroyed much of the aquatic habitat required by brookies. Rainbow trout (*Salmo gairdneri*) were shipped in from western states and stocked in the hopes of restoring a fishery. Hardier than brook trout and better able to adapt to the existing conditions, rainbows thrived, and soon took over as the anglers' main quarry.

Later, brown trout (*Salmo trutta*) became prevalent in many Smokies waters, but these fish migrated upstream from stockings made by Tennessee and North Carolina in waters outside the park.

There is only one record of brown trout ever being introduced into Smokies streams after the park was established: a single stocking of the Oconaluftee River in 1965. Some fishermen may have no problem with exotic species, but Park Service policy requires the removal of non-natives wherever feasible.

Brook trout from northern sources were also introduced, but some biologists and local fishermen believed these fish were different from those native to the southern mountains. In the early 1990s, using genetic fingerprinting, researchers were able to prove conclusively that the northern brookies are definitely a different strain. Further testing showed there are three distinct brook trout populations present: a native strain that migrated to the Smokies long ago to escape the freezing conditions of the Wisconsin glaciation farther north, a northern strain derived from hatchery stock, and a hybrid strain.

These findings brought about a second phase of the study intended to inventory native fish throughout eastern Tennessee, including the GSMNP. Most of the streams from which the trout were collected were above 3,000 feet, remote waters that are not likely to have ever been stocked. Of 1,385 brook trout sampled, 57 percent fit the genetic profile of the southern strain, 15 percent were northern strain fish, and 28 percent were hybrids.

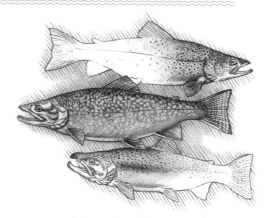

(From top to bottom)
BROWN TROUT
(Salmo trutta)
BROOK TROUT
(Salvelinus fontinalus)
RAINBOW TROUT
(Oncorhynchus mykiss)
The brook trout is the only fish of these three that is native to the Appalachians; the others are stocked.

Shortly after these findings were revealed, the Park Service initiated the Native Brook Trout Restoration Program, aimed at identifying, restoring, monitoring, and protecting the locations where they survive. Records indicating where stockings of northern and hatchery strains of brook trout occurred in the past aided the park in finding many high-elevation streams where fish of the native strain were present. Many of these locations are closed to all fishing, and efforts are being made to remove and relocate rainbows below natural barriers to upstream migration. Waterfalls at least 8 feet high are being utilized in an effort to restore the native brookie.

For fishermen in high-elevation park streams where native brook trout live along with rainbows, the stream is open to fishing. However, brook trout must currently be released. Because the rocks in and along the streams can be slippery, and therefore hazardous, crepe-soled boots and a companion are good ideas.

Other than in the closed waters, fishing is allowed year-round, and those possessing either a Tennessee or North Carolina license can fish anywhere in the park. In Tennessee, both residents and nonresidents ages 13 and older require a license. Residents age 65 prior to March 1 of the current year are exempt. They are only required to show proof of age and of Tennessee residence.

Licenses are not available at the visitor centers and must be obtained in nearby towns. Copies of the regulations and a map showing the locations of closed waters can be obtained at park visitor centers.

Biodiversity

With the approach of the Pleistocene ice sheets, hundreds of plants and animals living in areas far to the north retreated to the higher elevations of the Smokies to escape the climactic impact of the Wisconsin glaciation, in some instances later returning to their former range as conditions improved.

Cold-loving alpine plants and spruce and fir forests were restricted to the highest peaks in the Smokies as a warming trend began about 16,000 years ago. The flora and fauna that found refuge in the Smokies evolved and eventually developed into complex plant communities.

The variety of conditions found within the Smokies on the 14-mile trip from Sugarlands to Newfound Gap is the ecological equivalent of a trip from Georgia to Canada. The average temperature drops up to 3 to 5 degrees Fahrenheit for each 1,000-foot gain in elevation. Altitude varies from 850 feet to 6,643 feet, and average rainfall ranges from 55 inches at Sugarlands to 85 inches on Clingmans Dome.

Within these broad ranges flourishes one of the most ecologically diverse systems in the world.

COVE HARDWOOD FORESTS

The cove hardwood forest is comprised of broadleaf trees that exist below 4,000 feet in valleys and coves. These forests were extensively logged because of the huge trees and the varieties this forest type produced.

Cove hardwood forests are filled with spring wildflowers supported by the canopy of white basswood (*Tilia americana* var. *heterophylla*), American beech, several varieties of birch, black cherry (*Prunus serotina*), Eastern hemlock, cucumbertree (*Magnolia acuminata*), and sugar maple (*Acer saccharum*). The trees not only provide shade for wildflowers but also their leaves control soil chemistry and provide nutrients as they decompose.

There are still excellent examples of cove hardwoods in a few places missed by loggers before the park was established, notably at the Chimneys Picnic Area on the Newfound Gap Road, at the Albright Grove near Cosby, and at the Greenbrier entrance to the Ramsey Cascades and Porters Flat trails.

OPEN PINE-OAK FORESTS

Open pine-oak forests are found below 4,000 feet on the thirsty southern and western slopes. These low and middle elevations also support yellow poplar or tuliptree, pignut hickory (*Carya glabra*), flowering dogwood, rosebay rhododendron (*Rhododendron maximum*), and mountain laurel (*Kalmia latifolia*) thickets in addition to table mountain pine, black oak (*Quercus velutina*), and chestnut oak (*Quercus prinus*), a favorite food source of deer. Some examples of pine-oak stands can be seen along the Laurel Falls Nature Trail.

CLOSED OAK FORESTS

Dogwoods, hickories (*Carya* sp.), black locusts (*Robinia pseudoacacia*), maples, oaks, and yellow poplars in closed oak forests account for a large part of the outstanding fall foliage displays.

HEMLOCK FORESTS

The hemlock forest is dominant on the moist, shady, northern slopes below 4,500 feet along streams. Some of the largest specimens can be seen on the Grotto Falls Trail off the Roaring Fork Motor Nature Trail, and the Alum Cave Bluffs Trail from the Newfound Gap Road. Hemlock forests support an understory of rhododendron, mountain laurel, and doghobble (*Leucothoe fontanesiana*).

NORTHERN HARDWOOD FOREST

Northern hardwood forests consist of yellow birch (*Betula alleghaniensis*), American beech, maple, and cherry and are found around 4,500 feet. These broadleaf trees, which occur at higher elevations in the GSMNP, are commonly found at lower elevations in northern states. There are examples of this forest type on the road between Newfound Gap and Clingmans Dome.

SPRUCE-FIR FOREST

The spruce-fir forest is the most easily recognized of all of the forest types, because the trees are evergreen: Fraser fir and red spruce (*Picea rubens*). They grow only on high peaks above 4,500 feet where the climate is similar to that of Maine or Quebec.

The Spruce-Fir Nature Trail along the Clingmans Dome Road from Newfound Gap, and the road itself, pass through stands of these trees. Spruce-fir forests are found along the Appalachian Trail between Clingmans Dome and Mount Guyot on peaks above 5,000 feet that are often cloaked in cloudy mists. Within these mists, suspended particles including sulfur dioxide and nitrogen oxides released during fossil fuel burning react with sunlight to form acids that return to the ground in the form of cloudwater, rain, snow particle, or gas deposition. These acids lower the pH and damage the chlorophyll-producing foliage of the mature Fraser fir and spruce trees. Fraser fir are also under attack from the balsam wooly adelgid, with about 91 percent of the mature Fraser fir population succumbing to the tiny European insect.

BALDS

Grassy and heath balds are high-altitude open areas that defy the natural laws of succession (*see* Balds, page 12). Most grassy balds are found in the western portion of the park including Gregory Bald, Spence Field, and Andrews Bald. Heath Balds, known locally as slicks due to the glossy leaves of the rhododendron and mountain laurel that cover them, are brilliant sights in June when spectacular rhododendron blooms cover them.

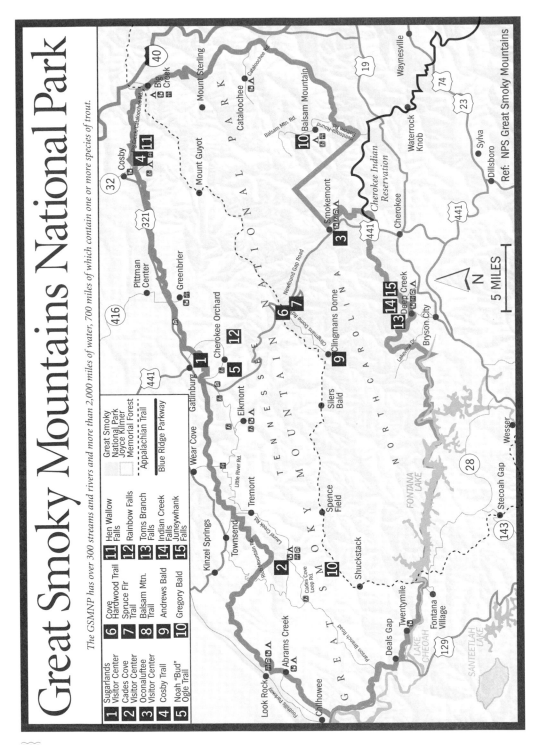

Great Smoky Mountains National Park

Fig. 45: Great Smoky Mountains National Park

The GSMNP has over 300 streams and rivers and more than 2,000 miles of water, 700 miles of which contain one or more species of trout.

1 Sugarlands Visitor Center
2 Cades Cove Visitor Center
3 Oconaluftee Visitor Center
4 Cosby Visitor Center
5 Noah "Bud" Ogle Trail
6 Cove Hardwood Trail
7 Spruce Fir Trail
8 Balsam Mtn. Trail
9 Andrews Bald
10 Gregory Bald
11 Hen Wallow Falls
12 Rainbow Falls
13 Toms Branch Falls
14 Indian Creek Falls
15 Juneywhank Falls

Great Smoky National Park
Joyce Kilmer Memorial Forest
Appalachian Trail
Blue Ridge Parkway

Ref: NPS Great Smoky Mountains

Major Peaks

From the lowest point in the park, the mouth of Abrams Creek, at an elevation of 840 feet, to the 6,643-foot summit of Clingmans Dome, there's more than a 5,800-foot change in elevation. More significantly, there are 16 peaks cresting above 6,000 feet, including six peaks that are among the highest east of the Rockies: Clingmans Dome, 6,643 feet; Mount Guyot, 6,621 feet; Mount LeConte, 6,593 feet; Cliff Top, 6,555 feet; Mount Buckley, 6,500 feet; and Mount Love, 6,446 feet. In addition, there are 58 places in the park with elevations of more than 1 mile (5,280 feet). Many of these locations lie on or along the Appalachian Trail (*see* Appalachian Trail, page 297).

Visitors Centers

There are three visitors centers within the park, two on the Tennessee side of the mountains and one on the North Carolina side. The Sugarlands Visitor Center is 2 miles south of Gatlinburg on US 441; Oconaluftee Visitor Center is 2 miles north of Cherokee, North Carolina on US 441; and Cades Cove is at the end of Laurel Creek Road that turns off TN 73 at an intersection approximately 2 miles east of Townsend.

▨ SUGARLANDS VISITOR CENTER

[Fig. 44(2), Fig. 45(1), Fig. 47(1)] Sugarlands takes its name from the abundance of sugar maple trees in this valley of the West Prong of the Little Pigeon River. Sugarlands Visitor Center is the northern entrance to the GSMNP. A short film, guidebooks, camping permits, and an abundance of written material assist the rangers in orienting thousands of visitors daily to the GSMNP. In addition to an excellent bookstore, visitors will find restrooms and a self-guiding nature trail.

Directions: US 441 south of Gatlinburg at the entrance to the GSMNP. The visitor center is at the intersection of US 441 and Little River Road.

Facilities: Introductory movie, displays, bookstore, restrooms, nearby handicapped-accessible nature trail, camping permits, and backcountry camping registration.

Dates: Open year-round with shorter hours in winter.

Fees: None.

Closest town: Gatlinburg, 2 miles.

For more information: Great Smoky Mountains National Park, 107 Park Headquarters Road, Gatlinburg, TN 37738. Phone (423) 436-1200.

▨ CADES COVE VISITOR CENTER

[Fig. 44(10), Fig. 45(2)] Adjacent to the John Cable Mill, the Cades Cove Visitor Center is about halfway around the 11-mile, one-way Cades Cove Loop Road. The visitor center is a modern construction and has exhibits, trail guides, and brochures. It is adjacent to the historic

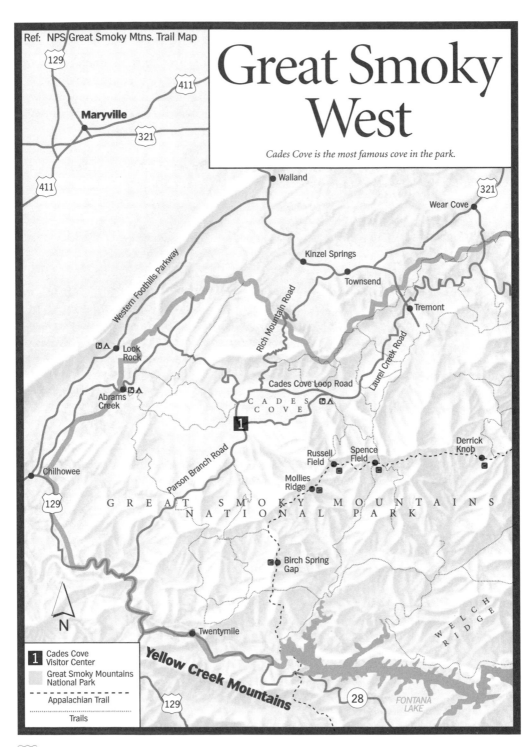

Ref: NPS Great Smoky Mtns. Trail Map

Great Smoky West

Cades Cove is the most famous cove in the park.

Maryville

Walland

Wear Cove

Kinzel Springs

Townsend

Tremont

Western Foothills Parkway

Rich Mountain Road

Laurel Creek Road

Look Rock

Abrams Creek

Cades Cove Loop Road

C A D E S   C O V E

1

Russell Field

Spence Field

Derrick Knob

Mollies Ridge

Parson Branch Road

Chilhowee

G R E A T   S M O K Y   M O U N T A I N S
N A T I O N A L   P A R K

Birch Spring Gap

W E L C H   R I D G E

N

Twentymile

Yellow Creek Mountains

1 Cades Cove Visitor Center

Great Smoky Mountains National Park

- - - Appalachian Trail

········ Trails

28

FONTANA LAKE

Cable Mill that has demonstrations and fresh-ground corn meal for sale.

Directions: From Sugarlands Visitor Center follow Little River Road to Laurel Creek Road and the entrance to Cades Cove. Follow Cades Cove Loop Road approximately 5.5 miles to the visitor center.

Facilities: Visitor center, restrooms, museum, and Cable Mill.

Dates: Open year-round.

Fees: None.

Closest town: Townsend, 8 miles.

For more information: Great Smoky Mountains National Park, 107 Park Headquarters Road, Gatlinburg, TN 37738. Phone (423) 436-1200.

OCONALUFTEE VISITOR CENTER

[Fig. 44(13), Fig. 45(3)] Spring through October at the Oconaluftee Visitor Center, GSMNP employees, in the garb of early pioneers, spin wool, weave cloth, make sorghum molasses, forge tools, and perform other daily chores of mountain people at the Mountain Farm Museum, a collection of historic structures. Visitors will find exhibits, brochures, trail maps, a bookstore and gift shop, and restrooms. Backcountry camping registration is available.

Directions: US 441 at the southern entrance to the GSMNP. From Gatlinburg follow US 441S through the GSMNP. From Cherokee, North Carolina proceed north on US 441 to the entrance to the GSMNP.

Activities: Tour the Mountain Farm Museum, ranger-guided walks, and exhibits.

Facilities: Visitor center, restrooms, bookstore, gift shop, theater, and museum.

Dates: Open year-round.

Fees: None.

Closest town: Cherokee, North Carolina, 2 miles.

For more information: Great Smoky Mountains National Park, 107 Park Headquarters Road, Gatlinburg, TN 37738. Phone (423) 436-1200.

RANGER-LED PROGRAMS

Starting in late spring and continuing through October, there is a schedule of ranger-led programs, designed for families, adults, and juveniles, conducted in areas throughout the park. These include a broad variety of activities: talks, demonstrations, daytime and nighttime walks, visits to historic and scenic sites, storytelling sessions, and wildlife viewing.

One of the highlights each week is the Junior Ranger Award Ceremony for young visitors who have completed their Junior Ranger booklet, a series of activities to acquaint youngsters with the Smokies.

Programs are held at the Cosby, Sugarlands, Elkmont, Cades Cove, Clingmans Dome, Smokemont, Oconaluftee, Balsam Mountain, and Deep Creek areas.

For more information: Great Smoky Mountains National Park, 107 Park Headquarters Road, Gatlinburg, TN 37738. Phone (423) 436-1200.

Auto Tours

There are over 350 miles of roads within the GSMNP, most of which extend a short way up the mountains and connect with foot trails. Persons who cannot or prefer not to hike the foot trails can use the auto tours to explore and enjoy some of the most scenic and spectacular park features. Signs along some of these routes mark Quiet Walkways, strolls of usually of less than 0.5 mile, where travelers can stop, stretch their legs, and enjoy some of the sounds and smells of the Smokies.

FOOTHILLS PARKWAY

[Fig. 45] The Foothills Parkway, a two-way scenic road that was to run alongside the Great Smoky Mountains National Park, is a dream that has yet to come true. In the 1920s, the concept of providing pristine scenic views of the Smokies using a parkway was developed, and a plan approved by Congress in 1944 calls for the Foothills Parkway to run 72 miles along the park's boundary from Cosby to Chilhowee Lake, through Cocke, Sevier, and Blount counties.

Since initial construction began in 1960, only two segments of the road have been completed and opened to the public: a 5.6-mile section from Cosby to I-40 and a 17-mile section from Walland to Chilhowee Lake. A 16-mile road from Walland in Blount County to Wear Valley in Sevier County was partially completed in 1980, but environmental problems and engineering challenges brought the work on the road to a halt.

Engineers couldn't decide how to bring the two sections of the road together across Caylor Gap, a 1.6-mile length of unstable, rocky ridges and ravines. The National Park Service developed a new design that minimizes large cuts and fills in the exceedingly rugged terrain. The work will require construction of 10 bridges.

For more information: Great Smoky Mountains National Park, 107 Park Headquarters Road, Gatlinburg, TN 37738. Phone (423) 436-1200.

THE FOOTHILLS PARKWAY-EAST

[Fig. 44(16)] The 5.5-mile Foothills Parkway-East connects I-40 with TN 32 near Cosby. Running through the foothills that overlook the lowlands between the parkway and English Mountain, is a section that looks toward the west and views of Mount Cammerer, Mount Guyot, and Greenbrier Pinnacle. The paved, two-way road is suitable for RVs and trailers and is a scenic, short approach to the northeastern edge of the GSMNP.

Directions: It runs from TN 32 near Cosby to I-40.

FOOTHILLS PARKWAY-WEST

[Fig. 45] The 17-mile mountain drive between Townsend and Chilhowee Lake known as the Foothills Parkway-West offers scenic overlooks of the western edge of the GSMNP from the top of 2,700-foot Chilhowe Mountain. The paved, two-way road is suitable for RV and trailers and takes about 30 minutes to drive. Across the road from the scenic overlook at Look Rock, a 15-minute walk leads to a lookout tower with a panoramic view of the western edge of the Smokies to the east and the Little Tennessee River valley, once the home of the Overhill Cherokee, to the west.

Horace Kephart

One of the earliest champions of the GSMNP, Horace Sowers Kephart was born in Pennsylvania in 1862. He lived in Iowa for a time and trained at several universities to be a librarian and scholar. As a 23-year-old, he lived and worked in Florence, Italy and had occasion to take walking trips in the Alps and the Apennines, acquainting him with the delights of the high country. He returned to resume his career as a librarian, this time at Yale, married, and started a family.

He moved to St. Louis where he compiled an excellent collection on American frontier history and awakened his own yearnings for adventure. He began to more spend time camping in the Ozarks and less time with his family and his job.

He determined that his life's work lay in a return to nature, and so he left his job and family forever. He moved to the remote southern flank of the Smokies in 1903, where he lived in a cabin along Hazel Creek and began his studies of the Smokies and their flora, fauna, and human inhabitants. He earned his living writing articles on outdoor life for major magazines and classic books including *Camping and Woodcraft* and *Our Southern Highlanders*.

By the mid-1920s, he had become an avid proponent of the creation of a national park in the mountains and was often visited at his boarding house in Bryson City by those seeking to learn more about the Smokies.

Although he died in an auto accident at 68, nine years before the park was dedicated, his name was given to one of the prominent peaks in the Smokies and a stream that arises on its slopes. His memorabilia and papers are housed at Western Carolina University in Sylva and the Pack Memorial Library in Asheville.

Directions: US 321 near Walland to US 129 near Chilhowee Lake.

GREENBRIER ROAD

[Fig. 47] Because this quiet, dead-end road is not suitable for RVs and trailers, most of the traffic you'll encounter will be hikers headed to Ramsay Cascades. The 4-mile trip to the trailhead passes the ranger station, where the pavement gives way to a good gravel road, and it passes a lovely, shady picnic shelter before reaching the sign for the road to the left to the trail to Ramsay Cascades. Ramsay Cascades is the highest waterfall accessible by trail in the GSMNP (*see* page 288). Along this same road you can access the Old Settlers Trail as well. The Old Settlers Trail passes numerous abandoned homesteads along its 15.9-mile length. It climbs less than 500 feet as it winds its way along and across the many creeks that drain the area between Greenbrier Cove and the intersection of the Old Settlers Trail with the Maddron Bald Trail and the Gabes Mountain Trail west of Cosby Campground.

Directions: 6 miles east of Gatlinburg off US 321.

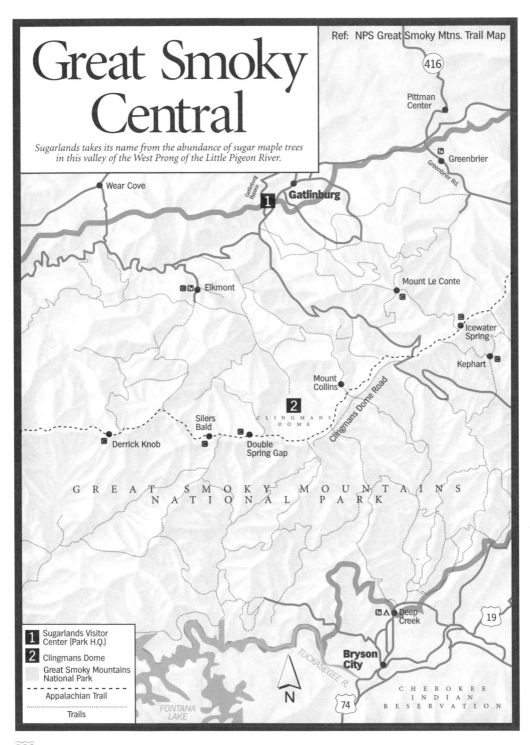

Great Smoky Central

Sugarlands takes its name from the abundance of sugar maple trees in this valley of the West Prong of the Little Pigeon River.

Ref: NPS Great Smoky Mtns. Trail Map

416

Pittman Center

Greenbrier

Greenbrier Rd.

Wear Cove

Gatlinburg bypass

Gatlinburg

1

Elkmont

Mount Le Conte

Icewater Spring

Kephart

Mount Collins

2

Silers Bald

C L I N G M A N S
D O M E

Clingmans Dome Road

Derrick Knob

Double Spring Gap

G R E A T   S M O K Y   M O U N T A I N S
N A T I O N A L   P A R K

Deep Creek

19

1 Sugarlands Visitor Center (Park H.Q.)

2 Clingmans Dome

Great Smoky Mountains National Park

- - - - Appalachian Trail

············ Trails

TUCKASEGEE R.

Bryson City

N

74

C H E R O K E E
I N D I A N
R E S E R V A T I O N

FONTANA LAKE

GATLINBURG BYPASS

[Fig. 47] This two-lane paved road exits US 441 between Pigeon Forge and Gatlinburg and rejoins it in 4.5 miles at the northern entrance to the GSMNP and the Sugarlands Visitor Center. On this road, visitors to the GSMNP not only avoid the considerable congestion through Gatlinburg, but also as the bypass climbs the side of Mt. Harrison, it offers peaceful views of the bustling activity of Gatlinburg, with Mount Le Conte looming large and lovely in the background.

Directions: Between US 441 north of Gatlinburg and the Sugarlands Visitor Center.

CHEROKEE ORCHARD ROAD

[Fig. 44(17)] Named for the 800-acre apple orchard of M.M. Whittle, this two-lane paved road allows RVs and trailers along its 3.5-mile length. Along the way, watch for wildflowers and tour the Noah "Bud" Ogle Place, a working farm from the 1800s, on a self-guiding nature trail that passes the house, barn, and tub mill. The Rainbow Falls trailhead is also on Cherokee Orchard Road (*see* page 288). Soon after passing the Ogle farm, the road joins the one-way Roaring Fork Motor Nature Trail (*see* below).

ROARING FORK MOTOR NATURE TRAIL

[Fig. 44(5)] An intimate, one-way, 5.5-mile paved drive, the Roaring Fork Motor Nature Trail is not suitable for RVs or trailers. It begins past the Ogle Farm on Cherokee Orchard Road, and it continues to explore abandoned farmsteads and offers one of the best opportunities for viewing wildflowers in the GSMNP, including bleeding heart, solomon's seal, and the spectacular showy orchis, a member of the orchid family. A favorite activity along the curvy, steep motor loop is the short hike to Grotto Falls from the Grotto Falls parking area.

Directions: Auto tour road beginning at Cherokee Orchard Road (*see* above).

NEWFOUND GAP ROAD

[Fig. 45] US 441, known as Newfound Gap Road in the park, travels between Gatlinburg and the northern entrance of the park at the Sugarlands Visitor Center and Cherokee, North Carolina and the southern entrance to the park at the Ocon-aluftee Visitor Center. The road takes its name from the gap found in the 1860s that was lower and easier to traverse than the old Indian Gap 2 miles distant. The Indian Gap was used by the old toll road until the discovery of the so-called Newfound Gap changed the course of the only road through the park. Also known as US 441, the 32-mile section allows RVs and trailers and is the most heavily traveled road in the GSMNP, requiring well over an hour to drive during peak tourist season.

From the Sugarlands Visitor Center, the road begins to slowly climb as it follows the West Prong of the Little Pigeon River on its way to the crest at Newfound Gap more than 5,000 feet above sea level. There are picnic areas, overlooks, nature trails, short walkways, stone tunnels, and an incredible 360-degree loop in the road on the way to the southern entrance to the GSMNP at Oconaluftee.

Newfound Gap Road travels between Mount Le Conte and Clingmans Dome and provides access to Clingmans Dome Road (*see* below). Trailheads for several trails, including Alum Cave Trail (*see* page 284) and Chimney Tops Trail (*see* page 284) are located along Newfound Gap Road, and the Appalachian Trail crosses the road at the gap.

CLINGMANS DOME ROAD

[Fig. 47] Clingmans Dome is the highest peak in the park at 6,643 feet. A 7-mile automobile spur road from Newfound Gap Road (US 441) winds up the side of the mountain to a parking lot. A 0.5-mile paved path leads to a concrete ramp topped by a large lookout tower with incredible views on clear fall mornings. The road is RV and trailer accessible. When the road is closed in winter, it's a favored destination after fresh snowfalls for cross-country skiers, as long as Newfound Gap Road remains open.

Directions: Newfound Gap Road to Clingmans Dome parking area.

LITTLE RIVER ROAD

[Fig. 45] Scenic TN 73, more commonly known as the Little River Road, travels 18 miles between the Sugarlands Visitor Center at the northern entrance to the park and Townsend. RVs and trailers also follow this winding, predominantly lower elevation road over portions of the old Little River Railroad bed.

From Sugarlands, the road climbs to Fighting Creek Gap where parking areas on both sides of the road are provided for those hiking the easy, 2.5-mile round trip to Laurel Falls. This hike is so popular the trail has been paved as far as the falls.

A bit farther along the road, the Elkmont Campground is open through November. The remains of the old Wonderland Hotel, a nature trail, and several hiking trails are located at Elkmont, the site of extensive logging operations before the park was formed.

There's a picnic area farther west at Metcalf Bottoms with a trail leading a little over 0.5 mile to the Little Greenbrier Schoolhouse, which was built by the surrounding community members in 1882 and was used to educate the children of the area until 1936 as the weather and funding would allow. From the school continue along a one-lane gravel road that originates on Wear Cove Gap Road and travels to the Walker Sisters Farmstead, an 1870s cabin that was the home of five maiden sisters until the last surviving sister died in 1964.

Continuing on Little River Road, you'll see a small parking area at The Sinks, a tumultuous cascade into a deep sinkhole created by loggers dynamiting to break up a log jam around the turn of the century. Keep a sharp eye out for Meigs Falls, which can be seen alongside the road where Meigs Creek empties into the Little River.

Before reaching Townsend, the Little River Road intersects Laurel Creek Road, the entrance to Cades Cove, at a scenic swimming hole known as the Y. The parking area next to the Y is frequently filled with people going to splash about in the clear, cold river, sunbathe on the big flat rocks, or hike the Chestnut Top Trail.

The Chestnut Top Trail is an outstanding wildflower trail, especially in April and May when star chickweed, spring beauty, bloodroot (*Sanguinaria canadensis*), bishop's cap (*Mitella diphylla*), purple phacelia (*Phacelia bipinnatifida*), and sweet white trillium (*Trillium simile*) are in bloom along the first 0.5 mile of the 4.3-mile trek.

LAUREL CREEK ROAD

[Fig. 45] This is the only paved, two-way road suitable for RVs and trailers entering Cades Cove. As you begin the 7-mile, 15-minute drive, you'll see the turn-off to Tremont, a former Job Corps Camp that is now operated as a year-round environmental education center by the Great Smoky Mountains Natural History Association. Several hiking trails crisscross the road as it approaches the Cades Cove Loop Road.

Directions: Access from the Little River Road between Townsend and the Visitor Center at Sugarlands.

CADES COVE LOOP ROAD

[Fig. 45] This 11-mile, one-way, paved road tours the most popular attraction in the most popular national park in the United States. There is the potential for traffic jams that could extend the usual one-hour driving time. That being said, it's still a beautiful drive with lots of interesting attractions.

Pioneer cabins, farmsteads, and barns and historic buildings dot the slopes ringing the cove. In addition to the campground, picnic area, and riding stable, the Cades Cove Visitor Center has exhibits, a bookstore, and information about the many hiking trails in the area, including the popular walk to Abrams Falls.

The drive is open from dawn to dusk and is suitable for RVs and trailers, but bicyclists have it to themselves early mornings on Wednesday and Saturday from spring through mid-September.

Directions: From the Sugarlands Visitor Center on Little River Road head west toward Townsend, continue straight on Laurel Creek Road 7 miles to the beginning of Cades Cove Loop Road.

RICH MOUNTAIN ROAD

[Fig. 45] This is one of two roads leading out of Cades Cove, except during winter when it's closed. This historic road was the route taken by early settlers in the cove. Today it is 7 miles one-way, steep, and curved until it crests at the park boundary at Rich Mountain Gap and is not suitable for RVs or trailers. It offers a great respite from the fall leaf-lookers creeping along the Cades Cove Loop Road and takes about one hour to drive. There is an excellent view of Cades Cove at a clearing on the side of the mountain, and there are views of Tuckaleechee Cove as you descend toward Townsend.

Directions: Cades Cove Loop Road across from the Missionary Baptist Church to US 321 in Townsend.

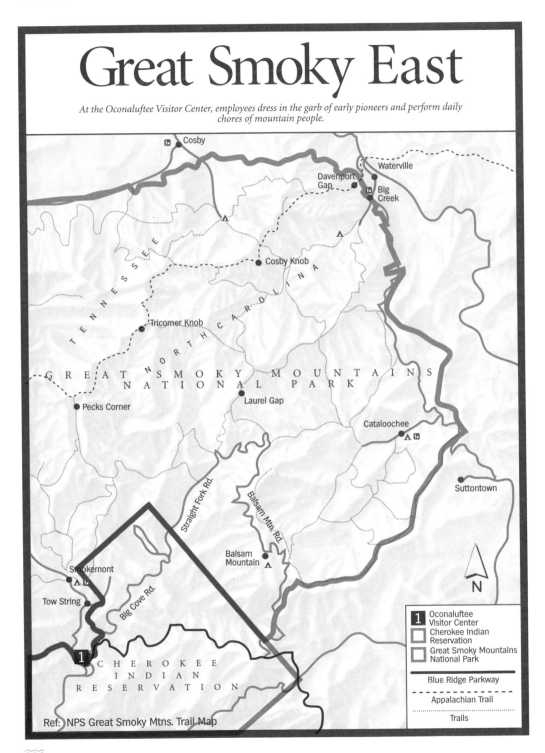

Great Smoky East

At the Oconaluftee Visitor Center, employees dress in the garb of early pioneers and perform daily chores of mountain people.

Cosby

Waterville

Davenport Gap

Big Creek

Cosby Knob

T E N N E S S E E

N O R T H   C A R O L I N A

Tricorner Knob

G R E A T   S M O K Y   M O U N T A I N S
N A T I O N A L   P A R K

Pecks Corner

Laurel Gap

Cataloochee

Suttontown

Straight Fork Rd.

Balsam Mtn. Rd.

Balsam Mountain

Smokemont

Tow String

Big Cove Rd.

N

1 | Oconaluftee Visitor Center
☐ | Cherokee Indian Reservation
☐ | Great Smoky Mountains National Park

——— Blue Ridge Parkway

- - - - - Appalachian Trail

.... Trails

1

C H E R O K E E
I N D I A N
R E S E R V A T I O N

Ref: NPS Great Smoky Mtns. Trail Map

PARSON BRANCH ROAD

[Fig. 45] This is the other historic road leading out of Cades Cove and it, too, is closed in winter and is not suitable for RVs and trailers. The 8-mile gravel road is one-way, steep, and curved, traveling through lush woodlands accented by cascading mountain streams. It once connected settlers in the cove with a toll road that followed the present route of US 129. The trailhead of the Gregory Bald Trail (*see* page 287) is on Parson Branch Road.

Since Parson Branch Road exits on US 129 near Calderwood Lake southwest of the terminus of the Foothills Parkway-West, visitors can create a nice extended driving tour by taking a right turn on US 129, travelling about 10 miles to the Foothills Parkway, following the Parkway 17 miles to its terminus near Townsend, and returning to Cades Cove via the Laurel Creek Road.

Directions: Cades Cove Loop Road just past the Visitor Center to US 129.

BIG CREEK/CATALOOCHEE ROAD (OLD NC 284)

[Fig. 45] The 27-mile Big Creek/Cataloochee Road follows the eastern edge of the GSMNP as it starts out as TN 32 west of Cosby. The pavement ends and the real trek begins about 11 miles later at the North Carolina line near the crossing of the Appalachian Trail at Davenport Gap.

The gravel road, now known as Old NC 284, is not suitable for RVs or trailers. It continues to the Mount Sterling Community where a left fork travels a couple of miles to I-40 via Waterville Road at Exit 451, and a right fork leads to the Big Creek Ranger Station and Campground (*see* page 276).

Old NC 284 sticks to the center and journeys 14 miles along a very curvy, one-lane road with two-way traffic that will take a couple of hours to negotiate as you travel through one of the most remote sections of the Smokies accessible by car.

Along the way, you'll pass the trailhead for the Mount Sterling Trail, a 2.8-mile trail that climbs nearly 2,000 feet from where Old NC 284 passes through Mount Sterling Gap to the summit at Mount Sterling. From the 60-foot steel fire tower on the summit, there are beautiful views of surrounding peaks as well as Cataloochee Valley to the south. A backcountry campsite (Number 38) has several sites among the Fraser fir.

The road continues past the community once known as Little Cataloochee, a smaller settlement of families related to the earlier settlers in the larger, neighboring community of Cataloochee. A gated road open to hikers and horseback riders bears to the right into Little Cataloochee with its few remaining historic structures and apple orchards that were once the source of commerce for the community.

Another couple of miles brings you to another split in the road. Bear to the left to return to I-40 at Exit 20, about 8 miles distant via Cove Creek Road. The right fork of the road continues to the long, narrow cove of the Cataloochee Valley (*see* page 275).

Directions: From Cosby, follow TN 32 until the pavement ends. Continue on the gravel road, now known as Big Creek/Cataloochee Road.

CATALOOCHEE ROAD

The entrance to Cataloochee Valley from US 276 is an 8-mile drive with paved and graveled sections. Travelers, including those in RVs and trailers, willing to face the challenge take Exit 20 off I-40 to US 276. Cove Creek Road, also known as Old NC 284, continues to Cove Creek Gap and bears to the right becoming a gravel surface, while Cataloochee Road begins at the left fork and descends into this once thriving community of 1,200 surrounded by peaks of the Smokies. Cataloochee Road continues as a paved road to the ranger station and campground, but becomes gravel as it passes the few remaining structures in the Cataloochee Historic District including a church, a school, houses, and barns. A auto tour guide is available at a roadside dispenser as you enter Cataloochee or from one of the GSMNP visitor centers. Cataloochee has one of the drive-in horse camps in the GSMNP (*see* page 281, 291).

Directions: From I-40, take Exit 20 to US 276 and turn right onto Cove Creek Road (Old NC 284). Follow Cove Creek Road to Cataloochee Road.

BLUE RIDGE PARKWAY

[Fig. 45] The Blue Ridge Parkway (BRP) was proposed in 1933 to link Virginia's Shenandoah National Park and the Great Smoky Mountains National Park. Initial funding for the 469-mile scenic parkway was approved in 1933 and surveyors were in the field the next year. The initial construction began during the summer of 1935 on a 12-mile section near the Virginia/North Carolina border. Ribbon-cutting ceremonies for the completion took place 52 years later following the construction of the last link, an engineering marvel known as the Linn Cove Viaduct that curves around Grandfather Mountain in North Carolina, minimizing the parkway's effect on the environment.

The southern terminus of the 469-mile BRP is at the southern edge of the GSMNP at the junction with US 441. On the BRP, the speed limit is 45 mph, unless otherwise posted, and the paved, two-way road is suitable for RVs and trailers to share with cyclists and motorists intent on enjoying the breathtaking scenery. Allowing for stops along the way, it will take you a minimum of three to four days to feel like you've had a chance to experience a sampling of all the BRP has to offer.

As you enter the BRP on the Oconaluftee River Bridge at an elevation of 2,000 feet, you immediately begin to climb, attaining an elevation of 5,000 feet within the first 10 miles. At Richland Balsam (mile marker 431.4) you'll reach the highest point on the BRP, an elevation of 6,053 feet. In addition to scenic overlooks and picnic areas, the BRP offers self-guiding nature trails, parks, and museums.

For more information: Superintendent, BRP, 400 BB&T Building, 1 Pack Square, Asheville, NC 28801. Phone 828-298-0398.

BALSAM MOUNTAIN ROAD

[Fig. 48] This 9-mile, paved, high mountain road begins as a spur of the Blue Ridge Parkway near Wolf Laurel Gap (mile marker 458.2). It leads drivers along the crest of Balsam Mountain with scenic overlooks on both sides. One highlight is the

Mile-High Overlook that scans the distant peaks of the Smokies to the left, including Clingmans Dome, Mount Le Conte, Mount Kephart, and Mount Guyot. To the right, the Balsam Mountains reach to the sky. After 3.3 miles, you re-enter the GSMNP. Picnic tables are available at Black Camp Gap. RVs and trailers are allowed on Balsam Mountain Road, which leads another 6 miles to Balsam Mountain Campground. At 5,310 feet, this is the highest camp accessible by road in the GSMNP (*see* page 279). Proceed past the campground to the Heintooga Overlook with its scenic view of the Smokies. The Balsam Mountain Road is closed in winter.

HEINTOOGA-ROUND BOTTOM ROAD

[Fig. 45] The Heintooga Overlook, at the end of Balsam Mountain Road near the Balsam Mountain Campground (*see* page 279), offers sweeping vistas of the high ranges of the Smokies. Just beyond the parking area for Heintooga Overlook, the 14-mile, one-way, gravel Heintooga-Round Bottom Road begins its curving route from an altitude of 5,535 feet to about 2,000 feet. This rough road is not suitable for RVs and trailers and is closed in winter. It will take about an hour to travel this route, which showcases the botanical diversity of the GSMNP through stands of beech and birch, followed by hemlocks, maples, and oaks. At the broad, flat area known as Round Bottom, the one-lane road becomes two-way before it joins the paved, two-way Big Cove Road north of Cherokee, North Carolina. Round Bottom has one of the drive-in horse camps in the GSMNP.

LAKEVIEW DRIVE

[Fig. 45] A dead-end road, Lakeview Drive travels 6 miles along the upper end of beautiful Fontana Lake. This lightly traveled road allows RVs and trailers and features scenic overlooks as well as good opportunities for fall foliage viewing. It was built in 1959 with the intention of replacing a North Carolina state road north of the lake that was flooded when Fontana Lake was created in 1944. Lakeview Drive was not completed for a variety of reasons, not the least of which was the desire to protect the roadless wild area at the southwestern end of the park.

Directions: From Bryson City, North Carolina follow Everett Street across the Tuckasegee River out of town to Lakeview Drive.

Cades Cove

Among the park's many outstanding topographic features, perhaps the most intriguing are the strange, flat-bottomed valleys surrounded by mountains that are known as coves. Of the several that appear throughout the southern Appalachians, Cades Cove is the most famous one inside the park. The coves vary in size and shape but are considered to be of similar geologic origin.

For the simplest explanation, consider them as windows, formed when a hole or break appeared in the older, harder rock that overthrust the younger rock during a mountain-building period. Erosion, acting on the softer rock underneath eventually carved out large, deep openings, leaving the harder rocks standing as ridges on all sides. Early settlers were attracted to these coves, and not just because they were level lands. Coves also have limestone bottoms and contain an accumulation of soil and gravel washed down from the mountain slopes above. As a result, cove soils are deep, rich, and extremely fertile—an anomaly, since the soil in most mountain lands is thin and poor.

Even though Cades Cove was a part of the Cherokee Nation until the signing of the Calhoun Treaty in 1819, in which the Indians relinquished their claim to the territory, several grants were issued for Cades Cove land as early as 1794. However, the first legal land title was granted in 1819, and in all, 36 land grants were issued from that date until 1890.

In the meantime, the population of the cove grew rapidly. The first families moved in in 1820, and by 1830 records show 44 households and a population of 271. Until that time there were only Indian trails between the cove and the outside world, but between 1830 and 1840, five roads were opened.

By the end of the decade the numbers had increased to 70 households with 471 people. By 1850, there were 132 households and a population of 685, but a slump followed that reduced the numbers significantly during a 10-year period. Another influx of settlers occurred in the late 1800s, and in 1900 the population reached its all-time peak of 125 families and 708 people.

From that point, due to World War I, the great flu epidemic of 1917–1918, people leaving the cove for employment elsewhere, and the initiation of the park movement, the population gradually diminished. Once all of the land in Cades Cove was purchased, a few residents were allowed to remain as lease-holders, but as soon as they died or moved out, the Park Service destroyed evidence of all but a handful of their homesteads, intending to allow the valley to return to its natural condition. Not all of the homes were log cabins, and the lifestyles of most of the families were far from primitive.

A closer look at the history of Cades Cove reveals that it was much more civilized than people outside the mountains might have imagined. There was a well-organized local government, as well as schools, churches, general stores, blacksmith shops, regular mail service, telephone communication, and even automobiles.

For many years Cades Cove wasn't well known because the valley was so prosperous that families could provide for their own needs. For many years the inhabitants were distant from any marketplaces and had little use for cash. They depended upon each other for the food and few comforts they enjoyed. Each household had its own vegetable garden, and they raised grain. Grain could be ground in tub mills into cornmeal and flour needed for the family's personal consumption. They also needed grain to feed their livestock, including the chickens and cows that supplied them with eggs and milk.

Grain was also used to produce moonshine whiskey, which continued to be made in the cove even after the government ceased to license distillers. There was also brandy distilled from fruit. Such spirits, along with apples (*Malus* sp.) and chestnuts, were items that were transported out of the cove and sold for cash in Maryville or Knoxville.

Today, Cades Cove is the most popular destination in the most popular park in the United States. The Cades Cove Campground, developed with bathrooms and 161 campsites, is open year-round. There's also a small general store, riding stables with saddle horses and guided tours from April to October, and a picnic area near the campground. The visitor center is located at Cable Mill about halfway around the Cades Cove Loop Road.

Each year more than 2 million people stream into Cades Cove to admire the sweeping views and get a look at what life in the Smokies was like in the old days. Also, the cove is a favorite wildlife viewing area since it's nearly impossible to travel the 11-mile loop road and not see deer, turkey, bear, or groundhogs. Other small animals and birds are common sights also.

The main purpose of the loop road is to allow visitors to see the old cabins, churches, barns, and other structures built by the original settlers and preserved by the Park Service.

The Cable Mill at the Cades Cove Visitor Center is a water-powered grist mill that is still in operation, and stone ground meal and other mountain products can be purchased at the gift shop. Living history demonstrations are held spring through fall at the complex and include the making of sorghum molasses, apple butter, and lye soap.

There are two one-way gravel roads leading out of the cove. To the north Rich Mountain Road leads to Townsend. To the south, Parsons Branch Road ends on US 129 near Calderwood Lake. Both are closed in winter.

Two gravel roads, Hyatt Lane and Sparks Lane, connect the northern and southern portions of the Cades Cove Loop Road. Both cross Abrams Creek, which offers excellent rainbow and brown trout fishing, and offer easy access by foot through the cove. Between the waterfall on Abrams Creek and the portion of the creek that flows through the cove, the Abrams Creek Trail travels downstream beside some very good rainbow and brown trout waters.

An excellent system of hiking trails surround the cove including self-guided nature trails and longer, more strenuous trails including one to Gregory Bald, a broad grass meadow known for its display of flame azalea (*Rhododendron calendulaceum*) in late June. There is also the Anthony Creek Trail that begins as an access road to the horse camp and travels along Anthony Creek on its way to the high country at Spence Field, Thunderhead Mountain, and Russell Field along the Appalachian Trail.

Numerous backcountry campsites in the vicinity are open year-round, and among them Cooper Road, Hesse Creek, Kelly Gap, Rich Mountain, Ace Gap, Anthony Creek, Beard Creek, Flint Gap, Rabbit Creek, and Scott Gap are available to horse parties with backcountry permits. Anthony Creek is a drive-in horse camp that can accommodate 12 horses and 12 people from April through October. The camps at Ledbetter Ridge and Sheep Pen Gap are rationed because of heavy use and require a phone call to the park's Backcountry Reservation Office.

For many years limited agricultural practices, including cattle farming, were allowed by permit, but present plans are to return to the patchwork of fields and grasses. Some fields will be cut and others burned, and native grasses from other areas of the cove will be planted in an effort to crowd out the fescue grass that was planted in the 1960s to graze cattle. No other agricultural practices will be conducted.

A long-time cattle farmer in the cove will be allowed to remain, but he is limited to 500 cattle, down from the previous 1,500, and upon his passing, grazing will be phased out.

Directions: To reach Cades Coves from the Sugarlands Visitors Center, follow TN 73 (Little River Road) 18 miles to the intersection east of Townsend just inside the park boundary, and go straight ahead 7 miles on the Laurel Creek Road.

To reach Cades Cove from Townsend, follow US 321 east of Townsend to its intersection with Scenic TN 73 (Little River Road). Follow Little River Road 2 miles to Laurel Creek Road. Continue an additional 7 miles on Laurel Creek Road to the entrance to Cades Cove.

Activities: Camping, horseback riding, bicycling, hiking, picnicking, wildlife viewing, fishing, scenic driving.

Facilities: Campground, camp store, visitor center with restrooms and museum, riding stable, picnic area, historic structures including Cable Mill, a working water-wheel powered mill, bike rental at Cades Cove Bicycle Shop, trails.

Dates: Visitor Center open daily mid-Apr. through Nov. and on a reduced schedule Dec. through Mar. Backcountry campsites and Cades Cove Campground are open year-round. Cades Cove Loop Road is closed until 10 a.m. on Wednesdays and Saturdays from late May through mid-September but otherwise is open from sunrise to sunset.

Fees: There is a charge for camping.

Closest town: Townsend.

For more information: Great Smoky Mountains National Park, 107 Park Headquarters Road, Gatlinburg, TN 37738. Phone (423) 436-1200. Backcountry Reservations, 107 Park Headquarters Road, Gatlinburg, 37738. Phone (423) 436-1231.

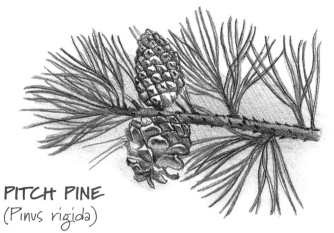

PITCH PINE
(Pinus rigida)

Cataloochee Valley

[Fig. 44(12)] Once the largest settlement in the Smokies, the areas known as Big Cataloochee and Little Cataloochee are located in the remote southeastern section of the North Carolina portion of the GSMNP. Settled in the 1830s, Big Cataloochee is an oval-shaped valley watered by Cataloochee, Rough Fork, and Pretty Hollow creeks and surrounded by towering peaks. Noland Mountain separates it from Little Cataloochee to the north.

Large tracts of land, including the land in Cataloochee, were granted to John Gray Blount, the brother of the Governor of the Southwest Territory, for services in lieu of cash. He, in turn, sold thousands of acres to Col. Robert Love, a Revolutionary War veteran and land speculator.

The first land entry in Cataloochee was 100 acres to Henry Caldwell in 1814. By the 1850s, Cataloochee was populated enough that adult children of the families living in the valley moved to Little Cataloochee to establish their own farmsteads. In 1900, the population was around 700 and most of the original log houses had been enlarged and weatherboarded. There were about 200 buildings scattered around the valley. Of these, less than a dozen remain.

In the early 1930s, Tom and Judy Alexander settled in Big Cataloochee to establish a tourist ranch with horseback riding, fishing, and hiking opportunities. At this time nearly 100 families lived in Cataloochee. By 1937 most of the families had moved out. The Alexanders stayed one more year before they, too, left, relocating their ranch to outside Maggie Valley, North Carolina.

Unlike Cades Cove, relatively few visitors to GSMNP discover Cataloochee, although it rewards visitors who meet the challenge of getting here with its peaceful beauty. When you arrive you'll find historic buildings, a shady campground, and a self-guiding auto tour.

Cataloochee Creek and its tributaries support a mixture of the largest rainbow and brown trout found in the valley. You can easily access the creek near the campground. Trails access other trout streams including Caldwell Fork; Palmer Creek, which has rainbows and brookies above 3,000 feet; Little Cataloochee Creek; and Rough Fork, which is near the Big Hemlock backcountry campsite (site # 40), a favorite camp of anglers seeking rainbow trout. No rationing is involved at this site.

Directions: To reach Cataloochee, exit I-40 at US 276 (Exit 20) and turn right onto Cove Creek Road after 0.2 mile. Follow Cove Creek Road as it becomes a gravel road for a portion of the 11-mile drive to Cataloochee.

Activities: Camping, hiking, wildlife viewing, bicycling, scenic driving, and trout fishing.

Facilities: Primitive campground with 27 sites and ranger station.

Dates: Campground open mid-Apr. though Oct. Backcountry campsites open year-round.

Fees: There is a charge for camping.

Closest town: Maggie Valley, North Carolina, 13 miles.

For more information: Great Smoky Mountains National Park, 107 Park Head-quarters Road, Gatlinburg, TN 37738. Phone (423) 436-1200. Backcountry Reservations, 107 Park Headquarters Road, Gatlinburg, 37738. Phone (423) 436-1231.

Camping

The GSMNP has 1,008 developed sites in 10 campgrounds maintained by the Park Service. The developed campgrounds have tent sites, limited trailer space, water, fireplaces, picnic tables, and restrooms with flush toilets, but there are no hot showers or hookups for trailers and RVs.

Sewage disposal stations are at Smokemont, Cades Cove, Deep Creek, and Cosby campgrounds and across the road from the Sugarlands Visitors Center. They are not available for use in the winter.

Reservations are required from May 15 through October 31 for year-round campgrounds including Cades Cove, Elkmont, and Smokemont. The length of stay is limited to seven consecutive days during the reservation period. Otherwise, the maximum stay is 14 days. You may call (800) 365-2267 for these reservations up to 12 weeks in advance, otherwise the system operates on a first-come, first-serve basis. The number of campsites available in year-round campgrounds decreases seasonally.

For more information: Great Smoky Mountains National Park, 107 Park Head-quarters Road, Gatlinburg, TN 37738. Phone (423) 436-1200.

CAMPGROUNDS
BIG CREEK

[Fig. 45] Located in the extreme northeastern corner on the North Carolina side of the GSMNP, this was one of the areas extensively logged before the formation of the park. Under the aegis of the Park Service, the area has recovered and Big Creek is one of the prettiest streams in the Smokies. A trail originating in the campground follows the creek as it cascades over massive boulders into deep plunge pools.

Directions: From I-40 between Newport and Asheville, take Exit 451, which is the Waterville Road. Follow it through Waterville, southwest about 1.5 miles to the campground.

Activities: Camping (tents only, all walk-in sites), fishing, and hiking.

Facilities: 12 sites, cold running water, fire rings, trail, and sanitary facilities.

Dates: Open mid-Mar. to Nov.

TULIP TREE OR
YELLOW POPLAR
(Liriodendron tulipifera)

Fees: There is a charge for camping.

Closest town: Waterville, North Carolina, 1.5 miles.

For more information: Great Smoky Mountains National Park, 107 Park Headquarters Road, Gatlinburg, TN 37738. Phone (423) 436-1200.

COSBY

[Fig. 45] Cosby has a lovely, relatively underutilized campground on the northeastern edge of the park. Several hiking trails originate from the campground including the Cosby Nature Trail, which is good for spring wildflower walks. Little Cosby Creek, a lovely stream bordered by hemlocks, offers angling opportunities for rainbow trout in its lower portions and access for tubing. It is restricted above the Low Gap Trail crossing for protection of brookies. The Low Gap Trail begins at the parking area to the left of the Cosby campground and crosses Cosby Creek in less than 1 mile.

Directions: Off TN 32 approximately 1.2 miles east of Cosby. Drive 2 miles on Cosby Cove Road to the Cosby Campground.

Activities: Camping, ranger/naturalist programs, fishing, and hiking.

Facilities: 175 campsites, sanitary facilities, disposal station, picnic tables, cold running water, and fire grills.

Dates: Open mid-Mar. to Nov.

Fees: There is a charge for camping.

Closest town: Cosby, 3 miles.

For more information: Great Smoky Mountains National Park, 107 Park Headquarters Road, Gatlinburg, TN 37738. Phone (423) 436-1200.

ELKMONT

[Fig. 45] Elkmont is off Little River Road and is the closest campground to Gatlinburg. Although it was the site of extensive logging operations before the formation of the park, the Elkmont Campground is tree-shaded with many campsites located along the confluence of Jakes Creek and the Little River.

Fishing access is plentiful along Jake's Creek Trail, which begins about 0.4 mile beyond the abandoned Elkmont Summer Colony, a cluster of former vacation homes built in the 1920s and now property of the GSMNP.

Elkmont was also the site of the historic Wonderland Hotel, one of two facilities offering overnight accommodations inside the park. The GSMNP declined to renew the lease for the Wonderland in 1992. The building, which does not fall under protective guidelines, is targeted for eventual removal.

Directions: Off TN 73 between Townsend and the Sugarlands Visitors Center, 9 miles west of Gatlinburg.

Activities: Picnicking, camping.

Facilities: 220 sites, some wheelchair accessible, sanitary facilities, fire grills, picnic tables, and cold running water.

Dates: Open mid-Mar. to Nov.

Fees: There is a charge for camping

Closest town: Gatlinburg, 9 miles.

For more information: Great Smoky Mountains National Park, 107 Park Headquarters Road, Gatlinburg, TN 37738. Phone (423) 436-1200.

CADES COVE

[Fig. 44] Cades Cove is on the western edge of the park and is one of three developed campgrounds open year-round. The campground provides easy access to horseback riding at the stable in Cades Cove, bicycle rental, hiking, and picnicking as well as fishing in Abrams Creek and visits to the historic structures and visitor center in Cades Cove (*see* Cades Cove, page 271).

Directions: From Townsend take TN 73 approximately 2 miles to Laurel Creek Road. Follow Laurel Creek Road to the Cades Cove Campground on the left just before Laurel Creek becomes the one-way Cades Cove Loop Road.

Activities: Camping, horseback riding, bicycling, hiking, ranger/naturalist programs, and picnicking.

Facilities: 161 sites (some wheelchair accessible), sanitary facilities, fire grills, picnic tables, cold running water, bike rentals, disposal station, firewood for sale, pay phone, vending machines, and stable nearby.

Dates: Open year-round.

Fees: There is a charge for camping.

Closest town: Townsend, 10 miles.

For more information: Great Smoky Mountains National Park, 107 Park Headquarters Road, Gatlinburg, TN 37738. Phone (423) 436-1200.

ABRAMS CREEK

[Fig. 45] Although it is the smallest campground on the Tennessee side of the park, it is one of the prettiest sites. The section of Abrams Creek near the campground offers excellent trout fishing in several long, deep pools. A steep walk up Little Bottoms Trail leads to Abrams Falls, a 25-foot cascade into a deep, trout-filled pool.

Directions: From US 129 approximately 1 mile east of junction with Western Foothills Parkway near Chilhowee Lake, turn onto Happy Valley Road and continue 7 miles to the Abrams Creek ranger station and campground.

Activities: Camping and fishing.

Facilities: 16 sites for tents and trailers up to 12 feet in length (some wheelchair accessible), cold running water, fire rings, and sanitary facilities.

Dates: Open mid-Mar. to Nov.

Fees: There is a charge for camping.

Closest town: Maryville, 15 miles.

For more information: Great Smoky Mountains National Park, 107 Park Headquarters Road, Gatlinburg, TN 37738. Phone (423) 436-1200.

LOOK ROCK

[Fig. 45] On the Western Foothills Parkway, Look Rock offers hiking and scenic overlooks.

Directions: Look Rock is on the Western Foothills Parkway between Walland and US 129.

Activities: Camping, hiking.

Facilities: 92 sites, sanitary facilities, picnic tables, cold running water, and fire grills.

Dates: Open late May to Nov.

Fees: There is a charge for camping.

Closest town: Maryville, 11 miles.

For more information: Great Smoky Mountains National Park, 107 Park Headquarters Road, Gatlinburg, TN 37738. Phone (423) 436-1200.

Wilderness Wildlife Week

This week-long series of free events for wilderness lovers takes place each January in Pigeon Forge, Tennessee, a few miles north of the Great Smoky Mountains National Park. During the week there are hikes and field trips ranging from easy, 1-mile jaunts to strenuous overnight hikes in the park, along with more than 100 slide shows and lectures conducted by various experts from the National Park Service, the U.S. Fish and Wildlife Service, Tennessee Wildlife Resources Agency, the University of Tennessee, and the Smoky Mountain Field School. For more information contact the Pigeon Forge Department of Tourism at (800) 946-8373 or the Office of Special Events at (423) 429-7350.

CATALOOCHEE

[Fig. 48] Located in one of the most remote sections of the park, Cataloochee provides excellent access to trout fishing and hiking.

Directions: Exit I-40 west of Asheville at Exit 20 to NC 276. Turn right and go west to Cove Creek Road, then turn left and drive north on a dirt road to a paved road that runs through the Cataloochee Valley where several buildings remain from the former settlement of 1,200 residents.

Activities: Camping, hiking, fishing.

Facilities: 27 sites, sanitary facilities, cold running water, and fire rings.

Dates: Open mid-Mar. to Nov.

Fees: There is a charge for camping.

Closest town: Maggie Valley, North Carolina, 13 miles.

For more information: Great Smoky Mountains National Park, 107 Park Headquarters Road, Gatlinburg, TN 37738. Phone (423) 436-1200.

BALSAM MOUNTAIN

[Fig. 48] Balsam Mountain Campground sits 5,310 feet above sea level north of the Blue Ridge Parkway on the North Carolina side of the park. A nature trail originating at the campground introduces campers to life in the high reaches of the Smokies.

Directions: 10 miles north of Soco Gap, exit the Blue Ridge Parkway between mile markers 458 and 459 on Balsam Mountain Road.

Activities: Camping and hiking.

Facilities: 46 sites, fire grills, picnic tables, cold running water, and sanitary facilities.

CHESTNUT OAK
(Quercus prinus)
This is also called
rock oak because of
its preference for a
rocky habitat.

Dates: Open late May through Sept.
Fees: There is a charge for camping.
Closest town: Cherokee, 18 miles.
For more information: Great Smoky Mountains National Park, 107 Park Headquarters Road, Gatlinburg, TN 37738. Phone (423) 436-1200.

SMOKEMONT

[Fig. 48] Smokemont is a lovely, shady campground on the southern edge of the park with many streamside sites. It is the largest campground on the North Carolina side of the park.

Directions: Off US 441 approximately 6 miles north of Cherokee, North Carolina.

Activities: Camping, fishing, horseback riding, ranger/naturalist programs, and hiking.

Facilities: 140 sites (some wheelchair accessible), disposal station, sanitary facilities, firewood for sale, cold running water, picnic tables, and fire grills.

Dates: Open year-round.

Fees: There is a charge for camping.

Closest town: Cherokee, North Carolina, 6 miles.

For more information: Great Smoky Mountains National Park, 107 Park Headquarters Road, Gatlinburg, TN 37738. Phone (423) 436-1200.

DEEP CREEK

[Fig. 45] Deep Creek Campground is very popular with anglers because of its proximity to the Deep Creek Trail, which offers about 10 miles of access to good to excellent rainbow and brown trout fishing on Deep Creek. Horace Kephart, a noted author and early proponent of the park, frequented this area. There are several backcountry campsites along Deep Creek that are frequented by anglers also. The campground is within 2 miles of Juneywhank Falls, Indian Creek Falls, and Toms Branch Falls.

Directions: Take the Deep Creek Campground Road 3 miles north from Bryson City, North Carolina.

Activities: Camping, fishing, ranger/naturalist programs.

Facilities: 108 sites, disposal station, sanitary facilities, cold running water, fire grills, firewood for sale, and picnic tables.

Dates: Open Apr. to Nov.

Fees: There is a charge for camping.

Closest town: Bryson City, North Carolina, 3 miles.

For more information: Great Smoky Mountains National Park, 107 Park Headquarters Road, Gatlinburg, TN 37738. Phone (423) 436-1200.

▨ BACKCOUNTRY CAMPING

In addition to the developed campgrounds, there are 98 backcountry campsites and 16 trail shelters. All require a free use permit. Approximately 30 of the sites can be reserved up to one month in advance, and the remainder are first-come, first-serve sites. The latter may be obtained by self-registering at any ranger station. You may stay up to three consecutive nights at a campsite, but should plan to spend only one night at any shelter. Since some sites are rationed because of heavy use, it may be necessary to obtain permission to camp from the Backcountry Reservation Office.

Camping is permitted only at designated sites and shelters. The maximum camping party size is eight. You should not bathe or wash dishes with soap in any park stream. All water should be boiled for one minute before drinking. A small camp stove is a good idea since open fires are allowed only at designated campsites and only wood that is dead and on the ground may be collected. Food should be stored so that it is inaccessible to bears, and all food and trash must be packed out.

All rules and regulations are listed on the Great Smoky Mountains Trail Map available from the Great Smoky Mountain Natural History Association.

For more information: Backcountry Reservations, 107 Park Headquarters Road, Gatlinburg, 37738. Phone (423) 436-1231.

▨ EQUESTRIAN CAMPS

There are also automobile-accessible horse camps with primitive horse stalls that may be reserved up to 30 days in advance and used for a maximum of 7 days. Some of the sites are rationed due to heavy use. Horses are restricted to trails designated for horse use. They may not be left unattended or allowed to graze. All food must be packed in. Horses should not be tied within 100 feet of trail shelters, sleeping areas of campsites, or stream or water sources.

For more information: Backcountry Reservations, 107 Park Headquarters Road, Gatlinburg, 37738. Phone (423) 436-1231.

Hiking Trails

There are more than 150 hiking trails in the park, with origins that represent an almost encyclopedic history of the area, dating back to long before the appearance of the first white man. Some of the earliest were game trails created by migrating bison, elk, and other large animals. Many became Indian traces used for trading between tribes and for warpaths.

When settlers moved into the Smokies, some of these became sled and wagon roads. Later, when the big lumber companies came to harvest the timber, a vast number of logging roads and railroads were built that traveled far back into the mountains.

Many hiking trails follow all or parts of these routes, but there are many others that were developed by the CCC, Park Service, and hiking clubs to reach scenic places, historic locations, or other interesting features.

The most famous is the 72.1-mile section of the Appalachian Trail (*see* Appalachian Trail, page 297), which follows the crest of the mountains from the Pigeon River to the Little Tennessee River.

The system of trails in the park is complex and extremely varied in regard to length, degree of difficulty, and condition. They range from short, level, well-maintained paths that are accessible to the handicapped, to rugged, nearly vertical trails that should be attempted only by well-conditioned hikers.

Some of the most popular trails are the day loops that require only a light pack, and these can be found at locations throughout the park. There are also plenty of overnight hikes that utilize the backcountry campsites.

The self-guided nature trails are popular because there is easy access to these short, casual walks.

NATURE TRAILS

Ranging from 0.5 to 1 mile round-trip, the nature trails are loops featuring natural history, beauty, and accessibility. These are generally easy trails with minimal changes in elevation that are suitable for all ages. Brochures available at the trailheads or at one of the visitor centers describe highlights.

For more information: Great Smoky Mountains National Park, 107 Park Headquarters Road, Gatlinburg, TN 37738. Phone (423) 436-1200.

COSBY

[Fig. 45(4)] This 1-mile, round-trip trail is a good spot for spring wildflowers including bleeding heart (*Dicentra eximia*), showy orchis (*Orchis spectabilis*), and the nodding Vasey's trillium (*Trillium vaseyi*) in April and May. The trail follows a portion of Cosby Creek across numerous footbridges and past old house sites.

The arching, glossy green leaves of dog-hobble grow so thick in many areas of the Smokies, including along the Cosby Nature Trail, that bears could escape the hunting dogs of early settlers by crashing through the dense growth that hobbled or tangled the pursuing dogs.

Directions: Starts near the amphitheater at Cosby Campground (*see* page 277).

NOAH "BUD" OGLE

[Fig. 45(5)] This 0.75-mile round trip is known for its abundance of white trillium and solomon's seal (*Smilacina racemosa*) and its route by an old log home, barn, and water-powered tub mill. This is one of the best wildflower walks in the Smokies.

Directions: From Gatlinburg, take Airport Road at traffic light number 8. As the road re-enters the GSMNP, it becomes Cherokee Orchard Road. Approximately 3 miles from traffic light number 8 and 0.5 mile from the entrance to the paved, one-way Roaring Fork Motor Nature Trail, the Bud Ogle Place Nature Trail begins.

SUGARLANDS

[Fig. 47(1)] Many wildflowers flourish along this 1-mile, round-trip trail including touch-me-nots (*Impatiens pallida*), doll's-eyes (*Actaea pachypoda*), little brown jug (*Asarum arifolium*) of the Birthwort family, and foamflower (*Tiarella cordifolia*). Native shrubs in the area include hearts-a-bustin' (*Euonymus americanus*) and sweetshrub, or Carolina allspice (*Calycanthus floridus*).

The trail follows a tumbling creek through rhododendron thickets and second-growth forest and past the restored log cabin of John Ownby.

Directions: Begins near Sugarlands Visitors Center (*see* page 259).

ELKMONT

[Fig. 47] This 0.8-mile, round-trip trail travels through an area logged by the Little River Lumber Company nearly 70 years ago. On the drier southern slopes, a pine-oak forest prevails, while a cove hardwood forest and wildflowers blanket the northern slopes. The brochure directs you in reading the landscape to discover portions of Elkmont's past visible in the forest terrain.

Directions: Begins at parking lot opposite Elkmont Campground (*see* page 277).

CADES COVE

[Fig. 44] A dry pine-oak forest with a dogwood understory is visited on this 0.75-mile, round-trip hike. You may spot pink lady's slipper (*Cypripedium acaule*) on this trail in April or May. The trail introduces visitors to native plants and their uses by early settlers in the cove.

Directions: Begins on Cades Cove Loop Road 0.5 mile from Cable Mill junction (*see* page 267).

COVE HARDWOOD

This popular, 0.75-mile, round-trip trail traverses some second-growth forest as well as mature cove hardwoods. Wildflowers are abundant on the moist slopes beneath Eastern hemlock, buckeye, basswood, yellow poplar, white ash (*Fraxinus americana*), black locust (*Robinia pseudo-acacia*), flowering silverbell (*Halesia carolina*), and sugar maple. Yellow trillium (*Trillium luteum*), trout lily (*Erythronium americanum*), Dutchman's breeches (*Dicentra cucullaria*), false solomon's seal (*Maianthemum racemosum*), white trillium (*Trillium grandiflorum*), tiny fringed phacelia (*Phacelia fimbriata*), and sharp-lobed hepatica (*Hepatica nobilis*) may be spotted along the trail.

Directions: Begins at Chimney Tops Picnic Area on Newfound Gap Road (US 441).

SPRUCE-FIR

[Fig. 47] The yellow variety of Clinton's lily, or ead lily (*Clintonia borealis*), and wood sorrel (*Oxalis montana*) are found along the 0.5-mile, round-trip hike through old-growth red spruce and Fraser fir trees, which are under attack from the balsam woolly adelgid.

Directions: From Gatlinburg follow Newfound Gap Road (US 441) about 15 miles south to Clingmans Dome Road.

SMOKEMONT

[Fig. 44(14)] Watch for yellow trillium and great chickweed (*Stellaria pubera* var. *silvatica*) along this 0.75-mile round trip that crosses Bradley Fork Creek. Although not indigenous, Norway spruces (*Picea abies*) found their way here from burned areas that were reforested before the area was part of the park. The effects of logging and farming are examined.

Directions: Begins at Smokemont Campground (*see* page 280).

BALSAM MOUNTAIN

[Fig. 48] This 0.75-mile, one-way trail takes you through hardwood forests of beech, birch, and maple followed by spruce-fir forest. You're likely to spot spring beauties (*Claytonia caroliniana*) and trout lilies along the trail in April and May. The northern hardwood forest growing at more than 1 mile above sea level is explored in a brochure available at the trailhead or one of the visitor centers.

Directions: Begins at Balsam Mountain Campground (*see* page 279).

DAY TRIPS

The following hiking trips range from four to eight hours hiking time and range from moderate to strenuous.

ALUM CAVE TRAIL

[Fig. 44(8)] This is one of the most popular walks in the GSMNP, initially passing through an old-growth forest of yellow buckeye (*Aesculus octandra*), beech, Eastern hemlock, and an understory of rhododendron. The trail then climbs stone steps through Arch Rock, a natural tunnel created by erosion, and onto a large heath bald covered with sand myrtle (*Leiiophyllum lyoni*), mountain laurel, and purple rhododendron before reaching Alum Cave Bluffs, a 100-foot-high cliff of black slate about 2.2 miles from the trailhead. Another 2.5 miles brings you to the top of Mount Le Conte near Le Conte Lodge (*see* page 292).

Directions: The trailhead is off the Newfound Gap Road (US 441) between the Chimney Tops and Newfound Gap.

Trail: 4.7 miles, one-way.

Elevation: Change, 1,100 feet.

Degree of difficulty: Moderate.

Surface: Forest floor.

CHIMNEY TOPS TRAIL

[Fig. 44(4)] Because of the steepness of this trail, it isn't recommended for hikers who are not in good physical condition. The first portion of the trail passes over the Walker Camp Prong of the Little Pigeon River and passes a large Fraser magnolia (*Magnolia fraseri*) with eight trunks. If you pass this way in April or May you may see its large creamy white blooms.

Beyond is another creek crossing, Road Prong, with stands of yellow buckeye (*Aesculus flava*), the only tree in the park with five leaflets joined in the center to form a compound leaf. Early settlers thought the dark, shiny brown nut of the tree looked like the eye of a deer. There are some large specimens along the trail. You will also find a profusion of wildflowers in the spring. After this placid streamside walk, from the beginning of the ascension to the pinnacles, the going is rocky and rugged.

Directions: The Chimney Tops trailhead is on the Newfound Gap Road 6.7 miles from the park entrance at the Sugarlands Visitor Center.

Trail: 2 miles, one-way.

European Wild Hogs

The European wild hog (*Sus scrofa*) is an exotic animal that has caused problems in the park, and the extent of damage it has done in the past and continues to do annually is of major concern.

These animals were first brought to the southern mountains from Europe in 1912 by an American who was establishing a hunting preserve at Hoppers Bald in western North Carolina, just a few miles southwest of the park boundary in what is now the Nantahala National Forest. The hogs later escaped the penned areas and began roaming freely through the hills and interbreeding with the free-roaming domestic hogs owned by the mountain people. It is believed that a few of these animals reached the park not many years after this initial escape, but it is believed the main invasion was in 1940.

The present-day wild hogs still exhibit the main characteristics of the European strain, including black hair, a distinct shoulder hump, and formidable-appearing tusks, but sometimes a white blaze on their face indicates that hybridization has occurred in the past.

Wild hogs do various kinds of damage. They root and furrow the forest floor and damage and destroy many plant species, some of which are rare or take several years to bloom. Like domestic hogs, wild hogs will eat almost anything: small mammals, salamanders, snakes, bird eggs, snails, mushrooms, and carrion. Wild hogs have no sweat glands, so they wallow in wet spots, springs, and small creeks, contaminating the water with coliform.

Park wildlife managers pursue a vigorous program of control measures, and since 1977, over 6,500 hogs have been removed by shooting or trapping. Funding from the National Resource Preservation Program gave the program a big boost, and since its initiation in 1986, over 3,800 hogs have been removed. A rooting survey is performed to learn the distribution of the hogs, and currently it is estimated that only a few hundred remain. Complete elimination of the hogs may not be possible, but it is believed that a very low population level can be maintained.

Elevation: Change, 1,300 feet
Degree of difficulty: Strenuous.
Surface: Forest floor.

MOUNT CAMMERER TRAIL

[Fig. 44(18)] The Lower Mount Cammerer Trail to the Mount Cammerer Fire Tower begins in the Cosby Campground and generally keeps to the lower sides of ridges as it weaves in and out of creek valleys. It begins as a gravel road passing old house sites in the former settlement area, but soon it begins to climb the western edge of Sutton Ridge.

The areas along the western ridges are drier with open oak forests. Hollows support wildflower colonies of spring beauties, hepatica, Indian cucumber (*Medeola virginiana*), and trillium, including the maroon wake robin trillium (*Trillium erectum*). Rhododendron and mountain laurel are abundant. The trail continues to weave along the dry western edges, rounding the points and cutting back to the moist eastern coves created by several creeks as it winds its way along the side of Mount Cammerer.

After traveling through forests of hemlocks and maple with an understory of flowering dogwoods, the trail intersects the Appalachian Trail (AT) 7.4 miles from the campground. Travel 2.3 miles along the AT through mountain laurel, rhododendron, hemlock, and spruce before reaching the craggy pinnacle and the Mount Cammerer Fire Tower, a 1930s project of the Civilian Conservation Corps.

The octagonal fire tower and its wooden catwalk were restored in 1995. The outstanding 360-degree views from this vantage point on the eastern end of the park extend to the Unaka Mountains to the east, Mount Sterling with its fire tower 5 miles to the south, and the Pigeon River valley and Douglas Lake to the north.

Directions: From Cosby, proceed 1.2 miles on TN 32 and turn right on Cosby Cove Road and drive 2 miles to the campground. The trailhead begins at the back of the Cosby Campground.

Trail: Approximately 10 miles, one-way

Elevation: 1,300 feet.

Degree of difficulty: Moderate.

Surface: Forest floor and rocks.

THE APPALACHIAN NATIONAL SCENIC TRAIL

[Fig. 44, Fig. 45, Fig. 46, Fig. 47] The Appalachian Trail (*see* page 297) is a 2,100-mile hiking trail stretching along the crest of the Appalachian Mountains from Springer Mountain in Georgia to Mount Katahdin in Maine. The 70 miles of the trail within the GSMNP are primarily located along the highest part of the main ridge that runs through the Smokies from southwest to northeast.

Balds

The origin of the grassy balds within the Smokies is uncertain. Early white settlers found these treeless patches on top of mountains well suited to provide summer pasture for their cattle and sheep. Both Andrews Bald and Gregory Bald are maintained by the Park Service against encroaching vegetation (*see* Balds, page 12).

ANDREWS BALD

[Fig. 45(9)] As you descend from the parking lot at Clingmans Dome on the Forney Ridge Trail, you pass through a forest of red spruce and Fraser fir trees under attack by the deadly balsam woolly adelgid, a non-native, sap-sucking insect. Andrews Bald is a large grassy bald named for Andrews Thompson, a settler who grazed his cattle on the bald in the 1850s. It is the easiest bald to reach, and it is known for its outstanding views of June's display of orange flame azalea and pink Catawba rhododendron. The trail passes through thickets of blackberries (*Rubus allegheny*) and raspberries (*Rubus idaeus*) that ripen in late July or early August.

Directions: Trailhead at Clingmans Dome Parking Area at the end of Clingmans Dome Road (*see* page 266) off US 441.

Trail: 4.2 miles, round-trip.

Elevation: Change, 500 feet.

Degree of difficulty: Moderate.

Surface: Rock and forest floor.

YELLOWWOOD (Cladrastis kentukea) The clear yellow heartwood of this tree turns light brown on exposure and has been used as a source of yellow dye.

GREGORY BALD

[Fig. 45(10)] Also known for its broad vistas and fine display of flame azalea in June, this broad grassy meadow also supports blueberries (*Vaccinium* sp.) that ripen in August.

Directions: The Gregory Bald Trail begins at Sam's Gap on Parson Branch Road (*see* page 269) off Cades Cove Loop Road.

Trail: 4.5 miles, one-way

Elevation: Change, 2,660 feet.

Degree of difficulty: Moderate.

Surface: Forest floor.

Waterfalls

There are a great many waterfalls and cascades in the park, but the following are the most impressive and the most accessible. Three of these can be seen from roads: The Sinks and Meigs Falls are visible from the Little River Road between the Sugarlands Visitor Center and Townsend, and the Place of a Thousand Drips. The latter, located along the Roaring Fork Motor Trail (*see* page 265) is classified as a sometimes waterfall, with water flow varying dramatically between wet and dry weather periods.

HEN WALLOW FALLS

[Fig. 45(11)] The hike to the falls is a pleasant walk through a poplar and hemlock forest and large rhododendron thickets. The waterfall is narrow at the top, but the water fans out as it drops.

Directions: Trailhead at Cosby Campground (*see* page 277).
Trail: 4 miles, round-trip.
Elevation: Change, 900 feet.
Degree of difficulty: Moderate.
Surface and blaze: Forest floor and rock.

RAMSAY CASCADES

[Fig. 44(6)] The falls is the highest in the park, and the trail to the cascade follows along the Middle Prong of the Little Pigeon River and Ramsay Prong, one of its tributaries. The trail initially follows an old road, but soon it begins to climb and cross streams along the way to a section of old-growth forest containing large yellow poplar, hemlocks, and black cherries. You're also likely to spot large specimens of silverbell and basswood, or linden as it's also called. The cascade is a 90-foot vertical plunge of whitewater down a series of rocky ledges.

Directions: Take US 321 approximately 6 miles east of Gatlinburg to Greenbrier Road. Travel past the ranger's station and turn left at the sign for Ramsay Cascades onto Ramsey Prong Road and continue 1.5 miles to the Ramsay Cascades Trail trailhead at the parking area.
Trail: 8 miles, round-trip.
Elevation: Change, 2,140 feet.
Degree of difficulty: Strenuous.
Surface and blaze: Forest floor and rock.

RAINBOW FALLS

[Fig. 45(12)] The trail to the falls passes along Le Conte Creek through hardwood forests with beautiful displays of wildflowers, like pink turtlehead (*Chelone lyonii*), in the spring and low-growing flowering shrubs including trailing arbutus (*Epigaea repens*) and teaberry (*Gaultheria procumbens*). Hikers will also see taller shrubs like pepper bush, or summer-sweet (*Clethra acuminata*), a member of the white alder family. The waterfall drops straight down for 80 feet, spraying a fine mist.

Directions: From Gatlinburg, take Airport Road at traffic light number 8. As the road re-enters the GSMNP, it becomes Cherokee Orchard Road. The Rainbow Falls Parking Area is on the right and the Rainbow Falls Trail trailhead is here.
Trail: 5.5 miles, round-trip.
Elevation: Change, 500 feet.
Degree of difficulty: Moderate.
Surface and blaze: Forest floor and rock.

GROTTO FALLS

[Fig. 44(19)] The wide, packed dirt trail to this falls passes through a cool hemlock forest with large American beeches, maples, and silverbells and an understory of rosebay rhododendrons. The 30-foot Grotto Falls is formed by the cascading Roaring Fork, which has its headwaters near the summit of Mount Le Conte. Above the falls, the trail, also known as the Trillium Gap Trail, continues to Mount Le Conte. This route is taken by llamas used to carry food and linens to Le Conte Lodge twice weekly from late March to Thanksgiving (*see* page 292).

Directions: From Gatlinburg take Airport Road at traffic light number 8 to the Roaring Fork Motor Nature Trail. During spring, summer, and fall, park in the Grotto Falls parking lot about 2 miles into the Roaring Fork Motor Nature Trail. Access road closed in winter. The Grotto Falls Trail begins at the parking area and soon joins the Trillium Gap Trail on its way to Grotto Falls.

Trail: 3 miles, round-trip.

Elevation: Change, 500 feet.

Degree of difficulty: Easy.

Surface and blaze: Forest floor and rock.

LAUREL FALLS

[Fig. 44(7)] Mid-May is the best time to see the abundant laurel blossoms for which this falls is named. A paved trail to Laurel Falls leads through a pine-oak forest with an understory of flowering dogwoods and is wheelchair accessible, although steep in spots. Along the way to the falls, you may spot trailing arbutus flowering in early spring. The shiny leaves of galax are visible year-round. The trail crosses the 75-foot cascade on a wooden bridge. At this point, the paved trail ends and a steep, rocky trail climbs above the falls before continuing up the ridge.

Directions: The trail begins at the Laurel Falls Parking Area on TN 73 (Little River Road) at Fighting Creek Gap between the Sugarlands Visitor Center and Elkmont Campground.

Trail: 2.6 miles, round-trip.

Elevation: Change, 450 feet.

Degree of difficulty: Easy.

Surface and blaze: Paved.

ABRAMS FALLS

[Fig. 44(9)] A large volume of water pours over this famous 20-foot falls into a broad plunge pool. The wide trail to it leads through rhododendron thickets and over a pine ridge as it travels along Abrams Creek past Arbutus Ridge.

Directions: Travel 5 miles along Cades Cove Loop Road before turning right onto a gravel road after passing sign post #10. Follow the gravel road 0.5 mile to the parking area and the trailhead for the Abrams Falls Trail.

Trail: 5 miles, round-trip.

Degree of difficulty: Moderate.

Surface and blaze: Forest floor and rock.

Information Sources

Those planning a trip to the park can obtain full information in advance by writing or calling Great Smoky Mountains National Park, 107 Park Headquarters Road, Gatlinburg, TN 37738, phone (423) 436-1200, and specifying your needs.

Another excellent source of information is the Great Smoky Mountains Natural History Association (GSMNHA), 115 Park Headquarters Road, Gatlinburg, TN 3738, phone (423) 436-7318. This is a nonprofit organization that assists the Park Service in educational and scientific projects. Funded entirely by private contributions and membership dues, it publishes a quarterly park newspaper and a variety of books and brochures, and operates the bookstores at the park's Sugarlands Visitor Center, Oconaluftee Visitor Center, and the Cades Cove Visitor Center.

The GSMNHA also operates the Great Smoky Mountains Institute at Tremont inside the park near Townsend. The institute is a conference and environmental educational facility where wilderness programs and activities are presented to school groups and families.

Information on the park is also available at visitor centers in Townsend, Gatlinburg, Pigeon Forge, Sevierville, and Knoxville in Tennessee as well as in Cherokee and Franklin, North Carolina.

TOMS BRANCH FALLS

[Fig. 45(13)] This falls is partially obscured by foliage during the summer months. It can be best seen during the late fall and winter months. It cascades about 60 feet into Deep Creek.

Directions: Deep Creek Road near Bryson City, North Carolina to Deep Creek Campground (*see* page 280). Continue on Deep Creek Road to the gate, where the trail to the falls begins.

Trail: 0.5 mile, round-trip.

Elevation: Change, 100 feet.

Degree of difficulty: Easy.

Surface and blaze: Forest floor and rock.

INDIAN CREEK FALLS

[Fig. 45(14)] The trail to the falls follows an old logging road paralleling Indian Creek and passes through a mixed forest with oaks, hemlocks, pines, and rhododendron on its way to a steep water slide.

Directions: Deep Creek Road near Bryson City, North Carolina to Deep Creek Campground (*see* page 280). Continue on Deep Creek Road to the gate, where the Deep Creek Trail begins. Follow the trail 0.7 mile to the Indian Creek Trail. This intersection is 0.1 mile from Indian Creek Falls.

Trail: 2 miles, round-trip.

Elevation: Change, 200 feet.
Degree of difficulty: Easy.
Surface and blaze: Forest floor and rock.

JUNEYWHANK FALLS

[Fig. 45(15)] This is a lovely cascade that is reached on a trail that winds through a pine-oak forest lined with maiden-hair ferns and solomon's seal. There is a foot bridge across the 90-foot cascade.

Directions: From Bryson City, North Carolina follow signs to Deep Creek Campground (*see* page 280). Go to the end of Deep Creek Road to park and walk 0.1 mile downstream to the trailhead.
Trail: 1.5 miles, round-trip.
Degree of difficulty: Moderate.
Surface and blaze: Forest floor and rock.

Other Activities

HORSEBACK RIDING

Equestrians have plenty of access to the park, and the trails are considered by many to be the best in the eastern U.S. Owners of horses should contact Park Headquarters at (423) 436-1200 for information on riding in the park. A free packet contains information on regulations, trails, and camping sites.

Rental horses are also available from private stables located within the park. Horses are rented by the hour or half-day, and the Park Service requires concessionaires to send guides with rental horses.

For more information: Cades Cove, phone (423) 448-6286; Smokemont, phone (704) 497-2373; and Deep Creek, phone (704) 497-7503. Others concessionaires in the park are McCarter's Riding Stable, on Newfound Gap Road near Park Headquarters, phone (423) 436-5354; and Smoky Mountains Riding Stable, 2 miles east of Gatlinburg on US 321, phone (423) 436-5634.

BICYCLING

Bicycles are allowed on paved roads and in campgrounds. Few areas in the park offer good opportunities for bicycling, mainly because the hiking trails are off-limits, and most of the paved roads are very steep and narrow and carry heavy traffic.

To help accommodate cyclists, the park closes the 11-mile loop road traffic around Cades Cove to automobiles until 10 a.m. on Wednesdays and Saturdays from late May through mid-September. This allows bikers time to make a leisurely tour of the valley.

Cataloochee Valley offers additional opportunities for bicyclists (*see* page 275).

For more information: Great Smoky Mountains National Park, 107 Park Headquarters Road, Gatlinburg, TN 37738. Phone (423) 436-1200.

Surrounding Communities

▓ COSBY

Once known as the Moonshine Capital of the World, Cosby sits at the northeastern corner of the GSMNP. On the first Sunday in May, the annual Ramp Festival brings thousands to this tiny community to celebrate the potent oniony-tasting ramp (*Allium tricoccum*) roots, an experience deemed quite noxious by those who haven't acquired the taste.

The Schilling Family Folk Life Center hosts festivals with traditional mountain music and dancing throughout the year in addition to making and selling dulcimers, publishing books, and releasing recordings of mountain music.

Directions: From I-40, take the Western Foothills Parkway to Cosby. From Gatlinburg, take US 321.

For more information: Newport/Cocke County Tourism Council, 360 E. Main Street, Suite 141, Newport, TN 37821. Phone (423) 625-9675.

▓ GATLINBURG

Located at the northern entrance to the GSMNP, Gatlinburg is a favorite mountain getaway for millions of visitors headed for the park. Gatlinburg began to attract tourists when Andy Huff built the Mountain View Motel in 1916, before the formation of the park.

Although thousands of overnight accommodations are available, none have been welcoming visitors longer than Le Conte Lodge, high atop Mount Le Conte. Founded in 1926 by Jack Huff, the lodge is only accessible by five hiking trails ranging from 4.9 to 8.9 miles one-way. Your accommodations are less than deluxe, there's no electricity or running water, but the sunsets from Cliff Top and the sunrises at Myrtle Point are legendary.

The Buckhorn Inn is one of Gatlinburg's few remaining historic inns. Built in 1938, the Buckhorn is nestled on 40 acres overlooking Mount Le Conte on Tudor Mountain Road.

Since 1950, Gatlinburg has been the site of an Annual Wildflower Pilgrimage, which is now the largest and best known of the walks in Tennessee. Trip leaders direct motorcades of up to a dozen autos to prime viewing areas in late April each year. During Pilgrimage weekend, wildflower enthusiasts gather for nature walks, bird walks, wildflower sketch walks, propagation workshops, slide shows, and photographic tours.

Gatlinburg has a craft tradition born of necessity and supported by the first national sorority for women, Pi Beta Phi. Pi Beta Phi established the Arrowcraft Shop in 1926 to provide a market to the outside world for mountain handicrafts. The Arrowcraft Shop continues to sell the handicrafts of members of the Southern Highlands Craft Guild, an association of fine craftsmen. The Arrowmont School next door was also founded by Pi

Beta Phi in 1912. Once the source of public education for the children of Gatlinburg, the school grew to include crafts instruction and offers summer classes ranging from wood-turning to weaving, pottery, and basketry.

The Gatlinburg crafts tradition continues in the Smoky Mountain Arts and Crafts Community off US 321 east of town.

Directions: From I-40, take Exit 407 and follow TN 66 to Sevierville. From Sevierville follow US 441 through Pigeon Forge to Gatlinburg.

For more information: Gatlinburg Convention and Visitors Bureau, 234 Airport Road, Gatlinburg, TN 37738. Phone (800) 343-1475. Gatlinburg Chamber of Commerce, phone (800) 568-4748.

TOWNSEND

Known, at least for a while yet, as the quiet side of the Smokies, Townsend is closest to Cades Cove and the Western Foothills Parkway. Several national franchise motels join hundreds of cabins and campsites in welcoming visitors to Townsend, the western gateway to the Smokies.

The Little River Railroad Lumber Company Museum is a very good place to learn more about the history of logging and railroads in the Smokies. The Shay engine sitting out front is typical of the geared steam locomotive engines used to haul timber down the steep mountain grades.

The Richmont Inn Bed and Breakfast is a modern construction inspired by the cantilevered barns found in areas like Cades Cove. A few miles from the entrance to the Western Foothills Parkway north of Townsend, the Inn at Blackberry Farm offers deluxe accommodations, dining, and recreational activities ranging from swimming and cycling to hiking and trout fishing on 1,100 acres in the shadows of the distant high peaks of the Smokies. Many visitors come to Townsend to enjoy the Spring Festival and Wildflower Celebration in April or Old Timer's Day in late September.

Directions: Exit I-40 near Kingston onto US 321 and go through Maryville to Townsend. From the north and east, exit I-40 in Knoxville at US 129 to join US 321 at Maryville. From the south and west on I-75, take Exit 18 to US 321. From GSMNP, take Little River Road to Townsend.

For more information: Townsend Visitor Center/Smoky Mountain Visitors Bureau, 7906 E. Lamar Alexander Parkway, Townsend, TN 37882. Phone (800) 525-6834.

CHEROKEE INDIAN RESERVATION

The town of Cherokee stretches along US 441 south of the GSMNP within the 56,000 acres of scattered tracts that make up the Qualla Boundary, home of the Eastern Band of the Cherokee.

The removal of most of the Cherokee from their ancestral homelands in this area was hastened by the discovery of gold on Cherokee land in northern Georgia in 1828. Georgia annexed Cherokee lands, sold lots by lottery to whites, and removed all legal recourse for the Cherokees who took their grievances to the United States Supreme Court.

Although the court supported the suit of the Cherokee, Georgia persisted, and the federal government based its course of action on a treaty agreeing to removal that had been rejected by the Cherokee people in October 1835. On May 26, 1838 the arrest and removal of the Cherokee began. Nearly 4,000 of the 16,000 Cherokee who traveled to lands west of the Mississippi River on the Trail of Tears died along the way.

Some 1,000 Cherokee fled to the high reaches of the Smokies with their chief, Yonaguska. The outdoor drama held each summer in Cherokee, *Unto These Hills*, tells the story of what happened next. An older Cherokee named Tsali killed a soldier while defending his wife. Gen. Winfield Scott, who was in charge of the removal, struck a deal. Tsali would face execution, but the pursuit of the Cherokee holdouts in their remote mountain hideouts would cease.

Col. William Holland Thomas, a white trader who had been adopted by Chief Yonaguska as a boy, remained at Oconaluftee to negotiate on behalf of the Cherokee. The Cherokee received compensation from the United States government totaling about $50 each for the lands they lost east of the Mississippi as a result of the removal.

Although the Cherokee were prevented by law from owning property, Thomas was able to purchase property and hold it in trust for them while serving as the Principal Chief of the Eastern Band of the Cherokee. Eventually, North Carolina recognized the right of the Cherokee to own property, and the lands purchased by Thomas became the Qualla Boundary in 1876, encompassing 56,000 acres of land, presently bordering the southern entrance of the GSMNP. In 1889, the charter forming the Eastern Band of the Cherokee was granted after the North Carolina legislature established the rights of the Cherokee living in North Carolina.

LARGE-FLOWERED TRILLIUM
(Trillium grandiflorum)

The city of Cherokee is heavily dependent on tourism revenues. To this end, there are more than 1,500 rooms and 2,200 campsites here. The Oconaluftee Indian Village is a re-creation of Cherokee village life before the removal. The Museum of the Cherokee Indian has artifacts, exhibits, and videotape presentations to acquaint you with the history of the Cherokee Nation.

Trout fishing is popular in about 30 miles of streams on the Qualla Boundary and three well-stocked ponds on Big Cove Road outside Cherokee. A $5 daily Tribal Fishing Permit is required and may be purchased at several businesses and campgrounds in Cherokeee. No state license is required.

The Big Cove community is a quiet, pretty area with several campgrounds and the spectacular 120-foot Mingo Falls about 5 miles up Big Cove Road from Cherokee. There's a small sign indicating the 0.25-mile walk to the falls beginning at the parking area beside Mingo Falls Campground.

Directions: From I-40 north of Asheville, N.C. take Exit 20 to Maggie Valley and continue on US 19W to Cherokee. From Gatlinburg, follow US 441 through the GSMNP to Cherokee.

For more information: Cherokee Visitor Center, POB 460, Cherokee, NC 28719. Phone (800) 438-1601.

BRYSON CITY, NORTH CAROLINA

Bryson City is one of the Western North Carolina towns served by the Smoky Mountain Railway, an excursion train offering round-trip train rides through the foothills of the Smokies.

Bryson City is also home to the historic Fryemont Inn, a National Register of Historic Places property built in 1923 by timber baron Amos Frye. The 37 rooms with private baths are paneled in chestnut, and huge stone fireplaces grace the lobby and the dining room, where the dinner menu features several trout dishes. The long porch is filled with rocking chairs and the inn's exterior is covered with poplar bark. The main lodge is open from mid-April through October. Other historic bed and breakfasts in Bryson City include the Randolph House Country Inn, also built by Amos Frye and open from April to October, and the 1920s Folkestone Inn, open year-round.

Directions: From Cherokee take US 19 west to Bryson City. From I-40 near Asheville take Exit 27 to US74W to Exit 67 at Bryson City. From I-40 near Knoxville, take Exit 407 to TN 66 to US 441 through GSMNP to Cherokee, then US 19S to Bryson City.

For more information: Swain County Chamber of Commerce, PO Box 509 Bryson City, NC 28713. Phone (704) 488-3681.

FONTANA VILLAGE

Fontana Dam, at 480 feet, is the highest dam in the eastern United States. The construction of the dam began on January 1, 1942, a few weeks after the bombing of Pearl Harbor. Fontana Village was quickly built to house the workers and their families, providing not only housing but also churches, schools, and a hospital. Laborers toiled 24 hours a day, seven days a week for more than two years to build Fontana Dam and provide the electricity needed for Alcoa Aluminum, which produced aircraft components for World War II.

This village evolved into Fontana Village Resort along the shores of beautiful Fontana Lake. Accommodations include historic and modern cottages, an inn with a cafeteria and a restaurant, houseboats, and campgrounds. The AT crosses over Fontana Dam.

Directions: From I-40 near Knoxville, exit onto US 129. Then travel southwest on US 411 to US 129 south and follow NC 28 west to Fontana. From Cherokee, NC, follow US 19 southwest to NC 28 to Fontana.

For more information: Fontana Village Resort, Highway 68, Fontana Dam, NC 28733. Phone (800) 849-2258.

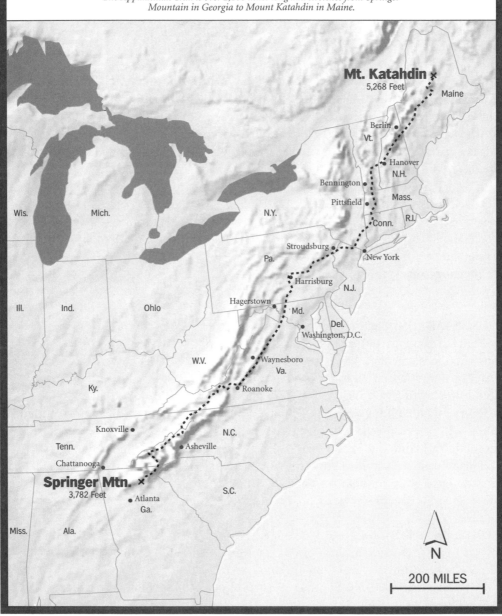

Appalachian Trail

The Appalachian Trail is over 2,100 miles long and stretches from Springer Mountain in Georgia to Mount Katahdin in Maine.

Mt. Katahdin ✕
5,268 Feet

Maine

Berlin

Vt.

Hanover
N.H.

Bennington

Pittsfield

Mass.

Conn.

R.I.

Stroudsburg

New York

N.Y.

Harrisburg

Pa.

N.J.

Hagerstown

Md.

Del.
Washington, D.C.

W.V.

Waynesboro

Va.

Ky.

Roanoke

Knoxville

N.C.

Tenn.

Asheville

Chattanooga

Springer Mtn. ✕
3,782 Feet

Atlanta
Ga.

S.C.

Miss.

Ala.

Wis.

Mich.

Ill.

Ind.

Ohio

N

200 MILES

Appalachian Trail

The Appalachian Trail (AT), America's most traveled long footpath, extends for 2,160 miles along 250,000 acres of the finest mountain terrain remaining in the eastern United States. Beginning at Katahdin, a granite monolith in central Maine, the white-blazed trail follows the crest of the Appalachian Mountains all the way to Springer Mountain in Georgia. Each year more than 3 million people hike all or parts of the trail.

For most of its journey through 14 states, the AT travels through public land. Virginia contains the longest section of the trail, 545 miles, while West Virginia contains the shortest, 26 miles. The lowest elevation is 124 feet above sea level near the Hudson River in New York, and the highest is 6,643 at Clingman's Dome in the Great Smoky Mountains. In the southern Appalachians, most of the trail passes through deciduous, hardwood forests, although spruce-fir stands are encountered at higher elevations. There are

[*Above:* The Tennessee portion of the Appalachian Trail is one of the most popular segments]

also balds and large areas blanketed with laurel and rhododendron thickets. In the spring a variety of wildflowers can be seen: several kinds of trillium and violets, bloodroot (*Samguinaria canadensis*), crested dwarf iris (*Iris cristata*), mayapple (*Podophyllum peltatum*), jack-in-the-pulpit (*Arisaema triphyllum*), flame azalea (*Rhododendron calendulaceum*), and numerous other. There are also spring displays of serviceberry (*Amelanchier arborea*), dogwood (*Cornus alternifolia*), and redbud (*Cercis canadensis*). In the fall, the many kinds of hardwoods provide superb color displays.

The initial proposal for such a trail was made by Benton MacKaye, a regional planner from Shirley, Massachusetts. MacKaye published an article in the October 1921 issue of the *Journal of the American Institute of Architects* entitled, "An Appalachian Trail, a Project in Regional Planning." The article described a vision of a footpath along the entire Appalachian ridgeline.

MacKaye's challenge ignited interest. At the time, almost all of the hiking clubs that could assist in such a venture were east of the Hudson River, and there were existing trail systems that could be incorporated into the AT. These systems included a series of trails in New England maintained by the Appalachian Mountain Club and the 130-mile Long Trail being developed in Vermont by the Dartmouth Outing Club. All of the efforts to build an AT were consolidated in 1925 with the formation of the Appalachian Trail Conference (ATC), a nonprofit educational organization of individuals and clubs of volunteers dedicated to managing, maintaining, and protecting the AT and its adjacent lands.

Arthur Perkins, a retired judge from Hartford, Connecticut, provided additional momentum to the trail movement by persuading groups to locate and cut the designated footpath through the wilderness, especially in the South where few trails and fewer clubs existed. More progress followed when Perkins interested Myron H. Avery, a Washington, DC attorney, to assist in the project. Avery enlisted the aid and coordinated the work of hundreds of volunteers who completed the trail on August 14, 1937, when the Civilian Conservation Corps (CCC) opened the last section.

That same year, an ATC member successfully proposed a plan for an Appalachian Trailway that would set apart an area on each side of the trail. The plan culminated in 1939 with an agreement between the National Park Service (NPS) and the U.S. Forest Service (USFS). The protection would extend 1 mile on each side of the Appalachian Trailway, no new parallel roads would be built, and no timber cutting would be permitted within 200 feet of the trail. Similar agreements creating a zone 0.25 mile in width were signed with most states along the AT's length.

A national system of trails was established by Congress in 1968, and the Appalachian Trail was included. The act directs the secretary of the interior, in consultation with the secretary of agriculture, to administer the AT primarily as a footpath and to protect it from incompatible activities. Supplemental agreements in 1970 among the NPS, USFS, and the ATC established the specific responsibilities of these organizations. Then in 1978 the slow progress of federal efforts led Congress to strengthen the National Trails System Act with amendments that emphasized the need for protecting the AT and set aside $90 million for acquiring a corridor through the lands outside the NPS and USFS lands. The acquisition program is scheduled to be completed in 2000. In 1984, the Interior Department formally delegated the responsibility of managing these AT corridor lands to the ATC.

The Conference, with 4,000 volunteers in 31 independent local clubs, plays the major role in maintaining the footpath, and the ATC publishes information on constructing and maintaining hiking trails, official AT guides, and general information on hiking and trail use.

Most trail guidebooks, including the *Appalachian Trail Guide to Tennessee-North Carolina* published by the ATC, cover the Tennessee and northwestern North Carolina sections of the AT together since the trail meanders back and forth over the border of these two states as it travels north/south. Tennessee and North Carolina offer a combined 376 miles of trail, much of it along ridgecrests above 5,000 feet. This portion of the AT offers some of the best wilderness and primitive areas along the trail's route as well as incredible scenic vistas from the high peaks.

Much of the trail in this region exists within the Cherokee National Forest in Tennessee, the Pisgah National Forest in North Carolina, and the Great Smoky Mountains National Park. This public ownership of trail lands ensures the AT's protection and improves hikers' chances of seeing a great variety of plant and animal life. In the Great Smoky Mountains National Park alone there are more species of trees than in all of Europe. Animals along the trail range from woodchucks, salamanders, and turkey vultures, to moles, mice, and skunks.

For more information: Appalachian Trail Conference, PO Box 807, Harpers Ferry, WV 25425-0807. Phone (304) 535-6331.

AT Road Crossings

These are the names or numbers of roads that the AT crosses. These are easy places to access the trail. Few crossings offer parking along the highways, and many highway crossings are not marked. It is recommended that all hikers carry an AT guidebook and map that details the section of the trail they intend to hike.

~ US 421 between Shady Valley, TN, and Bristol, TN.
~ TN 91 between Elizabethton, TN, and Shady Valley, TN.
~ TN 67 between Hampton, TN, and Mountain City, TN.
~ US 321 between Hampton, TN, and Boone, NC.
~ US 19E between Roan Mountain, TN, and Elk Park, NC.
~ TN 143/NC 261 between Roan Mountain, TN, and Bakersville, NC.
~ TN 107/NC 226 between Unicoi, TN, and Bakersville, NC.
~ TN 395/NC 197 between Erwin, TN, and Bakersville, NC.
~ US 19W between Ernestville, TN, and Burnsville, NC.
~ US 23 between Flag Pond, TN, and Mars Hill, NC.

Appalachian Trail

*The Appalachian Trail crosses 14 eastern state and eight national forests,
six national parks, and more than 75 public land areas.*

1 US 421 to TN 91

2 TN 91 to Watauga Dam Rd.

3 Watauga Dam Rd. to Dennis Cove Rd.

4 Dennis Cove to US 19E at Bear Branch Rd.

5 US 19E to Carvers Gap

6 Carvers Gap to Hughes Gap

7 Hughes Gap to Iron Mt. Gap

8 Iron Mt. Gap to Nolichucky R.

9 Nolichucky R. TN to Spivey Gap, NC

10 Spivey Gap, NC to Sams Gap

11 Sams Gap to Devils Fork Gap

12 Devil Fork Gap to Allen Gap

13 Allen Gap to Hot Springs NC

14 Hot Springs, NC to Max Patch Rd.

15 Max Patch Rd. to Davenport Gap

16 Davenport Gap to Newfound Gap

17 Newfound Gap to Little TN River

Great Smoky Mt National Park

Appalachian Trail

VIRGINIA

Asheville

BLUE RIDGE PARKWAY

TENNESSEE

NORTH CAROLINA

NORTH CAROLINA

SOUTH CAROLINA

GEORGIA

10 MILES

Ref: NPS Appalachian Trail

N

~ TN 352/NC 212 between Rocky Fork, TN, and Hot Springs, NC.
~ TN 70/NC 208 between Greeneville, TN, and Hot Springs, NC.
~ US 25/70 between Newport, TN, and Hot Springs, NC.
~ I-40 at the TN/NC state line.
~ TN 32 between Cosby, TN, and Mt. Sterling, NC.
~ US 441 between Gatlinburg, TN, and Cherokee, NC.
~ NC 28 at Fontana Dam, NC.
~ US 64 between Murphy, NC, and Franklin, NC.

Trail Descriptions

The portion of the AT that passes through the mountains of Tennessee and North Carolina and is covered in this book begins at Low Gap on US 421 just south of the Tennessee/Virginia state line, and it ends at Fontana Dam, North Carolina. The description of the trail given below is from north to south, and is a condensed version of the directions given in *Appalachian Trail Guide to Tennessee-North Carolina* published by the Appalachian Trail Conference. Copies of the book, as well as guides to the other 14 states covered by the AT, are available at bookstores or can be ordered from the ATC, PO Box 807, Harpers Ferry, WV 25425. Phone (304) 535-6331.

All of the AT is blazed with white, 2-by-6-inch, rectangular markers painted on trees and rocks. A double blaze, one above the other, warns of turns, junctions, or other places where hikers should be alert. Blue blazes mark AT side trails, which usually lead to shelters, a water supply, or viewpoints.

US 421 TO TN 91, 7.0 MILES

[Fig. 50(1)] 0.0 Begin at roadside park on US 421 (3,384 feet).

0.1 Reach ridgecrest and excellent campsite.

2.6 Pass over Locust Knob (4,020 feet).

3.5 Reach trail junction where AT leaves Holston Mountain. Double Springs Shelter is about 200 feet beyond junction, and spring is about 100 yards from shelter.

3.8 Reach crest of Cross Mountain.

4.3 Good spring and campsite located on the left.

7.0 Reach TN 91.

TN 91 TO WATAUGA DAM ROAD, 16.0 MILES

[Fig. 50(2)] 0.0 Begin on eastern side of TN 91 (3,470 feet).

2.7 Pass over a summit (4,120 feet).

4.5 Reach Iron Mountain Shelter. Water located 0.2 mile farther south on AT.

5.0 Reach top of broad summit.

6.2 Reach Turkeypen Gap (3,970 feet).

6.6 Reach level, grassy area with good tent sites, but no water.

7.4 At top of rise is grassy area with good tent sites.

10.1 Enter Big Laurel Wilderness.

11.5 Reach Vandeventer Shelter. To reach water, continue south on AT for 300 feet, then turn right on blue-blazed trail and descend 0.2 mile to old road track. Bear right 0.3 mile off road into hollow to spring.

13.3 Pass spring.

16.0 Reach Watauga Dam Road and end of Big Laurel Branch Wilderness Area.

WATAUGA DAM ROAD TO DENNIS COVE ROAD, 12.8 MILES

[Fig. 50(3)] 0.0 From high point of Watauga Dam Road (2,240 feet), climb western bank on stone steps and begin trail.

0.8 Turn right on paved dam-access road.

1.2 Walk across Watauga Dam.

2.2 Turn right onto old road paralleling stream. Beyond, where AT crosses stream, blue-blazed trail leads 50 yards uphill to Watauga Lake Shelter.

3.3 Swing right onto dirt road.

3.9 Reach USFS Shook Branch Recreation Area with picnic tables, sandy beach, drinking water, and toilets (open in warm weather). This is the start of a new 3.4-mile section of the AT that eliminated 5.7 miles of the former route.

4.5 Enter 4,365-acre Pond Mountain Wilderness.

7.1 Reach Pond Flats, a level area affording excellent camping.

7.4 Spring located in rocky bottom of drainage.

8.8 To left of trail, a small ledge offers a magnificent scenic view of Laurel Fork Gorge, with Potato Top, White Rocks Mountain, and Roan Mountain to the left.

10.6 Pass Waycaster Spring on left.

10.9 Reach summit of low, narrow ridge. Continue up ridge crest about 300 feet to Laurel Fork Shelter. Follow a path 150 feet from shelter to water.

11.6 Reach Laurel Falls.

12.8 Cross USFS parking lot to paved Dennis Cove Road to end of section. To left USFS 50 leads 1 mile to USFS Dennis Cove Recreation Area on Laurel Fork with a campground (fee) and running water.

DENNIS COVE (USFS 50) TO US 19E AT BEAR BRANCH ROAD, 19.4 MILES

[Fig. 50(4)] 0.0 From USFS parking lot in Dennis Cove (2,510 feet), cross USFS 50 to the south and climb bank to enter woods.

2.8 Reach White Rocks Mountain fire tower.

3.6 Reach field and pass former site of Canute Place, named for early settlers. All that remains of the Canute Place are scattered rocks from the house's foundation, and it is mostly covered with briars. This is a possible campsite.

5.8 Reach Moreland Gap (3,813 feet) and Moreland Gap Shelter. Spring a short distance down hollow opposite shelter.

6.1 Last major summit (4,121 feet) in this section.

7.2 Descend into hollow where several streams converge. Excellent campsite, but water should be purified.

10.0 Cross USFS logging road.

10.4 Trail crosses undulating terrain with several springs and possible campsites.

11.2 Excellent scenic view to south encompassing Hump, Little Hump, and Yellow mountains and Grassy Ridge, Jane Bald, Round Bald, and Roan High Knob. Straight ahead on trail to the east is a view of Buck Mountain, and in the distance is the outline of Grandfather Mountain.

12.7 Reach Walnut Mountain Road.

13.2 Turn left onto old gravel road in Slide Hollow.

13.6 Reach northeastern summit of Big Pine Mountain.

14.9 Turn right on old logging road in bottom of Sugar Hollow. Good campsite ahead.

15.9 Cross plank bridge over Jones Branch. Go through overgrown field and turn left on paved Campbell Hollow Road.

16.3 Turn left from Campbell Hollow Road and climb bank into overgrown field.

17.3 Reach summit (about 3,820 feet). White Rocks Mountain can be seen to the west, Beech Mountain to the east.

17.6 Spring is located at base of tree near ruins of house.

18.1 Leave woods and descend through Bishop Hollow.

19.1 Cross Bear Branch on bridge. Water is contaminated; do not use.

19.4 Cross US 19E to AT sign on southern side of highway and end of section.

▓ US 19E TO CARVERS GAP (TN 143/NC 261), 13.4 MILES

[Fig. 50(5)] 0.0 From US 19E (2,880 feet), descend former driveway and cross bridge over stream.

0.5 Apple House Shelter is on right. Seasonal piped spring is 0.1 mile west, up the hollow.

2.1 Reach summit (about 3,820 feet).

2.6 Reach crest of rocky spur.

3.0 Enter Doll Flats (4,560 feet). Level area offers excellent campsites.

5.4 Pass plaque dedicated to the memory of Stan Murray, former ATC chairman, and cross summit of Hump Mountain.

6.3 Reach wide, grassy Bradley Gap (4,960 feet), which has good campsites. Two springs are nearby, but water must be purified.

6.9 Reach a small gap, then soon ascend to flat, grassy summit of Little Hump Mountain, with outstanding views and campsites.

8.7 Reach Yellow Mountain Gap (4,682 feet), which has good campsites. Historic Bright's Trace crosses gap, and to the left and back along Bright's Trace about 300 yards is a spring. Blue-blazed trail through fence to the left leads 0.3 mile downhill past spring to Overmountain Shelter.

10.4 Reach Low Gap and Stan Murray Shelter. Spring is about 100 yards left down ridge on blue-blazed trail.

12.6 Pass through Engine Gap.

13.4 Cross rail fence and descend stone steps to TN 143/NC 261 through Carvers Gap. USFS picnic area with spring and toilets is beyond parking area straight across the highway.

CARVERS GAP (TN 143/NC 261) TO HUGHES GAP, 4.6 MILES

[Fig. 50(6)] 0.0 From Carvers Gap (5,512 feet), proceed to right of log fence along Cloudland Road to spring below picnic area.

1.3 Blue-blazed trail leads to summit of Roan High Knob (6,285 feet), and Roan High Knob Shelter. Spring is 50 feet past cabin.

2.8 Reach Ash Gap (5,340 feet), with good tent sites. Faint trail to left leads 0.1 mile to spring.

3.3 Reach summit of Beartown Mountain (5,481 feet).

4.6 Reach end of section at Hughes Gap. Small spring that trickles from rocks is 700 feet to right.

HUGHES GAP TO IRON MOUNTAIN GAP (TN 107/NC 226), 8.1 MILES

[Fig. 50(7)] 0.0 From Hughes Gap (4,040 feet), proceed north on old woods road.

1.3 Reach top of cliff on Little Rock Knob (4,918 feet).

2.1 Blue-blazed trail to right leads 200 yards to Clyde Smith Shelter and 300 yards to spring.

4.1 Reach Greasy Creek Gap (4,034 feet). Spring and good campsite are 300 yards to right on blue-blazed trail.

5.8 Pass overhanging rock, which may provide shelter for one or two people.

6.6 Blue-blazed trail leads downhill 0.1 mile to small stream, a good source of water.

8.1 Reach Iron Mountain Gap and end of section.

IRON MOUNTAIN GAP (TN 107/NC 226) TO NOLICHUCKY RIVER, 19.1 MILES.

[Fig. 50(8)] 0.0 From highway at Iron Mountain Gap (3,723 feet), cross small, flat area at left of gravel road and enter woods.

1.2 Reach summit of Little Bald Knob (4,459 feet).

2.7 Reach Cherry Gap Shelter. Spring is 250 yards southwest on blue-blazed trail.

3.7 Reach Low Gap (3,900 feet).

4.7 Reach spring.

5.4 Pass benchmark on summit of Unaka Mountain (5,180 feet).

7.0 Reach Deep Gap (4,100 feet). Meadow to right is excellent campsite. Concrete-boxed spring is on right at eastern end of gap.

8.0 Reach nearly level trail, and soon cross bog. On western side of bog, blue-blazed trail to north leads 150 yards to spring and spacious campsite.

8.5 Reach Beauty Spot summit (4,437 feet), a natural grassy bald that provides excellent scenic views of Road Mountain, the Blacks, Big Bald, and Flattop Mountain, and the upper Toe River Valley.

10.8 Reach Indian Grave Gap (3,360 feet). Ascend steps across road, and re-enter woods.

13.6 Pass spring on left.

14.8 Reach Curley Maple Gap Shelter on left. Spring is 100 feet farther down AT on left.

17.8 Pass Nolichucky Gorge Campground (hiker hostel) and Nolichucky Expeditions building.

19.0 Cross railroad tracks. Take care; trains are quiet and may not signal approach.

19.1 Reach end of section at western end of Nolichucky River Bridge.

NOLICHUCKY RIVER, TENNESSEE TO SPIVEY GAP, NORTH CAROLINA, 10 MILES

[Fig. 50(9)] 0.0 From western end of highway bridge across Nolichucky River (1,700 feet), turn left and follow road 250 feet, then turn right and climb steep bank on steps.

2.6 Reach access road to site of former Temple Hill fire tower.

3.3 Enter Temple Hill Gap (2,850 feet).

5.7 Reach No Business Knob Shelter. Spring is about 20 yards ahead on AT.

8.3 Reach overgrown logging road through Devils Creek Gap.

8.4 Cross state line into North Carolina in gap.

9.6 Reach saddle, descend, and soon reach Oglesby Branch.

10.4 Descend stone steps to US 19W, cross to southern side of highway and end section.

SPIVEY GAP, NORTH CAROLINA (US 19W) TO SAMS GAP, TN/NC (US 23), 13.6 MILES

[Fig. 50(10)] 0.0 AT resumes 0.3 mile east of Spivey Gap (3,200 feet).

2.3 Reach small clearing and good campsite at Whistling Gap.

4.3 Reach top of Little Bald (5,185 feet).

5.3 On old road, reach sign on tree designating water. To right, blue-blazed trail leads down into Big Bald Creek. Good spring is 0.2 mile down this trail.

5.7 Side trail goes north 0.1 mile to Bald Mountain Shelter. Spring is 50 feet down a side trail between AT and shelter.

6.8 Reach summit of Big Bald Mountain (5,516 feet).

7.6 Reach blue-blazed trail on right, which leads 100 yards down slope to spring.

9.8 Blue-blazed trail on right leads 20 yards to spring.

11.0 Reach Street Gap (4,100 feet).

13.6 Reach Sams Gap and end of section on west side of US 23.

SAMS GAP (US 23) TO DEVILS FORK GAP (NC 212), 8.2 MILES

[Fig. 50(11)] 0.0 Enter wide path 150 feet south of US 23 crest at Sams Gap (3,800 feet).

1.7 Reach High Rock (4,460 feet).

2.2 Blue-blazed trail to the left leads 0.1 mile to Hogback Ridge Shelter. Spring is 440 yards from shelter on trail to the west.

3.3 Reach Rice Gap (3,800 feet).

4.3 Reach Big Flat and a fair campsite.

6.4 Reach Sugarloaf Gap (4,000 feet). Sugarloaf Knob (4,560 feet) is to the left.

7.7 Reach and cross Boone Cove Road.

8.2 Reach NC 212 at Devils Fork Gap.

🔲 DEVIL FORK GAP (NC 212) TO ALLEN GAP (NC 208/TN 70), 20.2 MILES

[Fig. 50(12)] 0.0 From the road at Devil Fork Gap (3,107 feet), climb steps on northern side of road, and turn right in field.

1.8 The site of the old Locust Ridge Shelter (removed in 1982) is a possible campsite. Water is down the left side in ravine.

2.7 Pass spring, cross two branches, then go 100 feet to reach Flint Mountain Shelter. Latrine is 75 feet west.

3.5 Reach Flint Gap (3,425 feet).

5.4 Reach blue-blazed dirt road to left, which leads 125 yards downhill to spring.

8.6 Reach Chestnut Log Gap (4,150 feet) and in 100 yards, the Jerry Cabin Shelter. A good spring is on a side trail 100 yards northwest of the shelter.

11.1 Pass spring on left bank above trail.

11.8 Reach Bearwallow Gap.

12.3 Pass spring on left below trail.

13.2 Reach old lumber road.

15.3 Reach Little Laurel Shelter on left. Blue-blazed side trail on right bears back 100 yards to boxed spring.

18.3 Reach fork. AT bears left, south of crest. Straight ahead is former AT route.

20.2 Reach end of section at TN 70 in Allen Gap.

🔲 ALLEN GAP (NC 208/TN 70) TO HOT SPRINGS, NORTH CAROLINA, 14.7 MILES

[Fig. 50(13)] 0.0 From TN 70, 0.1 mile west of Allen Gap (2,234 feet), bear left in woods at foot of slope.

2.0 Reach Deep Gap.

3.7 Reach Spring Mountain Shelter. Spring is 75 yards down North Carolina side, opposite shelter.

5.4 Reach Hurricane Gap.

6.4 Cross head of ravine with good spring on right, and good campsite.

8.8 Cross old US 25/70 (no longer in use), then follow path of concrete overpass of new US 25/70.

9.8 In saddle, turn right downhill to pond. Pass above intermittent boxed spring and along pond. Excellent campsite.

11.4 Reach Pump Gap.

13.3 Reach sharp edge of crest. Lovers Leap Rock extends straight ahead to northwest.

14.2 Trail reaches small road bridge. Nantahala Outdoor Center is at right.

14.3 Follow US 25/70 over highway bridge across French Broad River.

14.6 Hot Springs Post Office, with AT hikers' registration book in lobby is on right. Beyond, on left, is USFS ranger district headquarters.

14.7 Reach end of section at junction of US 25/70 with NC 209.

HOT SPRINGS, NORTH CAROLINA, TO MAX PATCH ROAD (NC 1182), 20.2 MILES

[Fig. 50(14)] 0.0 From junction with US 25/70 and NC 208, go 0.3 mile and turn right from highway, follow old roadbed for 30 feet, and climb steep bank to left.

3.2 Reach Gregg Gap. To left 75 yards is Deer Park Mountain Shelter. Spring is halfway between Gregg Gap and shelter.

4.5 Reach Little Bottom Branch Gap, and 0.3 mile farther, ascend Lamb Knob.

6.6 Pass under powerline and descend steps to Garenflo Gap (2,500 feet).

7.5 Cross old road grade and USFS road from Garenflo Gap.

8.9 Big Rock Spring is 50 yards ahead in ravine.

10.3 Reach top of Bluff Mountain (4,686 feet).

11.2 Pass Catpen Gap to left.

14.0 Reach small clearing in Lemon Gap (about 3,550 feet), adjacent to NC 1182, which enters Tennessee as TN 107 at Del Rio.

16.6 Trail passes beautiful cascades and ascends among hemlocks.

18.2 Pass through fence line and emerge in open meadow on western slope of Buckeye Ridge.

19.0 Trail passes through fence line onto open meadows of Max Patch.

19.4 Trail crosses open summit of Max Patch (4,629 feet).

20.2 Trail reaches end of section at Max Patch Road (NC 1182).

MAX PATCH ROAD (NC 1182) TO DAVENPORT GAP (TN 32/NC 284), 15.2 MILES

[Fig. 50(15)] 0.0 From Max Patch Road about 0.5 mile southwest of summit, follow AT west through woods along ridge.

2.7 Reach Browns Gap (3,500 feet). To right, in Tennessee, occasional spring is 100 yards down dirt road.

5.6 In Deep Gap, also known as Groundhog Creek Gap (about 2,900 feet), trail to left down old dirt road in North Carolina leads to Groundhog Creek Shelter. Beyond shelter, trail leads 100 yards to stream.

6.9 Reach Turkey Gap, bear left and ascend eastern peak of Snowbird Mountain, also called Wildcat Top (4,201 feet).

8.1 Trail passes side trail to white FAA building on western peak of Snowbird Mountain (4,623 feet).

10.5 Cross small creek. Blue-blazed trail to left crosses Painter Creek and leads to excellent campsite and good spring.

13.3 Descend steps in rock cut, and turn right on Waterville School Road to pass under I-40 to Pigeon River. Cross concrete bridge over river.

14.5 Pass under powerline in cleared strip.

15.2 End of section at Davenport Gap on NC 284, which becomes TN 32 at the state line just to the north.

Davenport Gap to the Little Tennessee River

From Davenport Gap to the Little Tennessee River, most of the 72.1 miles of the AT lies within the boundaries of the Great Smoky Mountains National Park along the crest of the Great Smokies. The trails within the park are maintained primarily by the National Park Service (NPS). The AT within the park is managed jointly by the NPS and the Smoky Mountains Hiking Club, based in Knoxville, Tennessee.

The NPS requires permits for both camping and use of the shelters and approved campsites along the AT, and it is a violation of NPS regulations, punishable by fine, for overnight hikers to travel in the GSMNP without a (free) camping permit.

To prevent overcrowding at shelters, the NPS issues for a given night only as many camping permits as the capacity of the shelter. Between April 1 and June 15, three bunk spaces are reserved in the park at each AT shelter for through-hikers. Camping adjacent to the shelters, as well as at unauthorized places along the trail, is forbidden. Hikers planning trips of more than one day should write to or phone Great Smoky Mountains National Park, Gatlinburg, TN 37738, phone (423) 436-1200, for regulations on shelter use and camping.

▨ DAVENPORT GAP (TN 32/NC 284) TO NEWFOUND GAP (US 441), 31.3 MILES

[Fig. 50(16)] 0.0 From Davenport Gap (1,975 feet), follow graded trail west.

0.9 Davenport Gap Shelter, with built-in bunks that accommodate 12, is located 100 yards to right of trail.

1.9 Chestnut Branch Trail leads 2.0 miles to Big Creek Ranger Station and campground.

2.8 Reach lower Mt. Cammerer Trail, leading 7.8 miles to Cosby Campground on Tennessee side.

5.2 Graded side trail on right leads 0.6 mile to Mt. Cammerer tower.

6.7 Cross crest of Rocky Face Mountain.

8.0 Cosby Knob Shelter is 150 feet to the left, with built-in bunks that accommodate 12. Spring nearby.

9.5 Reach Camel Gap (4,645 feet).

11.9 Reach Snake Den Ridge Trail, which joins AT from Tennessee side.

12.8 Reach Deer Creek Gap (6,020 feet). Fantastic views of Mt. Guyot, Luftee Knob, Balsam Corner, and Mt. Sterling can be seen from here.

13.6 Reach gap between Mt. Guyot and Old Black.

15.7 Come to trail junction. AT bears right. Left fork leads 100 yards to Tri-Corner Knob Shelter. Built-in bunks accommodate 12. Spring nearby.

18.2 Reach high point of Mt. Guyot (6,000 feet).

20.9 Reach Hughes Ridge Trail on left. This trail leads to Pecks Corner Shelter. Built-in bunks accommodate 12. Spring nearby.

25.5 Reach Porters Gap (5,500 feet) on state line.

27.1 Pass Dry Sluice Gap Trail. Via this trail and Grassy Branch Trail, it is 3.8 miles to Kephart Shelter, which accommodates 14. Creek water.

28.3 Reach Icewater Spring Shelter on left. This shelter is closed for overnight use except to long-distance hikers.

28.6 Boulevard Trail enters on right. On Boulevard Trail, it is 5.3 miles to LeConte Lodge and Shelter. Accommodations are available at lodge from late March to early November. There is a fee, and reservations are recommended. Phone (423) 429-5704. Shelter accommodates 12.

31.3 Reach US 441 at Newfound Gap parking area.

❧ NEWFOUND GAP (US 441) TO LITTLE TENNESSEE RIVER (FONTANA DAM), 39.2 MILES

[Fig. 50(17)] 0.0 From junction of Newfound Gap (5,045 feet) and trail, cross parking area to its western end and descend through opening in guard wall.

1.2 Reach crest of Mt. Mingus ridge. Follow crest and bear left.

1.7 Reach Indian Gap. Enter woods on western slope.

4.5 Take left fork. Sugarland Mountain Trail to right leads to Mt. Collins Shelter. Built-in bunks accommodate 12. Spring nearby.

5.0 Reach summit of Mt. Collins (6,188 feet).

6.7 Reach summit of Mt. Love (6,446 feet).

7.9 Reach Clingmans Dome (6,643 feet), highest point on the AT.

8.4 Ascend to summit of Mt. Buckley (6,582 feet).

10.8 Reach Double Springs Gap (5,507 feet) and Double Springs Shelter. Built-in bunks accommodate 12. Best spring is 15 yards from crest on North Carolina slope.

12.5 At edge of woods, trail to right leads 100 yards to spring. Just beyond this trail, pass Silers Bald Shelter. Built-in bunks accommodate 12.

16.0 Cross Cold Spring Knob (5,240 feet).

18.0 Pass Derrick Knob Shelter on right. Built-in bunks accommodate 12. Spring nearby.

19.9 Enter Starkey Gap (4,500 feet).

22.5 Reach summit of Thunderhead Mountain (5,527 feet). Views from Thunderhead are outstanding.

23.1 Cross Rocky Top (5,441 feet).

25.4 Reach Little Bald.

26.8 Reach eastern end of Russell Field and Russell Field Shelter. Built-in bunks accommodate 12. Spring is 150 yards down trail toward Cades Cove.

29.4 At Gant Lot, pass Mollies Ridge Shelter. Built-in bunks accommodate 12. Spring nearby.

31.7 Reach summit of Doe Knob (4,520 feet). Trail leaves crest of Great Smokies and turns south along spur ridge.

34.0 Reach Birch Springs Gap (3,834 feet). Birch Spring Shelter is 100 yards to right down slope. Built-in bunks accommodate 12. Spring nearby.

36.2 Come onto ridge crest. To left, old road leads 0.1 mile to firewarden's cabin and fire tower on crest of Shuckstack Mountain (4,020 feet).

38.6 Reach hard-surfaced road. Turn right and almost immediately reach intersection with dirt road (abandoned NC 288). Follow hard-surfaced road 0.6 mile along lakeshore to northern end of Fontana Dam and end of section.

39.2 Hard-surfaced road leads downstream 0.2 mile to overlook, which has spectacular view of Fontana Dam and powerhouse. Trail crosses dam. Continue on road past visitor center (showers and toilets) to reach Fontana Dam Shelter on left at top of hill.

Fontana Village

Located 3 miles from Fontana Dam, Fontana Village is a favorite stopover for through-hikers. The village offers a 16-bed hostel with bunk beds, two bathrooms, hot showers, kitchen, and living area, all at very little charge. Also, there are private cottages with kitchen and bath, some of which can be shared by up to eight hikers. The shopping area has a cafeteria, short-order grill, grocery store for resupply, ice cream parlor, post office, recreation building with indoor pool, and laundromat. Hikers in need of backpacking supplies can order toll-free from Black Dome Outfitters in Asheville, North Carolina, with overnight delivery (ask about this service at registration desk).

Some of the facilities at Fontana Village are available on a seasonal basis.

For more information: Fontana Village, Fontana Dam, Box 68, NC 28733. Phone (800) 849-2258.

Side Trails in Great Smoky Mountains National Park

Side trails include all trails that branch directly from the AT and most of those that diverge from them.

Most of the trails are standard, 4-foot, graded paths; a few are narrower, graded foot trails; and other may be substandard. The trails may be good or quite rough in places, and they might be overgrown in summer. Due to curtailing of some trail maintenance, especially after storms, even some of the less-used "grade A" trails may be overgrown in summer.

🟦 SIDE TRAILS

1. Chestnut Branch Trail. Leaves AT 1.9 miles from Davenport Gap, leads south 2 miles to Big Creek Road near ranger station and campground.

2. Lower Mt. Cammerer Trail. Leaves AT 2.8 miles west of Davenport Gap; leads north 7.8 miles to public road at Cosby Campground.

3. Mt. Cammerer Trail. Leaves AT 5.2 miles west of Davenport Gap; leads northeast 0.6 mile along crest to Mt. Cammerer fire tower.

4. Low Gap Trail. Crosses AT at Low Gap; leads north 2.5 miles to Cosby Campground.

5. Camel Gap Trail. Leaves AT at Camel Gap; leads 10.1 miles to Big Creek Primitive Campground near Mt. Sterling village.

6. Snake Den Trail. Leaves AT 2.4 miles west of Camel Gap; leads 5.3 miles to Cosby Campground.

6-A. Maddron Bald Trail. Leaves Snake Den Trail (*see* above) 0.8 mile north of AT; crosses Maddron Bald and leads 7.2 miles to US 321.

7. Balsam Mountain Trail. Leaves AT at Tri-Corner Knob; leads 10.8 miles to Pin Oak Gap, where it intersects with Balsam Mountain Road.

7-A. Gunter Fork Trail. Leaves Balsam Mountain Trail (*see* above) 5.6 miles south of AT; leads left 5 miles to Walnut Bottoms.

7-B. Mt. Sterling Ridge Trail. Leaves Balsam Mountain Trail (*see* above) 6.5 miles south of AT; leads left 7.2 miles to NC 284 at Mt. Sterling Gap.

7-C. Beech Gap Trail. Leaves Balsam Mountain Trail (*see* above) 8.5 miles south of AT; leads right 3.5 miles to public road at Round Bottom on Straight Fork.

8. Hughes Ridge Trail. Leaves AT at Pecks Corner; leads south 12 miles to Smokemont Campground.

8-A. Bradley Fork Trail. Leaves Hughes Ridge Trail (*see* above) 2.2 miles south of AT; leads right via Taywa Creek and Bradley Fork to public road at Smokemont.

8-B. Enloe Creek Road. Leaves Hughes Ridge Trail (*see* above) 4.7 miles south of AT; leads left 3.6 miles to Hyatt Ridge Trail.

8-C. Chasteen Creek Trail. Leaves Hughes Ridge Trail (*see* above) 5 miles south of AT; leads right 5.5 miles via Chasteen Creek to public road at Smokemont.

9. Dry Sluice Gap Trail. Leaves AT at Dry Sluice Gap; leads south 3.8 miles to Cabin Flats Trail via Bradley Fork Trail to public road at Smokemont.

9-A. Grassy Branch Trail. Leaves Dry Sluice Gap Trail (*see* above) 1.8 miles south of AT; leads right 4.5 miles via Grassy Branch and Kephart Prong to US 441.

10. Boulevard Trail. Leaves AT at crest of AT on shoulder of Mt. Kephart; leads north 5.3 miles to Mt. LeConte.

10-A Jump-Off Trail. Leaves Boulevard Trail (*see* above) 0.1 mile north of AT. Leads right 0.8 mile to the Jump-Off, offering spectacular view into valleys of Porter Creek watershed.

10-B. Trillium Gap Trail. Leaves Mt. LeConte (*see* Boulevard Trail above). Leads 5 miles to public road at Cherokee Orchard.

10-C. Rainbow Falls Trail. Leaves Mt. LeConte (*see* Boulevard Trail above); leads 6.5 miles to public road at Cherokee Orchard.

11. Sweat Heifer Creek Trail. Leaves AT 1 mile west of crest of AT on shoulder of Mt. Kephart; leads south 5.7 miles via Sweat Heifer Creek and Kephart Prong to US 441.

12. Road Prong Trail. Leaves AT at Indian Gap; leads north 3.3 miles to US 441.

12-A. Chimneys Tops Trail. Leaves Road Prong Trail (*see* above) 3.4 miles north of AT; leads left about 1.1 miles to top of Chimneys.

13. Fork Ridge Trail. Leaves AT 0.8 mile east of Mt. Collins; leads south 14.7 miles to public road at Deep Creek Campground.

14. Sugarland Mountain Trail. Leaves AT 0.4 mile east of Mt. Collins; leads north 12.1 miles to Little River Road at Fighting Creek Gap.

14-A. Rough Creek Trail. Leaves Sugarland Mountain Trail (*see* above) about 4.8 miles from AT; leads left 5 miles to public road 1 mile south of Elkmont.

14-B. Huskey Gap Trail. Crosses Sugarland Mountain Trail (*see* above) about 9 miles from AT; leads left 2.1 miles to Little River Trail south of Elkmont. Leads right 2 miles to US 441.

15. Clingmans Dome Trail. Leaves AT at 7.9 miles, leads 50 yards to tower, and then it follows a paved path 0.5 mile downhill to Forney Ridge parking area at end of Clingmans Dome Road.

16. Clingmans Dome Bypass Trail. Leaves AT at 8.9 miles, leads 1 mile to Forney Ridge Trail, which begins at end of Clingmans Dome Road.

17. Forney Ridge Trail. Leaves Forney Ridge parking area and leads 11.5 miles to Fontana Lake.

17-A. Forney Creek Trail. Leaves Forney Ridge Trail (*see* above) 1 mile south of Forney Ridge parking area; leads 10.8 miles via Forney Creek to Fontana Lake.

17-B. Springhouse Branch Trail. Crosses Forney Ridge Trail (*see* above) 6.6 miles south of AT; leads left 3 miles to gravel road on Noland Creek, and right 4 miles via Bee Gum Branch to Forney Creek Trail.

18. Goshen Prong Trail. Leaves AT 0.8 mile east of Double Springs Gap; leads north 10 miles to public road 1 mile south of Elkmont.

19. Welch Ridge Trail. Leaves AT 0.2 mile east of Silers Bald; leads south 7.5 miles on crest of Welch Ridge to High Rocks.

19.A. Hazel Creek Trail. Leaves Welch Ridge Trail (*see* above) 1.5 miles south of AT; leads 14 miles via Hazel Creek and Lakeshore trails to Fontana Lake.

19-B. Jonas Creek Trail. Leaves Welch Ridge Trail (*see* above) 2.0 miles south of AT; leads left 4.5 miles to Forney Creek Trail.

19-C. Bear Creek Trail. Leaves Welch Ridge Trail (*see* above) 6.4 miles south of AT; leads left 6.8 miles to Fontana Lake.

20. Miry Ridge Trail. Leaves AT 0.1 mile west of Buckeye Gap; leads north 8.2 miles to public road at Elkmont.

20-A. Lynn Camp Prong Trail. Leaves Miry Ridge Trail (*see* above) 2.5 miles north of AT; leads left 2.4 miles to Middle Prong Trail above Tremont Ranger Station.

20-C. Panther Creek Trail. Leaves Miry Ridge Trail (*see* above) at Jakes Gap, 4.9 miles north of AT; leads left 2.2 miles to Middle Prong Trail above Tremont Ranger Station.

21. Greenbriar Ridge Trail. Leaves AT 0.2 mile east of Derrick Knob Shelter; leads north 8.3 miles via Middle Prong Trail above Tremont Ranger Station.

22. Jenkins Ridge Trail. Leaves AT at eastern end of Spence Field; leads 6 miles to Pickens Gap on Lakeshore Trail.

23. Bote Mountain Trail. Leaves AT near center of Spence Field; leads north 7.2 miles to Laurel Creek Road.

23-A. Anthony Creek Trail. Leaves Bote Mountain Trail (*see* above) 1.7 miles north of AT; leads left 3.2 miles to public road in eastern end of Cades Cove.

23-B. Lead Cove Trail. Leaves Bote Mountain Trail (*see* above) 2.9 miles and leads 1.8 miles to Laurel Creek Road.

23-C. Finley Cane Trail. Leaves Bote Mountain Trail (*see* above) 5.4 miles and leads 2.7 miles to Laurel Creek Road.

23-D. West Prong Trail. Leaves Bote Mountain Trail (*see* above) 6 miles north of AT; leads right 2.7 miles to public road on Middle Prong Little River above Tremont Ranger Station.

24. Eagle Creek Trail. Leaves AT near center of Spence Field; leads south 8 miles to Fontana Lake.

25. Russell Field Trail. Leaves AT at Russell Field; leads north 4.8 miles to public road in eastern end of Cades Cove.

26. Gregory Bald Trail. Leaves AT at Doe Knob; leads west 7.2 miles to Parson Branch Road between Cades Cove and US 129.

26-A. Long Hungry Ridge Trail. Leaves Gregory Bald Trail (*see* above) at Rich Gap (also known as Gant Lot); leads south 8 miles via Twenty-mile Trail to NC 28.

26-B. Gregory Ridge Trail. Leaves Gregory Bald Trail (*see* above) at Rich Gap; leads north 4.9 miles to Forge Creek Road in western end of Cades Cove.

26-C. Wolf Ridge Trail. Leaves Gregory Bald Trail (*see* above) 3.1 miles from AT; leads south 6.5 miles to Twenty-mile Trail about 0.7 mile from NC 27.

27. Twenty-mile Trail. Leaves AT at Sassafras Gap 0.5 mile north of Shuckstack firetower; leads right 5 miles to NC 28.

28. Lost Cove Trail. Leaves AT at Sassafras Gap; leads left 3.5 miles to Eagle Creek and Lakeshore Trail.

Tennessee Valley Authority Lakes

There are 14 Tennessee Valley Authority lakes.

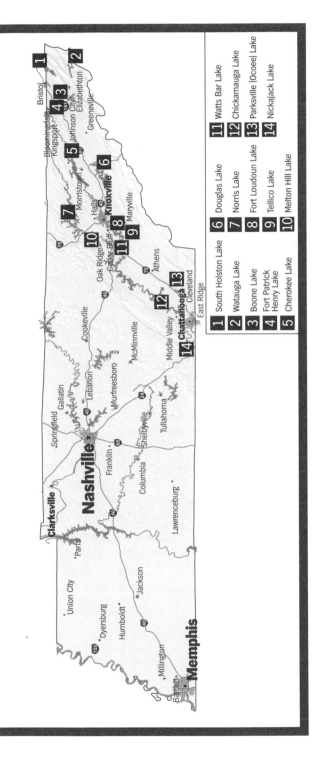

1	South Holston Lake	6	Douglas Lake	11	Watts Bar Lake
2	Watauga Lake	7	Norris Lake	12	Chickamauga Lake
3	Boone Lake	8	Fort Loudoun Lake	13	Parksville (Ocoee) Lake
4	Fort Patrick Henry Lake	9	Tellico Lake	14	Nickajack Lake
5	Cherokee Lake	10	Melton Hill Lake		

Tennessee Valley Authority

N o force outside nature has shaped the destiny of the Great Valley and the Tennessee mountains more than the Tennessee Valley Authority (TVA). It all began over six decades ago. In 1933, only 37 days after he was sworn into office, President Franklin D. Roosevelt asked Congress to create TVA. "It should be charged," he said, "with the broadest duty of planning for the proper use, conservation, and development of the natural resources of the Tennessee River drainage basin and its adjoining territory for the general social and economic welfare of the nation." On May 18, 1933, Congress approved his proposal.

It was an idea that had solid background. President Theodore Roosevelt and his conservation adviser, Gifford Pinchot, had worked together to establish the national parks system and the U.S. Forest Service in an effort to conserve the nation's natural resources. However, the administrations that followed failed to maintain the national policy to conserve the nation's

[*Above:* Tennessee has many beautiful rivers, including the Big South Fork River]

natural resources, and there was nationwide exploitation of them, including depletion of the once-fertile agricultural lands that led to the disastrous dust bowl conditions.

The TVA plan was broad, focusing principally on building a series of dams in the Tennessee River system for flood control and power production, but also aimed at improving the social and economic welfare of the people. By the 1930s, the valley was in sad shape, even by Depression standards. The soil on most of the land was eroded as a result of being farmed too much for too long. The timber had been cut, and what woodlands remained were regularly burned for grazing. Families that once prospered had fallen on hard times. Timber companies had ravaged the mountains to the east, and to the west, the Cumberland Plateau had been stripped of coal, iron, and timber.

Senator George W. Norris of Nebraska, the most powerful proponent of the TVA plan, was determined to gain its passage, and he used an issue that had been debated in Congress for several years to further his cause. It was obvious that addressing all of the problems would require a multifaceted approach, and it happened that some of the tools were already available. The government had a complex of idle chemical plants and a hydroelectric dam at Muscle Shoals, Alabama, that had been built during World War I to produce nitrates needed to make explosives. The nitrates could be converted to make fertilizers for farmers, and the dam could produce electricity. Senator Norris felt strongly that the public rather than private companies should receive the benefits from the government's investments, and this argument was a key to gaining congressional approval.

TVA began by helping provide the tools for the region to restore its basic natural resources, the water, the soil, and the forests. In less than a year there were two construction projects under way to build dams to harness the region's vast water resources and put them to work, and to provide flood control. New fertilizers were developed, and state agricultural extension services were enlisted to teach farmers how to use their land to grow more crops and protect it from erosion. Forests were replanted, and wildlife and fish populations were improved.

The most dramatic impact on the people came from electricity generated by the TVA dams. Electric lights and modern appliances such as electric stoves, refrigerators, and washing machines made life easier and more productive. The abundance of inexpensive electricity also drew industries into the area and provided desperately needed jobs.

The gates on the first TVA dam, named for Senator Norris, were closed in 1936, and the revitalization of the valley was well under way. Great progress was being made; then only a little more than four years after Norris Dam began operation, World War II broke out. TVA was faced with another challenge: producing the immense amounts of electricity the aluminum plants needed to produce aluminum for airplanes, as well as electricity for the top-secret Oak Ridge project. New records were set in building new dams. Between 1941 and 1945, five major dams were completed, and a 650-mile, year-round navigational channel on the Tennessee River from Knoxville, Tennessee, to Paducah, Kentucky, was created.

In total, from 1936 to 1977, 15 dams were constructed in the region, and in addition to the original purposes, the impoundments had other benefits. Fishing, boating, pic-

SNAIL DARTER
(Percina tanasi)

This small fish, which reaches lengths of 80 millimeters as an adult, inhabits larger creeks where it frequents sand and gravel shoal areas. It may also be found deeper in rivers where there is a current.

nicking, camping, and swimming became family pastimes, and early on TVA began developing lakeside parks and recreational areas to meet these recreational needs.

In the 1950s as the demand for electricity was outstripping the capacity of its hydro-electric units, TVA began a 20-year process of building coal-fired electric plants. By 1973 these steam plants accounted for three-fourths of TVA's generating capacity. They also created controversies over the strip-mining of coal and the pollution resulting from the burning of coal in the power-generating plants. Law suits led TVA to work out an agreement to clean up the air around these plants.

TVA entered the nuclear era in 1966 when estimates showed that a nuclear plant could produce electricity cheaper than a coal plant. The first project, the Browns Ferry Nuclear Plant, the largest in the nation, went into operation in 1974. In addition, work was begun on six other plants, but as energy needs changed due to soaring costs, construction was stopped on three of the plants in the late 1970s and early 1980s.

A huge controversy erupted in 1967 when TVA began work on the Tellico Dam project on the Little Tennessee River. Conservationists and environmentalists claimed that the project couldn't be justified on the basis of flood control, power production, navigation, recreation, or industrial development. Dam opponents were supported not only by independent studies but also by TVA's own statistics. Regardless, the dam was built, and TVA's image was badly marred.

At the heart of the controversy was a small fish not found anywhere else in the world. The snail darter (*Percina squamata*) became the rallying cry for environmentalist. The snail darter was on the national endangered species list, but Congress voted to wipe out this species with the blessings of the Supreme Court. This act became a lightning rod, attracting the ire of the environmentalists. The environmentalists eventually lost to TVA and Congress, and the dam was built.

This all took place before the small fish was located in other streams in 1973. Today the fish lives in many tributaries of the Tennessee River in Tennessee and in one in Alabama. The Snail Darter Recovery Team recommended the darter be reclassified as a threatened species. This was done in 1984.

Over the years TVA gained control of power production at all of the dams in the Tennessee River drainage system, some of which are outside the state's borders. This allows the agency to coordinate the flow of electricity throughout the system and maintain suitable levels under all circumstances.

Despite some bumps in the road, TVA has adjusted to present realities and remains a vital force with a variety of new projects under way. Electric cars and experimental batteries are being tested in Chattanooga, and agricultural and forestry scientists are studying ways to turn farm products and wood into alcohol for fuel. A pilot plant is now experimenting with methods for burning coal more efficiently and cleanly. Partnerships programs with local communities are turning urban waste into new fuel and fertilizer sources. Solar water heaters and other conservation technologies have been placed in valley homes. The agency also operates one of the nation's foremost training centers for nuclear plant personnel.

For more information: A map of the TVA lake system and a listing of all of the commercial resorts, campgrounds, and marinas can be obtained from Communications/Public Relations, TVA, 400 West Summit Hill Drive, Knoxville, TN 37902-1499. Phone (423) 632-6263.

TVA Lakes

[Fig. 51] The system of TVA lakes begins in northeastern Tennessee on the major tributaries of the Tennessee River, and all of the lakes offer water-oriented recreational opportunities. At many locations, state, county, and city parks are located on their shores, further broadening the scope of outdoor experiences.

Because flood control is one of the principal functions of the upper lakes, they experience considerable seasonal fluctuation, but southwest from Knoxville, where the mainstream Tennessee River begins, these water level changes are minor. This is because the river is navigational for the rest of its length, and certain channel depths must be maintained.

All of the lakes are excellent fisheries, and throughout the system there is a great variety of species, including largemouth bass, smallmouth bass, spotted bass (*Micropterus punctulatus*), white bass, rock bass, striped bass (*Roccus saxatilis*), striped bass/white bass hybrids, crappie, bluegill, walleye, sauger, several kinds of catfish, rainbow trout, brown trout, lake trout (*Salvelinus namaycush*), and numerous kinds of rough fish.

Also, the tail waters, water below dams or waterpower developments, provide good fishing. Most are warm-water fisheries, but areas below dams that discharge water from the lower depths of the reservoirs are cold-

WARPAINT SHINER
(*Luxilus coccogenis*)

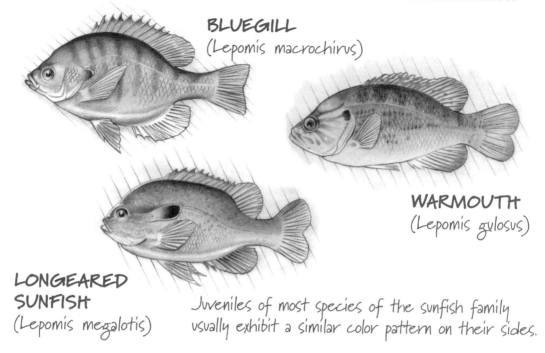

BLUEGILL
(Lepomis macrochirus)

WARMOUTH
(Lepomis gulosus)

LONGEARED SUNFISH
(Lepomis megalotis)

Juveniles of most species of the sunfish family usually exhibit a similar color pattern on their sides.

water fisheries that contain trout. The South Holston, Watauga, and Clinch tailraces all produce trophy specimens.

In recent years, TVA has done much to improve the quality of tailwaters by eliminating low dissolved oxygen levels and intermittent riverbed dry-out in areas below the dams. The solutions are site-specific and include the following: turbine venting, which is designed to provide an entrance for air as water passes through the turbines, making the water that is expelled at the end more oxygen rich; surface water pumps, which work like big ceiling fans to push water from the oxygen-rich surface to the oxygen-depleted bottom; oxygen injection, which is a large-scale version of the same basic principle that aerates home aquariums except it uses liquid oxygen instead of air; and aerating weirs, which are like man-made waterfalls.

Small hydropower units that kick in when the main units aren't operating, reregulating weirs, and pulsing operations are being used to sustain minimum flows.

The water flow below the dams is controlled from a central point, and computers determine power generation schedules. However, by calling (800) 238-2264, it is possible to learn when discharges are predicted through midnight of the following day. This toll-free line also provides details about current lake levels, future lake levels, and flows on unregulated streams.

SOUTH HOLSTON LAKE

[Fig. 51(1)] South Holston Lake is in Sullivan County in the extreme northeastern portion of the state, and part of the reservoir extends into Virginia. South Holston River is the major tributary. The nearest city is Bristol, and the lake can be accessed on and from TN 421 between Bristol and Shady Valley or on TN 44, which branches off TN 421 and becomes VA 75.

Public areas on the lake are the South Holston Dam Reservation; two USFS recreation areas, Lone Oak and Jacob's Creek; Sullivan County Park; and Washington County Park.

Length of lake: 23.7 miles.
Shoreline miles: 168.
Surface acres: 7,580.
Date impounded: 1948.

WATAUGA LAKE

[Fig. 51(2)] Also located in the northeastern corner of the region, Watauga Lake lies in Johnson and Carter counties within the boundaries of the Cherokee National Forest. Watauga River and Elk River are the major tributaries. The closest city is Elizabethton. The best access is on US 321 between Elizabethton and Boone, North Carolina, and on TN 67 that branches off US 321 at the lake. There is also a secondary road from Elizabethton that leads to the dam.

Public areas on the lake are the Watauga Dam Reservation, and the USFS Carden's Bluff Campground.

Length of lake: 16.3 miles.
Shoreline miles: 106.
Surface acres: 6,430.
Date impounded: 1948.

BOONE LAKE

[Fig. 51(3)] Boone Lake in situated in Sullivan and Washington counties in the center of the Tri-Cities area of Kingsport, Johnson City, and Bristol. Watauga River is the major tributary. The best access is on secondary roads off of TN 36 between Johnson City and Kingsport, or from TN 75, which turns right off TN 36.

The only public area is the Boone Dam Reservation.

Length of lake: 32.7 miles.
Shoreline miles: 130.
Surface acres: 4,310.
Date impounded: 1952.

FORT PATRICK HENRY LAKE

[Fig. 51(4)] The dam at Fort Patrick Henry Lake is in the Kingsport city limits, and all of this small impoundment lies within Sullivan County. It is accessible from TN 36 between Kingsport and Johnson City.

The single public area is Warrior Path State Park.

Length of lake: 10.4 miles.
Shoreline miles: 37.
Surface acres: 872.
Date impounded: 1953.

CHEROKEE LAKE

[Fig. 51(5)] Impounding lands in both Grainger and Hamblen counties, Cherokee Lake is closest to Morristown. Its tributary is the Holston River. There are numerous ways to access the lake. US 25E crosses the lake at about mid-point, US 11W parallels it between Rogersville and Rutledge, and US 11E is adjacent to it between Morristown and Jefferson City.

Public areas include Cherokee Dam Reservation, Panther Creek State Park, Grainger County Park, and TVA's May Springs and Fall Creek recreation areas.

Length of lake: 54 miles.
Shoreline miles: 393.
Surface acres: 30,300.
Date impounded: 1941.

DOUGLAS LAKE

[Fig. 51(6)] Douglas Lake lies in Cocke, Jefferson, and Sevier counties. The French Broad River is its major tributary. The closest towns are Newport and Dandridge. Access can be gained on US 25E between Newport and White Pine; on US 25W/70 and TN 92, both of which turn left off US 411 southwest of Newport; and from TN 138, which parallels the western side of the lake.

Public areas are Douglas Dam Reservation and Sevier County Campground.

Length of lake: 43.1 miles.
Shoreline miles: 555.
Surface acres: 30,400.
Date impounded: 1943.

NORRIS LAKE

[Fig. 51(7)] Norris Lake, TVA's first dam-building project, is in Campbell, Knox, Union, Claiborne, Roane, and Anderson counties. Norris and Jacksboro are the closest towns to the southwestern end of the lake. The Powell and Clinch rivers are the major tributaries. There are several ways to access the lake: off US 441 off I-75 north of Knoxville; and off TN 61, TN 170, and TN 33, all of which run between Norris and Tazewell.

The public areas are Norris Dam Reservation, Norris Dam State Park, Cove Lake State Park, Anderson County Park, and Big Ridge State Park.

Length of lake: 129 miles.
Shoreline miles: 800.
Surface acres: 34,200.
Date impounded: 1936.

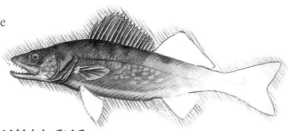

WALLEYE
(Stizostedion vitreum)

▧ FORT LOUDOUN

[Fig. 51(8)] Fort Loudoun Lake marks where the Holston and French Broad rivers converge to form the Tennessee River. The lake lies in Knox, Blount, and Loudon counties. The closest cities are Knoxville and Lenoir City. Access to Fort Loudoun can be gained from US 129 at Knoxville; TN 332 between Farragut and US 70; TN 333 between I-140 and US 321; and from US 321 at Lenoir City.

Public areas at Fort Loudoun Lake are Fort Loudoun Dam Reservation, Lenoir City Park, Concord Park, and TVA's Poland Creek Recreation Area.

Length of lake: 60.8 miles.
Shoreline miles: 360.
Surface acres: 14,600.
Date impounded: 1943.

▧ TELLICO LAKE

[Fig. 51(9)] Tellico Lake, on the Little Tennessee River, is in Loudon and Monroe counties. It is closest to Lenoir City. There is access to the lake at the dam at Lenoir City on TN 444; on TN 72 east of US 411 between Maryville and Madisonville; and on US 129, which turns left off US 411 south of Maryville.

Public areas include Tellico Dam Reservation, Fort Loudoun State Historic Park, and Toqua Recreation Area.

Length of lake: 33.2 miles.
Shoreline miles: 373.
Surface acres: 15,860.
Date impounded: 1977.

▧ MELTON HILL LAKE

[Fig. 51(10)] Melton Hill, near Oak Ridge, is in Anderson and Roane counties. The major tributary is the Clinch River. To access the lake take TN 162 a few miles southeast of Oak Ridge or take the TN 95 exit north from I-40 between Knoxville and Kingston.

The public areas are Melton Hill Dam Reservation, Melton Hill Park, and Haw Ridge Park.

Length of lake: 44 miles.
Shoreline miles: 173.
Surface acres: 4,180.
Date impounded: 1963.

▧ WATTS BAR LAKE

[Fig. 51(11)] Watts Bar is in Rhea, Meigs, and Roane counties. The Tennessee River is its major tributary. Kingston is the closest town. From I-40 take TN 58 to TN 304 or US 27 south from Rockwood to reach the lake.

Public areas are Watts Bar Dam Resort; TVA's Rhea Springs Fooshee Pass, Hornsby Hollow, and Riley Creek recreation areas; Roane County Park; and Kingston City Park.

Length of lake: 95.5 miles.
Shoreline miles: 771.
Surface acres: 39,000.
Date impounded: 1942.

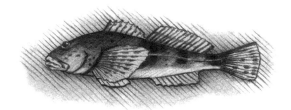

CHICKAMAUGA LAKE

[Fig. 51(12)] Chickamauga Dam is within the city limits of Chattanooga, but the lake, which lies in Hamilton, Meigs, and Rhea counties, stretches many miles to the north. US 27 parallels the lake on the west and TN

BANDED SCULPIN
(Cottus carolinae)
A bottom-dweller, the sculpin walks using leglike fins.

58 on the east, with numerous state and secondary roads branching off to the lake along their lengths. The major tributaries are the Tennessee, Hiwassee, Tellico, and Ocoee rivers.

There are numerous public areas: Chickamauga Dam Reservation; Booker T. Washington State Park; Harrison Bay State Park; Chester Frost County Park; TVA's Skull Island, Possum Creek, and Grasshopper Creek recreation areas; and Sale Creek Recreation Area.

Length of lake: 59.8 miles.
Shoreline miles: 810.
Surface acres: 35,400.
Date impounded: 1940.

PARKSVILLE (OCOEE) LAKE

[Fig. 51(13)] Parksville Lake on the Ocoee River is in Polk County between Cleveland and Ducktown, and US 64 parallels the lake for its entire length.

The Parksville Campground is the only public area, but the Ocoee River Recreation Area is nearby.

Length of lake: 7.5 miles.
Shoreline miles: 47.
Surface acres: 1,890.
Date impounded: 1911.

NICKAJACK LAKE

[Fig. 51(14)] Nickajack, the final TVA reservoir in the eastern region, lies in Marion County a few miles west of Chattanooga. Its major tributaries are the Tennessee and Sequatchie rivers. To reach the lake, take US 41/64/72 west from I-24 at Chattanooga.

The public areas are the Nickajack Dam Reservation, TVA's Maple View Recreation Area, Marion County Park, Walker's Landing, Ross's Landing Park, and Tennessee Riverpark.

Length of lake: 46.3 miles.
Shoreline miles: 192.
Surface acres: 10,370.
Date impounded: 1967.

Appendixes

A. Books and References

A Guide to Wildflowers of the Mid-South by Arlo I. Smith, Memphis State University Press, Memphis, TN, 1979

A Paddler's Guide to the Obey/Emory Watershed by Monte Smith, Menasha Ridge Press, Birmingham, AL, 1990.

Appalachian Trail Guide to Tennessee-North Carolina by the Appalachian Trail Conference, Harpers Ferry, WV, 1995.

Atlas of Tennessee Vascular Plants, Volumes 1 and 2 by Edward W. Chester, Eugene Wofford, and Robert Krall, Austin Peay State University, Clarksville, TN, 1993.

Big South Fork National River and Recreation Area by Russ Manning and Sondra Jamieson, Mountain Laurel Place, Norris, TN 1995.

Birth of a National Park in the Great Smoky Mountains by Carlos C. Campbell, The University of Tennessee Press, Knoxville, TN, 1960.

Boxes, Rockets, and Pens: A History of Wildlife Recovery in Tennessee by Doug Markham, The University of Tennessee Press, Knoxville, TN, 1997.

Canoeing and Kayaking Guide to the Streams of Tennessee, Volume II by Bob Sehlinger and Bob Lantz, Menasha Ridge Press, Birmingham, AL, 1983.

Conscience of a Conservationist by Michael Frome, The University of Tennessee Press, Knoxville, TN, 1989.

Eastern/Central Medicinal Plants by Steven Foster & James A. Duke, Houghton Mifflin Company, New York, NY, 1990.

Exploring the Big South Fork by Russ Manning, Mountain Laurel Press, Norris TN, 1994.

Fieldbook of Natural History by E. Laurence Palmer, McGraw Hill, New York, NY, 1975.

Footsteps of the Cherokees: A Guide to the Eastern Homelands of the Cherokee Nation by Vicki Rozema, John F. Blair, Winston-Salem, NC, 1995.

Highlands Trails by Kenneth Murray, The Overmountain Press, Johnson City, TN, 1997.

Hiking Tennessee by Kelly Roark, Falcon Press, Helena, MT, 1996.

Hiking Tennessee Trails by Evan Means, The Globe Peguot Press, Old Saybrook, CT, 1989.

Hiking the Big South Fork, Second Edition by Brenda Coleman and Jo Anna Smith, University of Tennessee Press, Knoxville, 1993.

Hiking the Big South Fork, Third Edition by Deaver, Smith, and Duncan, University of Tennessee Press, Knoxville, TN, 1998.

Hiking Trails of the Smokies edited by Don DeFoe, Beth Giddens, and Steve Kemp, Great Smoky Mountains Natural History Association, Gatlinburg, TN, 1994.

Hollows, Peepers, and Highlanders by George Constantz, Mountain Press Publishing Company, Missoula, MT, 1994.

Mammals of Great Smoky Mountains National Park by Alicia V. Linzey and Donald W. Linzey, University of Tennessee Press, Knoxville, TN, 1971.

Middle Tennessee On Foot by Robert Brandt, John F. Blair, Winston-Salem, NC, 1998.

Mountains of the Heart by Scott Weidensaul, Fulcrum Publishing, Golden, CO, 1994.

Mushrooms of the Great Smokies by L.R. Hesler, University of Tennessee Press, Knoxville, TN, 1960.

Natural Wonders of Tennessee: A Guide to Parks, Preserves and Wild Places by Ardi Lawrence and H. Lea Lawrence, Country Roads Press, Castine, ME,1994.

Our Restless Earth: The Geologic Regions of Tennessee by Edward T. Luther, The University of Tennessee Press, Knoxville, TN, 1977.

Strangers in High Places by Michael Frome, University of Tennessee Press, Knoxville, TN, 1980.

Tennessee Atlas & Gazetteer, DeLorme, Yarmouth, ME, 1997.

Tennessee Handbook by Jeff Bradley, Moon Publishing, Chico, CA, 1997.

Tennessee Hiking Guide edited by Robert S. Brandt, University of Tennessee Press, Knoxville, TN, Revised edition, 1992.

Tennessee Vacation Guide, Tennessee Department of Tourist Development, Journal Communications, Inc., Brentwood, TN, 1998.

Tennessee: A Guide to the State, Vanguard Press, New York, NY, 1939. Reprinted in softcover by The University of Tennessee Press, Knoxville, TN, 1986.

Tennessee's South Cumberland by Russ Manning and Sondra Jamieson, Mountain Laurel Press, Norris, TN, 1994.

The Appalachians by Maurice Brooks, The Naturalist's America series, Houghton Mifflin Company, Boston, MA, 1965.

The Audubon Society Field Guide to North American Birds by John Bull & John Farrand Jr., Alfred A. Knopf, New York, NY, 1977.

The Audubon Society Field Guide to North American Mammals by John O. Whitaker, Alfred A. Knopf, New York, NY, 1980.

The Audubon Society Field Guide to North American Reptiles and Amphibians by John L. Behler and F. Wayne King, Alfred A. Knopf, New York, NY, 1979.

The Audubon Society Field Guide to North American Trees by Elbert L. Little, Alfred A. Knopf, New York, NY, 1980.

The Audubon Society Field Guide to North American Wildflowers by William A. Niering and Nancy C. Arboretum, Alfred A. Knopf, New York, NY, 1979.

The East Tennessee Almanac by Robert Beverly, Sanctuary Press, Franklin, NC, 1992.

The Fishes of Tennessee by David A. Etnier and Wayne C. Starnes, The University of Tennessee Press, Knoxville, TN, 1993.

The Fly Fisherman's Guide to the Great Smoky Mountains National Park by H. Lea Lawrence, Cumberland House, Nashville, TN, 1998.

The Geologic History of Tennessee by Robert A. Miller, State of Tennessee, Department of Environment and Conservation, Nashville, TN, 1974.

The Highroad Guide to the Georgia Mountains by The Georgia Conservancy, Longstreet Press, Atlanta, GA, 1998.

The Highroad Guide to the North Carolina Mountains by Lynda McDaniel, Longstreet Press, Atlanta, GA, 1998.

The Highroad Guide to the Virginia Mountains by Deane and Garvey Winegar, Longstreet Press, Atlanta, GA, 1998.

The Great Smokies and the Blue Ridge edited by Roderick Peattie, Vanguard Press, New York, NY, 1943.

The Historic Cumberland Plateau by Russ Manning, The University of Tennessee Press, Knoxville, TN, 1993.

"The Natural History of the Blue Ridge" by Charles Wharton, *The Blue Ridge*, Natural Georgia Series, Georgia Wildlife Press, Conyers, GA, 1997.

The WPA Guide to Tennessee, The University of Tennessee Press, Knoxville, TN, 1986.

Touring the East Tennessee Backroads by Carolyn Sakowski, John F. Blair, Winston-Salem, NC, 1993.

Trails of the Big South Fork by Russ Manning and Sondra Jamieson, Mountain Laurel Press, Norris, TN, 1995.

Traveling Tennessee by Cathy and Vernon Summerlin, Rutledge Hill Press, Nashville, TN 1998.

Traveling the Southern Highlands by Cathy and Vernon Summerlin, Rutledge Hill Press, Nashville, TN 1997.

Trees of the Southeastern United States by Wilbur H. Duncan and Marion B. Duncan, The University of Georgia Press, Athens, GA, 1988.

Trees, Shrubs, and Woody Vines of Great Smoky Mountains National Park by Arthur Stupka, University of Tennessee Press, Knoxville, TN, 1964.

Trout Stream of Southern Appalachia by Jimmy Jacobs, Backcountry Publications, Woodstock, VT, 1994.

Waterfalls of Tennessee by Gregory Plumb, The Overmountain Press, Johnson City, TN, 1996.

Whistle Over the Mountain by Ronald G. Schmidt and William S. Hooks, Graphicom Press, Yellow Springs, OH, 1994.

Wilderness Trails of Tennessee's Cherokee National Forest edited by William H. Skelton, The University of Tennessee Press, Knoxville, TN, 1996.

Wildflower Folklore by Laura C. Martin, The East Woods Press, Charlotte, NC, 1984.

Wildflowers of the Southern Appalachians by Kevin Adams and Marty Casstevens, John F. Blair, Winston-Salem, NC, 1996.

B. Conservation Organizations

Appalachian Trail Conference, POB 807, Harpers Ferry, WV 25425. Phone (304) 535-6331. Publishes guidebooks and maps. Headquarters for hiking information about the AT.

Chattanooga Audubon Society, 900 North Sanctuary Road, Chattanooga, TN 37421. Phone (423) 892-1499. Dedicated to the preservation of wildlife and its habitat.

Great Smoky Mountains Institute at Tremont, 9275 Tremont Road, Townsend, TN 37882. Phone (423) 448-6709. Supporting teachers in their teaching about environmental education.

Sierra Club, Tennessee Chapter, POB 5152, Kingsport, TN 37663. Monthly meeting and year-round outing programs related to environmental protection.

Tennessee Conservation League, 300 Orlando Avenue, Nashville, TN 37209. Phone (615) 353-1133. Advocate for outdoor enthusiasts. Encourages responsible management of Tennessee's natural resources.

Tennessee Conservationist Magazine, Department of Energy and Conservation, 401 Church Street, Nashville TN 37243. Phone (615) 532-0060. A magazine about conserving Tennessee's wildlife and natural resources.

Tennessee Environmental Council, 1700 Hayes Street, Suite 101, Nashville, TN 37203. Phone (615) 321-5075. Educates and advocates for the protection of Tennessee's environment, public health, and natural resources.

Tennessee Forestry Association, POB 290693, Nashville, TN 37229. Phone (615) 883-3832. A conservation association dedicated to lobbying and educational programs and publicizing forestry issues and programs.

Tennessee Native Plant Society, Department of Botany, University of Tennessee, Knoxville, TN 37996. Furthering education on Tennessee's native plants.

Tennessee Parks and Recreation, 7th Floor L&C Tower, 401 Church Street, Nashville, TN 37243. Phone (615) 532-0001 or (800) 421-6683. Maintains Tennessee's state parks.

Tennessee River Gorge Trust, 25 Cherokee Boulevard, Suite 104, Chattanooga, TN 37405. Phone (423) 266-0314. Dedicated to enriching the community by conservation of the Tennessee River gorge through land protection, education, and promotion of good land stewardship.

Tennessee Outdoor Writers Association, 5550 Boy Scout Road, Franklin, TN 37064. Phone (615) 790-0487. Outdoor communicators disseminating information about Tennessee's outdoor opportunities and resources.

The Nature Conservancy of Tennessee, 50 Vantage Way, Suite 250, Nashville, TN 37228. Phone (615) 255-0303. Dedicated to preserving natural resources including rare plants, and animals and their habitats.

The Wildlife Society, Tennessee Chapter, Tennessee Wildlife Resources Agency, **Ellington Agricultural Center**, POB 40747, Nashville, TN 37204. Phone (615) 781-6612. Professional organization for wildlife managers to keep up to date with wildlife managing techniques.

Trust for the Future, 2704 12th Avenue South, Nashville, TN 37204. Phone (615) 297-2269. Education, promotion, and advocacy for conservation nationwide.

C. Outfitters

Appalachian Rivers Raft Company, 302 Great Glen Road, Greenville, SC 29615. Phone (803) 244-0168. Rafting the French Broad and Nantahala Rivers.

Appalachian Trail Conference, POB 807, Harpers Ferry, WVA 25425-0807. Phone (304) 535-6331. Information source for hiking the Appalachian Trail.

B-Cliff Whitewater Rafting, 390 Wilburdan Road, Elizabethton, TN 37643. Phone (423) 542-2262. Rafting the Watauga River.

Canoe the Sequatchie, Box 211, Dunlap, TN 37327. Phone (423) 949-4400. Canoeing the Sequatchie River.

Carolina Wilderness, 13077 Highway 19 West, Bryson City, NC 28713. Phone (800) 872-7437. Rafting the French Broad, Big South Fork, Obed, and Nolichucky Rivers.

Cherokee Adventures, 2000 Jonesboro Road, Erwin, TN 37650. Phone (423) (743) 7733 or (800) 445-7238. Rafting on Nolichucky, overnight trips, and mountain biking.

Cherokee Rafting, POB 111, Ocoee, TN 37361, (423) 338-5124 or (800) 451-7238. Rafting the Ocoee River.

Cripple Creek Expeditions, POB 98, Ocoee, TN 37361. Phone (423) 338-8441 or (800) 338-RAFT. Rafting the Ocoee River.

Cumberland Rapid Transit, 2365 Leatherword Ford Road, Jamestown, TN 38556. Phone (931) 879-4818. Rafting, rock climbing, rappelling, and cave tours in the Big South Fork Area.

French Broad Rafting Company, 376 Walnut Drive, Marshall, NC 28753. Phone (704) 649-3574 or (800) 842-3189. Rafting the French Broad River.

High Country, Inc., Route 1, Box 538, Ocoee, TN 37361. Phone (423) 338-8634 or (800) 233-8594. Fishing guide service for Watauga, Nolichucky, and South Holston Rivers.

High Mountain Expeditions, POB 1299, Blowing Rock, NC 28605. Phone (800) 262-9036. Rafting the Nolichucky River.

Hiwassee Trout Service, Route 1, Box 90, Reliance, TN 37369. Fishing guide service for Hiwassee River.

Hiwassee Outfitters, Inc., POB 62, Reliance, TN 37369. Phone (423) 338-8115. Rafting the Hiwassee River.

Hiwassee Outpost, POB 72, Ocoee, TN 37361. Phone (423) 338-2438. Rafting the Hiwassee River.

Jack Peppers, Fly Fishing Guide, 7733 River Road, Townsend, TN 37882. Phone (423) 448-9533 or (888) 892-5877. Fishing guide for the Smokies.

Little River Outfitters, PO Box 505, Townsend, TN 37882. Phone (423) 448-9459. Full fishing fly shop, backpacking, hiking, adventure travel gear, clothing, and fishing guides for the Smokies.

Nantahala Outdoor Center, 13077 Highway 19W, Bryson City, NC 28713-9114. Phone (704) 488-6900 or (800) 232-RAFT. Rafting on Chattooga, Ocoee, Nolichucky, Nantahala, and French Broad Rivers, and overnight trips.

Ocoee Inn Rafting, Inc., Route 1 Box 347, Benton TN 37307. Phone (423) 338-2064 or (800) 272-7238. Rafting the Ocoee River and restaurant, motel, and marina.

Ocoee Outdoors, Inc., POB 72, Ocoee, TN 37361. Phone (423) 338-2438 or (800) 533-7767. Rafting the Ocoee River.

Ocoee Rafting, Inc., POB 966, Ducktown, TN 37326. Phone (423) 496-3388 or (800) 251-4800. Rafting the Ocoee River.

Old Smoky Outfitters, 511 Parkway, Suite 201, Gatlinburg, TN 37738. Phone (423) 430-1936. Guide service for wild trout in the Smokies, and float trips for smallmouth on the Nolichucky River, Little River, and Little Pigeon River.

Outdoor Adventure Rafting, POB 109, Ocoee, TN 37361. Phone (423) 338-5746 or (800) 627-7636.

Rafting the Ocoee River, tubing on lower Ocoee River, ropes course, climbing, rappelling, and camping.

Outland Expeditions, 6501 Waterlevel Highway, Cleveland, TN 37323. Phone (423) 478-1442 or (800) 827-1442. Rafting on the Ocoee River, backpacking, climbing, and hiking in the Cherokee National Forest, cabins, and full service travel agency.

Pigeon River Outdoors, POB 592, Gatlinburg, TN 37738. Phone (423) 436-5008 or (800) PRO-RAFT. Rafting on the Pigeon River.

Quest Expeditions, POB 499, Benton, TN 37307. Phone (423) 338-2979 or (800) 277-4537. Rafting the Ocoee River.

Raccoon Mountain Riding Stables, 4312 Cummings Highway, Chattanooga, TN 37419. Phone (423) 825-1175. Guided horseback riding with scenic overlooks and hayrides on Aetna Mountain.

Rafting in the Smokies, Pigeon River Outfitters, POB 592, Gatlinburg, TN 37738. Phone (423) 436-5008. Rafting the French Broad and Nantahala Rivers.

Rafting, Inc., Highway 64, POB 106, Ocoee, TN 37361. Phone (423) 338-8441. Rafting the Ocoee River.

Rock Creek Outfitters, 100 Tremont Street, Chattanooga, TN 37405. Phone (423) 265-5969. Full line of backpacking, hiking, climbing, canoeing, and snowboarding equipment.

Rolling Thunder River Company, POB 88, Almond, NC 28702. Phone (704) 488-2030 or (800) 408-7238. Rafting the Ocoee and Nantahala Rivers, and camping.

Saddle Valley Campground, HC 61 Box 217-R, Jamestown, TN 38556. Phone (931) 879-6262 or (423) 984-0668. Campsites, stables, and corrals in the Big South Fork Area.

Sheltowee Trace Outfitters, POB 1060, Whitley City, KY 42653. Phone (606) 679-5026 (in the off-season) or (800) 541-RAFT. Rafting and canoeing the Russell, Cumberland, and Big South Fork Rivers, and shuttle service for hikers.

Smokey Mountain Expeditions, Inc., Highway 64, POB 98, Ocoee, TN 37361. Phone (423) 338-8441 or (800) 338-RAFT. Rafting the Ocoee River.

Smoky Mountain Angler, 376 East Parkway, PO Box 241, Gatlinburg, TN 37738. (423) 436-8746. Fly fishing guide to the Smokies.

Southeast Pack Trips, 299 Dewey Burk Road, Jamestown, TN 38556. Phone (931) 879-2260. Horseback riding and camping in the Big South Fork Area.

Southeastern Expeditions, 50 Executive Park South Suite 5016, Atlanta, GA 30329. Phone (404) 329-0433 or (800) 868-RAFT. Rafting, canoeing, and kayaking the Chattooga and Ocoee Rivers, and horseback riding.

Sunburst Adventures, POB 329, Benton, TN 37307. Phone (423) 338-8388 or (800) 247-8388. Rafting the Ocoee River.

The Eagle Adventure Company, 375 Eagle Ranch Road, Copperhill, TN 37317. Phone (800) 288-3245. Rafting the Ocoee River, climbing, rappelling, and horseback riding at the dude ranch.

U.S.A. RAFT, POB 277, Rowlesburg, WV 26425. Phone (800) USA-RAFT. Rafting on Ocoee, Pigeon, and Nolichucky Rivers.

Wahoo's Adventures, POB 1915, Boone, NC 28607. Phone (704) 262-5774 or (800) 444-RAFT. Rafting the Ocoee, Nolichucky, and French Broad Rivers.

Webb Bros. Float Service, Inc., Hiwassee River Box 61, Reliance, TN 37369. Phone (423) 338-2373. Rafting the Hiwassee River.

Whitewater Tennessee, POB 72, Ocoee, TN 37361. Phone (423) 338-2438 or (800) 533-7767. Rafting the Ocoee and Hiwassee Rivers.

Wildwater, Ltd., PO Box 309, Long Creek, SC 29658. Phone (423) 496-4904 or (800) 451-9972. Rafting on Nantahala, Pigeon, Ocoee and Chattooga Rivers, and overnight trips.

D. Tourism Information

Anderson County Chamber of Commerce, 245 North Main Street, Suite 200, Clinton, TN 37716. Phone (423) 457-2559.

Athens Area Chamber of Commerce, 13 North Jackson Street, Athens, TN 37303. Phone (423) 745-0334.

Blount County Chamber of Commerce, 201 South Washington Street, Maryville, TN 37804. Phone (423) 983-2241.

Bristol Chamber of Commerce, PO Box 519, Bristol, VA 24203. Phone (423) 989-4850.

Byrdstown/Pickett County Chamber of Commerce, West Main Street, Byrdstown, TN 38549. Phone (931) 864-7195.

Campbell County Chamber of Commerce, PO Box 305, Jacksboro, TN 37757. Phone (423) 566-0329.

Chattanooga Convention and Visitors Bureau, 1001 Market Street, Chattanooga, TN 37402. Phone: (423) 756-8687.

Claiborne County Chamber of Commerce, PO Box 332, Tazewell, TN 37879. Phone (423) 626-4149.

Cleveland/Bradley County Chamber of Commerce, PO Box 2275, Cleveland, TN 37320-2275. Phone (423) 472-6587 or (800) 472-6588.

Cookeville/Putnam County Chamber of Commerce, 302 South Jefferson Avenue, Cookeville, TN 38501. Phone (931) 526-2211.

Copper Basin Chamber of Commerce, PO Box 292, Ducktown, TN 37326.

Cumberland County Chamber of Commerce, 34 South Main Street, Crossville, TN 38557. Phone (931) 484-8444.

Dale Hollow/Clay County Chamber of Commerce, PO Box 69, Celina, TN 38551. Phone (931) 243-3338.

Dayton Chamber of Commerce, 107 Main Street, Dayton, TN 37321. Phone (423) 775-0361.

East TN Heritage & Community Tourism Development, 531 Henly Street, Seventh Floor, Room 703, Knoxville, TN 37902. Phone (423) 594-5500.

Elizabethton/Carter County Chamber of Commerce, PO Box 190, Elizabethton, TN 37644. Phone (423) 547-3850 or (800) 347-0208.

Erwin/Unicoi County Chamber of Commerce, PO Box 713, Erwin, TN 37650. Phone (423) 743-3000.

Etowah Area Chamber of Commerce, PO Box 458, Etowah, TN 37331. Phone (423) 263-2228.

Farragut Chamber of Commerce, PO Box 22461, Farragut, TN 37933. Phone (423) 675-7057.

Gatlinburg Chamber of Commerce, PO Box 527, Gatlinburg, TN 37738. Phone (423) 436-4178 or (800) 822-1998.

Greene County Tourism Council, 115 Academy Street, Greeneville, TN 37743. Phone (423) 638-4111.

Grundy County Chamber of Commerce, PO Box 387, Gruetli-Laager, TN 37339. Phone (931) 779-3238.

Historic Jonesborough, 117 Boone Street, Jonesborough, TN 37659. Phone (423) 753-5961.

Historic Rugby, PO Box 8, Rugby, TN 37733. Phone (423) 628-2441.

Jamestown/Fentress County Chamber of Commerce, PO Box 1294, Jamestown, TN 38556. Phone (931) 879-9948.

Jefferson County Chamber of Commerce, 532 Patriot Drive, Jefferson City, TN 37760-3216. Phone (423) 397-9642.

Jellico Tourism, 849 Fifth Street, Suite 1, Jellico, TN 37762. Phone (423) 784-3275

Johnson City Convention and Visitors Bureau, PO Box 180, Johnson City, TN 37605. Phone (423) 461-8000.

Kingsport Chamber of Commerce, PO Box 1403, Kingsport, TN 37662. Phone (423) 392-8820 or (800) 743-5282.

Kingston/Roane County Chamber of Commerce, PO Box 876, Kingston, TN 37763. Phone (423) 376-5572.

Knoxville Chamber of Commerce, 601 West Summit Hill Drive, Suite 300, Knoxville, TN 37902. Phone (423) 637-4550.

Lake City Chamber of Commerce, PO Box 1054, Lake City, TN 37769. Phone (423) 426-9595.

Livingston/Overton County Chamber of Commerce, 208-B West Broad Street, Livingston, TN 38570. Phone (931) 823-6421.

Loudon County Chamber of Commerce/Visitors Bureau, PO Box 909, Loudon, TN 37774. Phone (423) 458-2067.

McMinnville/Warren County Chamber of Commerce, PO Box 574, McMinnville, TN 37110. Phone (931) 473-6611.

Meigs County Chamber of Commerce, PO Box 611, Decatur, TN 37322. Phone (423) 334-5496.

Morristown Area Chamber of Commerce, PO Box 9, Morristown, TN 37815. Phone (423) 586-6382.

Mountain City Chamber of Commerce, PO Box 1, Mountain City, TN 37683. Phone (423) 727-5800.

Newport-Cocke County Chamber of Commerce, 433B Prospect Avenue, Newport, TN 37821. Phone (423) 623-7201.

Oak Ridge Chamber of Commerce, 1400 Oak Ridge Turnpike, Oak Ridge, TN 37830. Phone (423) 483-1321.

Pigeon Forge Department of Tourism, 2450 North Parkway, PO Box 1390, Pigeon Forge, TN 37868. Phone (423) 453-8574 or (800) 251-9100.

Pikeville/Bledsoe County Chamber of Commerce, PO Box 205, Pikeville, TN 37367. Phone (423) 447-2791.

Polk County Chamber of Commerce, PO Box 560, Benton, TN 37307. Phone (423) 338-5040 or (800) 633-7655.

Rogersville/Hawkins County Chamber of Commerce, 107 East Main Street, Suite 100, Rogersville, TN 37857. Phone (423) 272-2186.

Rutledge/Grainger County Chamber of Commerce, PO Box 126, Rutledge, TN 37861. Phone (423) 828-3513.

Scott County Chamber of Commerce, PO Box 4442, Oneida, TN 37841. Phone (423) 569-6900 or (800) 645-6905.

Sequatchie County Chamber of Commerce, PO Box 595, Dunlop, TN 37327. Phone (423) 949-3479.

Sevierville Chamber of Commerce, 866 Winfield Dunn Parkway, Sevierville, TN 37876. Phone (423) 453-6411 or (800) 255-6411.

Smoky Mountain Visitors Bureau, 201 South Washington Street, Maryville, TN 37804. Phone (423) 983-2241 or (800) 525-6834.

Sparta/White County Chamber of Commerce, 16 West Bockman, Sparta, TN 38583. Phone (931) 836-3552.

Spring City Chamber of Commerce, PO Box 355, Spring City, TN 37381. Phone (423) 365-5210.

The Greater Cumberland Gap Chamber of Commerce, PO Box 528, Cumberland Gap, TN 37724. Phone (423) 869-3660.

Townsend Visitors Center, 7906 East Lamar Alexander Parkway, Townsend, TN 37882. Phone (423) 448-6134.

Van Buren County Chamber of Commerce, PO Box 814, Spencer, TN 38584. Phone (931) 946-7033.

E. Map Sources

Big South Fork National River and Recreation Area, 4564 Leatherwood Road, Oneida, TN 37841. Phone (423) 569-9778.

U.S. Geological Survey, Map Sales, Box 25286, Denver, CO 80225. Phone (800) USA-MAPS.

U.S. Forest Service, PO Box 2010, Cleveland, TN 37320. Phone (423) 476-9700.

Great Smoky Mountains National Park, 107 Park Headquarters Road, Gatlinburg, TN 37738. Phone (423) 436-1207.

The Nature Conservancy, 50 Vantage Way, Suite 250, Nashville, TN 37228. Phone (615) 255-0303.

Tennessee Division of Maps and Publications, L&C Tower, 13th Floor, 401 Church Street, Nashville, TN 37243-0445. Phone (615) 532-1500.

Tennessee Valley Authority, Map Store, 311 Broad Street, Chattanooga, TN 37402. Phone (423) 751-6277.

The Map Store, 1900 Dutch Valley Road, Knoxville, TN 37918. Phone (423) 688-3608.

Timely Discount Topos, 9769 119th Drive, Suite 9, Broomfield, CO 80021. Phone (800) 821-7609.

Tennessee Atlas and Gazetteer, DeLorme Drive, POB 298, Yarmouth, ME 04096. Phone (207) 846-7000.

F. Special Events, Fairs, and Festivals

JANUARY

Wilderness Wildlife Week of Nature—More than 88 international experts in the fields of wildlife, conservation, and nature. Free hikes, lectures, displays, and demonstrations on a broad range of subjects. Pigeon Forge Department of Tourism. Phone (800) 251-9100.

FEBRUARY

Annual Smoky Mountains Storytelling Festival—Some of the best storytellers anywhere. They can take you away with their words, and your imagination, to places far or near. Pigeon Forge Department of Tourism. Phone (800) 251-9100.

MARCH

Norris Dam's Annual Spring Wildflower Walks—Guided hikes along trails of the state park and TVA reservation will acquaint participants with the identification, natural history, and folklore of the beautiful display of spring wildflowers. March–April. Norris Dam State Park, Lake City. Phone (423) 426-7461.

APRIL

Dogwood Arts Festival—Knoxville. Its been called "the best 17 days of spring in America." It's one festival after another—arts and crafts, music and dance, sports, more than 60 miles of glorious dogwood trails, and fabulous garden tours. Dogwood Arts Festival Office. Phone (423) 637-4561.

Great Smoky Arts & Crafts Community Spring Show—A welcome to springtime, featuring handmade arts and crafts by Craft Community members. Gatlinburg. Phone (423) 436-4448.

Loudon County Dogwood Festival—Includes beautiful gardens, mile run, fashion show, and other events. Also includes the Spring Festival at Loudon Valley Winery. Loudon County Beautification Board. Phone (423) 458-1987.

Annual Spring Wildflower Pilgrimage—A three-day program of wildflower walks, motorcades, and photographic tours in the Great Smoky Mountains National Park. Gatlinburg, Great Smoky Mountain National Park. Phone (423) 436-1262.

Annual Spring Fling—Celebrating the beauty of spring in beautiful downtown historic Rogersville. Includes arts, crafts, food, car show, gun/knife show, children's activities, and a chili cookoff. Historic downtown Rogersville. Rogersville/Hawkins County Chamber of Commerce. Phone (423) 272-2186.

Townsend in the Smokies Spring Festival—A celebration of spring with weekday wildflower walks, weekend story-telling, and a barbecue cook-off on the last Saturday of the festival. Begins the last weekend in April and continues through the first weekend in May. Bluegrass music on weekends. There are also arts and crafts demonstrations and old-fashioned kid games. Admission is free, and food and beverages are for sale. Townsend Visitors Center. Phone (423) 448-6134 or (800) 525-6834. www.smokymountains.org.

Spring Garden Fair—Gardeners will find acres of herbs, flowers, and related items, along with professional advice on the care and feeding of a wide variety of plants. Herbs, wildflowers, annuals, and garden crafts are available. Exchange Place, Kingsport. Phone (423) 288-6071.

MAY

The Cosby Ramp Festival—Huge dinner-on-the-ground, featuring the ramp, the "sweetest tasting, vilest smelling plant that grows." Held the first Sunday of May, festivities include gospel and country music, with large servings of ramps. Don't forget the mouthwash! Cosby. Contact Dr. Jack Clark. Phone (423) 623-5410

Annual Iris Festival—Juried arts & crafts show that also features a food court, entertainment stage, kid's korner, and premier wood carving show. Historic downtown Greeneville. Phone (423) 638-4111.

JUNE

Riverbend Festival—This nine-day event draws nearly half a million spectators each year. Features over 100 musical artists who perform on five stages including rock, country, blues, jazz, and folk. Other highlights include sporting events, family activities, fine arts exhibits, food, and a spectacular fireworks display. Ross's Landing, downtown Chattanooga. Phone (423) 265-4112 or (423) 756-2212.

Annual Rhododendron Festival—This festival focuses on the 600-acre garden of rhododendrons, the largest natural rhododendron gardens in the U.S., in full bloom atop Roan Mountain. Native arts and crafts, music, food festivals, beauty pageants, and wildlife tours. Roan Mountain State Park. Phone (423) 772-3303.

JULY

Kingsport Fun Fest—Over 150 events including hot-air balloon races, a beach party, block parties, celebrity entertainment, sports events, and much more. Fun Fest Office, Kingsport Chamber of Commerce. Phone (423) 392-8800.

AUGUST

Cherokee Days of Recognition—The festival features native dance, games, crafts, and food. Red Clay State Historic Park, Cleveland. Phone (423) 478-0339.

African American Cultural Festival—Local dancers, writers, and musical entertainment including choral, gospel, and jazz. African marketplace with clothing, food, jewelry, crafts, drama, and other special attractions. Miller Plaza, Chattanooga. Chattanooga African American Museum. Phone (423) 267-1076.

SEPTEMBER

Scott County Sorghum Festival—An Old Fashioned Stir-Off, sorghum making by the Mennonites. Horses pull the mill that squeezes the juice from the stalks that are boiled, gradually turning the stalks into a thick, golden colored, delicious sorghum syrup. Scott County Chamber of Commerce. Phone (423) 569-6900 or (800) 645-6905.

Fall Folk Arts Festival, Kingsport—This crafts show is held during a special, open house weekend at the Exchange Place Historic Site. Phone (423) 288-6071.

OCTOBER

National Storytelling Festival—A three-day celebration that showcases storytellers, stories, and traditions from across America and around the world. National Storytelling Association, Jonesborough. Phone (423) 753-2171.

Standing Stone Celebration—During this event, members of the Cherokee nation of Oklahoma make their annual pilgrimage to Monterey's Whittaker Park, site of ancient worship grounds. A ceremony commemorating the forced marches of the Cherokees from Georgia to Oklahoma in 1838–1839, includes laying a corn wreath on the Standing Stone Monument. Phone (931) 528-8350.

Heritage Days—Historic Downtown Rogersville. Harvest festival, arts and crafts, food, entertainment, children's activities, quilt show, demonstrations, parade, and antique car show. Phone (423) 272-1961.

NOVEMBER

Smoky Mountain Christmas—Over a million lights plus spectacular holiday shows transform Dollywood into a winter wonderland for a traditional, old-fashioned holiday celebration. Special holiday food and attractions also highlight this celebration. Dollywood, Pigeon Forge. Phone (423) 428-9488 or (800) Dollywood.

Rock City's Enchanted Garden of Lights—Over a quarter of a million twinkling bulbs used to create more than 30 holiday scenes. November–January. Rock City, Chattanooga. Phone (706) 820-2531.

DECEMBER

Christmas in Olde Jonesborough—An old-fashioned Christmas celebration with events all month long. Includes tour of homes, special museum exhibits, a parade, recipe swap, Christmas tree exhibit, and traditionally decorated streets. Jonesborough Visitor Center. Phone (423) 753-5961.

G. Glossary

Anticline—Arching rock fold that is closed at the top and open at bottom. Oldest formation occurs in the center of an anticline.

Basement—Complex of igneous and metamorphic rock that underlies the sedimentary rocks of a region.

Biotic—Pertaining to plants and animals.

Boreal—Relating to the northern biotic area characterized by the dominance of coniferous forests.

Carbonate rock—Collective term including limestone and dolomite.

Coniferous—Describing the cone-bearing trees of the pine family; usually evergreen.

Continental drift—Theory that the continental land masses drift across the earth as the earth's plates move and interact in a process called plate tectonics.

Deciduous—Plants that shed their leaves seasonally and are leafless for part of the year.

Endemic—Having originated in and being restricted to one particular environment.

Escarpment—Cliff or steep rock face formed by faulting that separates two comparatively level land surfaces.

Extinct—No longer existing.

Extirpated—Extinct in a particular area.

Feldspar—Complex of silicates that make up bulk of the earth's crust.

Fold—Warped rock including synclines and anticlines.

Gneiss—Metamorphic granitelike rock showing layers.

Granite—Igneous rock composed predominantly of visible grains of feldspar and quartz. Used in building.

Igneous—Rock formed by cooled and hardened magma within the crust or lava on the surface.

Karst—Area of land lying over limestone and characterized by sinkholes, caves, and sinking streams.

Lava—Magma which reaches the surface of the earth.

Magma—Molten rock within the earth's crust.

Metamorphic—Rock which has been changed into present state after being subjected to heat and pressure from the crust, or chemical alteration.

Monadnock—Land that contains more erosion-resistant rock than surrounding area and therefore is higher.

Orogeny—A geologic process which results in the formation of mountain belts.

Outcrop—Exposed bedrock.

Overthrust belt—An area where older rock has been thrust over younger rock.

Rapids—Fast-moving water that flows around rocks and boulders in rivers; classified from I to VI according to degree of difficulty navigating.

Schist—Flaky, metamorphic rock containing parallel layers of minerals such as mica.

Sedimentary—Rocks formed by the accumulation of sediments (sandstone, shale) or the remains of products of animals or plants (limestone, coal).

Shale—Sedimentary rock composed of clay, mud, and silt grains which easily splits into layers.

Syncline—A rock fold shaped like a U that is closed at the bottom and open at the top. The youngest rock is at the center of a syncline.

Talus—Rock debris and boulders that accumulate at the base of a cliff.

Watershed—The area drained by a river and all its tributaries.

Index